GUIDE TO THE
BIRDS
OF ALASKA

GUIDE TO THE
BIRDS
OF ALASKA

Robert H. Armstrong

Alaska Northwest Books™
Anchorage • Seattle

Third Edition 1990

Library of Congress Cataloging-in-Publication Data:

Armstrong, Robert H., 1936-
Guide to the birds of Alaska/
    Robert H. Armstrong. —Rev. ed
        p.   cm.
Includes bibliographical references.
ISBN 0-88240-367-2
1. Birds — Alaska —Identification.   I. Title.
QL 684.A4A75   1990
598.29798—dc20   89-17979   CIP

Cover: Tufted Puffin
Photo by Dave Menke

Photographs by Robert H. Armstrong
and others (see Photo Credits)

Paintings by John C. Pitcher
Book design by Alice Merrill Brown
Cover Design by Alyson Hallberg
and Alice Merrill Brown

Alaska Northwest Books™
22026 20th Avenue S.E.
Bothell, WA 98021
A division of GTE Discovery Publications, Inc.

Printed in Hong Kong

CONTENTS

FOREWORD

Watching birds is fun! Being able to identify the birds you are watching increases this pleasure. And watching birds in Alaska has its special excitement, both for resident observers and visitors.

This photographic book on Alaska's birds is designed to enhance your enjoyment of birds by helping you to identify them, understand their habits and know where to find them.

Seeing birds that have adapted to the harsh environments of the boreal forest, tundra and sea ice of the North and that cannot be seen farther south is one exciting aspect of observing birds in Alaska. Even those bird species that visit more southern climes during migration and winter often look and behave quite differently when on their northern breeding grounds. Not only may their plumage be strikingly different from in winter, but they may occupy entirely different habitats (e.g., many sandpipers and other shorebirds nest in Alaska's mountains, far from seashores and marshes) and they may be singing and executing various courtship antics that are performed only on their northern breeding grounds.

In addition to the northern-adapted species, two other groups of geographically restricted birds add particular zest to bird watching in Alaska. The first is a group of endemics that apparently differentiated, historically, in the Bering-Chukchi sea area ("Beringia") in isolated glacial refugia. These birds still have their centers of abundance in this relatively inaccessible region, and many have not extended their ranges much beyond the Aleutian Islands or southcoastal Alaska. Hence, it is necessary to visit Alaska (or Siberia) to see many of these geographically restricted species (e.g., Red-faced Cormorant; Emperor Goose; Red-legged Kittiwake; Aleutian Tern; Parakeet, Least and Whiskered auklets; and McKay's Bunting).

The second group is sometimes referred to as the "Asiatics," birds that have their origins in Asia and most of which can be seen in North America only in Alaska. Some are regular breeders (Bar-tailed Godwit, Bluethroat, Arctic Warbler, White Wagtail and Yellow Wagtail), but most are migrants or are casual or accidental visitants. The occurrence of these Asiatics is facilitated by the nearness of Siberia, with some species passing across parts of Alaska — especially the western Aleutian Islands and the islands of the Bering Sea — during migration. A few even straggle occasionally as far as mainland Alaska (e.g., Spot-billed Duck, Common Crane, Common Ringed Plover, Eurasian Dotterel, Wood Sandpiper, Terek Sandpiper, Great Knot, Sharp-tailed Sandpiper, Hoopoe, Eurasian Wryneck, Common House-Martin, Eyebrowed Thrush, Dusky Thrush, Fieldfare, Brambling, Eurasian Bullfinch, etc.).

One of the most exciting aspects of watching birds in Alaska is that there is so much yet to be learned about them. We are still at the frontier of knowledge about so many aspects of Alaska's bird life that any observant bird watcher has a good chance of contributing new and valuable information about them — range extensions; dates of migration, eggs, young, fledglings; clutch and brood sizes; food habits; flight speeds and distances; habitat requirements during nesting, migration, winter; behavior relative to others of their own species, to different species and under various kinds of stress, including that caused by man; behavioral means of adapting to the rigors of northern life; and *ad infinitum*.

Watching birds is indeed fun, whether you watch birds casually or seriously. Whether your enjoyment comes from watching birds through a window of your home as they sing or feed; from adding new kinds of birds to your life list; from seeing birds with different plumages, habits and behavior patterns; from studying the natural history or ecology of a species; or from matching wits with game birds during the hunting season, you will be glad to have this Alaska bird guide, with its beautiful illustrations, close at hand.

Brina Kessel
Professor of Zoology and Curator
Terrestrial Vertebrates Collection
University of Alaska, Fairbanks
23 July 1979

ACKNOWLEDGMENTS

THE HELP OF MANY PEOPLE made this book possible. Frank Glass, an attorney and self-taught ornithologist, reviewed the manuscript and offered useful suggestions and ideas. Jim King, U.S. Fish and Wildlife Service biologist, reviewed the sections on swans, geese and ducks and added items based on his extensive experience with this group in Alaska. Ed Bailey, U.S. Fish and Wildlife Service biologist, reviewed the seabird sections of the book and provided additional information.

The timely publication of this book was made possible by my receiving a copy of the manuscript on the *Status and Distribution of Alaska Birds* several months prior to its publication from its author, Dr. Brina Kessel, professor of zoology and curator of Terrestrial Vertebrates Collection, University Museum, University of Alaska, Fairbanks. She also worked up a seasonal checklist of birds for the eastern interior of Alaska which helped a great deal in compiling the status and distribution charts for each species. Many others provided information on local abundance of birds which helped in compiling the charts: Bruce Paige, National Park Service biologist, for Glacier Bay National Monument; John C. Pitcher, for the Anchorage area; Richard MacIntosh, National Marine Fisheries Service biologist, for Kodiak Island; and Doug Murphy, ornithologist and former seasonal ranger at Denali National Park and Preserve, for Denali National Park.

Technical reviewers made significant contributions to the quality of this book. Dr. Dennis Paulson, zoologist, instructor and consultant in Seattle, Washington, added considerable information to the identification section for each species, commented on the format and content of the manuscript and provided valuable assistance in selection of the photographs. Pete Isleib, commercial fisherman and self-taught ornithologist, filled out status and distribution charts for all species not covered by *Status and Distribution of Alaska Birds*. Dr. Don McKnight, research chief, Game Division, Alaska Department of Fish and Game, and working under funding from the Federal Aid in Wildlife Restoration Program, reviewed the entire manuscript and offered useful suggestions.

I am grateful to Dan Gibson of the University Museum, University of Alaska, for his constructive criticism of the manuscript and his review of the photographs.

Special thanks go to the many photographers who allowed me to tie up their photographs for many months through the selection and printing process.

To John C. Pitcher, whose excellent paintings enabled me to reach my goal of illustrating all of the bird species that occur in Alaska, I am especially grateful.

Many voice descriptions used in the book are from *The Audubon Society Field Guide to North American Birds, Western Region* (1977), text by Miklos D. F. Udvardy, and reprinted here by permission of Alfred A. Knopf.

Assistance in updating the 1983 and 1990 versions of the book was received from several people. Dan Gibson reviewed the text changes and new photographs and provided references for status and distribution changes. Pete Isleib assisted in updating the status and distribution charts and in providing new information on species identification. Richard Gordon of Juneau assisted in updating the status and distribution charts for southeastern Alaska. Bob Day of the University of Alaska, Fairbanks, provided new information on seabirds. Jim King, U.S. Fish and Wildlife Service, provided new information on swans, geese and ducks and made other helpful comments. Dan Timm, game biologist, Alaska Department of Fish and Game, Anchorage, provided new information on the status and distribution of Canada Goose subspecies in Alaska. Dr. Richard Chandler, photographic consultant for *British Birds*, assisted in the location of several photographs of the new Asiatic species. The help of all of these people is greatly appreciated.

BALD EAGLE

INTRODUCTION

THIS REVISED EDITION OF *Guide to the Birds of Alaska* covers the 437 species of birds known to have occurred in Alaska as of September 1, 1989. Detailed information on identification, status, distribution and habitat is provided for 372 of these species. The remaining 65 are accidental in Alaska; these species and where they have occurred are listed in the back of the book.

This book was designed to aid in the identificaton of birds of Alaska and to provide the reader with information that is unavailable in other guides. All species except accidentals are illustrated: I have used photographs for many species and paintings for those species for which photos were lacking. As much as possible, I have attempted to present birds in a natural setting as they would normally be viewed at close range. Not all of the photographs were taken in Alaska, but the species shown are the same as those that do occur in the state. While I feel that the illustrations will help in field identification, I also realize the limitations of the photographic approach. Paintings of similar-looking birds, with size relationships and appropriate field marks emphasized, will and should remain the standard approach to field identification guides for birds. For this reason the reader may also want to use, in conjunction with this book, one of the other field guides on the market when attempting to identify birds in the field.

Individual species are organized by families. The reader is encouraged to become familiar with family characteristics, since this can save a great deal of time when identifying birds in the field. The order of the species and their common and scientific names follow *The A.O.U. Check-list of North American Birds* (6th Edition, 1983; and the 35th, 36th and 37th Supplements). The length of each bird is an approximate average from the literature and represents a measurement taken from the tip of the bill to the tip of the tail of museum specimens. For identification I encourage the reader to use the text with the illustrations. For most birds the photograph or painting will provide the basic descriptive features, and I have added information only on field marks important to identification. Voice descriptions are included where I feel they aid identification. Written descriptions of a bird's voice, while helpful, often vary and are difficult to interpret. I encourage readers to learn voices through actual field study and by listening to recordings. Once these are learned, most birds can be readily identified by voice alone. For some species, learning the voice is essential for positive identification.

The status and distribution of each bird in Alaska is presented according to the 6 biogeographic areas (see the map on page 6) recognized by Kessel and Gibson (1978). Knowing when a particular bird occurs in an area and its status can be helpful in narrowing the choices leading to final identification. This information on distribution is based on Kessel (1989); Kessel and Gibson (1978); Gabrielson and Lincoln (1959); seasonal bird sightings as reported by Gibson (1978–1986) and Gibson, Tobish and Isleib (1987–1989); several published checklists; and the knowledge of individuals familiar with specific areas. For simplicity and to make the areas more comparable, I have combined some of the terms presented by Kessel and Gibson (1978) and others.

The habitat in which a bird usually occurs is included for most species. For some species, especially those rare and casual ones, I present the locations within the region where they have been found rather than their habitat. Most designations are understandable and need no definition. Exceptions are inshore and offshore marine waters. Inshore refers to all marine waters within 3 nautical miles of the outer coast and islands of Alaska including all waters of the inside passages of southeastern Alaska. Offshore marine waters encompass all marine waters beyond 3 nautical miles of the outer coast and islands of Alaska.

In summary, many factors are useful in identifying birds. In conjunction with field marks, learning a bird's voice, habits and habitat can be very helpful. Also knowing where and when individual species normally occur and their status in selected areas of Alaska are important. I hope this will be a useful guide and that appreciation of Alaska's birds will be enhanced through the use of this book.

THE SIX BIOGEOGRAPHIC REGIONS OF ALASKA

Delineated by dotted lines. Status and Distribution charts accompanying the text outline the distribution of individual species within these regions.

Key to National Wildlife Refuges
(numbers correspond with those on the map)

1. Alaska Maritime NWR
   In addition to the Aleutian Islands Unit the refuge includes an enormous number of offshore islands, islets, rocks, reefs and spires.
2. Alaska Peninsula NWR
3. Arctic NWR
4. Becharof NWR
5. Innoko NWR
6. Izembek NWR
7. Kanuti NWR
8. Kenai NWR
9. Kodiak NWR
10. Koyukuk NWR
11. Nowitna NWR
12. Selawik NWR
13. Tetlin NWR
14. Togiak NWR
15. Yukon Delta NWR
16. Yukon Flats NWR

This map reflects the addition of about 53 million acres to the existing 23 million acres of National Wildlife Refuges in Alaska by the Alaska National Interest Lands Conservation Act of 1980. Bird lists for some of the refuges and other information is available from the Regional Director, U.S. Fish and Wildlife Service, 1011 E. Tudor Road, Anchorage, Alaska 99503.

Bering Strait
Cape Prince of Wales • Wales
Se

• Gambell
Saint Lawrence Island
1

W E S T E R N

Hooper Bay

15

Nunivak Island

Bering Sea

St. Paul Island
1 Pribilof Islands
St. George Island

S O U T H W E S T E R N

Attu Island

Agattu Island   Shemya Island

A l e u t i a n

Buldir Island

Amchitka Island

I s l a n d s

Adak Island

Bogoslof Island • Unalaska

Izembek Bay 6
Alaska
Cold Bay
Sandman Reefs   Shuma Island

2

1

Pacific Ocean   1   1

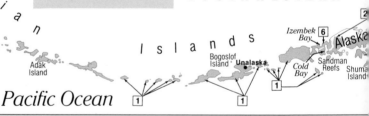

TOPOGRAPHY OF A BIRD

Although birds will vary radically in the specifics of their anatomy, they all share the same basic structures. Shown here are the basic features (far right) and wing feathers (right).

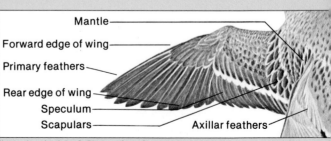

Mantle
Forward edge of wing
Primary feathers
Rear edge of wing
Speculum
Scapulars
Axillar feathers

Illustrations by John C. Pitcher / CartoGraphics by Jon.Hersh

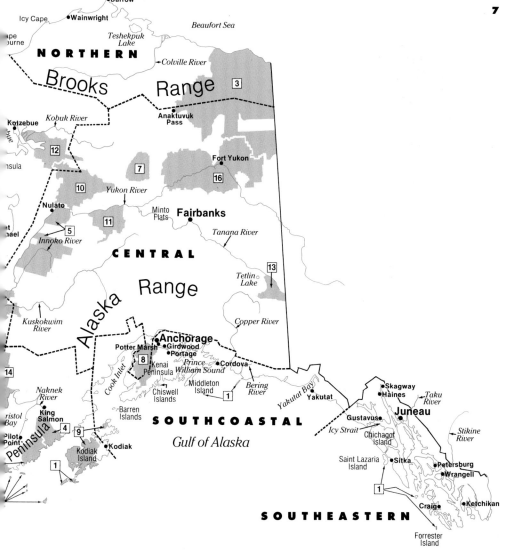

Arctic Ocean

Barrow
Icy Cape
Wainwright
Beaufort Sea
Teshekpuk Lake

NORTHERN

Colville River

Brooks Range

3

Kobuk River
Kotzebue
Anaktuvuk Pass

12

Fort Yukon
7
16

10
Yukon River

Nulato
Minto Flats
Fairbanks

11

5
Innoko River
Tanana River

CENTRAL

13
Tetlin Lake

Range

Alaska Range

Copper River

Kuskokwim River

Anchorage
Potter Marsh
Girdwood
Portage
8
Cordova
Kenai Peninsula
Cook Inlet
Prince William Sound

Middleton Island
1
Bering River
Yakutat Bay
Yakutat

14

Naknek River
Chiswell Islands

Skagway
Haines
Taku River

Barren Islands

SOUTHCOASTAL

Juneau

King Salmon

Gustavus
Icy Strait
Chichagof Island

Stikine River

4
9

Bristol Bay

Pilot Point

Kodiak Island
Kodiak

Gulf of Alaska

Saint Lazaria Island
Sitka

Petersburg
Wrangell

1

Peninsula

1

1
Craig

Ketchikan

SOUTHEASTERN

Forrester Island

Crown (cap)
Nape
Mantle
Scapulars
Rump
Upper tail coverts

Upper mandible
Lower mandible
Throat
Breast
Belly
Under tail coverts
Outer tail feathers

A GUIDE TO THE FAMILY HEADINGS AND STATUS AND DISTRIBUTION CHARTS IN THIS BOOK

Each family of birds is introduced by a heading giving the family scientific name. Under the family heading, one or two numbers appear indicating (1) the number of species with casual or more frequent occurrence and (2) the number of species appearing accidentally in the state of Alaska. For example:

Family *Ardeidae*
BITTERNS, HERONS
(5 + 4)

Number of species with casual or more frequent occurrence. Number of accidental species.

The total of the 2 numbers is the total number of species from that family occurring in the state.

CHART

For each species, a Status and Distribution Chart is provided. The charts outline the occurrence of individual species in various biogeographic regions of Alaska (see map, pages 6 and 7). Symbols in the charts and their meanings are:

Status & Distribution	Spring	Summer	Fall	Winter	*Breeder*
Southeastern	C	C	C	R	•
Southcoastal	C	C	C	R	•
Southwestern	C	C	C	R	•
Central	–	–	A	–	
Western	–	U	U	–	
Northern	–	–	–	–	

C: Common — Birds normally considered abundant, common and most of those considered fairly common.

U: Uncommon — Birds normally considered uncommon and some of those considered fairly common.

R: Rare — Birds considered rare or very rare.

A: Casual/Accidental — Birds considered casual or accidental.

– : No Records — Not known to occur.

• : *Breeder* — Known breeder or probable breeder in a region.

DEFINITIONS

Definitions for the terms, taken from *Birds of the North Gulf Coast — Prince William Sound Region, Alaska* by M. E. Isleib and Brina Kessel (Biological Papers of the University of Alaska, Number 14, November 1973), are:

Abundant Species occurs repeatedly in proper habitats, with available habitat heavily utilized, and/or the region regularly hosts great numbers of the species.

Common Species occurs in all or nearly all proper habitats, but some areas of presumed suitable habitat are occupied sparsely or not at all and/or the region regularly hosts large numbers of the species.

Fairly Common Species occurs in only some of the proper habitat, and large areas of presumed suitable habitat are occupied sparsely or not at all and/or the region regularly hosts substantial numbers of the species.

Uncommon Species occurs regularly, but utilizes very little of the suitable habitat, and/or the region regularly hosts relatively small numbers of the species; not observed regularly even in proper habitats.

Rare Species occurs, or probably occurs, regularly within the region, but in very small numbers.

Casual Species has been recorded no more than a few times, but irregular observations are likely over a period of years.

Accidental Species has been recorded only a time or two; it is so far from its usual range that subsequent observations are considered unlikely.

CHECKLIST OF ALASKAN BIRDS

This checklist includes all birds found in Alaska, including Accidentals (A). Readers may wish to use this list to record the species they have seen. Birds are listed by family, which is also the order of appearance of birds in the text. Birds that have appeared in Alaska accidentally are also listed at the back of the book along with the places where they have been seen (page 324).

LOONS
- Red-throated Loon
- Arctic Loon
- Pacific Loon
- Common Loon
- Yellow-billed Loon

GREBES
- Pied-billed Grebe
- Horned Grebe
- Red-necked Grebe
- Western Grebe

ALBATROSSES
- Short-tailed Albatross
- Black-footed Albatross
- Laysan Albatross

FULMARS, PETRELS, SHEARWATERS
- Northern Fulmar
- Mottled Petrel
- Cook's Petrel (A)
- Pink-footed Shearwater
- Flesh-footed Shearwater
- Buller's Shearwater
- Sooty Shearwater
- Short-tailed Shearwater

STORM-PETRELS
- Fork-tailed Storm-Petrel
- Leach's Storm-Petrel

PELICANS
- American White Pelican (A)

CORMORANTS
- Double-crested Cormorant
- Brandt's Cormorant
- Pelagic Cormorant
- Red-faced Cormorant

FRIGATEBIRDS
- Magnificent Frigatebird (A)

BITTERNS, HERONS
- American Bittern
- Chinese Little Bittern (A)
- Great Blue Heron
- Great Egret
- Chinese Egret (A)

- Snowy Egret (A)
- Cattle Egret
- Green-backed Heron (A)
- Black-crowned Night-Heron

SWANS, GEESE, DUCKS
- Tundra Swan
- Whooper Swan
- Trumpeter Swan
- Bean Goose
- Greater White-fronted Goose
- Snow Goose
- Ross' Goose
- Emperor Goose
- Brant
- Canada Goose
- Wood Duck
- Green-winged Teal
- Baikal Teal
- Falcated Teal
- American Black Duck
- Mallard
- Spot-billed Duck (A)
- Northern Pintail
- Garganey
- Blue-winged Teal
- Cinnamon Teal
- Northern Shoveler
- Gadwall
- Eurasian Wigeon
- American Wigeon
- Common Pochard
- Canvasback
- Redhead
- Ring-necked Duck
- Tufted Duck
- Greater Scaup
- Lesser Scaup
- Common Eider
- King Eider
- Spectacled Eider
- Steller's Eider
- Harlequin Duck
- Oldsquaw
- Black Scoter
- Surf Scoter
- White-winged Scoter
- Common Goldeneye
- Barrow's Goldeneye
- Bufflehead

❑ Smew
❑ Hooded Merganser
❑ Common Merganser
❑ Red-breasted Merganser
❑ Ruddy Duck

AMERICAN VULTURES
❑ Turkey Vulture

**HAWKS, EAGLES,
HARRIERS,
OSPREYS**
❑ Osprey
❑ Bald Eagle
❑ White-tailed Eagle
❑ Steller's Sea-Eagle
❑ Northern Harrier
❑ Sharp-shinned Hawk
❑ Northern Goshawk
❑ Swainson's Hawk
❑ Red-tailed Hawk
❑ Rough-legged Hawk
❑ Golden Eagle

FALCONS
❑ Eurasian Kestrel
❑ American Kestrel
❑ Merlin
❑ Northern Hobby
❑ Peregrine Falcon
❑ Gyrfalcon

**GROUSE,
PTARMIGANS**
❑ Spruce Grouse
❑ Blue Grouse
❑ Willow Ptarmigan
❑ Rock Ptarmigan
❑ White-tailed Ptarmigan
❑ Ruffed Grouse
❑ Sharp-tailed Grouse

**RAILS, GALLINULES,
COOTS**
❑ Virginia Rail (A)
❑ Sora
❑ Eurasian Coot (A)
❑ American Coot

CRANES
❑ Sandhill Crane
❑ Common Crane (A)

PLOVERS
❑ Black-bellied Plover
❑ Lesser Golden-Plover
❑ Mongolian Plover
❑ Common Ringed Plover
❑ Semipalmated Plover
❑ Little Ringed Plover
❑ Killdeer
❑ Eurasian Dotterel

OYSTERCATCHERS
❑ Black Oystercatcher

STILTS, AVOCETS
❑ Black-winged Stilt (A)
❑ American Avocet (A)

PRATINCOLES
❑ Oriental Pratincole (A)

SANDPIPERS
❑ Common Greenshank
❑ Greater Yellowlegs
❑ Lesser Yellowlegs
❑ Marsh Sandpiper (A)
❑ Spotted Redshank
❑ Wood Sandpiper
❑ Green Sandpiper
❑ Solitary Sandpiper
❑ Willet (A)
❑ Wandering Tattler
❑ Gray-tailed Tattler
❑ Common Sandpiper
❑ Spotted Sandpiper
❑ Terek Sandpiper
❑ Upland Sandpiper
❑ Eskimo Curlew (A)
❑ Little Curlew (A)
❑ Whimbrel
❑ Bristle-thighed Curlew
❑ Far Eastern Curlew
❑ Black-tailed Godwit
❑ Hudsonian Godwit
❑ Bar-tailed Godwit
❑ Marbled Godwit
❑ Ruddy Turnstone
❑ Black Turnstone

❑ Surfbird
❑ Great Knot
❑ Red Knot
❑ Sanderling
❑ Semipalmated Sandpiper
❑ Western Sandpiper
❑ Rufous-necked Stint
❑ Little Stint
❑ Temminck's Stint
❑ Long-toed Stint
❑ Least Sandpiper
❑ White-rumped Sandpiper
❑ Baird's Sandpiper
❑ Pectoral Sandpiper
❑ Sharp-tailed Sandpiper
❑ Rock Sandpiper
❑ Dunlin
❑ Curlew Sandpiper
❑ Stilt Sandpiper
❑ Spoonbill Sandpiper
❑ Broad-billed Sandpiper
❑ Buff-breasted Sandpiper
❑ Ruff
❑ Short-billed Dowitcher
❑ Long-billed Dowitcher
❑ Jack Snipe (A)
❑ Common Snipe
❑ Wilson's Phalarope
❑ Red-necked Phalarope
❑ Red Phalarope

**JAEGERS, GULLS,
TERNS**
❑ Pomarine Jaeger
❑ Parasitic Jaeger
❑ Long-tailed Jaeger
❑ South Polar Skua
❑ Franklin's Gull
❑ Common Black-headed Gull
❑ Bonaparte's Gull
❑ Black-tailed Gull (A)
❑ Mew Gull
❑ Ring-billed Gull
❑ California Gull
❑ Herring Gull
❑ Thayer's Gull
❑ Slaty-backed Gull
❑ Western Gull (A)
❑ Glaucous-winged Gull
❑ Glaucous Gull
❑ Black-legged Kittiwake

❑ Red-legged Kittiwake
❑ Ross' Gull
❑ Sabine's Gull
❑ Ivory Gull
❑ Caspian Tern
❑ Common Tern
❑ Arctic Tern
❑ Forster's Tern (A)
❑ Aleutian Tern
❑ White-winged Tern (A)
❑ Black Tern

ALCIDS
❑ Dovekie
❑ Common Murre
❑ Thick-billed Murre
❑ Black Guillemot
❑ Pigeon Guillemot
❑ Marbled Murrelet
❑ Kittlitz's Murrelet
❑ Ancient Murrelet
❑ Cassin's Auklet
❑ Parakeet Auklet
❑ Least Auklet
❑ Whiskered Auklet
❑ Crested Auklet
❑ Rhinoceros Auklet
❑ Tufted Puffin
❑ Horned Puffin

PIGEONS, DOVES
❑ Rock Dove
❑ Band-tailed Pigeon
❑ Rufous Turtle Dove (A)
❑ White-winged Dove (A)
❑ Mourning Dove

CUCKOOS
❑ Common Cuckoo
❑ Oriental Cuckoo

TYPICAL OWLS
❑ Oriental Scops-Owl (A)
❑ Western Screech-Owl
❑ Great Horned Owl
❑ Snowy Owl
❑ Northern Hawk Owl
❑ Northern Pygmy-Owl
❑ Barred Owl
❑ Great Gray Owl
❑ Long-eared Owl

❑ Short-eared Owl
❑ Boreal Owl
❑ Northern Saw-whet Owl

GOATSUCKERS
❑ Common Nighthawk
❑ Whip-poor-will (A)
❑ Jungle Nightjar (A)

SWIFTS
❑ Black Swift
❑ Chimney Swift (A)
❑ Vaux's Swift
❑ White-throated Needletail
❑ Common Swift (A)
❑ Fork-tailed Swift

HUMMINGBIRDS
❑ Ruby-throated
    Hummingbird (A)
❑ Anna's Hummingbird
❑ Costa's Hummingbird (A)
❑ Rufous Hummingbird

HOOPOES
❑ Hoopoe (A)

KINGFISHERS
❑ Belted Kingfisher

WOODPECKERS
❑ Eurasian Wryneck (A)
❑ Yellow-bellied Sapsucker
❑ Red-breasted Sapsucker
❑ Great Spotted
    Woodpecker (A)
❑ Downy Woodpecker
❑ Hairy Woodpecker
❑ Three-toed Woodpecker
❑ Black-backed Woodpecker
❑ Northern Flicker

TYRANT FLYCATCHERS
❑ Olive-sided Flycatcher
❑ Western Wood-Pewee
❑ Yellow-bellied Flycatcher
❑ Alder Flycatcher
❑ Willow Flycatcher (A)
❑ Least Flycatcher
❑ Hammond's Flycatcher
❑ Dusky Flycatcher

❑ Pacific-slope Flycatcher
❑ Say's Phoebe
❑ Western Kingbird
❑ Eastern Kingbird

LARKS
❑ Eurasian Skylark
❑ Horned Lark

SWALLOWS
❑ Purple Martin
❑ Tree Swallow
❑ Violet-green Swallow
❑ Northern Rough-winged
    Swallow
❑ Bank Swallow
❑ Cliff Swallow
❑ Barn Swallow
❑ Common House-Martin

**JAYS, MAGPIES,
CROWS**
❑ Gray Jay
❑ Steller's Jay
❑ Clark's Nutcracker
❑ Black-billed Magpie
❑ American Crow
❑ Northwestern Crow
❑ Common Raven

CHICKADEES
❑ Black-capped Chickadee
❑ Mountain Chickadee
❑ Siberian Tit
❑ Boreal Chickadee
❑ Chestnut-backed Chickadee
❑ Great Tit (A)

NUTHATCHES
❑ Red-breasted Nuthatch

CREEPERS
❑ Brown Creeper

WRENS
❑ Winter Wren

DIPPERS
❑ American Dipper

OLD WORLD WARBLERS AND FLYCATCHERS, KINGLETS, THRUSHES

- ❏ Middendorff's Grasshopper-Warbler
- ❏ Lanceolated Warbler (A)
- ❏ Wood Warbler (A)
- ❏ Dusky Warbler
- ❏ Arctic Warbler
- ❏ Golden-crowned Kinglet
- ❏ Ruby-crowned Kinglet
- ❏ Narcissus Flycatcher (A)
- ❏ Red-breasted Flycatcher
- ❏ Siberian Flycatcher
- ❏ Gray-spotted Flycatcher
- ❏ Asian Brown Flycatcher (A)
- ❏ Siberian Rubythroat
- ❏ Bluethroat
- ❏ Siberian Blue Robin (A)
- ❏ Red-flanked Bluetail
- ❏ Northern Wheatear
- ❏ Stonechat (A)
- ❏ Mountain Bluebird
- ❏ Townsend's Solitaire
- ❏ Gray-cheeked Thrush
- ❏ Swainson's Thrush
- ❏ Hermit Thrush
- ❏ Eyebrowed Thrush
- ❏ Dusky Thrush
- ❏ Fieldfare
- ❏ American Robin
- ❏ Varied Thrush

MIMIC THRUSHES

- ❏ Northern Mockingbird
- ❏ Brown Thrasher (A)

ACCENTORS

- ❏ Siberian Accentor

WAGTAILS, PIPITS

- ❏ Yellow Wagtail
- ❏ Gray Wagtail
- ❏ White Wagtail
- ❏ Black-backed Wagtail
- ❏ Brown Tree-Pipit (A)
- ❏ Olive Tree-Pipit
- ❏ Pechora Pipit
- ❏ Red-throated Pipit
- ❏ American Pipit

WAXWINGS

- ❏ Bohemian Waxwing
- ❏ Cedar Waxwing

SHRIKES

- ❏ Brown Shrike
- ❏ Northern Shrike

STARLINGS

- ❏ European Starling

VIREOS

- ❏ Solitary Vireo (A)
- ❏ Warbling Vireo
- ❏ Philadelphia Vireo
- ❏ Red-eyed Vireo

WOOD WARBLERS, TANAGERS, SPARROWS, BUNTINGS, BLACKBIRDS

- ❏ Tennessee Warbler
- ❏ Orange-crowned Warbler
- ❏ Northern Parula (A)
- ❏ Yellow Warbler
- ❏ Magnolia Warbler
- ❏ Cape May Warbler
- ❏ Yellow-rumped Warbler
- ❏ Townsend's Warbler
- ❏ Black-throated Green Warbler (A)
- ❏ Prairie Warbler (A)
- ❏ Bay-breasted Warbler (A)
- ❏ Palm Warbler
- ❏ Blackpoll Warbler
- ❏ Black-and-white Warbler (A)
- ❏ American Redstart
- ❏ Ovenbird (A)
- ❏ Northern Waterthrush
- ❏ Kentucky Warbler (A)
- ❏ Mourning Warbler (A)
- ❏ MacGillivray's Warbler
- ❏ Common Yellowthroat
- ❏ Wilson's Warbler
- ❏ Canada Warbler (A)
- ❏ Scarlet Tanager (A)
- ❏ Western Tanager
- ❏ Rose-breasted Grosbeak (A)
- ❏ Blue Grosbeak (A)
- ❏ Rufous-sided Towhee (A)
- ❏ American Tree Sparrow
- ❏ Chipping Sparrow

- ❏ Clay-colored Sparrow (A)
- ❏ Savannah Sparrow
- ❏ Fox Sparrow
- ❏ Song Sparrow
- ❏ Lincoln's Sparrow
- ❏ Swamp Sparrow
- ❏ White-throated Sparrow
- ❏ Golden-crowned Sparrow
- ❏ White-crowned Sparrow
- ❏ Harris' Sparrow
- ❏ Dark-eyed Junco
- ❏ Lapland Longspur
- ❏ Smith's Longspur
- ❏ Little Bunting
- ❏ Rustic Bunting
- ❏ Yellow-breasted Bunting (A)
- ❏ Gray Bunting
- ❏ Pallas' Reed-Bunting
- ❏ Common Reed-Bunting
- ❏ Snow Bunting
- ❏ McKay's Bunting
- ❏ Bobolink (A)
- ❏ Red-winged Blackbird
- ❏ Western Meadowlark
- ❏ Yellow-headed Blackbird
- ❏ Rusty Blackbird
- ❏ Brewer's Blackbird
- ❏ Common Grackle
- ❏ Brown-headed Cowbird
- ❏ Northern Oriole (A)

FINCHES

- ❏ Brambling
- ❏ Rosy Finch
- ❏ Pine Grosbeak
- ❏ Common Rosefinch
- ❏ Purple Finch
- ❏ Cassin's Finch (A)
- ❏ Red Crossbill
- ❏ White-winged Crossbill
- ❏ Common Redpoll
- ❏ Hoary Redpoll
- ❏ Pine Siskin
- ❏ Oriental Greenfinch
- ❏ Eurasian Bullfinch
- ❏ Evening Grosbeak
- ❏ Hawfinch

OLD WORLD SPARROWS

- ❏ House Sparrow (A)

BIRD FAMILIES

Family *Gaviidae*
LOONS
(5)

Loons are large swimming birds with webbed feet and sharply pointed bills. In flight the head is held lower than the body, giving the loon a hunchbacked appearance. Loons are considered among the most proficient of the diving birds; when underwater they propel themselves with only their feet. They feed mostly on fish, which they chase, usually in shallow water, and grasp with their bill. Because they have a specific gravity near that of water, loons can disappear quietly below the surface with hardly a ripple.

Red-throated Loon

(Gavia stellata)
Length: 25$^1/_2$ in.

Identification: Summer adult has dark gray head, red throat patch and plain brown back. Bill is slender, and carried slightly uptilted. All plumages at close range have the back speckled with white instead of the scaly or all-dark appearance of the other loons. Head always pale gray, contrasting little with the white throat. Voice is long series of quacking notes on breeding grounds; otherwise silent.

Habitat: Breeding — lakes, usually smaller and shallower than those inhabited by other loons. Nests on shores and islands of lakes. In migration and winter — inshore marine waters.

Status & Distribution	Spring	Summer	Fall	Winter	Breeder	Key
Southeastern	C	U	C	U	•	C Common
Southcoastal	C	C	C	U	•	U Uncommon
Southwestern	C	C	C	U	•	R Rare
Central	U	U	U	–	•	A Casual/Accidental
Western	C	C	C	–	•	– No Records
Northern	C	C	C	–	•	

RED-THROATED LOON, *Winter*

RED-THROATED LOON, *Summer*

Arctic Loon

(Gavia arctica)
Length: 28 in.

Identification: Very difficult to distinguish from the Pacific Loon. In all plumages, the Arctic Loon is larger than the Pacific Loon and has a proportionately heavier bill. The Arctic Loon may show a clear white patch on its rear flanks; the Pacific Loon lacks this patch. In breeding plumage the sub-species of Arctic Loon occurring in Alaska *(G. a. viridigularis)* has a green sheen to its throat rather than the purple or violet gloss of most Pacific Loons. But this color is difficult to see in the field, and a small percentage of Pacific Loons have green throats. Also, in breeding plumage the Arctic Loon has a darker (smokey-gray) nape than the pale (pearl-gray) nape of the Pacific Loon. This feature, like throat color, may be difficult to see except under excellent lighting conditions.

Habitat: Apparently very similar to Pacific Loon's; both species occur on the Seward Peninsula near Wales and Nome.

Status & Distribution	Spring	Summer	Fall	Winter	Breeder	Key
Southeastern	A	–	–	–		C Common
Southcoastal	–	–	–	–		U Uncommon
Southwestern	?	–	?	?		R Rare
Central	–	–	–	–		A Casual/Accidental
Western	R	R	R	–	•	– No Records
Northern	–	A	–	–		? Status Uncertain

ARCTIC LOON, Summer

ARCTIC LOON; Summer, left; Winter, right

Pacific Loon

(Gavia pacifica)
Length: 26 in.

Identification: In summer, adult has a gray nape and black throat. White checkers on the back are separated into several large patches. In Common Loon and Yellow-billed Loon the checkers cover the entire back. In winter, similar to Common Loon but smaller in size with a more slender bill. Dark color of the cap reaches below the eye in a well-marked straight dark line. In contrast, the Common Loon has considerable white around the eyes and an irregular border between the cap and throat colors. Voice is a barking *caw wow* and a variety of wailing and honking notes.

Habitat: Breeding — lakes on tundra or in coniferous forests. Nests on projecting points or small islands. In migration and winter — inshore and offshore marine waters.

PACIFIC LOON, *Winter*

Status & Distribution	Spring	Summer	Fall	Winter	Breeder	Key
Southeastern	C	R	C	C		C Common
Southcoastal	C	U	C	C	•	U Uncommon
Southwestern	C	C	C	R	•	R Rare
Central	C	C	C	–	•	A Casual/Accidental
Western	C	C	C	–	•	– No Records
Northern	C	C	C	–	•	

PACIFIC LOON, *Summer*

Common Loon
(Gavia immer)
Length: 32 in.

Identification: In summer, adult has an all-black head with a broken white collar that separates it from the Red-throated, Pacific and Arctic loons. Similar to the Yellow-billed Loon but has a straight black bill rather than the upturned yellow bill. Winter adults and young similar to other loons. Large size and noticeably heavy straight bill useful for identification in winter. In flight, looks more ponderous than the smaller Red-throated, Pacific and Arctic loons, and has distinctly slower wingbeats. Distinctive loud, resonant yodeling call on breeding grounds.

COMMON LOON, *Summer*

Status & Distribution	Spring	Summer	Fall	Winter	Breeder	Key
Southeastern	C	U	C	U	•	C Common
Southcoastal	C	U	C	U	•	U Uncommon
Southwestern	U	U	U	U	•	R Rare
Central	C	C	C	–	•	A Casual/Accidental
Western	U	U	U	–	•	– No Records
Northern	–	A	–	–		

Habitat: Breeding — lakes in coniferous forests and heath in the Aleutian Islands. Nests on a mound of vegetation near water, often on small islands, sometimes on top of old muskrat houses. Prefers secluded lakes away from human activity. Highly territorial; usually only a single pair is found on the smaller lakes. In winter — inshore marine waters.

COMMON LOON, *Winter*

Yellow-billed Loon

(Gavia adamsii)
Length: 35 in.

Identification: An adult in any plumage can be distinguished from the Common Loon by the larger, whitish-yellow, chisel-shaped, slightly upturned bill. In the first fall, immatures of both species are similar, but the head pattern of the Yellow-billed Loon has a dark smudge behind the ears, the bill is usually held up at a slight angle, and the head and back often appear browner than in the Common Loon. Voice is similar to that of the Common Loon, although this species is described as less vocal.

Habitat: Breeding — tundra lakes, ponds and rivers. May visit inshore marine waters to feed. Nests in vegetation on small islands or on shore. In migration and winter — inshore and offshore marine waters.

YELLOW-BILLED LOON, *Winter*

Status & Distribution	Spring	Summer	Fall	Winter	Breeder	Key
Southeastern	U	R	R	U		C Common
Southcoastal	U	R	R	U		U Uncommon
Southwestern	R	–	R	R		R Rare
Central	A	–	A	–		A Casual/Accidental
Western	U	U	U	–	•	– No Records
Northern	U	U	U	–	•	

YELLOW-BILLED LOON, *Summer*

Family *Podicipedidae*
GREBES
(4)

Grebes are thin-necked diving birds that are smaller than loons. Compared with loons they have a relatively long neck and rarely fly. Their legs are set well back on their bodies, they have flat lobes on their toes and a virtually nonexistent tail. Young, except for the Western Grebe, have striped heads. They feed primarily on fish.

Pied-billed Grebe

(Podilymbus podiceps)
Length: 13 in.

Identification: Only grebe that is all brown in all plumages, with no indication of the angular head of the other species and with a much shorter, almost chickenlike white bill. In summer, the throat is black and the bill has a black band across it.

Habitat: Inshore marine waters and lakes.

Status & Distribution	Spring	Summer	Fall	Winter	Breeder	Key
Southeastern	A	A	R	R		C Common
Southcoastal	A	A	A	A	•	U Uncommon
Southwestern	–	–	–	–		R Rare
Central	–	–	–	–		A Casual/Accidental
Western	–	–	–	–		– No Records
Northern	–	–	–	–		

PIED-BILLED GREBE, *Breeding*

Horned Grebe

(Podiceps auritus)
Length: 13 1/2 in.

Identification: In breeding plumage, recognized by broad buffy ear tufts conspicuous against a black head and red neck. In winter, clear white cheeks, short neck and short slender bill separate it from other grebes.

Status & Distribution	Spring	Summer	Fall	Winter	Breeder	Key
Southeastern	C	A	C	U		C Common
Southcoastal	C	U	C	C	•	U Uncommon
Southwestern	C	U	C	C	•	R Rare
Central	C	C	C	–	•	A Casual/Accidental
Western	R	R	R	–	•	– No Records
Northern	–	A	–	–		

Habitat: Breeding — freshwater ponds, sloughs and lakes, usually in areas containing emergent vegetation. Nests are floating platforms of vegetation and mud anchored to growing vegetation in shallow lakes. In migration and winter — inshore marine waters.

HORNED GREBE, *Breeding*

Red-necked Grebe

(Podiceps grisegena)
Length: 20 in.

(Pictured on right)
Identification: In breeding plumage has black crown, conspicuous white cheeks and throat and chestnut-red neck. In winter, similar to other grebes, with gray to brown upperparts and white underparts. Larger than Horned Grebe, with longer yellowish bill and brownish neck. Slightly smaller and shorter necked than Western Grebe. Lacks strong contrast of Western Grebe's black and white on head and neck. More often seen in flight than other grebes. Only grebe with narrow, white wing patch on both front and rear edge of each wing.

Status & Distribution	Spring	Summer	Fall	Winter	Breeder	Key
Southeastern	C	U	C	U		C Common
Southcoastal	C	U	C	U	•	U Uncommon
Southwestern	U	R	U	U	•	R Rare
Central	C	C	C	–	•	A Casual/Accidental
Western	U	U	U	–	•	– No Records
Northern	–	A	–	–	•	

Habitat: Breeding — freshwater lakes, marshes and slow-moving rivers. Nests float and are placed in vegetation along the margins of shallow lakes. In winter — inshore marine waters.

Western Grebe
(Aechmophorus occidentalis)
Length: 26 in.

Identification: Largest of North American grebes. Identified by long, very slender neck, contrasting black-and-white coloration and slender yellow bill.

Status & Distribution	Spring	Summer	Fall	Winter	Breeder	Key
Southeastern	U	A	U	U		C Common
Southcoastal	–	–	A	A		U Uncommon
Southwestern	–	–	A	A		R Rare
Central	–	–	A	–		A Casual/Accidental
Western	–	–	–	–		– No Records
Northern	–	–	–	–		

Habitat: Inshore marine waters mostly in the southern part of southeastern Alaska from mid-September through early May. Not known to breed in Alaska.

WESTERN GREBE

RED-NECKED GREBE, *Breeding*

Family *Diomedeidae*
ALBATROSSES
(3)

Albatrosses are goose-sized seabirds that frequent the open ocean. They have long, narrow, bowed wings, and fly low over the water with scarcely a wingbeat on windy days. The bill is strongly hooked at the tip and has tubular nostrils near the base. Albatrosses do not breed north of the central and western Pacific islands. They feed mostly at night on marine animals such as squid and cuttlefish; some follow ships at sea to feed on refuse.

Short-tailed Albatross
(Diomedea albatrus)
Length: 35 in.

Identification: Adult is distinguished from Laysan Albatross by an entirely white back. Immature is chocolate brown, with conspicuous pale bill and feet.

Habitat: Mostly offshore marine waters. Endangered species.

Status & Distribution	Spring	Summer	Fall	Winter	Breeder	Key
Southeastern	A	–	–	–		C Common
Southcoastal	–	–	A	–		U Uncommon
Southwestern	A	A	A	–		R Rare
Central	–	–	–	–		A Casual/Accidental
Western	–	–	–	–		– No Records
Northern	–	–	–	–		

SHORT-TAILED ALBATROSS, *Adult*

Black-footed Albatross

(Diomedea nigripes)
Length: 32 in.
Wingspan: 7 ft.

Identification: Dark-bodied, with dark feet and bill. Some older birds have white rumps and considerable white on the head.

Status & Distribution	Spring	Summer	Fall	Winter	Breeder	Key
Southeastern	C	C	C	–		C Common
Southcoastal	C	C	C	R		U Uncommon
Southwestern	C	C	C	–		R Rare
Central	–	–	–	–		A Casual/Accidental
Western	R	R	R	–		– No Records
Northern	–	–	–	–		

Habitat: Mostly offshore marine waters. Most often seen from vessels crossing the Gulf of Alaska and near the Aleutian Islands.

BLACK-FOOTED ALBATROSS

Laysan Albatross

(Diomedea immutabilis)
Length: 32 in.
Wingspan: 6¹/₂ ft.

Identification: Huge, long-winged seabird with white body and black back and wings.

Status & Distribution	Spring	Summer	Fall	Winter	Breeder	Key
Southeastern	R	A	–	–		C Common
Southcoastal	R	R	R	–		U Uncommon
Southwestern	U	U	U	R		R Rare
Central	–	–	–	–		A Casual/Accidental
Western	R	R	R	–		– No Records
Northern	–	–	–	–		

Habitat: Inshore and offshore marine waters. The western and central Aleutian Islands are good areas to view this species.

Notes: This species is not nearly as common as the Black-footed Albatross. Estimates of yearly populations in the southcoastal region are in the hundreds, whereas estimates for the Black-footed Albatross for the summer alone number in the thousands and possibly the tens of thousands.

LAYSAN ALBATROSS

Family *Procellariidae*
FULMARS, PETRELS, SHEARWATERS
(7 + 1)

Fulmars, petrels and shearwaters are gull-sized seabirds that resemble gulls but have longer, more slender wings and tubular nostrils. Sailing over the open sea with occasional rapid wingbeats, they are often seen skimming low over the waves on stiff, bowed wings. The Northern Fulmar is the only member of this family that breeds in Alaska.

Northern Fulmar

(Fulmarus glacialis)
Length: 18 in.

Identification: Color varies from light to dark. In the lighter phase (gray back and wings, otherwise white) it resembles an adult gull, but it is distinguished from any gull by its stubby large bill with large nostrils, held pointing downward, thick neck and stiff-winged flight. In the darker phase (all dark gray) it may be mistaken for a dark shearwater but is much heavier built, paler, and again has a thicker, down-pointing, yellow bill.

Status & Distribution	Spring	Summer	Fall	Winter	Breeder	Key
Southeastern	U	U	U	U		C Common
Southcoastal	C	C	C	U		U Uncommon
Southwestern	C	C	C	U	•	R Rare
Central	–	–	–	–		A Casual/Accidental
Western	U	C	U	R	•	– No Records
Northern	–	R	–	–		

Habitat: Inshore and offshore marine waters. Nests in colonies on sea cliffs on some of the outlying islands including the Semidi, Aleutian and Pribilof islands.

Notes: A fulmar usually feeds from the surface of the sea on small fish and squid. Often it follows ships or concentrates near canneries to feed on refuse.

NORTHERN FULMAR, *Light Phase*

NORTHERN FULMAR, *Dark Phase*

Mottled Petrel

(Pterodroma inexpectata)
Length: 14 in.

Identification: At close range a patchy pattern of gray is visible above, with a dark cap and forward edge of the wing; mixed dark and white below. Gray belly and dark line under the wing contrast with white breast and undertail. Flight is much like that of other shearwaters but more rapid and often higher above the surface of the water. This species sometimes flies in great loops.

Habitat: Mostly offshore marine waters. Occasionally inshore waters in summer. Usually seen singly or in small groups on the open North Pacific.

Status & Distribution	Spring	Summer	Fall	Winter	Breeder	Key
Southeastern	U	U	U	–		C Common
Southcoastal	U	U	U	–		U Uncommon
Southwestern	U	U	U	–		R Rare
Central	–	–	–	–		A Casual/Accidental
Western	–	R	–	–		– No Records
Northern	–	–	–	–		

MOTTLED PETREL

Pink-footed Shearwater
(Puffinus creatopus)
Length: 19 in.

Identification: One of 3 white-bellied shearwaters that might be seen offshore. Drab light brown above with an irregular line where the 2 colors meet. Considerable brown in the white wing linings. Pink bill.

Status & Distribution	Spring	Summer	Fall	Winter	Breeder	Key
Southeastern	R	R	R	–		C Common
Southcoastal	R	R	R	–		U Uncommon
Southwestern	–	–	A	–		R Rare
Central	–	–	–	–		A Casual/Accidental
Western	–	–	–	–		– No Records
Northern	–	–	–	–		

Habitat: Inshore and offshore marine waters.

PINK-FOOTED SHEARWATER

Flesh-footed Shearwater
(Puffinus carneipes)
Length: 19¹/₂ in.

Identification: Large, entirely chocolate brown with conspicuous pink bill and feet. Wing linings are dark, even darker than in most Short-tailed Shearwaters. A slow wingbeat is the best field mark at a distance.

Status & Distribution	Spring	Summer	Fall	Winter	Breeder	Key
Southeastern	–	–	–	–		C Common
Southcoastal	–	A	A	–		U Uncommon
Southwestern	–	A	A	–		R Rare
Central	–	–	–	–		A Casual/Accidental
Western	–	–	–	–		– No Records
Northern	–	–	–	–		

Habitat: Inshore and offshore marine waters.

FLESH-FOOTED SHEARWATER

Buller's Shearwater
(Puffinus bulleri)
Length: 16¹/₂ in.

Identification: Small, crisply gray above, with a black cap and tail and black M-pattern across the wings and back. Snowy white beneath, including the wing linings. The flash of the white wing linings is the best distant field mark.

Status & Distribution	Spring	Summer	Fall	Winter	Breeder	Key
Southeastern	A	–	–	–		C Common
Southcoastal	A	R	A	–		U Uncommon
Southwestern	–	–	–	–		R Rare
Central	–	–	–	–		A Casual/Accidental
Western	–	–	–	–		– No Records
Northern	–	–	–	–		

Habitat: Offshore marine waters.

Notes: This species travels in flocks more than other shearwaters do.

BULLER'S SHEARWATER

Sooty Shearwater
(Puffinus griseus)
Length: 17 in.

Identification: Appears dark at a distance. Often seen gliding over waves with narrow, rigidly held wings. Has dark bill and feet. Most have whitish wing linings and uniformly dark head; some have dark wing linings.

Habitat: Inshore and offshore marine waters. Approaches the coastline more often than other shearwaters.

Status & Distribution	Spring	Summer	Fall	Winter	Breeder	Key
Southeastern	C	C	C	–		C Common
Southcoastal	C	C	C	–		U Uncommon
Southwestern	C	C	C	A		R Rare
Central	–	–	–	–		A Casual/Accidental
Western	–	–	–	–		– No Records
Northern	–	–	–	–		

Notes: In some years these birds are estimated to number in the millions in Alaska's offshore waters.

SOOTY SHEARWATER

Short-tailed Shearwater

(Puffinus tenuirostris)
Length: 14 in.

Identification: Difficult to distinguish from Sooty Shearwater. Usually the underside of the wing is plain gray rather than whitish as in the Sooty Shearwater. Short-tailed Shearwater has a shorter, thinner bill than Sooty Shearwater, but this may be difficult to see in the field. Throat is often whitish.

Habitat: Inshore and offshore marine waters. Most abundant near the Aleutian Islands and in the Bering Sea. Occurs less frequently along the coast of Alaska to Forrester Island in southeastern Alaska and north along the coast to Point Barrow. This species and the Northern Fulmar are the only shearwaters likely to be found in far northern waters.

Status & Distribution	Spring	Summer	Fall	Winter	Breeder	Key
Southeastern	R	R	R	–		C Common
Southcoastal	U	C	U	A		U Uncommon
Southwestern	C	C	C	A		R Rare
Central	–	–	–	–		A Casual/Accidental
Western	C	C	C	–		– No Records
Northern	–	R	R	–		

Notes: This species, like the Sooty Shearwater, sometimes occurs in numbers estimated to be in the millions. Short-tailed Shearwater feeds on fish, squid, crustaceans and refuse thrown from ships.

SHORT-TAILED SHEARWATER

Family *Hydrobatidae*
STORM-PETRELS
(2)

Storm-petrels are small blackbird-sized birds of the open sea with a forked or notched tail. They are often seen hovering over or diving onto the ocean surface in search of their food — small fishes, shrimp, squid, other marine animals and even oil from wounded whales or seals.

FORK-TAILED STORM-PETREL

Fork-tailed Storm-Petrel
(Oceanodroma furcata)
Length: $8^{1}/_{2}$ in.

Identification: Pearl gray color distinguishes this species from Leach's Storm-Petrels, which are dark brown. Phalaropes, which fly steadily and are often seen in flocks, are the only other small, pale birds to be seen at sea.

Habitat: Inshore and offshore marine waters. Nests in colonies on offshore islands. Breeding pairs dig burrows in the soil or, more commonly, occupy rock crevices. Breeding locations include Saint Lazaria and Forrester islands in southeastern Alaska, the Aleutian Islands and Barren, Chiswell, Semidi and Shumagin islands.

Status & Distribution	Spring	Summer	Fall	Winter	Breeder	Key
Southeastern	C	C	C	R	•	C Common
Southcoastal	C	C	C	R	•	U Uncommon
Southwestern	C	C	C	R	•	R Rare
Central	–	–	A	–		A Casual/Accidental
Western	–	U	U	–		– No Records
Northern	–	–	–	–		

Notes: Although this species congregates at food sources, it does not flock; each bird is independent in flight. Often attracted to boat lights at night. Commonly seen near shore, especially in fall.

Leach's Storm-Petrel

(Oceanodroma leucorhoa)
Length: 8 in.

Identification: Dark brown above and below, with a forked tail and conspicuous white rump patch.

Habitat: Inshore and offshore marine waters. Nests on islands in colonies, with each nest placed at the end of a shallow burrow. Breeds on the Aleutian, Semidi and Shumagin islands; in the Sandman Reefs, south of the Alaska Peninsula; and on Saint Lazaria and Forrester islands off southeastern Alaska.

Status & Distribution	Spring	Summer	Fall	Winter	Breeder	Key
Southeastern	U	C	C	–	•	C Common
Southcoastal	R	R	R	–	•	U Uncommon
Southwestern	U	C	C	–	•	R Rare
Central	–	–	–	–		A Casual/Accidental
Western	–	A	–	–		– No Records
Northern	–	–	–	–		

Notes: Feeds nocturnally near its breeding grounds; hence it is rarely seen at sea near shore.

LEACH'S STORM-PETREL

Family *Phalacrocoracidae*
CORMORANTS
(4)

Cormorants are large, dark, water birds with slender bills. All 4 of the toes on each foot are connected by webs. They hold the bill up at an angle and are longer tailed and broader winged than loons. Unlike ducks their feathers are not completely waterproof, so they often go to shore and hold their wings out to dry. They feed mostly on small fish.

Double-crested Cormorant
(Phalacrocorax auritus)
Length: 33 in.

Identification: Distinguished from other cormorants by orange-yellow throat pouch and pale bill, and in breeding season by side-by-side crests on the head. Bulky neck is kinked in flight. Immatures have pale brownish breast. Often flies much higher than other cormorants, which tend to stay low over the water except at breeding colonies.

Status & Distribution	Spring	Summer	Fall	Winter	Breeder	Key
Southeastern	U	U	U	U	•	C Common
Southcoastal	C	C	C	U	•	U Uncommon
Southwestern	C	C	C	U	•	R Rare
Central	–	A	–	–		A Casual/Accidental
Western	–	–	–	–		– No Records
Northern	–	–	–	–		

Habitat: Lakes, rivers, inshore marine waters. Nests in a variety of locations including cliff ledges, trees near either fresh or salt water or on the ground on small islands. Only cormorant to be seen on fresh water and in shallow estuaries.

DOUBLE-CRESTED CORMORANT

Brandt's Cormorant
(Phalacrocorax penicillatus)
Length: 34 in.

Identification: Shaped more like a
Pelagic Cormorant than a Double-crested
Cormorant, with a long, slender neck and
long, slender bill. Flies with a very slightly
crooked or a straight neck, and with the
head moderately distinct from the neck.
Bill looks heavier than that of the Pelagic
or Red-faced cormorants. Shorter tail than
for other cormorants, which is a good way
to distinguish Brandt's Cormorant from
smaller cormorants. At close range buffy
feathers are visible behind the naked dark
throat pouch. In breeding plumage, fine
white plumes appear on the sides of the neck
and back, and throat pouch becomes bright
blue. Immature is dark brown below, darker
than young Double-crested Cormorants but
paler than young Pelagic and Red-faced
cormorants.

Status & Distribution	Spring	Summer	Fall	Winter	Breeder	Key
Southeastern	–	R	A	–	•	C Common
Southcoastal	–	R	–	–	•	U Uncommon
Southwestern	–	–	–	–		R Rare
Central	–	–	–	–		A Casual/Accidental
Western	–	–	–	–		– No Records
Northern	–	–	–	–		

Habitat: Inshore marine waters, rocky
islands.

BRANDT'S CORMORANT

Pelagic Cormorant

(Phalacrocorax pelagicus)
Length: 25$^1/_2$ in.

Identification: Glossy greenish-black
color is similar to that of the Red-faced
Cormorant. Both Pelagic and Red-faced
cormorants have white flank patches in
breeding plumage and fore and aft crests
on the head. Pelagic Cormorant has a dull
red pouch and a small amount of dull red
on its face; small, dark bill. Immature is all
dark, without the iridescence of the adult.

PELAGIC CORMORANT

Status & Distribution	Spring	Summer	Fall	Winter	Breeder	Key
Southeastern	C	U	C	C	•	C Common
Southcoastal	C	C	C	C	•	U Uncommon
Southwestern	C	C	C	C	•	R Rare
Central	–	–	–	–		A Casual/Accidental
Western	C	C	C	A	•	– No Records
Northern	–	R	–	–		

Habitat: Inshore marine waters, sea cliffs,
rocky islands. Nests in colonies on small
islands and narrow cliff ledges near the sea.

Notes: Dives deeper than other cormorants
and swims underwater. Often approaches
schools of small fish from below, causing
them to jump about at the surface and thus
become easier to capture. Sometimes seen
on floating logs and icebergs.

Red-faced Cormorant

(Phalacrocorax urile)
Length: 29 in.

Identification: Likely to be confused only with Pelagic Cormorant, the only other small cormorant in Alaska. In breeding season has bright red face patch and blue throat and much greater area of bare skin about the base of bill. In duller immature plumage, distinguished at close range by a heavier bill, which is usually pale, and somewhat larger size than Pelagic Cormorant.

Status & Distribution	Spring	Summer	Fall	Winter	Breeder	Key
Southeastern	–	–	–	A		C Common
Southcoastal	C	C	C	C	•	U Uncommon
Southwestern	C	C	C	C	•	R Rare
Central	–	–	–	–		A Casual/Accidental
Western	–	A	–	–		– No Records
Northern	–	–	–	–		

Habitat: Inshore marine waters. Nests in colonies on ledges of sea cliffs, small piles of rocks and small shelves on volcanic cinder cones. In North America this bird appears only in Alaska.

RED-FACED CORMORANT

Family *Ardeidae*
BITTERNS, HERONS
(5 + 4)

Bitterns and herons are wading birds with a long neck, long legs and a rather long, straight, pointed bill. They usually capture their food by grasping it with the bill rather than by spearing it. Beware of picking up an injured member of this family, because it might, in self-defense, strike at your eyes with its sharp bill.

American Bittern
(Botaurus lentiginosus)
Length: 23 1/2 in.

Identification: Heavily striped with white and warm brown. Much more compact than larger Great Blue Heron, but has same long, pointed bill, longish neck, long legs and habit of folding the neck in flight. Flying at a distance, bittern looks very pointed at the front end and appears all brown with darker flight feathers.

Status & Distribution	Spring	Summer	Fall	Winter	Breeder	Key
Southeastern	R	R	R	–	•	C Common
Southcoastal	–	–	–	–		U Uncommon
Southwestern	–	–	–	–		R Rare
Central	–	–	–	–		A Casual/Accidental
Western	–	–	–	–		– No Records
Northern	–	–	–	–		

Habitat: Freshwater lakes and marshes with heavy aquatic vegetation. Nests have not been found in Alaska. Elsewhere nests consist of platforms of dead stalks in heavy vegetation. Found mostly along major mainland river systems of southeastern Alaska.

AMERICAN BITTERN

Great Blue Heron

(Ardea herodias)
Length: 47 in.
Wingspan: 6 ft.

Identification: Blue-gray and somewhat streaked. Likely to be confused only with Sandhill Crane, which is plain gray and streakless. In flight, the heron carries its neck doubled back, with its head against its shoulders; the crane carries its neck straight out. Heron is usually solitary; crane is often in pairs or flocks.

Status & Distribution	Spring	Summer	Fall	Winter	Breeder	Key
Southeastern	U	U	U	U	•	C Common
Southcoastal	U	U	U	U	•	U Uncommon
Southwestern	–	–	–	–		R Rare
Central	–	A	–	–		A Casual/Accidental
Western	–	–	–	–		– No Records
Northern	–	A	–	–		

Habitat: Tidal sloughs, saltwater inlets and beaches, lower reaches of salmon spawning streams, shallow lakes, freshwater ponds and marshes. Nests in colonies in upper parts of tall trees and more rarely in bushes or on the ground. Sometimes perches in trees.

Notes: Expert at fishing; captures prey by remaining motionless or by a very slow stalk and a rapid strike with the bill.

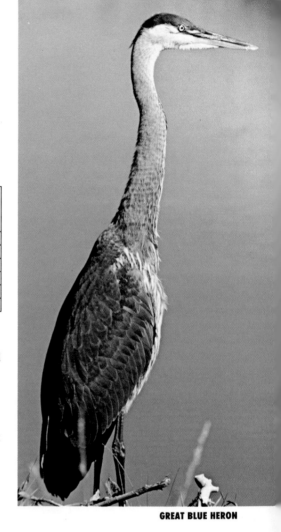

GREAT BLUE HERON

Great Egret

(Casmerodius albus)
Length: 39 in.

Identification: Large white heron with yellow bill, black legs and feet. In breeding plumage, it has long, lacy plumes on the back.

Status & Distribution	Spring	Summer	Fall	Winter	Breeder	Key
Southeastern	A	A	–	–		C Common
Southcoastal	A	A	–	–		U Uncommon
Southwestern	–	–	–	–		R Rare
Central	–	–	–	–		A Casual/Accidental
Western	–	–	–	–		– No Records
Northern	–	–	–	–		

Habitat: Marshes and mud flats. Has been found at Kodiak, Cordova, Glacier Bay and Juneau.

GREAT EGRET

Cattle Egret

(Bubulcus ibis)
Length: 20 in.

Identification: Small, stocky, short-necked white heron. Breeding adult is mostly white with orange-buff plumes on crown, back and upper breast. Nonbreeding adult and immature have a yellow bill and yellow or greenish legs. Some immatures may have black legs.

Status & Distribution	Spring	Summer	Fall	Winter	Breeder	Key
Southeastern	–	–	A	A		C Common
Southcoastal	–	–	A	–		U Uncommon
Southwestern	–	A	–	–		R Rare
Central	–	–	–	–		A Casual/Accidental
Western	–	–	–	–		– No Records
Northern	–	–	–	–		

Habitat: Open habitat, marshes and mud flats. Has been found at Ketchikan, Sitka, Whittier and Agattu Island.

CATTLE EGRET

Black-crowned Night-Heron

(Nycticorax nycticorax)
Length: 23–28 in.

Identification: Adult is distinctive with its black back and black cap. Gray wings, whitish underneath, and long white plumes on head in breeding plumage. Immature is brown with buffy spots on wings and back and streaks on head and underparts. Call is a loud, barking *Kwok!*

Status & Distribution	Spring	Summer	Fall	Winter	Breeder	Key
Southeastern	A	A	–	–	*	C Common
Southcoastal	–	–	–	–		U Uncommon
Southwestern	A	–	–	–		R Rare
Central	–	–	–	–		A Casual/Accidental
Western	–	–	–	–		– No Records
Northern	–	–	–	–		

Habitat: Has occurred on Shemya and Atka islands in the Aleutians, on Saint Paul Island in the Pribilofs and at Juneau.

BLACK-CROWNED NIGHT-HERON, *Adult*

Family *Anatidae*
SWANS, GEESE, DUCKS
(48 + 1)

This family of waterfowl is best described in the following groups:

Swans — Large waterfowl, in which the adults have an all white plumage and very long neck. Alaska swans do not pair until their third or fourth year but, once paired, tend to remain together for life. The usual family seen in fall or winter includes 2 white parents and 3 to 5 gray young. Young assume pure white adult plumage early in their second year. Three species occur in Alaska.

Geese — Geese are smaller than swans and larger than ducks. They walk better than ducks and feed more frequently on land. Seven species occur in Alaska.

Perching Ducks — Represented in Alaska by 1 species, the Wood Duck. This duck nests in holes in trees, has sharp claws and usually perches on branches near water.

Surface-feeding Ducks — Includes birds from Green-winged Teal through American Wigeon. Surface-feeding, or puddle, ducks have feet set in the middle of their bodies and walk well, often nesting far from the water in meadows or woodlands. They feed while walking or by tipping up in the water and "dabbling." These ducks leap from the water when taking flight. Most of them from Alaska winter in Pacific coast states. Fourteen species occur in Alaska.

Diving Ducks — Includes birds from Common Pochard through Bufflehead. They have feet set far back on their bodies and must balance in an awkward fashion when walking. They feed underwater and can dive to depths of a hundred feet or more in search of food. Diving ducks patter across the water in a long takeoff run before becoming airborne. Nineteen species occur in Alaska.

Mergansers — These are fish-eating ducks with slender bills equipped with sharp projections especially adapted for catching and holding fish. Four species occur in Alaska.

Stiff-tailed Ducks — Represented in Alaska by 1 species, the Ruddy Duck. They have stiff, elongated tail feathers and unusually large feet. They are nearly helpless on land and feed almost exclusively underwater.

Plumages: In the swans and geese, sexes are identical. In ducks, sexes are usually easily separated in winter and spring, with the males being the more colorful. After nesting, ducks undergo an eclipse molt, causing males to look much like females. This causes some confusion in identification; however, the distinctive speculum does not change, providing a handy way to identify ducks in flight. The pictures in this book are winter-spring plumages.

Notes: About 10 million swans, geese and ducks nest in Alaska each year, making the state "critical" habitat for North America's waterfowl. In North America some species and subspecies use Alaska as their exclusive nesting grounds (Emperor Goose, Cackling Canada Goose, Aleutian Canada Goose, Spectacled Eider and Steller's Eider), while over half the North American population of other species nest in the state (Trumpeter Swan, Tundra Swan, Vancouver Canada Goose, White-fronted Goose, Greater Scaup and Harlequin Duck).

Tundra Swan

(Cygnus columbianus)
Length: 52 in.
Wingspan: 6–7 ft.

Identification: Bright yellow teardrop on otherwise black bill is typical of Tundra Swan, although in some birds this spot is absent or too small to see.

Status & Distribution	Spring	Summer	Fall	Winter	Breeder	Key
Southeastern	U	–	C	R		C Common
Southcoastal	C	R	C	R		U Uncommon
Southwestern	C	C	C	R	•	R Rare
Central	C	U	C	–	•	A Casual/Accidental
Western	C	C	C	–	•	– No Records
Northern	U	U	U	–	•	

Habitat: In summer — tundra. Nests usually on dry upland sites sometimes many yards from water, and occasionally on small islands. In migration — salt water, wetlands, lakes and rivers.

Notes: Recent inventories show more than 100,000 Tundra Swans in their principal wintering areas in California, Maryland, Virginia and North Carolina. Two-thirds of this population probably nest in Alaska, with the birds from western Alaska migrating primarily to California and those from north of the Brooks Range making the long trek east.

Best places to watch for Tundra Swans include: Yukon-Kuskokwim delta, where nesting densities are highest; Naknek River near the King Salmon airport, where large flocks gather in spring and fall; upper Cook Inlet, including Potter Marsh and Portage; and wetlands near Cordova, Yakutat, Gustavus, Juneau and other southeastern coastal areas, particularly in October.

TUNDRA SWAN

Whooper Swan

(Cygnus cygnus)
Length: 52 in.
Wingspan: 6–7 ft.

Identification: Slightly smaller than
Trumpeter Swan, but otherwise resembles
that species except for extensive yellow
saddle covering half or more of upper bill
in the adult.

Status & Distribution	Spring	Summer	Fall	Winter	Breeder	Key
Southeastern	–	–	–	–		C Common
Southcoastal	–	–	A	–		U Uncommon
Southwestern	R	R	R	U		R Rare
Central	–	–	–	–		A Casual/Accidental
Western	R	R	–	–		– No Records
Northern	–	–	–	–		

Habitat: Mostly found in western and
central Aleutian Islands, where a few dozen
winter. Not known to breed in Alaska.

WHOOPER SWAN

Trumpeter Swan
(Cygnus buccinator)
Length: 65 in.
Wingspan: 6–8 ft.

Identification: Difficult to distinguish from Tundra Swan. Has an all-black bill, lacking the yellow spot usually found on the bill of the Tundra Swan. Substantially larger than Tundra Swan, and easily distinguished when the two are occasionally seen together during migration. Trumpeter Swan usually has an obvious pink area where upper and lower mandibles contact. Trumpeter's call is hornlike (often *ko-hoh*); Tundra's is high-pitched, often quavering (*oo-oo-oo*) and is accentuated in the middle.

Status & Distribution	Spring	Summer	Fall	Winter	Breeder	Key
Southeastern	U	R	U	R	•	C Common
Southcoastal	C	C	C	U	•	U Uncommon
Southwestern	–	–	–	A		R Rare
Central	U	U	U	–	•	A Casual/Accidental
Western	–	A	–	–	•	– No Records
Northern	–	R	–	–	•	

Habitat: Forest wetlands, lakes, marshes, rivers with dense vegetation. Nests in water by making a platform 6 to 12 feet in diameter from surrounding vegetation.

Notes: Recognized as the largest of the 7 swans found worldwide and is one of the heaviest flying birds at 25 to 35, and occasionally 40, lbs. Eighty percent of world's population of Trumpeter Swan nests in Alaska, yet at 7,000 to 8,000 birds it is outnumbered 15 to 1 by smaller Tundra Swan. Best places to see Trumpeter Swans in summer are Kenai National Wildlife Refuge, Minto Flats near Fairbanks, and along the highway east from Cordova. In winter they are often seen at Eyak Lake in Cordova and Blind Slough in Petersburg.

TRUMPETER SWAN

Bean Goose
(Anser fabalis)
Length: 28–36 in.

Identification: Closely resembles Greater White-fronted Goose at a distance, but is generally larger and more ponderous, darker and longer necked. Has no white around the bill. Has unspotted belly similar to young Greater White-fronted Goose. Bill is black with irregularly shaped orange ring around the middle.

Status & Distribution	Spring	Summer	Fall	Winter	Breeder	Key
Southeastern	–	–	–	–		C Common
Southcoastal	–	–	–	–		U Uncommon
Southwestern	R	A	–	–		R Rare
Central	–	–	–	–		A Casual/Accidental
Western	A	–	–	–		– No Records
Northern	–	–	–	–		

Habitat: Asiatic goose found mostly in western and central Aleutian Islands during spring. Not known to breed in Alaska.

BEAN GOOSE

Greater White-fronted Goose

(Anser albifrons)
Length: 28¹/₂ in.

Identification: Brown with white tail coverts. Shorter neck than similarly sized Canada Goose, although the 2 species may closely resemble one another at a distance. Adult has a white patch on the front of the face. Immature lacks white patch but has yellow or orange legs and feet, which no other Alaska geese have except much rarer Bean Goose and easily distinguished Emperor Goose. Young have very light black breast spotting, while older birds become heavily spotted or blotched underneath.

Habitat: Breeding — nests on flats or slight hummocks often bordering a stream or lake. In migration — coastal saltwater grass flats and inland open grassy fields.

Status & Distribution	Spring	Summer	Fall	Winter	Breeder	Key
Southeastern	U	A	U	–		C Common
Southcoastal	C	R	C	A	•	U Uncommon
Southwestern	C	C	C	A	•	R Rare
Central	C	U	C	–	•	A Casual/Accidental
Western	C	C	C	–	•	– No Records
Northern	C	C	C	–	•	

Notes: Nests over most of Alaska north of Alaska Range. There are 2 separate populations: birds from Yukon River delta go to California, and birds from eastern and northern Alaska migrate southeast to Canadian prairies, the central flyway and eastern Mexico.

GREATER WHITE-FRONTED GOOSE

Snow Goose
(Chen caerulescens)
Length: 28 in.

Identification: Adult is pure white with black wing tips visible at a great distance. Immature is pale gray. This species is most vociferous of all waterfowl; call is a high-pitched yelp similar to bark of a small dog. The blue phase, very rare in Alaska, could be confused with the Emperor Goose (see photo).

Habitat: Breeding — low, grassy tundra. Nests in grassy areas on the tundra. In migration — may occur along almost all coastal areas of Alaska, except the Aleutian Islands, and in several locations in the interior including Yukon and Tanana river valleys.

Status & Distribution	Spring	Summer	Fall	Winter	Breeder	Key
Southeastern	U	–	U	–		C Common
Southcoastal	C	–	C	–		U Uncommon
Southwestern	C	–	C	–		R Rare
Central	C	A	C	–		A Casual/Accidental
Western	C	R	C	–	•	– No Records
Northern	C	U	C	–	•	

Notes: Spectacular migration occurs from Wrangel Island in Siberia to Seward Peninsula early in September, thence to Yukon River delta where flocks fatten on berries for a month. In October often seen at Pilot Point on north coast of the Alaska Peninsula, Cook Inlet, Cordova, Yakutat and on Stikine River delta near Wrangell. Canadian birds visit Arctic National Wildlife Refuge in large numbers, foraging in the uplands before following Canada's Mackenzie River Valley south.

SNOW GOOSE, *Blue Phase*

SNOW GOOSE

Ross' Goose

(Chen rossii)
Length: 24 in.

Identification: Petite version of the Snow Goose, very much like it at a distance. Bill is much smaller than Snow Goose and lacks the distinct black "lips." A bit of bluish-gray at the bill base is visible at extremely close range. Immature is pale gray but smaller and has a smaller bill than a Snow Goose.

Habitat: Has been found at the mouth of the Stikine River in southeastern Alaska. On the Arctic coast, it has been found near Teshekpuk Lake, and a nest was found on Duck Island, in the Sagavarnirktok River delta.

ROSS' GOOSE

Status & Distribution	Spring	Summer	Fall	Winter	Breeder	Key
Southeastern	A	–	–	–		C Common
Southcoastal	–	–	–	–		U Uncommon
Southwestern	–	–	–	–		R Rare
Central	–	–	–	–		A Casual/Accidental
Western	–	–	–	–		– No Records
Northern	–	A	–	–	•	

Emperor Goose

(Chen canagica)
Length: 27 in.

Identification: Adult is medium blue-gray, scaled with black and white, and identified by a white head and hind neck. From the rear in flight the white tail is prominent. Immature is dark in September but grows white feathers of adult plumage throughout the fall. In all plumages, only goose in Alaska with white *tail* and dark tail *coverts* (reverse is true of all other species).

Habitat: Breeding — low, wet tundra near the coast, often near lakes and ponds. Nests near water in grassy marsh habitat on an island, bank or in a large tussock. In winter — saltwater beaches.

Notes: Bulk of world's population nests in Yukon-Kuskokwim delta. A few nest farther north to Kotzebue Sound; a few nest in eastern Siberia. Most Emperor Geese, including the Siberians, work their way down the coast of western Alaska in fall and most winter in the Aleutian Islands. Only rarely is an Emperor Goose seen east or south of Kodiak.

EMPEROR GOOSE

Status & Distribution	Spring	Summer	Fall	Winter	Breeder	Key
Southeastern	A	–	–	A		C Common
Southcoastal	R	A	R	U		U Uncommon
Southwestern	C	U	C	C	•	R Rare
Central	–	–	–	–		A Casual/Accidental
Western	C	C	C	–	•	– No Records
Northern	–	R	–	–		

Brant
(Branta bernicla)
Length: 26 in.

Identification: Very dark. Lacks white cheeks of Canada Goose. Adult has narrow, barred, white patch on the sides of the neck. In flight, looks dark with a conspicuous white posterior. Calls infrequently. Voice is a croaking sound very different from calls of other geese.

Status & Distribution	Spring	Summer	Fall	Winter	Breeder	Key
Southeastern	U	R	R	R		C Common
Southcoastal	C	R	R	A		U Uncommon
Southwestern	C	R	C	R		R Rare
Central	A	–	–	–		A Casual/Accidental
Western	C	C	C	–	•	– No Records
Northern	C	C	C	–	•	

Habitat: Breeding — lowland, coastal tundra, usually just above high tide line. Perhaps half the population nests on the Yukon-Kuskokwim delta on low, grassy flats dissected by numerous tidal streams. The rest nest farther north in coastal Alaska, Siberia and Canada. In migration — saltwater bays and estuaries.

Notes: Best place to see Brant is Yukon River delta near Hooper Bay in early summer or at Izembek Bay near Cold Bay on the Alaska Peninsula in fall. At Izembek Bay in the fall the entire population spends a month or more fattening in the largest eel grass pasture in the world. In early November they fly en masse across the Gulf of Alaska, many reaching Mexico before making landfall.

BRANT

Canada Goose
(Branta canadensis)

Identification: Most authorities agree there are 11 subspecies of Canada Goose in North America, of which 6 occur in Alaska. All have a brown back, a white rump patch, a long black neck and white cheeks. Size, range and habits separate these subspecies. Because they mate for life and the young accompany their parents on their first round-trip migration, mixing among these subspecies is minimal. Larger subspecies make the familiar honk, while smaller ones have a higher pitched call.

Distribution and Habitat: Great sub-specific diversity in breeding habitats and range makes a concise summary difficult. See next page for discussion of separate subspecies.

Status & Distribution	Spring	Summer	Fall	Winter	Breeder	Key
Southeastern	C	C	C	C	•	C Common
Southcoastal	C	C	C	U	•	U Uncommon
Southwestern	U	R	C	A	•	R Rare
Central	C	C	C	–	•	A Casual/Accidental
Western	C	C	C	–	•	– No Records
Northern	C	C	C	–	•	

CANADA GOOSE, *Vancouver Subspecies*

The 6 subspecies of Canada Goose that occur in Alaska, and their distribution and habitat, are discussed below.

Vancouver Canada Goose — *B. c. fulva:* Dark goose, weighing up to 16 pounds. Nests from British Columbia throughout southeastern Alaska and perhaps to Prince William Sound. Nests are widely scattered and tend to be well hidden in the woods. Winters primarily within its breeding range in flocks up to 500, thus is essentially nonmigratory. It is probably most often seen at the tideflats near the Juneau airport; some individuals are present there almost all year.

Dusky Canada Goose — *B. c. occidentalis:* Superficially similar to but slightly smaller than Vancouver Canada Goose. Mostly nests in one great colony in grasslands of Copper River delta and migrates to Willamette River Valley in Oregon.

Lesser Canada Goose — *B. c. parvipes:* Medium-sized goose distributed in summer from Cook Inlet north through interior valleys. Most often seen at Potter Marsh near Anchorage and Minto Flats near Fairbanks. Major staging areas are islands in the Yukon River, the Yukon delta and Cook Inlet. Winters in Pacific Coast states.

Taverner's Canada Goose — *B. c. taverneri:* The validity of taxonomic distinction and extent of breeding ranges of Taverner's Canada Goose and Lesser Canada Goose are controversial. However, scientists now believe *parvipes* nests generally in interior, forested areas while *taverneri* nests on the tundra. Up to 73,500 Taverner's Canada Geese have been counted staging for their fall migration in Cold Bay area.

Aleutian Canada Goose — *B. c. leucopareia:* Small goose with a broad white ring at the base of the neck. Rarest of all Canada Geese. Formerly nested over most of the Aleutian Islands but foxes introduced by fur farmers exterminated this subspecies on all islands except Buldir in western Aleutians and Chagulak in the eastcentral Aleutians. Closed hunting areas in California and Oregon, release of captive reared birds, and a decline of foxes in the Aleutians are allowing an increase in this rare bird. Winters in western Oregon, northwestern and central California. Movements of this subspecies within Alaska are not well known, and Aleutian Canada Goose can be easily confused with more abundant Cackling Canada Goose, which can have a white neck-ring.

Cackling Canada Goose — *B. c. minima:* Smallest of all Canada Geese. Not much larger than a Mallard. Nests in a loose colony along 100 miles of coastline between mouths of Kuskokwim and Yukon rivers. Winters in California.

Wood Duck

(Aix sponsa)
Length: 18 in.

Identification: Male has striped, crested head, bright red at base of the bill and around the eye, dark red breast, finely barred sides, and iridescent blue wings. Female has a similar but shorter crest, is generally drab brown but with a conspicuous white patch around the eye and some iridescent blue on the wings. Wood Duck has a long tail, conspicuous in flight, and high, squeaky *whoo-eeek* call.

Status & Distribution	Spring	Summer	Fall	Winter	Breeder	Key
Southeastern	A	A	A	A		C Common
Southcoastal	–	–	A	A		U Uncommon
Southwestern	–	–	–	–		R Rare
Central	–	–	–	–		A Casual/Accidental
Western	–	–	–	–		– No Records
Northern	–	–	–	–		

Habitat: Has been found on Mendenhall River near Juneau, and in a slough along Stikine River in southeastern Alaska. Not known to breed in Alaska.

WOOD DUCK, Female

WOOD DUCK, Male

Green-winged Teal

(Anas crecca)
Length: 14 in.

Identification: Small size, all dark color at a distance and bright green speculum distinguish this species from other Alaskan ducks. Male has white vertical stripe before the wing, and creamy buff patches under the tail.

Habitat: Breeding — freshwater ponds, marshes and shallows of lakes surrounded by woods. Nests on the ground in long grass, usually near water. In migration and winter — brackish intertidal areas near the mouths of streams.

Status & Distribution	Spring	Summer	Fall	Winter	Breeder	Key
Southeastern	C	U	C	U	•	C Common
Southcoastal	C	C	C	R	•	U Uncommon
Southwestern	C	C	C	U	•	R Rare
Central	C	C	C	–	•	A Casual/Accidental
Western	C	C	C	–	•	– No Records
Northern	U	U	U	–	•	

Notes: Smallest duck found in Alaska and one of the swiftest fliers. Green-winged Teal breeding in the western and central Aleutians resembles a Eurasian subspecies that has been recorded in the Pribilofs. Males of these subspecies have a horizontal white stripe above the wings and lack the vertical white stripe on side of body.

GREEN-WINGED TEAL; *Male, left; Female, right*

Baikal Teal

(Anas formosa)
Length: 18 in.

Identification: Male is unmistakable, with a striking face pattern. Otherwise male resembles Green-winged Teal, but is a bit larger and has an all-dark undertail pattern. Female similar to female Green-winged Teal, but has distinctive white spot at the base of the bill.

Status & Distribution	Spring	Summer	Fall	Winter	Breeder	Key
Southeastern	–	–	–	–		C Common
Southcoastal	–	–	–	–		U Uncommon
Southwestern	–	A	A	–		R Rare
Central	–	–	–	–		A Casual/Accidental
Western	A	A	A	–		– No Records
Northern	A	A	A	–		

Habitat: Asiatic teal found along the coast and on islands in the Bering Sea and along Arctic Ocean coastline. Not known to breed in Alaska.

BAIKAL TEAL, *Male*

Falcated Teal

(Anas falcata)
Length: 19 in.

Identification: Adult male is gray with conspicuously crested dark green and purple head. White spot on forehead, just above bill, distinctive at a distance. White throat is bordered behind with a black line. Speculum is dark, glossy green, and the basal wing feathers are long and sickle-shaped, hanging off the back. Female is similar to female Gadwall in size and shape but with a dark speculum and gray rather than orange bill.

Status & Distribution	Spring	Summer	Fall	Winter	Breeder	Key
Southeastern	–	–	–	–		C Common
Southcoastal	–	–	–	–		U Uncommon
Southwestern	R	A	A	A		R Rare
Central	–	–	–	–		A Casual/Accidental
Western	–	–	–	–		– No Records
Northern	–	–	–	–		

Habitat: Most often seen in western and central Aleutian Islands. Breeds in central and eastern Siberia. Not known to breed in Alaska.

FALCATED TEAL, *Male*

American Black Duck

(Anas rubripes)
Length: 22 in.

Identification: Very dark, similar to
Mallard in size and shape. Wing linings
white, contrasting greatly with overall
color. Head conspicuously paler than body.
Speculum darker blue than in Mallard,
with a narrower white border. Sexes alike.

Habitat: Has occurred near Fairbanks,
Cordova and Gustavus. Not known to breed
in Alaska.

AMERICAN BLACK DUCK

Status & Distribution	Spring	Summer	Fall	Winter	Breeder	Key
Southeastern	–	–	–	A		C Common
Southcoastal	A	–	A	A		U Uncommon
Southwestern	–	–	–	–		R Rare
Central	A	–	–	–		A Casual/Accidental
Western	–	–	–	–		– No Records
Northern	–	–	–	–		

Mallard

(Anas platyrhynchos)
Length: 20¹/₂–28 in.

Identification: Male has green head and
narrow white collar. Whitish outer sides
of the tail, white wing linings, and white-
bordered blue speculum on both male and
female are good flight identifying marks.
Voice of female is the familiar *quack*; male
emits a quiet *reeb* or low *kwek*.

Habitat: Marshes, sloughs, lakes, rivers
and most flooded land. Forages on land,
especially upper tideland habitats. Seems to
prefer fresh to salt water but will frequent
estuarine areas, especially in winter. Nests
on the ground, sometimes far from water
and on rare occasions in trees.

Status & Distribution	Spring	Summer	Fall	Winter	Breeder	Key
Southeastern	C	C	C	C	•	C Common
Southcoastal	C	C	C	C	•	U Uncommon
Southwestern	C	C	C	C	•	R Rare
Central	C	C	C	R	•	A Casual/Accidental
Western	C	C	C	–	•	– No Records
Northern	R	R	–	–	•	

Notes: Most widespread duck in the world.
Most domestic ducks come from Mallard
stock. Male has a little curled feather above
the tail, which often indicates the origin of
domestic ducks that otherwise do not
resemble Mallards.

MALLARD; Male, left; Female, right

Northern Pintail

(Anas acuta)

Length: Male, 25–29 in.

Female, 20 1/2–22 1/2 in.

Identification: Male has long, slender neck, conspicuous white breast and brown head, and pointed tail. Female is plain brown, lacks eye stripe that characterizes most female dabblers, and has a gray bill. Both sexes at a distance and in flight present a slender, elegant appearance.

NORTHERN PINTAIL, *Male*

Status & Distribution	Spring	Summer	Fall	Winter	Breeder	Key
Southeastern	C	U	C	U	•	C Common
Southcoastal	C	C	C	U	•	U Uncommon
Southwestern	C	C	C	U	•	R Rare
Central	C	C	C	A	•	A Casual/Accidental
Western	C	C	C	–	•	– No Records
Northern	C	C	C	–	•	

Habitat: Breeding — marshy, low country with shallow freshwater lakes, brackish estuaries and sluggish streams with marshy borders. Nests on the ground usually near fresh water in tall grass, occasionally some distance from water. In migration and winter — salt and brackish waters along the coast.

Notes: Most widely distributed and abundant puddle duck in Alaska, its major breeding ground.

NORTHERN PINTAIL, *Female*

Garganey
(Anas querquedula)
Length: 15 in.

Identification: Breeding male has reddish-purple head and broad white stripe over the eye. Female very similar to female Green-winged Teal, but tends to be more grayish and shows a more conspicuous pale spot at the base of its bill. Uninterrupted eyeline helps separate it from female Baikal Teal.

Habitat: Asiatic species that has occurred most often as a spring and fall migrant in the western and central Aleutian Islands. Not known to breed in Alaska.

GARGANEY, Male

Status & Distribution	Spring	Summer	Fall	Winter	Breeder	Key
Southeastern	–	–	–	–		C Common
Southcoastal	–	–	A	–		U Uncommon
Southwestern	R	A	R	–		R Rare
Central	–	–	–	–		A Casual/Accidental
Western	–	–	–	–		– No Records
Northern	–	–	–	–		

Blue-winged Teal
(Anas discors)
Length: 15 in.

(Pictured on right and far right)
Identification: In the field the small size, large white crescent in front of the eye of the adult male, and blue forewing of both sexes are distinguishing. Blue forewing, conspicuous in flight, separates this species from all other ducks but Cinnamon Teal and Northern Shoveler. Northern Shoveler has a much larger bill. Adult male Cinnamon Teal is cinnamon red. Females and young Blue-winged and Cinnamon teals and Garganey cannot be safely separated in the field.

Habitat: Shallow muddy ponds, lakeshores and sloughs overgrown with aquatic vegetation. Prefers fresh water; not often found in salt or brackish water.

Notes: Breeding records are not numerous for Alaska, partly because of lack of abundance and perhaps partly because of well-concealed nests.

Status & Distribution	Spring	Summer	Fall	Winter	Breeder	Key
Southeastern	U	R	U	–	•	C Common
Southcoastal	R	R	R	A	•	U Uncommon
Southwestern	A	–	A	–		R Rare
Central	U	R	U	–	•	A Casual/Accidental
Western	–	–	–	–		– No Records
Northern	–	A	–	–		

BLUE-WINGED TEAL, Male

Cinnamon Teal
(Anas cyanoptera)
Length: 16 in.

Identification: Male is all cinnamon red with blue shoulder patches. Female cannot be distinguished in the field from female Blue-winged Teal. In late summer, when male has molted into a plumage much like that of the female, these 2 species cannot be distinguished from one another.

Status & Distribution	Spring	Summer	Fall	Winter	Breeder	Key
Southeastern	R	R	–	–		C Common
Southcoastal	A	A	–	–		U Uncommon
Southwestern	–	–	–	–		R Rare
Central	A	A	–	–		A Casual/Accidental
Western	–	–	–	–		– No Records
Northern	–	–	–	–		

Habitat: Intertidal wetlands, lakes. Not known to breed in Alaska.

CINNAMON TEAL, *Male*

CINNAMON TEAL, *Female*

BLUE-WINGED TEAL, *Female*

Northern Shoveler
(Anas clypeata)
Length: 18½ in.

Identification: Long bill and light blue forewing patch are good field identification marks for both sexes at all seasons. In flight adult male can be recognized at long distances by white breast contrasting markedly with dark head and belly. Female is mottled brown, like other dabblers.

Status & Distribution	Spring	Summer	Fall	Winter	Breeder	Key
Southeastern	U	R	U	R	•	C Common
Southcoastal	C	C	C	A	•	U Uncommon
Southwestern	R	R	R	A		R Rare
Central	C	C	C	A	•	A Casual/Accidental
Western	U	U	U	–	•	– No Records
Northern	R	R	R	–	•	

Habitat: Breeding — shallow, often muddy, freshwater marshes, sloughs and lakes. Nests on ground, often but not necessarily close to water. In migration and winter — coastal saltwater mud flats and shallow freshwater areas.

Notes: Long bill has more comblike straining devices along the margin than bills of other waterfowl and is especially adapted to straining tiny food particles from open shallow waters. Also feeds on seeds, tubers of aquatic plants and a variety of small fish, crustaceans, mollusks and insects.

NORTHERN SHOVELER, *Female*

NORTHERN SHOVELER, *Male*

Gadwall

(Anas strepera)
Length: 18¹/₂–23 in.

Identification: At a distance a flock of Gadwalls appears drab. Adult male looks gray with a black posterior. All Gadwalls can be distinguished from other puddle ducks in flight by the white speculum. A female at close range looks much like a Mallard, with a dark bill with orange sides; but she is slightly smaller and more slender, with a distinctly more slender bill and gray tail feathers. A female is difficult to distinguish unless she accompanies a male or exposes her wings.

Habitat: Sedge-grass marshes. Nests in heavy vegetation often several yards from water.

Status & Distribution	Spring	Summer	Fall	Winter	Breeder	Key
Southeastern	U	R	U	R	•	C Common
Southcoastal	C	U	C	U	•	U Uncommon
Southwestern	U	U	U	U	•	R Rare
Central	R	R	R	–		A Casual/Accidental
Western	–	A	A	–		– No Records
Northern	A	A	–	–		

Notes: Nests in small numbers in Alaska. Spring and fall migrants are more abundant on grass flats of Copper River delta than elsewhere. Hundreds winter in Prince William Sound, primarily at Port Wells and Port Fidalgo.

GADWALL; *Female, left; Male, right*

Eurasian Wigeon

(Anas penelope)
Length: 18 in.

Identification: Adult male can be
distinguished from American Wigeon
by a red-brown head topped with cream,
and gray back and sides. Most females
and immatures of the 2 species are too
similar for separation in the field, but some
Eurasian Wigeons have a reddish-tinged
head. Head of the female American Wigeon
is gray.

Habitat: This species is not known to breed
in North America and is only an uncommon
or rare visitor to scattered parts of Alaska.
Most sightings have been of only 1 or a few
birds, and greatest numbers are seen in the
Aleutian Islands. Habits are identical to
those of American Wigeon and, when
present, Eurasian Wigeon is almost always
found with American Wigeon.

Status & Distribution	Spring	Summer	Fall	Winter	Breeder	Key
Southeastern	R	A	A	A		C Common
Southcoastal	R	A	A	A		U Uncommon
Southwestern	U	R	U	R		R Rare
Central	R	A	–	–		A Casual/Accidental
Western	R	R	A	–		– No Records
Northern	–	A	–	–		

EURASIAN WIGEON, *Female*

EURASIAN WIGEON, *Male*

American Wigeon

(Anas americana)
Length: 20 in.

Identification: At a distance the white crown, wing patch and side spot create a contrasting brown-and-white pattern on males. White forewing patches are conspicuous in flight, and the high-pitched whistles (like a flock of rubber ducks) can often be heard. At closer range, brown female has distinctly reddish body and contrasting gray head, unlike other dabblers, which are more uniform. Small bill is blue-gray.

Habitat: Breeding — freshwater marshes, sloughs, ponds and marshy edges of lakes. Unlike most dabbling ducks, females and young frequent open water in the habitat. Nests on the ground, sometimes a considerable distance from water. In migration and winter — shallow coastal bays.

Notes: American Wigeons have a habit of stealing plant materials brought to the surface by other waterfowl such as Canvasbacks, Redheads and Tundra Swans.

Status & Distribution	Spring	Summer	Fall	Winter	Breeder	Key
Southeastern	C	U	C	U	•	C Common
Southcoastal	C	C	C	U	•	U Uncommon
Southwestern	C	C	C	R	•	R Rare
Central	C	C	C	A	•	A Casual/Accidental
Western	C	C	C	–	•	– No Records
Northern	U	U	U	–	•	

AMERICAN WIGEON, *Female*

AMERICAN WIGEON, *Male*

Common Pochard

(Aythya ferina)
Length: 18 in.

Identification: Resembles a hybrid between a Redhead and Canvasback, with the shape of the Redhead and the white body of the Canvasback. Bill of both sexes is dark with a blue-gray ring around the middle. Female is similar to a female Redhead and is difficult to distinguish by itself. Male Common Pochard is much paler than male Redhead.

Status & Distribution	Spring	Summer	Fall	Winter	Breeder	Key
Southeastern	–	–	–	–		C Common
Southcoastal	A	–	–	–		U Uncommon
Southwestern	R	A	A	–		R Rare
Central	–	–	–	–		A Casual/Accidental
Western	–	–	–	–		– No Records
Northern	–	–	–	–		

Habitat: Has been found in western and central Aleutian Islands and in the Pribilof Islands. Not known to breed in Alaska.

COMMON POCHARD, *Male*

Canvasback

(Aythya valisineria)
Length: 22 in.

Status & Distribution	Spring	Summer	Fall	Winter	Breeder	Key
Southeastern	U	A	U	A		C Common
Southcoastal	U	U	U	A	•	U Uncommon
Southwestern	R	A	R	R		R Rare
Central	U	U	U	–	•	A Casual/Accidental
Western	R	R	R	–	•	– No Records
Northern	A	–	–	–		

Identification: Long bill and sloping forehead are unlike those of any other duck. Male's back, belly and inner half of the wing are white, and male shows more white in flight than most other ducks. At a distance, dark reddish head may look black, as do breast and tail. Females are light brown and identified by head and bill shape. Both sexes have all-black bills.

Habitat: Breeding — marshes, sloughs and deep-water lakes with vegetated shorelines. Nests in marsh vegetation near open waters with sufficient depth for diving and abundant bottom vegetation. In migration — saltwater bays, large lakes and rivers.

CANVASBACK, *Female*

CANVASBACK, *Male*

Redhead

(Aythya americana)
Length: 20 in.

Identification: Male is distinguished by round red-brown head and pale blue bill, gray back, and black breast and tail. Female is brownish with a light patch about the base of the bill and is very similar to but paler than female Ring-necked Duck.

Habitat: Breeding — freshwater marshes and lakes. Most breed in eastern central Alaska in area of Tetlin Lakes and Yukon Flats. Nests in emergent vegetation over standing water or on a mass of plant material surrounded by water. In migration — saltwater bays, river deltas, freshwater lakes and marshes.

Status & Distribution	Spring	Summer	Fall	Winter	Breeder	Key
Southeastern	R	A	R	A	•	C Common
Southcoastal	R	R	R	A	•	U Uncommon
Southwestern	A	A	A	–		R Rare
Central	U	R	U	–	•	A Casual/Accidental
Western	A	A	A	–	•	– No Records
Northern	A	A	–	–		

Notes: This species sometimes places its eggs in the nests of other species.

REDHEAD, *Male*

Ring-necked Duck
(Aythya collaris)
Length: 16 in.

Identification: Resembles the scaups in appearance, behavior and flight. Male is distinguished from male scaups by black back, gray sides, white vertical blaze behind the black breast, and at closer range, by whitish ring around the bill. Bill ring and characteristic triangular or pointed head shape distinguish the female. Ring-necked Duck looks short-bodied and long-necked compared with scaups. Both Ring-necked Ducks and Redheads have dark wings with gray stripes on the rear of each wing; scaups have a single white stripe on each wing.

Habitat: Mostly fresh water, sometimes found in saltwater bays during migration. Breeds in eastern central Alaska in such places as Tetlin Lakes and on the Yukon Flats, and in lower southeastern Alaska. A rare breeder in Alaska.

RING-NECKED DUCK, Female

Status & Distribution	Spring	Summer	Fall	Winter	Breeder	Key
Southeastern	U	R	U	R	•	C Common
Southcoastal	R	R	R	R	•	U Uncommon
Southwestern	A	A	A	–		R Rare
Central	U	U	U	–	•	A Casual/Accidental
Western	–	A	–	–		– No Records
Northern	A	A	–	–		

RING-NECKED DUCK, Male

Tufted Duck
(Aythya fuligula)
Length: 17 in.

Identification: Adult male similar to Ring-necked Duck but has entirely white sides and usually a conspicuous tuft of feathers on back of the head. Female similar to a female scaup with a small head tuft, but rarely any white at the base of the bill as in female scaups. In flight Tufted Duck has a white wing stripe like Greater Scaup but male has much darker back.

Habitat: A Eurasian species that occurs mostly in western and central Aleutian Islands, where it has been found year round. Less numerous and less regular elsewhere, but has been found in eastern Aleutian Islands, Pribilof Islands, northern Bering Sea, southcoastal and northern Alaska. Not known to breed in Alaska.

TUFTED DUCK, *Male*

Status & Distribution	Spring	Summer	Fall	Winter	Breeder	Key
Southeastern	–	–	–	–		C Common
Southcoastal	A	A	A	A		U Uncommon
Southwestern	R	R	R	R		R Rare
Central	–	–	–	–		A Casual/Accidental
Western	A	A	–	–		– No Records
Northern	–	–	A	–		

TUFTED DUCK, *Female*

Greater Scaup
(Aythya marila)
Length: 19 in.

Identification: The 2 species of scaups are very similar in appearance, and only experienced observers can distinguish between them, under good conditions. In good light and at close range, Greater Scaup adult male has a greenish gloss to the head; the head of the Lesser Scaup male is dark purple, but this can vary. Head of the Greater Scaup is smoothly rounded, and that of the Lesser Scaup is more puffy with almost a point toward the rear of the crown. White wing stripe of the Greater Scaup extends farther toward the wing tip, a field mark noticeable only in flight. A bluish bill and broad white stripe on the trailing edge of the wing in flight are characteristic of both species.

Status & Distribution	Spring	Summer	Fall	Winter	Breeder	Key
Southeastern	C	U	C	C	•	C Common
Southcoastal	C	C	C	C	•	U Uncommon
Southwestern	C	C	C	C	•	R Rare
Central	C	C	C	A	•	A Casual/Accidental
Western	C	C	C	–	•	– No Records
Northern	U	U	U	–	•	

Habitat: Breeding — tundra or low forest closely adjacent to tundra. Freshwater lakes and ponds. Nests near water in dense vegetation. In winter — coastal saltwater bays.

GREATER SCAUP; *Male, left; Female, right*

Lesser Scaup
(Aythya affinis)
Length: 16 in.

Status & Distribution	Spring	Summer	Fall	Winter	Breeder	Key
Southeastern	C	R	C	R	•	C Common
Southcoastal	R	A	R	R		U Uncommon
Southwestern	A	–	–	A		R Rare
Central	C	C	C	A	•	A Casual/Accidental
Western	R	R	R	–	•	– No Records
Northern	A	A	–	–		

Identification: See Greater Scaup.

Habitat: Breeding — interior lakes and ponds, especially in the upper Yukon River Valley and its tributaries. Nests in dry grassy areas near lakeshores. In winter — saltwater bays, but in smaller numbers than Greater Scaup.

LESSER SCAUP, *Female*

LESSER SCAUP, *Male*

Common Eider
(Somateria mollissima)
Length: 25 in.

Identification: Largest wild duck in North America. Adult male is unique with white back and breast and black belly. Female is chunky, brown but paler than scoters, and obviously barred when seen at moderate or close range. Configuration where the head and bill meet is different for each eider species. In Common Eider the forehead feathers do not extend as far forward as do those on side of the bill.

Status & Distribution	Spring	Summer	Fall	Winter	Breeder	Key
Southeastern	R	R	R	R	•	C Common
Southcoastal	U	U	U	U	•	U Uncommon
Southwestern	C	C	C	C	•	R Rare
Central	–	–	–	–		A Casual/Accidental
Western	C	C	C	R	•	– No Records
Northern	C	C	C	–	•	

Habitat: Breeding — low-lying rocky marine shores with numerous islands. Nests on the ground, often in areas sheltered by rocks. In winter — inshore marine waters.

Notes: Flocks fly in long lines, often low over the water, and thousands may pass on peak migration days along the Arctic coast.

COMMON EIDER, *Female*

COMMON EIDER, *Male*

King Eider

(Somateria spectabilis)
Length: 22 in.

Status & Distribution	Spring	Summer	Fall	Winter	Breeder	Key
Southeastern	R	A	–	R		C Common
Southcoastal	U	–	U	U		U Uncommon
Southwestern	C	R	C	C		R Rare
Central	–	–	–	–		A Casual/Accidental
Western	C	U	C	R	•	– No Records
Northern	C	U	C	–	•	

Identification: At a distance male appears white in front and black behind, the only duck with this appearance. White shoulder patches are separated from white neck and breast by black back — markings that are very distinctive at great distances. Head of male has orange knoblike frontal shield outlined in black. Female and immature are difficult to distinguish from Common Eider, but they have crescent-shaped rather than straight bars on the back and sides, and feathering on forehead extends farther forward than that on sides of the bill. In mixed flocks, female King Eiders appear richer colored, more reddish-brown than female Common Eiders.

Habitat: Breeding — ponds and lakes on Arctic tundra or lakes and streams not far from the coast. In Alaska King Eider breeds in small numbers along the Arctic coast from Point Hope to Demarcation Point. Nests on the ground near lakes or islands in lakes and sometimes on almost bare hillsides. In migration and winter — inshore marine waters.

Notes: During migration a million or more King Eiders pass close to such places as Hooper Bay, Cape Lisburne, Wainwright and Point Barrow in their annual flight from the Bristol Bay-to-Kodiak area to Canadian nest sites.

KING EIDER, Female

KING EIDER, Male

Spectacled Eider

(Somateria fischeri)
Length: 21 in.

Identification: Both sexes identified by huge pale spectacles around the eyes. Male is much like a Common Eider at a distance but has a black instead of white breast. Female has feathering down the bill to the nostrils.

Habitat: Breeding — lowland tundra with small ponds. Nests in fairly high grass near ponds. Nests in a narrow coastal strip of Alaska from mouth of the Kuskokwim River north along Bering Sea coast to Arctic Ocean, and then east to Colville River delta. A few nest in Siberia, but this is a Bering Sea bird and largely an Alaskan species. Winter range is not known. An occasional winter bird has been sighted off Kodiak or near the tip of the Kenai Peninsula.

Status & Distribution	Spring	Summer	Fall	Winter	Breeder	Key
Southeastern	A	–	–	–		C Common
Southcoastal	–	–	–	A		U Uncommon
Southwestern	–	–	–	R		R Rare
Central	–	–	–	–		A Casual/Accidental
Western	C	C	C	–	•	– No Records
Northern	U	U	U	–	•	

SPECTACLED EIDER, Female

SPECTACLED EIDER, Male

Steller's Eider

(Polysticta stelleri)
Length: 18 in.

Identification: Adult male has white head and large white shoulder patch. Male's chestnut-colored breast and belly are especially obvious in flight. Dark brown female is similar to other eiders, but female is more mottled than barred and the wing has a blue speculum bordered by a white stripe, similar to Mallard.

Habitat: Breeding — lowland tundra adjacent to the coast. Nests on small elevations near tidewater, also in flat mossy tundra. In winter — inshore marine waters around Kodiak Island and the south side of the Alaska Peninsula, and the eastern Aleutian Islands. In autumn huge flocks of Siberian-reared Steller's Eiders frequent Izembek and other Alaska Peninsula lagoons.

Status & Distribution	Spring	Summer	Fall	Winter	Breeder	Key
Southeastern	A	–	–	R		C Common
Southcoastal	C	A	U	C		U Uncommon
Southwestern	C	U	C	C		R Rare
Central	–	–	–	–		A Casual/Accidental
Western	U	U	U	–	•	– No Records
Northern	U	U	U	–	•	

STELLER'S EIDER, Female

STELLER'S EIDER, Male

Harlequin Duck

(Histrionicus histrionicus)
Length: 17 in.

Identification: Male in nuptial plumage is mostly slate-blue with white spots and stripes and chestnut-colored flanks. Female is dusky brown with 3 round white spots on each side of the head, very much like a diminutive scoter with a very small bill. In flight the dark color, stripes on the male's back, and habit of flying just above the water's surface with very shallow wingbeats are good field marks.

Habitat: Breeding — cold, rapidly flowing streams, often but not always surrounded by forests. Nests on the ground, close to water and in areas protected by dense vegetation. Hole-nesting is not typical of this species in North America. In winter — inshore marine waters, rocky shores and reefs; often perches on rocks for preening and sleeping.

Status & Distribution	Spring	Summer	Fall	Winter	Breeder	Key
Southeastern	C	C	C	C	•	C Common
Southcoastal	C	C	C	C	•	U Uncommon
Southwestern	C	C	C	C	•	R Rare
Central	U	U	U	–	•	A Casual/Accidental
Western	U	U	U	A	•	– No Records
Northern	–	R	–	–	•	

Notes: More abundant in Alaska than in any other part of its range. Male, with its brilliant plumage, is responsible for the name "harlequin," taken from the clown or harlequin of old English pantomime.

HARLEQUIN DUCK; *Female, left; Male, right*

Oldsquaw

(Clangula hyemalis)
Length: 20 in.

Identification: Only sea duck with considerable white on the body and unpatterned dark wings. Male has long, pointed tail. Drastic plumage change between summer and winter, especially obvious in the male, is quite unusual among ducks and, of the Alaskan species, only the Ruddy Duck shares this characteristic. Oldsquaw is a noisy duck with a variety of calls, some of which are considered musical.

Habitat: Breeding — Arctic tundra near lakes or ponds and along the coast. Nests on the ground, often under low shrubs. In winter — inshore marine waters. Many Alaskan Oldsquaws winter in the Bering Sea, the Sea of Okhotsk and the Sea of Japan.

OLDSQUAW; *Summer, Male*

Status & Distribution	Spring	Summer	Fall	Winter	Breeder	Key
Southeastern	C	R	C	C	•	C Common
Southcoastal	C	U	C	C	•	U Uncommon
Southwestern	C	U	C	C	•	R Rare
Central	C	U	C	–	•	A Casual/Accidental
Western	C	C	C	C	•	– No Records
Northern	C	C	C	–	•	

OLDSQUAW; *Winter; Female, left; Male, right*

Black Scoter

(Melanitta nigra)
Length: 19 in.

Identification: Male solid black, with base
of bill bright yellow-orange. Female and
immature are dark brown, with darker cap
and pale cheeks and throat. Both sexes have
a shorter, more typically ducklike bill than
do other scoters. Primary feathers look quite
pale in flight.

Status & Distribution	Spring	Summer	Fall	Winter	Breeder	Key
Southeastern	U	R	U	U		C Common
Southcoastal	C	U	C	C		U Uncommon
Southwestern	C	C	C	C	•	R Rare
Central	R	R	R	–	•	A Casual/Accidental
Western	C	C	C	–	•	– No Records
Northern	–	A	–	–		

Habitat: Breeding — lakes, ponds or rivers
in tundra or woodlands. Nests on the
ground near water. In winter — inshore
marine waters.

BLACK SCOTER, *Male*

Surf Scoter

(Melanitta perspicillata)
Length: 20 in.

Status & Distribution	Spring	Summer	Fall	Winter	Breeder	Key
Southeastern	C	C	C	C		C Common
Southcoastal	C	C	C	C		U Uncommon
Southwestern	C	U	C	C		R Rare
Central	C	C	C	–	•	A Casual/Accidental
Western	C	C	C	–	•	– No Records
Northern	U	U	U	–	•	

Identification: Adult male has solid black color and white patches on crown and nape. Immature female usually has 2 whitish spots on each side of the head like White-winged Scoter, but lacks white wing patch. In an adult female these spots tend to disappear and are often replaced by a pale nape patch much like that of the male. This nape patch is absent in White-winged Scoter. In a female the base of the bill is unfeathered, with as much bill visible behind the nostril as in front of it.

Habitat: Breeding — not well known but probably like other scoters, i.e., freshwater ponds, lakes, rivers with shrubby cover or woodland nearby. In winter — inshore marine waters.

SURF SCOTER, Female

SURF SCOTER, Male

White-winged Scoter

(Melanitta fusca)
Length: 21 in.

Status & Distribution	Spring	Summer	Fall	Winter	Breeder	Key
Southeastern	C	C	C	C		C Common
Southcoastal	C	C	C	C	•	U Uncommon
Southwestern	C	C	C	C		R Rare
Central	C	C	C	–	•	A Casual/Accidental
Western	U	U	U	–	•	– No Records
Northern	U	U	U	–	•	

Identification: Largest scoter. Identified in flight, and often in the water, by white wing patches of both sexes. A male on the water is easily recognizable by white crescent around the eye. A female without the wing patches visible is distinguished from female Surf Scoter by feathering on side of the bill, which extends almost as far forward as the nostrils.

Habitat: Breeding — most definite breeding records are near interior streams and lakes, chiefly in the upper Tanana and on the Yukon Flats. Nests on the ground under shrubs and trees sometimes several hundred yards from water. In winter — inshore marine waters.

Notes: If several White-winged Scoters nest on the same lake, as frequently happens in the Interior, one female will dominate, drive away the others, and gather all the young into one immense brood of 20 to 60. Males leave soon after incubation starts in early June and return to the sea coast.

WHITE-WINGED SCOTER; *Male, left; Female, right*

Common Goldeneye

(Bucephala clangula)
Length: 18 in.

Identification: Adult male has round white spot behind bill. Head shape is distinctive, and head is glossy, sometimes appearing greenish. Female Common Goldeneye is difficult to distinguish from female Barrow's Goldeneye, but both are recognizable as goldeneyes by a gray body and contrasting brown puffy head. Female Common Goldeneye has yellow tip to the dark bill.

Status & Distribution	Spring	Summer	Fall	Winter	Breeder	Key
Southeastern	C	R	C	C	•	C Common
Southcoastal	C	R	C	C	•	U Uncommon
Southwestern	C	U	C	U	•	R Rare
Central	C	C	C	A	•	A Casual/Accidental
Western	U	R	U	–	•	– No Records
Northern	A	A	–	–		

Habitat: Breeding — ponds and lakes with adjacent stands of trees. Nests in a cavity in a tree. Nesting largely confined to the valleys of Yukon and Kuskokwim rivers. However, because of the difficulty of separating female Common and Barrow's goldeneyes during nesting, this breeding distribution is not certain. In winter — inshore marine waters.

COMMON GOLDENEYE; Female, left; Male, right

Barrow's Goldeneye

(Bucephala islandica)
Length: 18 in.

Identification: Adult male has large white crescent behind base of the bill. Male has more black on back than Common Goldeneye, a distinction that is noticeable from great distances. Female has gray body and puffy brown head. Female has an all-yellow bill in winter and spring.

Status & Distribution	Spring	Summer	Fall	Winter	Breeder	Key
Southeastern	C	U	C	C	•	C Common
Southcoastal	C	C	C	C	•	U Uncommon
Southwestern	C	U	C	C	•	R Rare
Central	C	C	C	–	•	A Casual/Accidental
Western	–	–	–	–		– No Records
Northern	–	–	–	–		

Habitat: Breeding — lakes and ponds, usually in wooded country. Nests in cavities in trees, or if not available, may nest in holes among rocks or cliffs. In winter — inshore marine waters and lakes and rivers if there is open water.

BARROW'S GOLDENEYE, *Male*

BARROW'S GOLDENEYE, *Female*

Bufflehead
(Bucephala albeola)
Length: 14 in.

Identification: Male distinguished by large white patch on head, black back and white sides. Female identified by small size, puffy brown head with oval white spot behind each eye.

Status & Distribution	Spring	Summer	Fall	Winter	Breeder	Key
Southeastern	C	A	C	C		C Common
Southcoastal	C	R	C	C	•	U Uncommon
Southwestern	C	U	C	C	•	R Rare
Central	C	C	C	A	•	A Casual/Accidental
Western	R	R	R	–	•	– No Records
Northern	–	A	–	–		

Habitat: Breeding — ponds and lakes in or near open woodland. Nests in cavities in trees, often in holes made by woodpeckers. In winter — inshore marine waters, fresh water if open.

BUFFLEHEAD, *Male*

BUFFLEHEAD, *Female*

Smew

(Mergellus albellus)
Length: 16 in.

Identification: Small merganser with
shorter bill than others of this group. Male
almost entirely white with narrow, black
markings on head and body and dark eye
patch. Female has gray body, contrasting
white cheeks and brown cap. Head in both
sexes is puffy.

Status & Distribution	Spring	Summer	Fall	Winter	Breeder	Key
Southeastern	–	–	–	–		C Common
Southcoastal	–	–	A	A		U Uncommon
Southwestern	R	A	R	R		R Rare
Central	–	–	–	–		A Casual/Accidental
Western	–	–	–	–		– No Records
Northern	–	–	–	–		

Habitat: Asiatic species found mostly in
western and central Aleutian Islands during
spring, fall and winter. Not known to breed
in Alaska.

SMEW, *Female*

SMEW, *Male*

Hooded Merganser

(Lophodytes cucullatus)
Length: 18 in.

Identification: From a distance male is black above, with dark, reddish sides and white breast. White head patch appears narrow when the crest is down and very conspicuous when the crest is erect. Female and young are all brown with narrow merganser bills and puffy brown crests. Females of the other 2 species of mergansers are larger, with more wispy crests and reddish-brown heads. Hooded Merganser flies very fast with rapid wingbeats and shows a more slender head and longer neck than other small ducks.

Habitat: Breeding — wooded streams and, to a lesser degree, wooded shorelines of lakes. Nests in cavities in trees or on the top of snags. In Alaska — nests along the valleys of larger mainland rivers in southeastern Alaska where cottonwoods occur. In migration and winter — freshwater ponds and streams and occasionally saltwater bays.

Status & Distribution	Spring	Summer	Fall	Winter	Breeder	Key
Southeastern	U	U	U	U	•	C Common
Southcoastal	R	R	R	R	•	U Uncommon
Southwestern	A	A	A	A		R Rare
Central	R	R	R	A		A Casual/Accidental
Western	–	–	–	–		– No Records
Northern	–	–	–	–		

HOODED MERGANSER, Female

HOODED MERGANSER, Male

Common Merganser

(Mergus merganser)
Length: 22–27 in.

Identification: Largest merganser. Adult male is white with black head and back. Only Common Goldeneye shares these characteristics at a distance, but the merganser has a long, slender, red bill and long, low silhouette. Female, like the female goldeneye, has a gray body and sharply set-off brown head. In flight, Common Merganser appears very pointed in the front and has especially rapid shallow wingbeats.

Habitat: Breeding — forested areas where ponds are associated with upper portions of rivers and clear, freshwater lakes. Nests in hollow trees, in crevices of cliffs, and on the ground under cover. In migration and winter — prefers fresh water but if not available, then saltwater bays and inlets.

COMMON MERGANSER, Female

Status & Distribution	Spring	Summer	Fall	Winter	Breeder	Key
Southeastern	C	C	C	C	•	C Common
Southcoastal	C	C	C	C	•	U Uncommon
Southwestern	C	C	C	C	•	R Rare
Central	R	R	R	R	•	A Casual/Accidental
Western	R	R	R	–		– No Records
Northern	–	–	–	–		

COMMON MERGANSER, Male

Red-breasted Merganser
(Mergus serrator)
Length: 23 in.

Status & Distribution	Spring	Summer	Fall	Winter	Breeder	Key
Southeastern	C	C	C	C	•	C Common
Southcoastal	C	C	C	C	•	U Uncommon
Southwestern	C	C	C	C	•	R Rare
Central	R	R	R	R	•	A Casual/Accidental
Western	C	C	C	A	•	– No Records
Northern	R	R	R	–	•	

Identification: Adult male has greenish-black, crested head and reddish breast band. Female and young similar to Common Merganser, but the lighter reddish-brown of the head blends into the light throat, whereas head color is more sharply cut off in female Common Merganser.

Habitat: Breeding — lakes, ponds, rivers, often near sea coast. Occasionally may nest along the coast or on coastal islands. Nests on the ground under overhanging branches of trees among tree roots or in a pile of driftwood. In migration and winter — inshore marine waters.

RED-BREASTED MERGANSER, *Female*

RED-BREASTED MERGANSER, *Male*

Ruddy Duck

(Oxyura jamaicensis)
Length: 15 in.

Identification: Small diving duck with long tail, often held up at an angle. Chunky and short-necked, with a disproportionately large bill. Very awkward on land and in the air. In breeding plumage, male has a cinnamon-red body, black cap, white cheeks and bright sky-blue bill. In winter, bill turns dark and body plumage becomes brown. A female is always brown, with a brown cap and 2 dark stripes across each light cheek.

Habitat: Breeding — interior lakes; broods have been sighted at Tetlin Lakes and Minto Lakes in central Alaska. In migration and winter — inshore marine waters, lakes.

Status & Distribution	Spring	Summer	Fall	Winter	Breeder	Key
Southeastern	A	–	A	A		C Common
Southcoastal	A	–	–	–		U Uncommon
Southwestern	–	–	–	–		R Rare
Central	A	A	A	–	•	A Casual/Accidental
Western	A	–	–	–		– No Records
Northern	–	–	–	–		

RUDDY DUCK, *Male*

Family *Cathartidae*
AMERICAN VULTURES
(1)

American vultures are large birds with long, broad wings and a naked head. They are scavengers that consume carrion.

Turkey Vulture
(Cathartes aura)
Length: 27 in.
Wingspan: 6 ft.

Identification: In flight, wings show two tones; flight feathers are light gray and wing linings are black. Otherwise a large blackish bird, with a red head and white bill in adult, and a dark head and bill in immature.

Status & Distribution	Spring	Summer	Fall	Winter	Breeder	Key
Southeastern	–	–	–	–		C Common
Southcoastal	–	–	–	–		U Uncommon
Southwestern	–	–	–	–		R Rare
Central	A	A	–	–		A Casual/Accidental
Western	–	–	–	–		– No Records
Northern	–	–	–	–		

Habitat: Open country. Has been found at Delta Junction, Tok and Porcupine River.

TURKEY VULTURE

Family *Accipitridae*
HAWKS, EAGLES, HARRIERS, OSPREYS
(11)

These birds of prey have hooked beaks and sharp, curved talons for catching and holding their prey. Eleven species occur in Alaska; they are divided into 4 groups:

Accipiters or bird hawks — Small- to medium-sized hawks with short, rounded wings and long tails. Two species are found in Alaska.

Buteos and eagles — Medium- to large-sized hawks with broad wings and fairly short tails. They are often seen soaring. Seven species occur in Alaska.

Harriers — Medium-sized hawks with long wings, slim bodies and long tails. This group is represented in Alaska by 1 species.

Ospreys — Large hawklike birds of prey with powerful talons and spines on the soles of the feet to aid in capturing live fish, their main food supply.

Osprey
(Pandion haliaetus)
Length: 20–25 in.
Wingspan: 4½–6 ft.

Identification: Fish-eating hawk, dark brown above and entirely white below, with a white head and dark eye stripe. In flight, wings are arched, with the wrist at the highest point. Adult female has dark marking on breast and forehead.

Habitat: Near lakes, rivers and sea coasts. Nests near water in trees or on cliffs. Occurs more frequently in Bristol Bay than elsewhere.

Status & Distribution	Spring	Summer	Fall	Winter	Breeder	Key
Southeastern	R	R	R	–	•	C Common
Southcoastal	R	R	R	–	•	U Uncommon
Southwestern	R	R	R	–	•	R Rare
Central	R	R	R	–	•	A Casual/Accidental
Western	R	R	R	–	•	– No Records
Northern	–	A	–	–		

Notes: Usually hovers then plunges into the water feet first after fish.

OSPREY, *Male*

Bald Eagle

(Haliaeetus leucocephalus)
Length: 30–43 in.
Wingspan: 6½–8 ft.

Identification: Adult with white head and tail is unmistakable. Immature has a dusky head and tail which it retains for up to 4 years. Immature may be confused with a Golden Eagle, but Bald Eagle has a diagonal white line on the underwing and a white spot in the wing linings where the wing meets the body.

Habitat: Coniferous forests, deciduous woodlands, rivers and streams, beaches and tidal flats, rocky shores and reefs. Nests in old-growth timber along the coast and larger mainland rivers. In treeless areas, nests on cliffs or on the ground.

Notes: There are more Bald Eagles in Alaska than in all the other states combined. They are scavengers more than predators and subsist mainly on dead and dying fish. When fish are not available, they will kill birds and sometimes small mammals. In the Aleutian Islands their main food supply is seabirds.

Status & Distribution	Spring	Summer	Fall	Winter	Breeder	Key
Southeastern	C	C	C	C	•	C Common
Southcoastal	C	C	C	C	•	U Uncommon
Southwestern	C	C	C	C	•	R Rare
Central	U	U	U	R	•	A Casual/Accidental
Western	R	R	R	–	•	– No Records
Northern	–	A	–	–		

BALD EAGLE, *Immature*

BALD EAGLE, *Adult*

White-tailed Eagle

(Haliaeetus albicilla)
Length: 27–35 in.
Wingspan: 6–7 1/2 ft.

Status & Distribution	Spring	Summer	Fall	Winter	Breeder	Key
Southeastern	–	–	–	–		C Common
Southcoastal	–	–	–	–		U Uncommon
Southwestern	R	R	R	R	•	R Rare
Central	–	–	–	–		A Casual/Accidental
Western	–	–	–	–		– No Records
Northern	–	–	–	–		

Identification: Adult paler than adult Bald Eagle, with only the tail white. Head may be pale and appear white at a distance. Immature all brown, often with whitish streaks on breast and dark wing linings. Most Bald Eagle immatures have pale wing linings. Distinguished from Golden Eagle by wedge-shaped tail.

Habitat: Asiatic bird that occurs primarily on islands in southwestern Alaska. Known to breed only on Attu Island, in western Aleutians.

WHITE-TAILED EAGLE

Steller's Sea-Eagle

(Haliaeetus pelagicus)
Length: 27–36 in.
Wingspan: 7–8 ft.

Status & Distribution	Spring	Summer	Fall	Winter	Breeder	Key
Southeastern	–	A	A	–		C Common
Southcoastal	–	–	–	–		U Uncommon
Southwestern	A	A	A	–		R Rare
Central	–	–	–	–		A Casual/Accidental
Western	–	–	–	–		– No Records
Northern	–	–	–	–		

Identification: Similar to Bald and White-tailed eagles in size, but has a larger bill and even more prominently wedge-shaped tail than White-tailed Eagle. Adult has white shoulders, thighs and tail that are distinctive. Immature is largely brown, with a mottled brown-and-white tail.

Habitat: Asiatic bird that has been reported from Unalaska in the Aleutian Islands, Kodiak Island, Saint Paul Island in the Pribilof Islands and Taku River in southeastern Alaska. Not known to breed in Alaska.

STELLER'S SEA-EAGLE, *Adult*

Northern Harrier

(Circus cyaneus)
Length: 20 in.
Wingspan: 3¹/₂–4¹/₂ ft.

Identification: Adult male is mostly gray,
turning to whitish on the spotted brown
belly. Adult female is brown above and buffy
below. Immatures of both sexes are brown
above and rich reddish brown below.
Diagnostic features are white rump patch
in both sexes and all plumages, and wings
held at an angle above the horizontal.

Habitat: Open country, especially tidal
marshes and freshwater marshes; open
mountain ridges of the Interior. Nests on
the ground in wet marshy areas.

Status & Distribution	Spring	Summer	Fall	Winter	Breeder	Key
Southeastern	U	R	U	R	•	C Common
Southcoastal	C	U	C	R	•	U Uncommon
Southwestern	U	U	U	R	•	R Rare
Central	U	U	U	A	•	A Casual/Accidental
Western	U	U	U	–	•	– No Records
Northern	R	R	R	–	•	

Notes: Differs considerably from all other
birds of prey; is not deep-chested as most
hawks but has a long, thin body with long,
strong wings and a long, thin tail. Northern
Harrier hunts close to the ground in search
of mice and small birds. Roosts on the
ground at night. During daylight it normally
perches on the ground or on stumps or
fence posts; only rarely does it perch in trees
or bushes. Only hawk that always chooses a
ground site for nesting.

NORTHERN HARRIER, *Female*

Sharp-shinned Hawk

(Accipiter striatus)
Length: 12 in.
Wingspan: 2 ft.

Identification: Small, with short, rounded wings and long tail. Adult has a blue-gray back and rusty, barred breast; immature has a brown back and streaked breast. Females are larger than males.

Status & Distribution	Spring	Summer	Fall	Winter	Breeder	Key
Southeastern	C	U	C	U	•	C Common
Southcoastal	C	U	C	U	•	U Uncommon
Southwestern	–	–	–	–		R Rare
Central	C	C	C	A	•	A Casual/Accidental
Western	R	R	R	–	•	– No Records
Northern	–	–	–	–		

Habitat: Coastal and interior coniferous forests, shrubs, mixed deciduous-coniferous woodlands, forest edges. Nests in conifers usually 20 to 60 feet from the ground.

Notes: Difficult to see because of small size and habit of hunting close to the ground and perching in thick conifers.

SHARP-SHINNED HAWK, *Adult*

Northern Goshawk

(Accipiter gentilis)
Length: 23 in.
Wingspan: 3 1/2–4 ft.

Identification: Long tail and short, rounded wings. This species is identified as an accipiter by its habit of flying with short rapid wingbeats, then sailing briefly. Much larger than Sharp-shinned Hawk, the only other accipiter found in Alaska. Adult has a blue-gray back, light stripe over its eye and gray underparts. Immature is brown above and white with brown streaks below. Immature has a light eye-line that distinguishes it from other large brown hawks, such as Red-tailed Hawk, when the whole bird is not clearly visible.

Status & Distribution	Spring	Summer	Fall	Winter	Breeder	Key
Southeastern	U	U	U	U	•	C Common
Southcoastal	U	U	U	U	•	U Uncommon
Southwestern	U	U	U	U	•	R Rare
Central	U	U	U	U	•	A Casual/Accidental
Western	R	R	R	–		– No Records
Northern	–	–	–	–		

Habitat: Coastal and boreal forests, forest edges. Nests in heavy timber, usually 30 to 40 feet up in a conifer.

Notes: Hunts for prey such as ptarmigan, rabbits and rodents by flying close to the ground usually near the edge of timber.

NORTHERN GOSHAWK, *Adult*

Swainson's Hawk

(Buteo swainsoni)
Length: 22 in.
Wingspan: 4–4¹/₂ ft.

Identification: More slender than Red-tailed Hawk, with narrower, more pointed wings held up at a slight angle when soaring. Tail is always gray with narrow, dark bands, looking all dark at a distance. Light-phase adult has a dark brown back and breast, white throat and belly — a different combination of light and dark underneath than any of the other buteos. Dark-phase adult is all dark, including flight feathers. Dark-phase Red-tailed and Rough-legged hawks have paler flight feathers. Immature is white below, with dark streaks all over.

SWAINSON'S HAWK, *Adult, Light Phase*

Status & Distribution	Spring	Summer	Fall	Winter	Breeder	Key
Southeastern	A	A	A	A		C Common
Southcoastal	A	–	A	A		U Uncommon
Southwestern	–	–	–	–		R Rare
Central	R	R	R	–	•	A Casual/Accidental
Western	–	–	–	–		– No Records
Northern	–	–	–	–		

Habitat: Open forests of the Interior. Nest locations are not well known in Alaska. Elsewhere they commonly nest in trees, usually deciduous, and sometimes on cliffs.

SWAINSON'S HAWK, *Immature*

Red-tailed Hawk

(Buteo jamaicensis)
Length: 19–25 in.
Wingspan: 4–4^1/$_2$ ft.

Identification: Large hawk with broad
wings and broad, relatively short, rounded
tail. Adult in coastal Alaska is reddish on
upperside of the tail. Most adults and
immatures show a dark belt of streaks across
the abdomen. Breast and belly may be
mostly white, reddish or dark brown to
black. In eastern Alaska a form occurs
(Harlan's Hawk) that is usually blackish with
a whitish mottled tail. Less commonly this
form is light underneath, with a whitish
mottled tail. Individuals with intermediate
plumage occur, even some with reddish tails.
Most common buteo in forested Alaska.

RED-TAILED HAWK, *Adult*

RED-TAILED HAWK, *Immature, Light Phase*

Status & Distribution	Spring	Summer	Fall	Winter	Breeder	Key
Southeastern	U	U	U	A	•	C Common
Southcoastal	R	R	R	A	•	U Uncommon
Southwestern	–	–	–	–		R Rare
Central	C	C	C	–	•	A Casual/Accidental
Western	–	A	–	–		– No Records
Northern	A	–	–	–		

Habitat: Coniferous forests and deciduous
woodlands with open areas for hunting.
Nests in trees or on cliffs.

Notes: Often soars in wide circles above
trees or mountain ridges, and perches on
dead limbs or top branches of tall trees.
Food consists of squirrels, rabbits, mice,
lemmings and occasional birds.

RED-TAILED HAWK, *Immature, Dark Phase*

Rough-legged Hawk

(Buteo lagopus)
Length: 19–24 in.
Wingspan: 4–4½ ft.

Identification: Large, with whitish tail with a dark terminal band, long, rounded wings and a habit of hovering in the air over one spot. Plumage is variable, but most common variant is a dark back, light breast and lower belly, with some streaking of dark brown or black, and a solid, wide band of black across lower breast and upper belly. Head always pale, unlike Swainson's and Red-tailed hawks, which usually have a dark head and light throat. Some Rough-legged Hawks are all dark but can be distinguished from other dark-phase birds by the conspicuous light undersides of the primaries and the usually visible light-and-dark tail. Often a flash of white is also visible on upperside of the primaries.

Status & Distribution	Spring	Summer	Fall	Winter	Breeder	Key
Southeastern	U	A	U	–		C Common
Southcoastal	R	A	R	A	•	U Uncommon
Southwestern	U	C	U	–	•	R Rare
Central	C	U	C	A	•	A Casual/Accidental
Western	U	C	U	–	•	– No Records
Northern	C	C	C	–	•	

Habitat: Upland tundra with cliffs and rocky outcrops. Nests on cliffs or trees.

ROUGH-LEGGED HAWK, *Light Phase*

Golden Eagle

(Aquila chrysaetos)
Length: 30–41 in.
Wingspan: 6$^{1}/_{3}$–7$^{2}/_{3}$ ft.

Identification: Adult is difficult to distinguish from an immature Bald Eagle, but clues are golden back of the neck, and legs fully feathered to the toes. Immature has a white tail with a contrasting dark terminal band and a white area only at base of the primary feathers in the spread wings. In flight, head of Golden Eagle projects forward less than half the extent of the tail, whereas in Bald Eagle head projects forward of wings more than half the extent of the tail.

GOLDEN EAGLE, *Immature*

Status & Distribution	Spring	Summer	Fall	Winter	Breeder	Key
Southeastern	R	R	R	R	•	C Common
Southcoastal	R	R	R	R	•	U Uncommon
Southwestern	U	U	U	R	•	R Rare
Central	C	C	C	A	•	A Casual/Accidental
Western	U	U	U	A	•	– No Records
Northern	U	U	U	–	•	

Habitat: Upland tundra, mountain ridges. Nests on cliffs and in the tops of trees.

Notes: Prey consists of rabbits, marmots, squirrels, various rodents and birds. Usually seen soaring over mountain ridges in search of food.

GOLDEN EAGLE, *Adult with young*

Family *Falconidae*
FALCONS
(6)

Falcons are fast-flying birds of prey that are characterized by long, pointed wings and medium-to-long, slender tails. Their pointed wings are designed for speed rather than for soaring, as in the broad-winged buteos and eagles.

Eurasian Kestrel

(Falco tinnunculus)
Length: 12–15 in.
Wingspan: 2 1/4–2 1/2 ft.

Identification: Noticeably larger than American Kestrel. Male distinguished from male American Kestrel by gray tail and head and chestnut-colored upper wing coverts. American Kestrel has reddish tail and gray upper wing coverts. Both adult and immature Eurasian Kestrels have 1 dark vertical bar on face; American Kestrel has 2 vertical bars. Merlins are smaller, slate-blue above (male) or brown above (female). Eurasian Kestrel has spotted chestnut-colored upperparts (male) or rusty, barred underparts (female).

Status & Distribution	Spring	Summer	Fall	Winter	Breeder	Key
Southeastern	–	–	–	–		C Common
Southcoastal	–	–	–	–		U Uncommon
Southwestern	A	–	A	–		R Rare
Central	–	–	–	–		A Casual/Accidental
Western	–	–	–	–		– No Records
Northern	–	–	–	–		

Habitat: Has been found on Attu and Shemya islands in western Aleutians. Breeds in Eurasia and Africa.

EURASIAN KESTREL, *Female*

American Kestrel

(Falco sparverius)
Length: 9–12 in.
Wingspan: 1³/₄–2 ft.

Identification: Only small falcon in Alaska with conspicuous reddish color in the tail and on the back. Black-and-white face pattern. Habitually hovers with wings beating rapidly, and, when perched, occasionally flicks tail.

Status & Distribution	Spring	Summer	Fall	Winter	Breeder	Key
Southeastern	C	A	C	A		C Common
Southcoastal	R	A	R	A	•	U Uncommon
Southwestern	–	–	–	–		R Rare
Central	C	C	C	–	•	A Casual/Accidental
Western	A	A	A	–	•	– No Records
Northern	A	–	–	–		

Habitat: Forest edges and openings. Nests in tree cavities.

Notes: Diet consists of insects, mice and occasionally small birds.

AMERICAN KESTREL, *Male*

Merlin

(Falco columbarius)
Length: 12 in.
Wingspan: 2 ft.

Identification: Because of small size, may be confused only with Sharp-shinned Hawk or American Kestrel. Pointed wings and steady wingbeat separate Merlin from Sharp-shinned Hawk. Lack of reddish in the tail and lack of conspicuous black face markings distinguish it from American Kestrel. Tail is barred dark and light (quite different from reddish tail of the kestrel), and flight is more rapid and powerful.

Status & Distribution	Spring	Summer	Fall	Winter	Breeder	Key
Southeastern	U	R	U	R	•	C Common
Southcoastal	R	R	R	R	•	U Uncommon
Southwestern	U	U	U	A	•	R Rare
Central	U	U	U	A	•	A Casual/Accidental
Western	R	R	R	–	•	– No Records
Northern	R	R	–	–		

Habitat: Open coastal and interior forests, particularly near tidal marshes and interior muskegs. Nests on cliff ledges, in a tree hollow or on the ground.

MERLIN, *Male*

Northern Hobby

(Falco subbuteo)
Length: 12 in.
Wingspan: 2½ ft.

Identification: Similar to Peregrine Falcon but smaller with narrower moustaches. Breast and belly heavily streaked, not barred. Thighs and under tail coverts chestnut-colored. Wings longer than tail when perched. Immature has heavier streaks on underparts and no chestnut color on thighs and under tail coverts.

Habitat: Generally in open areas. Has been found on Attu Island, Aleutian Islands, at sea near the western Aleutian Islands and Saint George Village, Pribilof Islands.

NORTHERN HOBBY, *Adult*

Status & Distribution	Spring	Summer	Fall	Winter	Breeder	Key
Southeastern	–	–	–	–		C Common
Southcoastal	–	–	A	–		U Uncommon
Southwestern	A	A	–	–		R Rare
Central	–	–	–	–		A Casual/Accidental
Western	–	–	–	–		– No Records
Northern	–	–	–	–		

NORTHERN HOBBY, *Adult*

Peregrine Falcon

(Falco peregrinus)
Length: 15–21 in.
Wingspan: 3¹/₄–3³/₄ ft.

Identification: Crow-sized falcon commonly referred to as the duck hawk. Head pattern characterized by broad-to-narrow black moustaches. Pointed wings, narrow tail and quick wingbeats identify it as a falcon. Adult has a slaty-colored back, often a dark cap, and a light, barred breast. Immature is brown above, with heavy streaking on white underparts. Birds of the Aleutian Islands and southcoastal areas of Alaska are darker than Arctic-breeding birds.

Status & Distribution	Spring	Summer	Fall	Winter	Breeder	Key
Southeastern	U	U	U	R	•	C Common
Southcoastal	U	R	U	R	•	U Uncommon
Southwestern	C	U	C	U	•	R Rare
Central	R	R	R	–	•	A Casual/Accidental
Western	R	R	R	–	•	– No Records
Northern	R	R	R	–	•	

Habitat: Open country, especially shores and marshes frequented by waterfowl and shorebirds, as well as cliffs on islands, along the coast and in the mountains. Nests on cliff ledges.

Notes: One of the swiftest birds in the world. Has been clocked at speeds up to 180 miles per hour, when diving after prey.

PEREGRINE FALCON, *Adult*

Gyrfalcon

(Falco rusticolus)
Length: 20–25 in.
Wingspan: 4 ft.

Identification: Largest falcon, with a streamlined body, pointed wings and long, narrow tail. Three color phases exist — black, gray and white. Gray phase is most common in Alaska. More uniformly colored than Peregrine Falcon, and lacks the dark hood of that species. Has broader wings and shallower wingbeat than Peregrine Falcon. Flies with short, rapid wingbeats and usually does not soar for long periods.

Status & Distribution	Spring	Summer	Fall	Winter	Breeder	Key
Southeastern	R	–	R	R		C Common
Southcoastal	R	R	R	R	•	U Uncommon
Southwestern	U	U	U	U	•	R Rare
Central	U	U	U	R	•	A Casual/Accidental
Western	U	U	U	U	•	– No Records
Northern	U	U	U	–	•	

Habitat: Open country. Nests on cliff ledges.

Notes: Primarily a bird hunter that feeds on ptarmigan and seabirds. When birds are unavailable, preys on small mammals.

GYRFALCON, White Phase

Family *Phasianidae*
GROUSE, PTARMIGANS
(7)

Grouse and ptarmigans are chickenlike birds that are distinguished by the presence of feathers over the nostrils, lower legs and, in ptarmigans, the entire foot. They forage for food on the ground or in the trees when the ground is snow-covered. Their foods include berries, flowers and leaves of herbaceous plants, conifer needles, buds and twigs of trees, seeds, catkins and various insects. To survive Alaska's winter, ptarmigans and the Ruffed Grouse often plunge under the snow where the temperature may be many degrees warmer than the air. Grouse and ptarmigans also possess a food storage organ, called a crop, that can be filled during the short winter day and the contents digested at night, allowing them to keep their metabolism and body temperature high during a cold winter night.

Spruce Grouse

(Dendragapus canadensis)
Length: 16 in.

Identification: Male gray, with a sharply defined black breast and some white spotting on the sides. Red comb over the eye is often visible. Female is rusty-brown and thickly barred, more heavily barred below than female Blue Grouse. A rusty-orange band at tip of the dark tail is characteristic; however, this band is missing in birds found in southeastern Alaska, which have a row of conspicuous white spots at base of the black tail instead.

Habitat: Coniferous forests and mixed deciduous-spruce woodlands, muskegs, forest edges and openings. Inhabits mixed woodlands of spruce/paper birch, black spruce bogs and, in lower southeastern Alaska, Sitka spruce and hemlock forests. Nests on the ground at the base of a tree or under a log.

Status & Distribution	Spring	Summer	Fall	Winter	Breeder	Key
Southeastern	R	R	R	R	•	C Common
Southcoastal	U	U	U	U	•	U Uncommon
Southwestern	R	R	R	R	•	R Rare
Central	C	C	C	C	•	A Casual/Accidental
Western	R	R	R	R	•	– No Records
Northern	–	–	–	–		

Notes: An individual bird will spend most of its life in one area of only a few acres. However, in September and October it may travel several miles to get grit along roads, streams and lakes. Spruce Grouse needs a large amount of grit to make the digestive change from a fall diet of berries and leaves to a winter diet of fibrous needles.

SPRUCE GROUSE, *Male*

SPRUCE GROUSE, *Female*

Blue Grouse

(Dendragapus obscurus)
Length: 15^1/$_2$–21 in.

Identification: Adult male is slate-colored with a yellow comb and a long, black tail tipped with pale gray. Female is browner and more heavily barred than male and is only a little over two-thirds as large, but she has the same distinctive tail tip. Tail pattern is diagnostic for each Alaska grouse species (except between Rock and Willow ptarmigans, which both have black tails).

Status & Distribution	Spring	Summer	Fall	Winter	Breeder	Key
Southeastern	C	C	C	C	•	C Common
Southcoastal	A	–	–	–		U Uncommon
Southwestern	–	–	–	–		R Rare
Central	–	–	–	–		A Casual/Accidental
Western	–	–	–	–		– No Records
Northern	–	–	–	–		

Habitat: Coniferous forests, muskegs and alpine meadows near treeline. Nests on the ground often near a tree, log or rock.

Notes: Male in courtship is well known for its booming or hooting notes given while sitting in a conifer. Locating one is difficult due to ventriloquial quality of the voice and grouse's habit of changing the direction of hooting every few minutes.

BLUE GROUSE, *Male*

BLUE GROUSE, *Female*

Willow Ptarmigan

(Lagopus lagopus)
Length: 16 in.

Identification: In winter lacks the black eye bar of male Rock Ptarmigan and the white tail of White-tailed Ptarmigan. In summer Willow and Rock ptarmigans are difficult to separate, but both sexes of Willow Ptarmigan are usually more reddish than Rock Ptarmigan and have slightly heavier bills. The male Willow molts head and neck plumage in spring and body plumage some months later. Usually the Willow Ptarmigan is found among willows and heavily vegetated tundra and slopes; the Rock Ptarmigan prefers the higher, more barren and rocky slopes. Male has a deep, raucous call that sounds much like *go back go back.*

Habitat: Willow shrub thickets, tundra, muskeg. Nests on the ground, usually in wetter places with more luxuriant vegetation than the other 2 species of ptarmigan.

Notes: Willow Ptarmigan was selected as the official state bird in a vote taken by school children just before Alaska became a state. Male Willow Ptarmigan often helps to care for the chicks, a habit unique among North American grouse and ptarmigans. If the female is killed, the male will take over all family responsibilities.

WILLOW PTARMIGAN, Winter

Status & Distribution	Spring	Summer	Fall	Winter	Breeder	Key
Southeastern	U	U	U	U	•	C Common
Southcoastal	U	U	U	U	•	U Uncommon
Southwestern	C	C	C	C	•	R Rare
Central	C	C	C	C	•	A Casual/Accidental
Western	C	C	C	C	•	– No Records
Northern	C	C	C	C	•	

WILLOW PTARMIGAN, Female, Summer

WILLOW PTARMIGAN, Male, Summer

Rock Ptarmigan

(Lagopus mutus)
Length: 14 in.

Identification: In white winter plumage
Rock Ptarmigan may be separated from the
other 2 species by a black bar through the
eye of the male. Black tail distinguishes it
from White-tailed Ptarmigan. In other
plumages Rock Ptarmigan is difficult to
separate from Willow Ptarmigan, although
it is somewhat smaller than the Willow.
Voice of the courting male Rock Ptarmigan
is a growling *kurr kurr*.

Habitat: Upland and coastal (Aleutian
Islands) tundra, especially rocky mountain
ridges, shrub thickets. Nests on the ground,
usually under shrubs.

Notes: Breeding Rock Ptarmigan frequents
higher and more rocky ground than Willow
Ptarmigan. In winter most males frequent
the lower edge of the breeding grounds and
females move to shrubby openings on low,
forested hills. Winter flocks wander from
place to place in search of food. They feed
and search for food during most of the
daylight hours. Rock Ptarmigan must eat
the equivalent of one-tenth to one-fifth of
their body weight each day.

ROCK PTARMIGAN, *Summer*

Status & Distribution	Spring	Summer	Fall	Winter	Breeder	Key
Southeastern	C	C	C	C	•	C Common
Southcoastal	C	C	C	C	•	U Uncommon
Southwestern	C	C	C	C	•	R Rare
Central	C	C	C	C	•	A Casual/Accidental
Western	U	U	U	U	•	– No Records
Northern	U	U	U	U	•	

ROCK PTARMIGAN, *Winter*

White-tailed Ptarmigan

(Lagopus leucurus)
Length: 13 in.

Identification: Smallest ptarmigan. Has all-white tail in all plumages. Other ptarmigans have a black tail, although the long, white tail coverts may obscure much of it. In summer, back feathers are more finely barred and color tone is grayish instead of brown. Voice consists of cackling notes, clucks and soft hoots.

Habitat: Upland tundra, especially high mountain ridges, shrub thickets. Nests on the ground on mossy mountain ledges or against big boulders to catch the sun's warmth. In summer, hens with broods stay high on the breeding grounds near moist areas, where they feed on young plant growth around edges of melting snow patches. Rock slides and boulder fields offer protection for chicks. In late fall White-tailed Ptarmigan usually moves lower and spends the winter on slopes or in high valleys among the alders, willows and birches that project above the snow.

WHITE-TAILED PTARMIGAN, *Summer*

Status & Distribution	Spring	Summer	Fall	Winter	Breeder	Key
Southeastern	U	U	U	U	•	C Common
Southcoastal	R	R	R	R	•	U Uncommon
Southwestern	–	–	–	–		R Rare
Central	U	U	U	U	•	A Casual/Accidental
Western	–	–	–	–		– No Records
Northern	–	–	–	–		

WHITE-TAILED PTARMIGAN, *Winter*

Ruffed Grouse

(Bonasa umbellus)
Length: 17$^1/_2$ in.

Identification: Two color phases exist: a reddish-brown phase with back and tail brown, and a gray phase with a gray tail. Gray phase is more common in Alaska. Dark band near the tip of the fan-shaped tail is diagnostic.

Status & Distribution	Spring	Summer	Fall	Winter	Breeder	Key
Southeastern	R	R	R	R	•	C Common
Southcoastal	–	–	–	–		U Uncommon
Southwestern	–	–	–	–		R Rare
Central	C	C	C	C	•	A Casual/Accidental
Western	–	–	–	–		– No Records
Northern	–	–	–	–		

Habitat: Deciduous woodlands — stands of aspen and birch mostly on drier south-facing slopes, willow and alder thickets along streams and rivers. Nests on the ground under dense cover, usually near the base of a tree. In central Alaska occurs in Yukon, Tanana and Kuskokwim valleys, and in southeastern Alaska occurs along Taku, Stikine, Unuk, Chickamin and Salmon rivers.

Notes: Males establish territory and begin courtship by making a drumming sound that suggests the starting of a motor in the distance. This sound is produced by quick forward and upward strokes of the wings while standing erect.

RUFFED GROUSE

Sharp-tailed Grouse

(Tympanuchus phasianellus)
Length: 15–20 in.

Identification: Medium-sized, with a short, stiff, dun-colored tail that shows white in flight. The "V"-marked underparts are diagnostic.

Habitat: Muskegs in interior coniferous forests, willow and stunted spruce thickets, forest edges in more open areas than preferred by the forest grouse. Nests on the ground in brush or grass.

Status & Distribution	Spring	Summer	Fall	Winter	Breeder	Key
Southeastern	–	–	–	–		C Common
Southcoastal	–	–	–	–		U Uncommon
Southwestern	–	–	–	–		R Rare
Central	U	U	U	U	•	A Casual/Accidental
Western	–	–	–	–		– No Records
Northern	–	–	–	–		

Notes: In the spring courtship ritual, males taxi like wind-up airplanes on display grounds. At dawn, cocks gather on their dancing ground, with dominant males in the center and subordinate males at the edge. They then follow a routine of feet drumming and circling, accompanied by tail rasping and popping sounds generated by their bulging air sacs.

SHARP-TAILED GROUSE

Family *Rallidae*
RAILS, GALLINULES, COOTS
(2 + 2)

These birds are small- to medium-sized marsh and water birds, with short tails and wings, and large feet. Coots have lobes on the sides of their toes.

Sora

(Porzana carolina)
Length: 8¹/₂ in.

Identification: Only rail in Alaska. Has striped brown back, gray underparts with barred sides, black face patch and bright yellow bill. Call is a descending whinny.

Habitat: Freshwater marshes and ponds. Nests — a basket of woven marsh grass attached to vegetation over water or on the ground near marsh or pond. Found mostly along mainland river systems of southeastern Alaska.

Status & Distribution	Spring	Summer	Fall	Winter	Breeder	Key
Southeastern	R	R	R	–	•	C Common
Southcoastal	–	A	A	–		U Uncommon
Southwestern	–	–	–	–		R Rare
Central	–	A	–	–		A Casual/Accidental
Western	–	–	–	–		– No Records
Northern	–	–	–	–		

Notes: This small bird skulks in marsh vegetation and is unlikely to be seen.

SORA

American Coot

(Fulica americana)
Length: 15 in.

Identification: All dark gray with a white bill. Has lobed rather than webbed feet.

Status & Distribution	Spring	Summer	Fall	Winter	Breeder	Key
Southeastern	A	A	R	R		C Common
Southcoastal	A	A	A	–		U Uncommon
Southwestern	–	–	A	–		R Rare
Central	R	R	R	–	•	A Casual/Accidental
Western	–	A	–	–		– No Records
Northern	–	A	–	–		

Habitat: Lakes, ponds, marshes. Intertidal ponds and sloughs. Floating nests of vegetation are attached to surrounding plants.

AMERICAN COOT

Family *Gruidae*
CRANES
(1 + 1)

Cranes are among the tallest birds in the world. They are large, long-legged, long-necked wading birds. Cranes are known for their trumpetlike notes reminiscent of French horn sounds that are produced through a modified windpipe. Sandhill Cranes eat a variety of foods including roots, seeds, berries, lemmings, earthworms, insects and small birds.

Sandhill Crane
(Grus canadensis)
Length: 34–48 in.
Wingspan: 6–7 ft.

Identification: Long-legged, long-necked gray bird, with a bold red crown in the adult. Flies with extended neck and with wings jerking upward with each beat. Flocks flying at a distance could be mistaken for geese if long legs and very long necks were not obvious. The somewhat similar Great Blue Heron is solitary, relatively silent, flies with neck retracted, and has more slender body. Cranes and herons are rarely seen in same habitat.

Status & Distribution	Spring	Summer	Fall	Winter	Breeder	Key
Southeastern	C	R	C	A	•	C Common
Southcoastal	C	R	C	–	•	U Uncommon
Southwestern	C	C	C	–	•	R Rare
Central	C	U	C	–	•	A Casual/Accidental
Western	C	C	C	–	•	– No Records
Northern	U	U	U	–	•	

Habitat: Breeding — lowland tundra marshes. Nests on the ground in grassy marshes. In migration — tidal flats, muskegs. Winters in southern California, Texas and Mexico.

Notes: Often observed flying in "V" formation or in a line at fairly high altitude. Courtship ritual involves elaborate head bowing, leaping into the air and wing flapping.

SANDHILL CRANE

Family *Charadriidae*
PLOVERS
(8 + 1)

Plovers are plump-bodied shorebirds with a thick pigeonlike bill, short legs and large eyes. Plovers characteristically run short distances and then stop. They feed mostly on insects when on land and on insects and small mollusks and crustaceans when along salt water.

Black-bellied Plover
(Pluvialis squatarola)
Length: 12 in.

Identification: Likely to be confused only with Lesser Golden-Plover. In winter, plumage shows contrasting black axillar feathers under the wing base like no other shorebird. Noisy; common call is plaintive whistled *whee-e-ee*.

BLACK-BELLIED PLOVER, *Juvenile*

Status & Distribution	Spring	Summer	Fall	Winter	Breeder	Key
Southeastern	C	–	C	–		C Common
Southcoastal	C	U	C	A		U Uncommon
Southwestern	C	–	C	–		R Rare
Central	R	R	R	–		A Casual/Accidental
Western	C	U	C	–	•	– No Records
Northern	U	U	U	–	•	

Habitat: Breeding — tundra, usually drier ridges within wet tundra areas. Nests on ground in tundra. In migration — tidal flats, saltwater and freshwater shores.

BLACK-BELLIED PLOVER, *Breeding*

Lesser Golden-Plover

(Pluvialis dominica)
Length: 10 in.

Identification: Always appears darker than similar but slightly larger Black-bellied Plover. In summer and winter back is golden brown; in breeding plumage entire underside of male Golden-Plover is black, while under tail coverts of Black-bellied Plover are white. Female of both species may have much white underneath, even in full breeding plumage. Lesser Golden-Plover appears all dark in flight in any plumage, with uniformly dark wings, rump and tail, while Black-bellied Plover has conspicuous white wing stripes and white tail and rump. Fast flier. Call a whistled *queedle*.

Status & Distribution	Spring	Summer	Fall	Winter	Breeder	Key
Southeastern	U	–	U	A		C Common
Southcoastal	C	A	C	–		U Uncommon
Southwestern	C	–	C	–		R Rare
Central	C	C	C	–	•	A Casual/Accidental
Western	C	C	C	–	•	– No Records
Northern	C	C	C	–	•	

Habitat: Breeding — tundra on drier hillsides. Nests on tundra in moss. In migration — tidal flats, usually the drier upper portions, and tundra.

Notes: A distinct subspecies *(P. d. fulva)* breeds at lower elevations on the Seward Peninsula in western Alaska. These birds are identified in breeding plumage by the white stripe on the head, neck and sides of breast that extends down to the flanks. On juveniles this subspecies has a very bright golden hue throughout. Some Lesser Golden-Plovers migrate south via Asia to winter in Japan, India, Australia and New Zealand. Others, like many Alaskans, make a nonstop flight across the ocean from Alaska to the Hawaiian Islands, a distance of up to 2,000 miles.

LESSER GOLDEN-PLOVER (P. d. dominica), Breeding

LESSER GOLDEN-PLOVER, Juvenile

Mongolian Plover
(Charadrius mongolus)
Length: 7 1/2 in.

Identification: In breeding plumage has
conspicuous rusty breast band and rust color
in the light head stripe. In winter much
duller, like a washed-out Semipalmated
Plover but larger. In flight shows a narrower
wing stripe and less conspicuous tail pattern
than Semipalmated or Common Ringed
plovers. Call is a short trill.

Status & Distribution	Spring	Summer	Fall	Winter	Breeder	Key
Southeastern	–	–	–	–		C Common
Southcoastal	–	A	–	–		U Uncommon
Southwestern	R	A	R	–	•	R Rare
Central	–	–	–	–		A Casual/Accidental
Western	R	A	A	–	•	– No Records
Northern	–	A	A	–		

Habitat: Most often seen in spring in
western Aleutian Islands and on Saint
Lawrence Island. Has been recorded nesting
on the mainland coast of western Alaska.
Asiatic bird.

MONGOLIAN PLOVER, *Breeding*

Common Ringed Plover

(Charadrius hiaticula)
Length: 7^{1}/$_{2}$ in.

Identification: Difficult to distinguish
from Semipalmated Plover, but in summer
plumage the black breast band is considerably wider and head markings are more
contrasting. Has webbing between the bases
of 2 toes, whereas in Semipalmated webbing
occurs between all 3 toes.

Habitat: Asiatic species that has occurred
as a spring migrant and breeder on Saint
Lawrence Island in the Bering Sea and as
a casual migrant in the Aleutian Islands.

Status & Distribution	Spring	Summer	Fall	Winter	Breeder	Key
Southeastern	–	–	–	–		C Common
Southcoastal	–	–	–	–		U Uncommon
Southwestern	A	–	A	–		R Rare
Central	–	–	–	–		A Casual/Accidental
Western	A	A	–	–	•	– No Records
Northern	–	–	–	–		

COMMON RINGED PLOVER, *Male, Breeding*

Semipalmated Plover

(Charadrius semipalmatus)
Length: 7 in.

Status & Distribution	Spring	Summer	Fall	Winter	Breeder	Key
Southeastern	C	C	C	–	•	C Common
Southcoastal	C	C	C	–	•	U Uncommon
Southwestern	C	C	C	–	•	R Rare
Central	C	C	C	–	•	A Casual/Accidental
Western	C	C	C	–	•	– No Records
Northern	U	U	U	–	•	

Identification: Small, with a single black breast band; duller in the fall. Legs and base of the bill are orange. In areas bordering the Bering Sea, potentially confused with Common Ringed Plover. Call is plaintive *chu-wi*.

Habitat: Breeding — gravelly or sandy beaches of lakes, ponds, rivers and glacial moraines. Nests on the ground in sand, gravel or moss. In migration — lakes, ponds, rivers, glacial moraines and tidal flats.

SEMIPALMATED PLOVER, *Breeding*

Little Ringed Plover

(Charadrius dubius)
Length: 7 in.

Identification: Similar to Semipalmated and Common Ringed plovers but smaller. Best distinguished in breeding plumage with yellow eye-ring and a white line separating gray-brown crown from black band across forehead. In flight shows no white wing stripe. Bill is mostly dark. Voice is a short descending *piu*.

Habitat: Beaches and estuaries. Has been found on Attu, Buldir and Shemya islands in the Aleutians.

LITTLE RINGED PLOVER, *Breeding*

Status & Distribution	Spring	Summer	Fall	Winter	Breeder	Key
Southeastern	–	–	–	–		C Common
Southcoastal	–	–	–	–		U Uncommon
Southwestern	A	A	–	–		R Rare
Central	–	–	–	–		A Casual/Accidental
Western	–	–	–	–		– No Records
Northern	–	–	–	–		

Killdeer

(Charadrius vociferus)
Length: 10 in.

Identification: Two black breast bands are diagnostic. In flight, tail looks longer than in other shorebirds, and its reddish base is conspicuous at close range. Call is raucous cry of *kill-dee, kill-dee*.

Habitat: Marshes, tidal sloughs, lake shores, rivers, ponds, grasslands. Nests on gravel shores or in fields or pastures.

KILLDEER, *Breeding*

Status & Distribution	Spring	Summer	Fall	Winter	Breeder	Key
Southeastern	U	U	U	R	•	C Common
Southcoastal	R	R	R	–	•	U Uncommon
Southwestern	A	A	–	–		R Rare
Central	R	R	R	–	•	A Casual/Accidental
Western	A	A	–	–		– No Records
Northern	A	A	–	–		

Eurasian Dotterel

(Charadrius morinellus)
Length: 8 1/2 in.

Identification: In summer has white stripe over the eye meeting at nape, white throat and narrow white band across the breast. Breast is gray, belly chestnut and black. In winter is sandy brown, but the head pattern and particularly the white breast band are diagnostic. From above in flight, much like Lesser Golden-Plover but smaller and unpatterned. Call is musical twitter or trill.

Status & Distribution	Spring	Summer	Fall	Winter	Breeder	Key
Southeastern	–	–	–	–		C Common
Southcoastal	–	–	A	–		U Uncommon
Southwestern	–	–	A	–		R Rare
Central	–	A	–	–		A Casual/Accidental
Western	R	R	–	–	•	– No Records
Northern	–	A	–	–	•	

Habitat: Asiatic shorebird most often seen in summer on mountains of Bering Strait islands and Seward Peninsula in western Alaska. Although it probably breeds in these mountains, no nests have been found.

EURASIAN DOTTEREL, *Breeding*

Family *Haematopodidae*
OYSTERCATCHERS
(1)

The oystercatcher family contains large, dumpy, short-legged shorebirds with long red bills that are flattened laterally. The oystercatcher, with its chisel-like bill tip, pries shellfish off rocks and also inserts its bill between the two shells of a mollusk to sever the strong abductor muscle. The oystercatcher's food includes mussels, clams, chitons, limpits and barnacles. Also it probes in the sand and mud for marine worms and other invertebrates.

Black Oystercatcher
(Haematopus bachmani)
Length: 17 in.

Identification: Crow-sized, all black shorebird with bright red bill and pinkish legs and feet. Rounded wings beat rapidly and are kept below the level of the body in flight, all of which distinguishes the oystercatcher from a crow at a distance. Call is a loud, whistled *wheee-whee-whee-whee*.

Status & Distribution	Spring	Summer	Fall	Winter	Breeder	Key
Southeastern	C	C	C	R	•	C Common
Southcoastal	C	C	C	U	•	U Uncommon
Southwestern	C	C	C	C	•	R Rare
Central	–	–	–	–		A Casual/Accidental
Western	–	–	–	–		– No Records
Northern	–	–	–	–		

Habitat: Rocky shores, reefs and islands. Nests in beach gravel, often near grass line.

BLACK OYSTERCATCHER

Family *Scolopacidae*
SANDPIPERS
(51 + 5)

Members of the Sandpiper family vary considerably in size, shape and color. The bill is more slender than the plovers', and is soft and rather flexible. Unlike plovers, sandpipers typically move slowly and continuously when foraging, probing or picking from the surface. These shorebirds typically inhabit lakeshores, intertidal areas or other moist places. They usually lay 4 eggs in shallow depressions in the ground. Before and after the breeding season most are gregarious and can be seen in large flocks, often several species together. Many travel long distances to reach Alaska, with some wintering in South America as far south as Patagonia, a distance of over 8,000 miles.

Common Greenshank

(Tringa nebularia)
Length: 12 in.

Identification: Similar to Greater Yellow-legs, but legs are greenish, not yellow, and in flight the white of the rump extends in a point up the back. Has very white tail, not densely barred like that of the yellowlegs. Leg color distinguishes this species from Spotted Redshank in winter plumage. Call is similar to Greater Yellowlegs.

Status & Distribution	Spring	Summer	Fall	Winter	Breeder	Key
Southeastern	–	–	–	–		C Common
Southcoastal	–	–	–	–		U Uncommon
Southwestern	R	A	A	–		R Rare
Central	–	–	–	–		A Casual/Accidental
Western	A	–	–	–		– No Records
Northern	–	–	–	–		

Habitat: Asiatic shorebird seen mostly in western Aleutian Islands. Not known to breed in Alaska.

COMMON GREENSHANK, *Breeding*

Greater Yellowlegs

(Tringa melanoleuca)
Length: 14 in.

Identification: Yellowlegs are slim, gray and white, with long, bright yellow legs. In flight they show a white rump and gray-and-white barred tail and no wing stripe. Greater and Lesser yellowlegs often appear together and can be distinguished by size. When separate, size can be confusing. Greater Yellowlegs have a longer, heavier and very slightly upturned bill. Voice is usually 3- or 4-note whistle sounding like *whew-whew-whew*. Display song is a repeated whistle *whee-oodle*.

Status & Distribution	Spring	Summer	Fall	Winter	Breeder	Key
Southeastern	C	C	C	–	•	C Common
Southcoastal	C	C	C	–	•	U Uncommon
Southwestern	C	C	C	–	•	R Rare
Central	R	R	R	–	•	A Casual/Accidental
Western	R	R	R	–	•	– No Records
Northern	–	A	–	–		

Habitat: Breeding — muskegs, freshwater marshes. Breeds from the lower Yukon River Valley to the Alaska Peninsula and south and east around the coast into southeastern Alaska. Nests on the ground in moss. In migration — tidal flats, lakes, ponds.

GREATER YELLOWLEGS, *Juvenile*

Lesser Yellowlegs

(Tringa flavipes)
Length: 11 in.

Identification: Smaller version of Greater
Yellowlegs with shorter, slighter, straight
bill. Voice is 1 or 2 notes like *tew tew.*
Display song is *wheedle-bree.*

Status & Distribution	Spring	Summer	Fall	Winter	Breeder	Key
Southeastern	C	R	C	–	•	C Common
Southcoastal	C	C	C	–	•	U Uncommon
Southwestern	R	–	R	–		R Rare
Central	C	C	C	–	•	A Casual/Accidental
Western	U	U	U	–	•	– No Records
Northern	–	A	–	–	•	

Habitat: Breeding — muskegs, freshwater
marshes. Breeds primarily from Kobuk
River Valley through Yukon-Kuskokwim
area to Kenai Peninsula and Yakutat Bay. In
migration — tidal flats, lakes, ponds.

Notes: Noisy. When approached, yellowlegs usually begin calling. During nesting
season they often stand on the topmost twig
of a small tree, and if disturbed, they will
dive at the intruder while making shrill
alarm noises.

LESSER YELLOWLEGS, Juvenile

Spotted Redshank

(Tringa erythropus)
Length: 12 in.

Identification: Shaped like Greater
Yellowlegs but with slightly shorter neck
and legs. Has bright red or red-orange legs
in all plumages. In summer mostly black,
with white spotting above; in winter gray
above and white below, and plainer than a
yellowlegs. In flight similar to a yellowlegs
but white of the rump extends up the back
in a point, similar to the pattern of a
dowitcher. Call is a loud, whistled *tew-it.*

Status & Distribution	Spring	Summer	Fall	Winter	Breeder	Key
Southeastern	–	–	–	–		C Common
Southcoastal	–	–	–	–		U Uncommon
Southwestern	A	–	R	–		R Rare
Central	–	–	–	–		A Casual/Accidental
Western	–	–	–	–		– No Records
Northern	–	–	–	–		

Habitat: Asiatic migrant that has occurred
in the western and central Aleutian Islands,
primarily in fall, and as a fall migrant in the
Pribilof Islands. Not known to breed in
Alaska.

SPOTTED REDSHANK, Nonbreeding

Wood Sandpiper

(Tringa glareola)
Length: 8 in.

Identification: Built like a Solitary
Sandpiper, but warm brown dorsally,
not olive. Legs are duller yellow than
those of the yellowlegs. Wings are light
underneath, more like yellowlegs than
Solitary Sandpiper. Resembles a pale
Solitary Sandpiper with bold white rump.
Flight call is a 3-note whistle.

Status & Distribution	Spring	Summer	Fall	Winter	Breeder	Key
Southeastern	–	–	–	–		C Common
Southcoastal	–	–	–	–		U Uncommon
Southwestern	U	R	R	–	•	R Rare
Central	–	–	–	–		A Casual/Accidental
Western	R	A	–	–		– No Records
Northern	–	A	–	–		

Habitat: Tundra, tidal flats. Asiatic
sandpiper frequently observed in recent
years in southwestern and western Alaska.
Now considered an uncommon to fairly
common spring migrant in western and
central Aleutian Islands, where it has been
seen in groups of 2 to 5 and occasionally
in flocks of 20 to 45. Nesting has been
recorded in western and central Aleutian
Islands.

WOOD SANDPIPER

Green Sandpiper
(Tringa ocrophus)
Length: 9¹/₂ in.

Identification: Dark above, dark streaking on breast; white eye-ring, rump patch and belly; dark underwings. Similar to Solitary Sandpiper in plumage, flight pattern and voice. Best distinguished in flight by a conspicuous white rump patch and white tail barred with black. (Solitary has a dark rump and tail. Tail has white sides barred with black.) Best distinguished from Wood Sandpiper by its dark underwings. Wood Sandpiper has white underwings. Common Sandpiper has dark rump, white wing stripes and whitish underwings.

Status & Distribution	Spring	Summer	Fall	Winter	Breeder	Key
Southeastern	–	–	–	–		C Common
Southcoastal	–	–	–	–		U Uncommon
Southwestern	A	–	A	–		R Rare
Central	–	–	–	–		A Casual/Accidental
Western	A	–	–	–		– No Records
Northern	–	–	–	–		

Habitat: Has been found on Attu Island in western Aleutians and on Saint Lawrence Island. Breeds in northern Eurasia.

GREEN SANDPIPER

Solitary Sandpiper

(Tringa solitaria)
Length: 8 in.

Identification: Shaped like yellowlegs.
Dark olive-brown above, with conspicuous
eye-ring, and shorter, greenish legs. In
flight shows blackish underwings, dark
rump and tail. Tail has flashy white sides
barred with black. Often flies high in the air
when flushed. Call is a high-pitched whistle
wheet-wheet-wheet-wheet.

Status & Distribution	Spring	Summer	Fall	Winter	Breeder	Key
Southeastern	U	R	U	–	•	C Common
Southcoastal	U	R	U	–	•	U Uncommon
Southwestern	A	R	–	–	•	R Rare
Central	U	U	U	–	•	A Casual/Accidental
Western	A	R	–	–	•	– No Records
Northern	A	A	–	–	•	

Habitat: Breeding — muskegs, freshwater
marshes, lakes, ponds. Nests in deserted
nests of other birds, such as robins and
thrushes. In migration — muddy shorelines
of ponds and streams in wooded areas.
Rarely occurs on salt water.

Notes: Usually solitary or with 1 or
2 others.

SOLITARY SANDPIPER

Wandering Tattler

(Heteroscelus incanus)
Length: 11 in.

Identification: This species is distinguished from others found along rocky coasts by the uniform dark gray on its upperparts, wings and tail. In breeding plumage has heavily barred underparts, unlike most other shorebirds. Noisy; call is a ringing series of whistled notes that can be easily heard over pounding surf or rushing water.

Status & Distribution	Spring	Summer	Fall	Winter	Breeder	Key
Southeastern	U	R	U	–	•	C Common
Southcoastal	C	U	C	–	•	U Uncommon
Southwestern	U	R	U	–	•	R Rare
Central	U	U	U	–	•	A Casual/Accidental
Western	U	U	U	–	•	– No Records
Northern	A	A	A	–	•	

Habitat: Breeding — gravel bars of mountain streams. Nests in gravel near streams. In migration — rocky saltwater beaches.

Notes: Usually found alone or with 1 or 2 others. Almost exclusively an Alaskan breeding bird. Elsewhere has been reported from only 1 small area in Yukon Territory.

WANDERING TATTLER, *Juvenile*

WANDERING TATTLER, *Breeding*

Gray-tailed Tattler

(Heteroscelus brevipes)
Length: 9½ in.

Identification: Very similar to Wandering
Tattler. In winter and juvenile plumages
the two tattlers are so similar they should be
separated by voice. In summer Gray-tailed
Tattler is distinguished by much less
prominently barred underparts, the center
of the belly and undertail being immaculate.
Bars are lighter and narrower than in
Wandering Tattler. Call is double whistle
too-weet.

Habitat: Asiatic migrant found mostly in
the Aleutian Islands and Bering Sea islands.
Not known to breed in Alaska.

Status & Distribution	Spring	Summer	Fall	Winter	Breeder	Key
Southeastern	–	–	–	–		C Common
Southcoastal	–	–	A	–		U Uncommon
Southwestern	R	A	R	–		R Rare
Central	–	–	–	–		A Casual/Accidental
Western	R	A	A	–		– No Records
Northern	A	A	–	–		

GRAY-TAILED TATTLER, *Breeding*

Common Sandpiper

(Actitis hypoleucos)
Length: 8 in.

Identification: In spring or summer easily distinguished from very similar Spotted Sandpiper by plain, unspotted underparts, streaked breast, greenish-gray legs and feet (Spotted Sandpiper's are flesh-pink) and all-dark bill. In fall these species are very similar. Common has a proportionately longer tail; at rest wings reach to base of tail whereas the Spotted's reach to mid-tail. In flight the Common's tail is outlined in white whereas the Spotted's tail contains dark bands extending into the white. Spotted Sandpiper is unknown on Bering Sea islands.

Habitat: Asiatic migrant in western and central Aleutian Islands, Pribilof Islands and Saint Lawrence Island.

COMMON SANDPIPER

Status & Distribution	Spring	Summer	Fall	Winter	Breeder	Key
Southeastern	–	–	–	–		C Common
Southcoastal	–	–	–	–		U Uncommon
Southwestern	R	A	R	–	•	R Rare
Central	–	–	–	–		A Casual/Accidental
Western	R	–	–	–		– No Records
Northern	–	–	–	–		

Spotted Sandpiper
(Actitis macularia)
Length: 7¹/₂ in.

Identification: Breeding adult unmistakable, with large black spots on white underparts. In autumn, spots disappear and plumage is brown above and white below, with a dark mark on the side at the bend of the wing. In all plumages has a narrow wing stripe and dark tail. Teeters almost constantly. Has shallow wing strokes in flight. Call is series of high-pitched whistles, much like Solitary Sandpiper but dropping toward the end of the series.

Habitat: Shores of rivers, streams, lakes and saltwater beaches. Nests near water in gravel or grass.

Notes: One of Alaska's most widely distributed breeding birds. When flushed, flies out over the water with short jerky wingbeats, only to swing back to shore a short distance away.

SPOTTED SANDPIPER, *Nonbreeding*

Status & Distribution	Spring	Summer	Fall	Winter	Breeder	Key
Southeastern	C	C	C	A	•	C Common
Southcoastal	C	C	C	A	•	U Uncommon
Southwestern	U	U	U	–	•	R Rare
Central	C	C	C	–	•	A Casual/Accidental
Western	U	U	U	–	•	– No Records
Northern	U	U	U	–	•	

SPOTTED SANDPIPER, *Breeding*

Terek Sandpiper

(Xenus cinereus)
Length: 9 in.

Identification: Larger than Spotted and
Common sandpipers. Plain gray above and
white below, with short yellow legs and
conspicuously upturned long bill (only small
shorebird with such a bill). In summer
shows a pair of black stripes down the back.
In flight plain above but with white patches
on the rear edge of each wing. Bobs like
Spotted and Common sandpipers. Call is a
fluted *tutututu*.

Habitat: Asiatic migrant found mostly in
western Aleutian Islands and along the
Bering Sea coast and islands. Not known to
breed in Alaska.

TEREK SANDPIPER, Breeding

Status & Distribution	Spring	Summer	Fall	Winter	Breeder	Key
Southeastern	–	–	–	–		C Common
Southcoastal	–	A	A	–		U Uncommon
Southwestern	R	A	A	–		R Rare
Central	–	–	–	–		A Casual/Accidental
Western	R	A	A	–		– No Records
Northern	–	–	–	–		

Upland Sandpiper

(Bartramia longicauda)
Length: 11¹/₂ in.

Identification: Large, buffy, with a long
neck, small head and straight bill that is
shorter than the head. Blackish lower back
and longish tail, both visible in flight.
Flies with wings held low like a Spotted
Sandpiper. Often holds wings up for a
moment on alighting. Voice on the breeding
grounds is a long, mournful, rolling whistle;
flight call similar to Whimbrel's.

Habitat: Open grassy fields and sparsely
vegetated uplands. Never associated with
water. Frequently perches on small trees
or fence posts. Occurs primarily in interior
Alaska, in areas such as Denali National
Park and open grassy ridges north of
Fairbanks.

UPLAND SANDPIPER

Status & Distribution	Spring	Summer	Fall	Winter	Breeder	Key
Southeastern	A	–	A	–		C Common
Southcoastal	A	–	A	–		U Uncommon
Southwestern	–	–	–	–		R Rare
Central	U	U	U	–	•	A Casual/Accidental
Western	–	A	A	–	•	– No Records
Northern	–	–	–	–		

Whimbrel

(Numenius phaeopus)
Length: 17 in.

Identification: At a distance appears
entirely plain brown. At close range a long
downcurved bill and striped crown are
visible. May be confused only with Bristle-
thighed Curlew or with the much rarer,
larger curlews with unstriped heads.
Whimbrels from Siberia occur regularly in
southwestern and western Alaska. They have
a conspicuous white back and dark-spotted
white rump. Call is a loud, repeated,
whistled *pi-pi-pi-pip*.

Habitat: Breeding — tundra. Nests in a
depression or on a mound of vegetation in
the tundra. In migration — tidal flats and
beaches. In migration this large shorebird
is quite conspicuous among the smaller
sandpipers. However, on the tundra
Whimbrel blends well with its surroundings
and is often difficult to see.

Status & Distribution	Spring	Summer	Fall	Winter	Breeder	Key
Southeastern	U	A	U	–		C Common
Southcoastal	C	U	C	–		U Uncommon
Southwestern	C	C	C	–		R Rare
Central	C	C	U	–	•	A Casual/Accidental
Western	C	C	U	–	•	– No Records
Northern	U	U	–	–	•	

WHIMBREL

Bristle-thighed Curlew
(Numenius tahitiensis)
Length: 17 in.

Identification: Similar to Whimbrel, with long, downcurved bill, large size and conspicuous head stripe. Tawnier all over than Whimbrel; pale salmon-colored on the rump and tail. Flight call is a slurred whistle.

Status & Distribution	Spring	Summer	Fall	Winter	Breeder	Key
Southeastern	A	–	–	–		C Common
Southcoastal	A	–	A	–		U Uncommon
Southwestern	R	A	R	–		R Rare
Central	A	–	–	–		A Casual/Accidental
Western	U	U	U	–	•	– No Records
Northern	R	R	–	–		

Habitat: Breeding — flat, dry tundra on exposed ridges. Nests in depressions on the tundra. In migration — drier coastal tundra, tidal flats and beaches.

Notes: Alaska is the only known nesting place for this species.

BRISTLE-THIGHED CURLEW

Far Eastern Curlew

(Numenius madagascariensis)
Length: 20–26 in.

Identification: Considerably larger than
Whimbrel and Bristle-thighed Curlew, with
plain brown back, wings and tail, and boldly
streaked beige underparts. Head is finely
streaked, without the conspicuous stripes of
other curlews.

Status & Distribution	Spring	Summer	Fall	Winter	Breeder	Key
Southeastern	–	–	–	–		C Common
Southcoastal	–	–	–	–		U Uncommon
Southwestern	A	A	–	–		R Rare
Central	–	–	–	–		A Casual/Accidental
Western	A	–	–	–		– No Records
Northern	–	–	–	–		

Habitat: Asiatic bird found mostly in spring
and summer on Aleutian Islands and
Pribilof Islands. Not known to breed in
Alaska.

FAR EASTERN CURLEW

Black-tailed Godwit

(Limosa limosa)
Length: 16 in.

Identification: In summer similar to Hudsonian Godwit but with an immaculate cinnamon head and breast, and paler flanks that are barred with bold black bars. Hudsonian Godwit has dark cinnamon breast and belly, and pale head. In all seasons Black-tailed Godwit has white wing linings rather than black as in the Hudsonian Godwit. Only godwit with a straight bill.

Habitat: This Asiatic shorebird has been found in western and central Aleutian Islands and on Bering Sea islands. Not known to breed in Alaska.

Status & Distribution	Spring	Summer	Fall	Winter	Breeder	Key
Southeastern	–	–	–	–		C Common
Southcoastal	–	–	–	–		U Uncommon
Southwestern	A	A	–	–		R Rare
Central	–	–	–	–		A Casual/Accidental
Western	A	–	–	–		– No Records
Northern	–	–	–	–		

BLACK-TAILED GODWIT, *Breeding*

Hudsonian Godwit

(Limosa haemastica)
Length: 15 in.

Identification: Large shorebird with long, slender, slightly upturned bill. In summer the underparts are extensively dark cinnamon, narrowly barred with black; the back is brown. In winter entirely pale brownish-gray. Shows a vivid pattern in flight, with a conspicuous white wing stripe, black underwings and white-based, black-tipped tail. Similarly sized Bar-tailed Godwit is drab in comparison.

Status & Distribution	Spring	Summer	Fall	Winter	Breeder	Key
Southeastern	R	A	A	–		C Common
Southcoastal	U	U	U	–	•	U Uncommon
Southwestern	A	R	R	–	•	R Rare
Central	R	A	–	–		A Casual/Accidental
Western	U	U	U	–	•	– No Records
Northern	–	R	R	–		

Habitat: Breeding — sedge-grass marshes, wet tundra, taiga bogs. In migration — tidal flats and beaches.

HUDSONIAN GODWIT, *Juvenile*

Bar-tailed Godwit

(Limosa lapponica)
Length: 16 in.

Identification: Has long, slightly upturned bill. Male is rich rufous below in breeding plumage; female is duller with more white. In all plumages looks rather plain above in flight, with poorly defined wing stripe, and rump and tail slightly lighter than the back. Some field guides portray a European subspecies that has a much more contrasting rump and tail than does the Alaska one.

Status & Distribution	Spring	Summer	Fall	Winter	Breeder	Key
Southeastern	A	–	A	–		C Common
Southcoastal	R	–	R	–		U Uncommon
Southwestern	C	U	C	–		R Rare
Central	–	–	–	–		A Casual/Accidental
Western	C	C	C	–	•	– No Records
Northern	U	U	U	–	•	

Habitat: Breeding — wet lowland tundra. Nests on the ground in moss. In migration — tidal flats.

BAR-TAILED GODWIT; *Female, left; Male, right*

Marbled Godwit

(Limosa fedoa)
Length: 16–20 in.

Identification: Largest godwit in Alaska. Resembles a larger, entirely tawny-brown version of the summer-plumaged Bar-tailed Godwit. At all seasons is evenly buff-colored ventrally. In flight, wings are conspicuously cinnamon. Juvenile Bar-tailed Godwit in fall has paler breast and belly and lighter tail than any Marbled Godwit. Call is a loud *kerreck*.

Habitat: Tidal flats. No nests have been found in Alaska.

MARBLED GODWIT, *Nonbreeding*

Status & Distribution	Spring	Summer	Fall	Winter	Breeder	Key
Southeastern	R	A	–	–		C Common
Southcoastal	R	–	A	–		U Uncommon
Southwestern	R	R	R	–	•	R Rare
Central	–	–	–	–		A Casual/Accidental
Western	–	–	–	–		– No Records
Northern	–	–	–	–		

Ruddy Turnstone

(Arenaria interpres)
Length: 9 in.

Identification: In spring and summer is striking black, white and russet. In autumn, adult and juvenile are brownish, but still show enough of their peculiar breast and wing pattern to be distinctive. A very dull Ruddy Turnstone can be separated from Black Turnstone by orangier legs, white throat, browner back and the double-rounded line where breast and belly colors meet. In flight both turnstones show a vivid calico pattern above. Voice is a chattering call, slower and lower pitched than Black Turnstone.

Habitat: Breeding — drier tundra areas, dunes. Nests in a depression on the ground. In migration — rocky shores, tidal flats and beaches.

RUDDY TURNSTONE, *Breeding*

RUDDY TURNSTONE, *Nonbreeding*

Status & Distribution	Spring	Summer	Fall	Winter	Breeder	Key
Southeastern	U	–	U	–		C Common
Southcoastal	C	R	U	–		U Uncommon
Southwestern	C	U	C	–		R Rare
Central	R	A	–	–		A Casual/Accidental
Western	C	C	C	–	•	– No Records
Northern	U	U	U	–	•	

Black Turnstone
(Arenaria melanocephala)
Length: 9 in.

Identification: Chunky, short-legged shorebird with blackish chest and white lower breast and belly. Black-and-white wing and back pattern can be seen in flight. Breast coloration meets that of the belly in a straight line, and legs vary from dull dark-yellowish to black. Voice is a high and shrill chattering call.

BLACK TURNSTONE, *Breeding*

Status & Distribution	Spring	Summer	Fall	Winter	Breeder	Key
Southeastern	C	R	C	U		C Common
Southcoastal	C	U	C	R		U Uncommon
Southwestern	C	U	C	R	•	R Rare
Central	–	A	A	–		A Casual/Accidental
Western	C	C	C	–	•	– No Records
Northern	A	–	–	–		

Habitat: Breeding — wet tundra. Nests on the ground in grassy areas near ponds. In migration and winter — rocky shores, tidal flats and beaches.

BLACK TURNSTONE, *Nonbreeding*

Surfbird

(Aphriza virgata)
Length: 10 in.

Identification: Chunky, short-legged and short-billed. In breeding plumage breast is heavily spotted and streaked, and back is reddish-brown. Shape, behavior, habitat and flight pattern are diagnostic. In winter plain gray, lighter than Black Turnstone, with which it is often associated. Also larger and thicker billed than the turnstones. In flight appears all dark, with a thin, white wing stripe and white rump and tail base contrasting with black tail tip. Unlike turnstones and tattlers, it is usually silent.

Status & Distribution	Spring	Summer	Fall	Winter	Breeder	Key
Southeastern	U	R	U	R		C Common
Southcoastal	C	U	C	U	•	U Uncommon
Southwestern	R	R	R	R	•	R Rare
Central	U	U	U	–	•	A Casual/Accidental
Western	R	R	R	–	•	– No Records
Northern	–	–	–	–		

Habitat: Breeding — alpine tundra along mountain ridges. Nests on the ground in rocky area interspersed with small clumps of vegetation. In migration and winter — rocky shores and rockier portions of tidal flats.

SURFBIRD, *Breeding*

SURFBIRD, *Juvenile*

Great Knot

(Calidris tenuirostris)
Length: 11½ in.

Identification: Shaped much like Red Knot, but is a bit larger and more heavily marked in all plumages. In summer back is marked with rufous, breast heavily blotched with black and sides covered with bold black heart-shaped or arrowhead-shaped spots. In winter breast is lightly spotted and the crown streaked. Legs are greenish as in Red Knot, and flight pattern is similar except that the paler rump contrasts considerably with the tail in Great Knot.

Habitat: Asiatic shorebird that has been found in western and central Aleutian Islands and on the Bering Sea coast and islands. Not known to breed in Alaska.

Status & Distribution	Spring	Summer	Fall	Winter	Breeder	Key
Southeastern	–	–	–	–		C Common
Southcoastal	–	–	–	–		U Uncommon
Southwestern	A	–	–	–		R Rare
Central	–	–	–	–		A Casual/Accidental
Western	A	–	–	–		– No Records
Northern	–	–	–	–		

GREAT KNOT, *Breeding*

Red Knot

(Calidris canutus)
Length: 10 1/2 in.

Identification: Chunky, short-legged
sandpiper of medium size that feeds on mud
flats. In spring breast is brick red, the back
mottled; in fall upperparts are light gray and
underparts white. In spring only dowitchers
and Red Phalaropes have plain reddish
underparts; Red Knot's short, straight black
bill separates it from those species. When
knots and dowitchers have their bills hidden,
which is often, the slightly lighter breast
color and white under tail coverts in Red
Knot are diagnostic. In fall Red Knot is the
only bird so evenly gray, with a straight bill
rather short for its body size. Flight pattern,
with white wing stripe and pale rump and
tail, separates it from all shorebirds but
Black-bellied Plover, which is larger and has
conspicuous black axillar feathers. Knots are
relatively silent; their 2-noted whistled song
is given from high in the air.

Status & Distribution	Spring	Summer	Fall	Winter	Breeder	Key
Southeastern	R	–	A	–		C Common
Southcoastal	C	A	R	–		U Uncommon
Southwestern	A	A	R	–		R Rare
Central	A	–	–	–		A Casual/Accidental
Western	U	U	U	–	•	– No Records
Northern	R	R	R	–	•	

Habitat: Breeding — gravelly ridges in
alpine tundra. Nests on the ground in
shallow depressions in gravel or rubble. In
migration — tidal flats. Locally abundant on
tidal flats of Copper and Bering river deltas
in the spring, where flocks of over 40,000
have been seen.

RED KNOT, *Breeding*

Sanderling
(Calidris alba)
Length: 8 in.

Identification: Small, with a short, heavy black bill, black legs and a conspicuous white wing stripe in flight. In spring is bright buffy, and much more uniformly reddish above than other small sandpipers. In fall migration is palest of small sandpipers, with pale gray back and snowy white underparts. The bend of its wing is conspicuously dark at this time. Call is a sharp *wick-wick*.

Habitat: Breeding — primarily in Canadian arctic islands and Greenland; very rarely in Alaska at Point Barrow. In migration and winter — sandy beaches, tidal flats and rocky beaches.

SANDERLING, *Juvenile*

Status & Distribution	Spring	Summer	Fall	Winter	Breeder	Key
Southeastern	U	R	U	R		C Common
Southcoastal	U	U	U	R		U Uncommon
Southwestern	U	–	U	R		R Rare
Central	R	–	R	–		A Casual/Accidental
Western	U	R	U	–		– No Records
Northern	U	R	U	–	•	

SANDERLING, *Juvenile*

Semipalmated Sandpiper

(Calidris pusilla)
Length: 6¹/₂ in.

Identification: One of 3 common, very small sandpipers, with the Western and Least sandpipers, that may be confused with each other. Semipalmated and Western sandpipers have black legs, easily seen at close range. Semipalmated has a short, thick bill; Western a longer, thinner bill with a slight droop at the tip. In breeding plumage Semipalmated is mottled with brown above; Western with gray and reddish. In drab fall plumage these species are more similar, but birds with any reddish remaining (often on the scapulars) are Westerns. Call of Semipalmated is shorter and lower than Western. Trills given on breeding grounds are simple and unmusical; song flight is relatively low and short.

Habitat: Breeding — wet tundra, sand dunes. Nests on the ground in tundra or short grass of sand dunes. In migration — tidal flats and beaches, lake shores.

Notes: Smaller Alaskan sandpipers are called peeps. In mixed flocks of peeps, comparing size can aid identification.

Status & Distribution	Spring	Summer	Fall	Winter	Breeder	Key
Southeastern	R	–	R	–		C Common
Southcoastal	U	R	U	–		U Uncommon
Southwestern	R	–	R	–		R Rare
Central	C	A	U	–	•	A Casual/Accidental
Western	U	U	U	–	•	– No Records
Northern	C	C	U	–	•	

SEMIPALMATED SANDPIPER, *Breeding*

SEMIPALMATED SANDPIPER, *Juvenile*

Western Sandpiper

(Calidris mauri)
Length: 6½ in.

Identification: Among Alaskan peeps,
Western Sandpiper is distinguished
from Least Sandpiper by black legs (not
yellowish-green) and longer bill, reddish-
marked head and back in spring and
summer, and paler back and less marked
breast in fall. Compared with Semipalmated
Sandpiper, Western shows much more
rusty color on the crown and upperparts in
breeding plumage. Is the only peep with
distinct, arrowhead-shaped flank spots in
breeding plumage. In autumn, separation of
the 2 species is difficult. Call is a thin, high
jeet. Breeding song is more varied than that
of Semipalmated Sandpiper, rising and
falling in pitch.

Habitat: Breeding — drier areas of the
tundra. Nests on the ground in short tundra
vegetation. In migration — tidal flats and
beaches.

Status & Distribution	Spring	Summer	Fall	Winter	Breeder	Key
Southeastern	C	R	C	–		C Common
Southcoastal	C	U	C	–		U Uncommon
Southwestern	C	R	C	–		R Rare
Central	R	A	R	–	•	A Casual/Accidental
Western	C	C	C	–	•	– No Records
Northern	U	U	U	–	•	

WESTERN SANDPIPER, *Breeding*

WESTERN SANDPIPER, *Juvenile*

Rufous-necked Stint
(Calidris ruficollis)
Length: 5 in.

Identification: In spring and summer has a rufous face, throat and upper breast, rufous feather edges on back, a whitish chin, short black bill and short dark legs. In winter plumage is very similar to Little Stint, Western and Semipalmated sandpipers.

Status & Distribution	Spring	Summer	Fall	Winter	Breeder	Key
Southeastern	–	–	A	–		C Common
Southcoastal	A	A	A	–		U Uncommon
Southwestern	R	A	R	–		R Rare
Central	–	–	–	–		A Casual/Accidental
Western	R	R	A	–	•	– No Records
Northern	R	R	R	–	•	

Habitat: Breeding — wet tundra. Nests in depressions in the tundra. In migration — tidal flats. Asiatic species.

RUFOUS-NECKED STINT, *Breeding*

Little Stint

(Calidris minuta)
Length: 5 in.

Identification: Small sandpiper with black legs and short bill tapering to a fine point. Very similar to Rufous-necked Stint. In breeding plumage the orange feather edges on back and coverts, rusty face and white throat help separate Little Stint from Rufous-necked Stint, which has rufous feather edges on back, bright chestnut-colored face, throat and upper breast. In winter plumage grayish above and white below, making it very difficult to distinguish from Rufous-necked Stint.

Habitat: Has been found at Point Barrow; the Pribilof Islands; Gambell, Saint Lawrence Island; and Buldir Island in western Aleutian Islands. Breeds in northern Eurasia.

LITTLE STINT, *Juvenile*

Status & Distribution	Spring	Summer	Fall	Winter	Breeder	Key
Southeastern	–	–	–	–		C Common
Southcoastal	–	–	–	–		U Uncommon
Southwestern	–	–	A	–		R Rare
Central	–	–	–	–		A Casual/Accidental
Western	A	–	–	–		– No Records
Northern	A	–	–	–		

LITTLE STINT, *Breeding*

Temminck's Stint

(Calidris temminckii)
Length: 5¹/₂ in.

Identification: In summer a gray peep with irregular black spots on back forming no pattern, and with short yellowish or greenish legs. A peep with yellowish legs in the Bering Sea area might be either a Temminck's Stint, Least Sandpiper or Long-toed Stint, none of which is common. In winter very plain gray above and white below, the plainest of the peeps or stints. Outer tail feathers are pure white rather than the gray of other peeps. Call is short, high-pitched trill.

Habitat: Asiatic shorebird that has been seen mostly as a migrant in western Aleutian Islands, Pribilof Islands and in the Bering Strait area. Not known to breed in Alaska.

Status & Distribution	Spring	Summer	Fall	Winter	Breeder	Key
Southeastern	–	–	–	–		C Common
Southcoastal	–	–	–	–		U Uncommon
Southwestern	R	A	R	–		R Rare
Central	–	–	–	–		A Casual/Accidental
Western	R	A	A	–		– No Records
Northern	–	–	–	–		

TEMMINCK'S STINT, *Juvenile*

TEMMINCK'S STINT, *Breeding*

Long-toed Stint

(Calidris subminuta)
Length: 5³/₄ in.

Identification: Looks enough like Least Sandpiper to be usually indistinguishable in the field, although Least Sandpiper is less likely to be observed in the western Aleutian Islands and Bering Sea islands. Under close observation toes are visible that are conspicuously longer than those of other peeps. Crown, ear and finely streaked breast band are washed with pale cinnamon in comparison with much browner Least Sandpiper. Call is a low, short, trilled *chrrup.*

Habitat: Asiatic shorebird that has been seen mostly as a migrant in the Aleutian Islands, Pribilof Islands and in the Bering Strait area. Not known to breed in Alaska, although may nest in years when enough birds are present to stimulate breeding activity.

LONG-TOED STINT

Status & Distribution	Spring	Summer	Fall	Winter	Breeder	Key
Southeastern	–	–	–	–		C Common
Southcoastal	–	–	–	–		U Uncommon
Southwestern	R	A	R	–		R Rare
Central	–	–	–	–		A Casual/Accidental
Western	R	–	–	–		– No Records
Northern	–	–	–	–		

Least Sandpiper

(Calidris minutilla)
Length: 5¹/₂ in.

(Pictured on right)
Identification: Yellowish rather than black legs distinguish this smallest sandpiper. Least Sandpipers are browner than Semipalmated Sandpipers in the fall and browner than Western Sandpipers in any plumage. Brown-breasted rather than gray-breasted as in the other 2 small peeps. Call is a thin, rising *pree-eet.*

Status & Distribution	Spring	Summer	Fall	Winter	Breeder	Key
Southeastern	C	U	C	–	•	C Common
Southcoastal	C	C	C	–	•	U Uncommon
Southwestern	C	C	C	–	•	R Rare
Central	C	U	U	–	•	A Casual/Accidental
Western	U	U	U	–	•	– No Records
Northern	U	U	R	–	•	

Habitat: Breeding — sedge-grass marshes near tidal flats, freshwater marshes, muskegs. Nests on the ground in both wet and dry grassy areas. In migration — tidal flats, lakes, ponds, marshes.

Notes: Often feeds among marsh vegetation and on mud flats. Rarely occurs in large flocks.

White-rumped Sandpiper
(Calidris fuscicollis)
Length: 7¹/₂ in.

Identification: Like Baird's, larger than other peeps and has longer wings. More rufous in summer and grayer in winter than Baird's Sandpiper, and colored somewhat like a Western Sandpiper. In flight white rump contrasts with darker tail. Call is a very high mouselike squeak.

Status & Distribution	Spring	Summer	Fall	Winter	Breeder	Key
Southeastern	–	–	–	–		C Common
Southcoastal	A	–	A	–		U Uncommon
Southwestern	–	–	–	–		R Rare
Central	R	–	–	–		A Casual/Accidental
Western	–	–	–	–		– No Records
Northern	R	R	–	–	•	

Habitat: Breeding — wet grassy tundra. Nests on the ground in tundra moss. In migration — tidal flats and beaches.

Notes: Like Pectoral and Curlew sandpipers only the female incubates the eggs and rears the young. Most other shorebirds share these duties.

WHITE-RUMPED SANDPIPER, *Female, Breeding*

LEAST SANDPIPER, *Breeding*

Baird's Sandpiper

(Calidris bairdii)

Length: 7 in.

Identification: Almost the size of a Sanderling. Wing tips extend beyond the tail tip when folded, because the wings are relatively longer than in the smaller species. In all plumages Baird's have black legs and an overall buffy appearance, not as bright or uniform as a Sanderling and with pale feather edges on the back presenting a somewhat scaly appearance. This is especially pronounced in young heading south in autumn. Call is a louder, deeper version of Least Sandpiper's. Breeding song is a loud, long trill, *durreee, durreee,* given from high in the air.

Habitat: Breeding — tundra, preferably drier portions. Nests on dry tundra. In migration — lakes, ponds, tidal flats and beaches often in drier areas.

Notes: Rarely occurs in flocks of more than a few individuals.

BAIRD'S SANDPIPER, *Juvenile*

Status & Distribution	Spring	Summer	Fall	Winter	Breeder	Key
Southeastern	U	–	U	–		C Common
Southcoastal	U	–	U	–		U Uncommon
Southwestern	R	–	U	–		R Rare
Central	U	U	U	–	•	A Casual/Accidental
Western	U	U	U	–	•	– No Records
Northern	C	C	C	–	•	

BAIRD'S SANDPIPER, *Breeding*

Pectoral Sandpiper

(Calidris melanotos)
Length: 9 in.

Status & Distribution	Spring	Summer	Fall	Winter	Breeder	Key
Southeastern	C	A	C	–		C Common
Southcoastal	C	A	C	–		U Uncommon
Southwestern	R	R	C	–		R Rare
Central	C	U	U	–		A Casual/Accidental
Western	C	C	C	–	•	– No Records
Northern	C	C	C	–	•	

Identification: Brown with yellowish legs, obvious light streaks on the back, and a heavily streaked brown breast with streaks sharply cut off from white of the belly. Male is somewhat larger than the female. Appears long-necked and alert, compared with other small- to medium-sized sandpipers. Call, when flushed, is rolling, somewhat like that of Baird's Sandpiper.

Habitat: Breeding — grassy areas in wet tundra. Nests on the ground within tundra vegetation. In migration — sedge-grass areas of tidal flats, grassy marshes, grassy edges of lakes and ponds.

Notes: Their "hooting" mating call given in low flights across the tundra is unique among American shorebirds. To call they fill the esophagus with air until breast and throat are inflated to at least twice normal size.

PECTORAL SANDPIPER

Sharp-tailed Sandpiper

(Calidris acuminata)
Length: 8¹/₂ in.

Identification: Breeding-plumaged adult has bold spotting on orange breast, rusty cap and upperparts. Juvenile has buffy breast only lightly streaked and not set off from the white belly, as in Pectoral Sandpiper. The back and especially the cap are ruddy-colored.

Habitat: In migration — grassy areas of tidal flats, marshes, lakes and ponds. Not known to breed in Alaska.

Status & Distribution	Spring	Summer	Fall	Winter	Breeder	Key
Southeastern	A	–	R	–		C Common
Southcoastal	–	–	R	–		U Uncommon
Southwestern	A	–	U	–		R Rare
Central	–	–	A	–		A Casual/Accidental
Western	A	A	U	–		– No Records
Northern	A	–	A	–		

Notes: Quite similar in appearance and behavior to more common Pectoral Sandpiper in juvenile plumage, and therefore probably has gone unnoticed in many areas.

SHARP-TAILED SANDPIPER, *Juvenile*

Rock Sandpiper

(Calidris ptilocnemis)
Length: 9 in.

Identification: In summer rust-colored on the crown and back, like a Dunlin, but darker and with a similar black patch on the breast rather than the belly. In winter medium-gray between the shades of Surfbird and Black Turnstone, with a slender, Dunlin-like bill and yellowish legs. In flight rather plain-looking with a narrow white wing stripe. Darker color, yellowish legs and bill base, and spotted sides distinguish Rock Sandpiper from similar Dunlin. Relatively silent in migration; summer song of Rock Sandpiper is loud and given high in the air over a rather large territory.

Habitat: Breeding — tundra. Nests on the ground in mossy or rocky tundra. In migration and winter — tidal flats and beaches usually in more rocky areas.

Notes: Of shorebirds commonly inhabiting rocky areas, this one is the smallest.

ROCK SANDPIPER, *Nonbreeding*

Status & Distribution	Spring	Summer	Fall	Winter	Breeder	Key
Southeastern	C	–	C	C		C Common
Southcoastal	C	–	C	C		U Uncommon
Southwestern	C	C	C	C	•	R Rare
Central	–	–	–	–		A Casual/Accidental
Western	C	C	C	–	•	– No Records
Northern	–	–	–	–		

ROCK SANDPIPER, *Breeding*

Dunlin
(Calidris alpina)
Length: 8 in.

Identification: Medium-sized sandpiper with a longish bill, noticeably downcurved near the tip. In spring and summer rich reddish above and white below, with a large black patch on the belly. In winter unpatterned grayish-brown above and on the breast, and white below. One of the most drab shorebirds in winter. In flight similar to most peeps, with a narrow white wing stripe and white sides to the rump. Call, often given in flight, is a high, rasping *cheezp.* Breeding song is a musical rising and falling trill delivered from the air over a smaller area than that of the Rock Sandpiper.

DUNLIN, *Breeding*

Status & Distribution	Spring	Summer	Fall	Winter	Breeder	Key
Southeastern	C	–	C	U		C Common
Southcoastal	C	R	C	U	•	U Uncommon
Southwestern	C	C	C	U	•	R Rare
Central	A	A	A	–		A Casual/Accidental
Western	C	C	C	–	•	– No Records
Northern	U	U	U	–	•	

Habitat: Breeding — wet grassy tundra and coastal sedge-grass marshes. Nests on the ground in grassy areas. In migration and winter — tidal flats and muddy and sandy beaches. Sometimes associated with Rock Sandpipers in rocky areas.

DUNLIN, *Winter*

Curlew Sandpiper

(Calidris ferruginea)
Length: 8¹/₂ in.

Identification: Long, evenly downcurved
bill is best field mark. Summer plumage is
bright rufous above and below. In winter
is gray, rather clear-breasted, and shows a
white rump in flight. Curlew Sandpiper is a
bit longer legged (the feet extending beyond
the tail in flight), and longer necked than a
Dunlin, giving it a more elegant appearance.
Call is a soft, whistled *chirrup*.

Status & Distribution	Spring	Summer	Fall	Winter	Breeder	Key
Southeastern	–	–	–	–		C Common
Southcoastal	A	A	–	–		U Uncommon
Southwestern	A	–	A	–		R Rare
Central	–	–	–	–		A Casual/Accidental
Western	A	–	A	–		– No Records
Northern	R	R	A	–	•	

Habitat: Dry tundra adjacent to the coast.
Asiatic sandpiper that has been found
breeding in northern Alaska at Barrow.
Elsewhere only a casual migrant.

CURLEW SANDPIPER, *Breeding*

Stilt Sandpiper

(Calidris himantopus)
Length: 8 in.

Identification: Summer adults have a
chestnut cheek patch and heavily barred
underparts; winter birds are streaked gray
above and mostly white below, rather like a
winter-plumaged Dunlin but with much
longer legs. In flight the wings lack stripes,
and tail and rump are white, as in yellowlegs
and Wilson's Phalarope. Bill is slightly
drooped like that of Dunlin. Call is a short,
single note, rarely heard.

Status & Distribution	Spring	Summer	Fall	Winter	Breeder	Key
Southeastern	A	–	R	–		C Common
Southcoastal	A	–	R	–		U Uncommon
Southwestern	A	–	–	–		R Rare
Central	R	–	A	–		A Casual/Accidental
Western	A	–	–	–		– No Records
Northern	R	R	R	–	•	

Habitat: Breeding — relatively open, dry
tundra, north of the tree line. Nests have
been found in the Arctic National Wildlife
Refuge. In migration — tidal flats, lake
shores, ponds and sloughs.

STILT SANDPIPER, Breeding

Spoonbill Sandpiper

(Eurynorhynchus pygmeus)
Length: 6¹/₂ in.

Identification: Broad spoon-shaped bill tip
is diagnostic but may be difficult to see in
side view. In summer and winter much like
Rufous-necked Sandpiper, with which it
occurs in Siberia, but in winter may be
recognized by more white on the forehead
and a more prominent white wing bar.

Status & Distribution	Spring	Summer	Fall	Winter	Breeder	Key
Southeastern	–	–	–	–		C Common
Southcoastal	–	–	–	–		U Uncommon
Southwestern	A	–	–	–		R Rare
Central	–	–	–	–		A Casual/Accidental
Western	–	–	–	–		– No Records
Northern	–	–	A	–		

Habitat: Asiatic sandpiper found in
northern Alaska at Wainwright and in the
western Aleutian Islands on Buldir Island
and on Attu Island. Not known to breed in
Alaska.

SPOONBILL SANDPIPER, *Breeding*

Broad-billed Sandpiper

(Limicola falcinellus)
Length: 6³/₄ in.

Identification: The thick, longish black bill that is slightly decurved, two white lines over the eye and conspicuous white "V" on the back help separate the Broad-billed from other sandpipers in any plumage.

Status & Distribution	Spring	Summer	Fall	Winter	Breeder	Key
Southeastern	–	–	–	–		C Common
Southcoastal	–	–	–	–		U Uncommon
Southwestern	–	–	A	–		R Rare
Central	–	–	–	–		A Casual/Accidental
Western	–	–	–	–		– No Records
Northern	–	–	–	–		

Habitat: Has been found on Adak and Shemya islands in the western Aleutians. Breeds in northern Europe and Asia.

BROAD-BILLED SANDPIPER, *Juvenile*

Buff-breasted Sandpiper

(Tryngites subruficollis)
Length: 8¹/₂ in.

Identification: Slender and small-headed, similar to but much smaller than an Upland Sandpiper, with a brown back and warm buffy underparts. No other shorebird is unmarked buff from throat to undertail. Legs are bright yellow, wing linings are white, contrasting strongly with the belly. Usually silent.

Habitat: Breeding — dry tundra ridges. Nests on the ground in dry areas. In migration — drier areas of tidal flats, sandy beaches, grassy fields and meadows.

Notes: Impressive display on the breeding grounds, with 1 or both wings raised to show the white linings.

Status & Distribution	Spring	Summer	Fall	Winter	Breeder	Key
Southeastern	A	–	A	–		C Common
Southcoastal	–	–	A	–		U Uncommon
Southwestern	–	–	A	–		R Rare
Central	R	–	A	–		A Casual/Accidental
Western	R	–	A	–		– No Records
Northern	R	R	R	–	•	

BUFF-BREASTED SANDPIPER

Ruff

(Philomachus pugnax)
Length: 11¹/₂ in.

Identification: Male is considerably larger
than female. In spring, breeding-plumaged
male has huge erectile ruffs of white, brown
or black. Fall male and female are warm
brown, similar to Pectoral or Sharp-tailed
sandpipers but with the back scaled, not
striped, the breast buffy and the belly white.
Legs are yellowish and the bill short and
straight with a pale base. In flight resembles
a large Pectoral Sandpiper with conspicuous
white patches at the base of the tail. Feet
project beyond tail in flight.

Status & Distribution	Spring	Summer	Fall	Winter	Breeder	Key
Southeastern	A	–	A	–		C Common
Southcoastal	–	–	A	–		U Uncommon
Southwestern	R	–	R	–		R Rare
Central	–	–	–	–		A Casual/Accidental
Western	R	A	R	–		– No Records
Northern	–	A	A	–	•	

Habitat: Asiatic shorebird that has been
found mostly in western and central
Aleutian Islands, on the Bering Sea islands
and on the Chukchi Sea coast. Only 1 nest
has been found, in northern Alaska.

RUFF, *Male, Breeding*

Short-billed Dowitcher

(Limnodromus griseus)
Length: 11¹/₂ in.

Identification: Medium-sized with a long
straight bill. White on the lower back and
rump, conspicuous in flight, penetrates
forward in a point, unlike white rumps of
many other shorebirds, which are cut
straight across. Field identification of the 2
species of dowitchers is difficult. They are
best distinguished by voice. Common call of
the Short-billed Dowitcher is a low, mellow
tu-tu-tu much like that of Lesser Yellowlegs;
call of the Long-billed Dowitcher is a high,
single or sometimes repeated *peep*.

Status & Distribution	Spring	Summer	Fall	Winter	Breeder	Key
Southeastern	C	R	C	–	•	C Common
Southcoastal	C	C	C	–	•	U Uncommon
Southwestern	C	C	C	–	•	R Rare
Central	–	A	–	–		A Casual/Accidental
Western	–	–	–	–		– No Records
Northern	–	–	–	–		

Habitat: Breeding — muskegs. Nesting
locations are not well known. One nest was
found in a muskeg and consisted of a small
hollow in the moss. In migration — tidal
flats and ponds, especially the muddy
portions.

SHORT-BILLED DOWITCHER, *Breeding*

Long-billed Dowitcher
(Limnodromus scolopaceus)
Length: 11¹/₂ in.

Identification: In the breeding Long-billed, the sides of breast are barred rather than spotted as in the Short-billed Dowitcher.

LONG-BILLED DOWITCHER, *Breeding*

Status & Distribution	Spring	Summer	Fall	Winter	Breeder	Key
Southeastern	U	–	U	A		C Common
Southcoastal	C	–	C	–		U Uncommon
Southwestern	U	–	U	–		R Rare
Central	C	U	U	–	•	A Casual/Accidental
Western	C	C	C	–	•	– No Records
Northern	C	C	C	–	•	

Habitat: Breeding — wet tundra. Nests on the ground in wet marshy areas. In migration — tidal flats and ponds, especially muddy areas.

LONG-BILLED DOWITCHER, *Juvenile*

Common Snipe

(Gallinago gallinago)
Length: 11 in.

Identification: Extremely long, slender bill distinguishes Common Snipe from almost all other Alaskan birds. Only dowitchers have comparable bills, and in any plumage they lack the stripes on the crown and back of Common Snipe. In flight the short, dark tail (orange at close range) and lack of white on wings and lower back separate Common Snipe from the dowitchers.

Habitat: Breeding — muskegs, freshwater marshes. Nests on the ground usually in grass. In migration and winter — sedge-grass meadows at the head of tidal flats and freshwater marshes.

Status & Distribution	Spring	Summer	Fall	Winter	Breeder	Key
Southeastern	C	C	C	U	•	C Common
Southcoastal	C	C	C	R	•	U Uncommon
Southwestern	C	C	C	A	•	R Rare
Central	C	C	C	–	•	A Casual/Accidental
Western	C	C	C	–	•	– No Records
Northern	C	C	C	–	•	

Notes: High, circling courtship flight is unusual. During this flight the bird makes a loud winnowing sound like *who who who who who who who*, increasing and then decreasing in intensity. The sound is made by stiffened tail feathers held at right angles to the body as the bird dives downward after each ascent. The wings are reported to produce the pulsations of sound.

COMMON SNIPE

Wilson's Phalarope

(Phalaropus tricolor)
Length: 9 in.

Identification: Larger and more slender than Red-necked and Red phalaropes, with a long, slender bill. In summer, females are gray above, with a black and rusty neck stripe and rusty back stripes, appearing considerably paler overall than Red-necked Phalaropes. Male is duller version of the same pattern. In these and in the plain winter-plumaged bird, breast and belly are immaculate white. In flight the impression is of a yellowlegs, with dark wings and white rump and tail, but with a whiter breast and much shorter, greenish legs.

Habitat: Freshwater marshes and ponds, usually those with open water surrounded by shallow vegetated areas. Nests near ponds or sloughs in grass-lined hollows in vegetation. Feeds on land much more readily than other phalaropes, and is not likely to be seen on the ocean.

WILSON'S PHALAROPE, *Male*

Status & Distribution	Spring	Summer	Fall	Winter	Breeder	Key
Southeastern	A	A	A	–		C Common
Southcoastal	A	A	–	–	•	U Uncommon
Southwestern	–	–	–	–		R Rare
Central	A	A	–	–	•	A Casual/Accidental
Western	A	–	–	–		– No Records
Northern	A	A	–	–		

WILSON'S PHALAROPE, *Female*

Red-necked Phalarope
(Phalaropus lobatus)
Length: 7 in.

Identification: Breeding female is gray above, with a patch of rufous on the neck and a white throat. Male is browner and more variable but similar in pattern, always with a white eye-line. In winter all are dark gray above and white below, the back heavily marked with pale lines. Call is a *tic, tic.*

Status & Distribution	Spring	Summer	Fall	Winter	Breeder	Key
Southeastern	C	U	C	A		C Common
Southcoastal	C	C	C	A	•	U Uncommon
Southwestern	C	C	C	–	•	R Rare
Central	C	C	C	–	•	A Casual/Accidental
Western	C	C	C	–	•	– No Records
Northern	C	C	C	–	•	

Habitat: Breeding — wet tundra, freshwater marshes, ponds and lakes. Nests on the ground in wet grassy areas near water. In migration — inshore and offshore marine waters, tidal ponds and sloughs, lakes and ponds.

Notes: Phalaropes differ from other shorebirds by having lobes or scalloped margins on their toes which enable them to swim with ease. Females are more brilliantly colored than the males and do all the courting. Males incubate and take care of the young.

RED-NECKED PHALAROPE, *Male, Breeding*

RED-NECKED PHALAROPE, *Female, Breeding*

RED-NECKED PHALAROPE, *Juvenile*

Red Phalarope

(Phalaropus fulicaria)
Length: 8 in.

Identification: Breeding female is brown
above and rich reddish below, with a black
crown, white face and yellow bill. Male is
very variable, from just duller than the
female but with a brownish, streaked crown
to virtually white beneath. In winter both
sexes are pale gray above and white below.
Young are darker backed, looking more like
Red-necked Phalaropes, but are larger, with
a thicker bill. In fall, Red Phalarope looks
paler than Red-necked Phalarope, without
the conspicuous back stripes. Both have
vivid white wing stripes and a dark mark
through the eye. Call note resembles *tic tic.*

Habitat: Breeding — wet tundra near ponds
and lakes. Nests on the ground in tundra. In
migration — inshore and offshore marine
waters, preferably offshore.

Status & Distribution	Spring	Summer	Fall	Winter	Breeder	Key
Southeastern	R	–	R	–		C Common
Southcoastal	C	R	C	–		U Uncommon
Southwestern	C	U	C	–		R Rare
Central	A	A	–	–		A Casual/Accidental
Western	C	C	C	–	•	– No Records
Northern	C	C	C	–	•	

RED PHALAROPE, *Female, Breeding*

RED PHALAROPE, *First Winter*

RED PHALAROPE, *Male, Breeding*

Family *Laridae*
JAEGERS, GULLS, TERNS
(25 + 4)

Jaegers are gull-like predatory seabirds with strongly hooked bills and sharp claws. Their wings are narrow, pointed and dark with white patches near the tip. They fly in a fast, falconlike manner, forcing gulls and terns to drop or disgorge just-caught fish. The agility of the jaegers during these maneuvers is breathtaking. Adults of the 3 jaegers have characteristic projecting central tail feathers.

Gulls and terns are long-winged birds that inhabit oceans, lakes and rivers. Plumages are mostly white below and gray above, often with black on the wing tips or head. The back and wings together are called the mantle. Most are colonial nesters and usually lay 2 to 3 eggs. Gulls are excellent scavengers and feed on almost anything edible by picking their food up from the water surface or ground. The bill is slightly hooked and the tail is usually square or rounded (except Sabine's Gull, which is shallowly forked). Terns dive into the water to pursue food. They have sharp-pointed bills and deeply forked tails.

Pomarine Jaeger
(Stercorarius pomarinus)
Length: 22 in.

Identification: At a distance recognized by purposeful flight and black wing linings, with a flash of white visible near the wing tip at closer range. Central tail feathers project from 1 to 4 inches and are blunt and usually twisted. Most adults are light beneath, with variable amounts of barring, but some are virtually all black. Immature jaegers can be very difficult to identify. Immature Pomarine is barred all over and lacks the longer tail feathers.

POMARINE JAEGER, *Adult*

Status & Distribution	Spring	Summer	Fall	Winter	Breeder	Key
Southeastern	R	R	U	–		C Common
Southcoastal	C	R	C	–		U Uncommon
Southwestern	C	U	C	–		R Rare
Central	–	A	–	–		A Casual/Accidental
Western	C	R	C	–	•	– No Records
Northern	U	U	U	–	•	

Habitat: Breeding — low wet tundra in areas interspersed with lakes and ponds. Nests on the ground in slight depressions. In migration — inshore and offshore marine waters.

Notes: Largest of the jaegers; usually chases large or medium-sized gulls.

Parasitic Jaeger

(Stercorarius parasiticus)
Length: 17 in.

Identification: Distinguished from the
Pomarine Jaeger by pointed central tail
feathers, shorter than those of adult Long-
tailed Jaeger. Adult is dark brown above and
often has a breast band, as in the Pomarine,
but lacks bars of that species. Some birds
are all dark, as in the Pomarine. First-year
birds of the 3 jaeger species are very difficult
to separate in the field.

Status & Distribution	Spring	Summer	Fall	Winter	Breeder	Key
Southeastern	U	U	U	–	•	C Common
Southcoastal	U	C	C	–	•	U Uncommon
Southwestern	C	C	C	–	•	R Rare
Central	–	R	–	–	•	A Casual/Accidental
Western	C	C	C	–	•	– No Records
Northern	C	C	C	–	•	

PARASITIC JAEGER, Adult, Light Phase

Habitat: Breeding — wet tundra, tidal flats
and beaches, coastal marshes. Nests on the
ground in depressions. In migration —
tundra, tidal flats, beaches, coastal marshes,
inshore and offshore marine waters.

PARASITIC JAEGER, Adult, Dark Phase

Long-tailed Jaeger

(Stercorarius longicaudus)
Length: 21 in.

Identification: Adult has long, streaming
central tail feathers. In molt, adult with only
partly developed tail feathers resembles
Parasitic Jaeger but has a gray-brown rather
than brown back, no breast band, and
bluish-gray instead of black legs. Dark-
phase birds are extremely rare. First-year
immature is difficult to separate from other
jaegers, but shows less white in the spread
wing and is slightly smaller and paler
than Parasitic Jaeger in similar plumage.
Long-tailed Jaeger has light, airy flight.

Habitat: Breeding — wet coastal tundra and
drier upland tundra of the Interior. Nests on
the ground. In migration — inshore and
offshore marine waters.

Status & Distribution	Spring	Summer	Fall	Winter	Breeder	Key
Southeastern	R	R	R	–		C Common
Southcoastal	R	R	R	A	•	U Uncommon
Southwestern	U	U	U	–	•	R Rare
Central	C	C	C	–	•	A Casual/Accidental
Western	C	C	C	–	•	– No Records
Northern	C	C	C	–	•	

LONG-TAILED JAEGER, *Adult*

South Polar Skua

(Catharacta maccormicki)
Length: 21 in.

Identification: All dark at a distance, with very broad, black wings that show a conspicuous white patch near the tip. At close range some show a golden nape. Heavier bodied and stockier than Pomarine Jaeger.

Habitat: Inshore and offshore marine waters; prefers offshore waters. Breeds in southern hemisphere.

Status & Distribution	Spring	Summer	Fall	Winter	Breeder	Key
Southeastern	–	–	–	–		C Common
Southcoastal	–	R	R	–		U Uncommon
Southwestern	–	R	A	–		R Rare
Central	–	–	–	–		A Casual/Accidental
Western	–	–	–	–		– No Records
Northern	–	–	A	–		

Franklin's Gull
(Larus pipixcan)
Length: 14¹/₂ in.

Identification: Summer adult has black head, reddish bill and dark gray wings with a white band across the tips. Larger than Bonaparte's Gull and much darker-looking above. Winter bird loses black on the head except for a dark patch on the hind neck. Immature is brownish-gray above, with dark nape patch and narrow black band at tail tip. Alaskan records are of breeding-plumaged adults.

Habitat: Inshore marine waters, offshore islands. Not known to breed in Alaska.

FRANKLIN'S GULL, *Breeding*

Status & Distribution	Spring	Summer	Fall	Winter	Breeder	Key
Southeastern	–	–	A	–		C Common
Southcoastal	A	A	–	–		U Uncommon
Southwestern	–	A	–	–		R Rare
Central	–	–	–	–		A Casual/Accidental
Western	–	–	–	–		– No Records
Northern	–	–	–	–		

Common Black-headed Gull
(Larus ridibundus)
Length: 14¹/₂ in.

Identification: Adults similar to Bonaparte's Gull, but larger with a longer, dark red bill. Has dark red, not pink, feet. Best distant field mark is dark gray lower surface of wing tips (white in Bonaparte's Gull). Immature is like immature Bonaparte's Gull, but bill is yellow with a black tip rather than black.

Habitat: Asiatic gull found in all coastal regions of Alaska except southeastern. Most often seen in western and central Aleutian Islands and Pribilof Islands. Not known to breed in Alaska.

COMMON BLACK-HEADED GULL, *Breeding*

Status & Distribution	Spring	Summer	Fall	Winter	Breeder	Key
Southeastern	–	–	–	–		C Common
Southcoastal	–	A	A	–		U Uncommon
Southwestern	R	R	A	–		R Rare
Central	A	–	–	–		A Casual/Accidental
Western	R	A	–	–		– No Records
Northern	–	A	–	–		

Bonaparte's Gull

(Larus philadelphia)
Length: 13 in.

Identification: Ternlike flight and largely white wing tips that flash conspicuously in flight at considerable distances are diagnostic. Summer adult has black head which turns mostly white in autumn and winter except for a conspicuous black ear spot. First-year bird is similar to winter adult but has a dark band at end of tail and brown markings on wings.

BONAPARTE'S GULL, *Breeding*

Status & Distribution	Spring	Summer	Fall	Winter	Breeder	Key
Southeastern	C	U	C	A	•	C Common
Southcoastal	C	C	C	A	•	U Uncommon
Southwestern	U	U	U	–	•	R Rare
Central	U	U	U	–	•	A Casual/Accidental
Western	U	U	U	–	•	– No Records
Northern	–	A	–	–		

Habitat: Breeding — coniferous woods near lakes and ponds. Nests in low conifers. In migration and winter — tidal flats, beaches, inshore marine waters, lakes, salmon streams.

Mew Gull

(Larus canus)
Length: 17 in.

Identification: Smallest of commonly seen white-headed gulls, with half the bulk of Glaucous-winged Gull, with which it is often seen. Narrow wings and rapid wingbeat allow distant identification; at closer range, delicate yellowish bill and greenish-yellow legs are diagnostic. Mantle darker than in larger species; underwing often looks dark. Brown eye. White spots in the black wing tips are larger and more prominent than in other gulls of this type, and often appear as a white band across the wing tip. First-year immature is grayish-brown with a dark terminal tail band and a short, ploverlike bill.

Status & Distribution	Spring	Summer	Fall	Winter	Breeder	Key
Southeastern	C	C	C	C	•	C Common
Southcoastal	C	C	C	C	•	U Uncommon
Southwestern	C	C	C	C	•	R Rare
Central	C	C	C	–	•	A Casual/Accidental
Western	C	C	C	–	•	– No Records
Northern	R	R	R	–	•	

Habitat: Breeding — tundra, lakes, rivers, streams, islands. Nests on tundra, in trees, on stumps, cavities in sand by water. In migration and winter — inshore and offshore marine waters, tidal flats and beaches, lakes, rivers, rocky shores and reefs.

MEW GULL, *Breeding*

Ring-billed Gull
(Larus delawarensis)
Length: 19¹/₂ in.

Identification: Very pale gray mantle and strongly contrasting black wing tips. Mantle is distinctly paler than in either California or Mew gulls, and wings are snowy white beneath. Bill is yellow, with a black ring near the tip, and legs are yellow. Immature is paler than young California or Mew gulls, with a narrow black band near the tail tip. In Mew and California gulls and still larger species, the tail band is broader.

Habitat: Inshore marine waters, tidal flats and beaches. Not known to breed in Alaska.

RING-BILLED GULL, Winter, Adult

Status & Distribution	Spring	Summer	Fall	Winter	Breeder	Key
Southeastern	R	R	R	R		C Common
Southcoastal	R	R	R	R		U Uncommon
Southwestern	–	A	A	–		R Rare
Central	A	–	–	–		A Casual/Accidental
Western	–	–	–	–		– No Records
Northern	–	–	–	–		

California Gull
(Larus californicus)
Length: 21¹/₂ in.

Identification: Medium-gray mantle (darker than Herring, Glaucous-winged or Ring-billed gulls) and black wing tips, more extensive than those of Herring Gull. Greenish legs. Yellow bill marked with both a red spot and a black spot near the tip. Eyes are dark. Immature is much like young Herring Gull but smaller, with a more slender bill that is flesh-colored for the basal two-thirds.

Habitat: Found mostly in southern part of southeastern Alaska along inshore marine waters and coastal beaches. Not known to breed in Alaska.

CALIFORNIA GULL, Breeding

Status & Distribution	Spring	Summer	Fall	Winter	Breeder	Key
Southeastern	R	R	R	A		C Common
Southcoastal	A	–	A	–		U Uncommon
Southwestern	–	–	–	–		R Rare
Central	–	–	–	–		A Casual/Accidental
Western	–	–	–	–		– No Records
Northern	–	–	–	–		

Herring Gull

(Larus argentatus)
Length: 24 in.

Identification: Adult Herring Gull much like Glaucous Gull, with red-spotted yellow bill and flesh-colored legs, but wing tips are jet black from above and below, with a few white spots at tips of the feathers. Eye is pale, cold yellow, giving bird a reptilian look. First-year bird is dusky gray-brown with a dark bill and eye. Head is pale but wings are much darker than in Glaucous and Glaucous-winged gulls. Second- and third-year birds are gray on the back, with dark wing tips, dark tail and light rump.

Status & Distribution	Spring	Summer	Fall	Winter	Breeder	Key
Southeastern	C	C	C	C	•	C Common
Southcoastal	C	U	C	U	•	U Uncommon
Southwestern	R	R	R	R		R Rare
Central	U	U	U	–	•	A Casual/Accidental
Western	U	U	U	–	•	– No Records
Northern	–	A	A	–	•	

Habitat: Breeding — lakes, rivers, islands, tidal flats and beaches. Nests on the ground in hollows, on sand, gravel, rocks and grassy fields, cliff ledges and trees. In migration and winter — lakes, rivers, tidal flats and beaches, garbage dumps, inshore marine waters.

Notes: Tend to occur more inland than other gulls. Scavengers. Like crows, will break open clam shells by dropping them on rocks from the air.

HERRING GULL, *Breeding*

Thayer's Gull

(Larus thayeri)
Length: 24 in.

Identification: Distinctly smaller bill than the larger gulls. Mantle varies from as light as that of Herring Gull to somewhat darker, eye is usually brown but may be almost as light as that of Herring Gull, and wing tips have more or less black on them. Usually more white in the wing tip than in Herring Gull. Best field mark is nature of the wing tip coloration: black above and gray below. In all plumages wing tips are colored like Herring Gull above and Glaucous-winged Gull below. This feature can be seen in flight or at rest.

Habitat: In migration and winter — similar to Herring Gulls. Not known to breed in Alaska.

Status & Distribution	Spring	Summer	Fall	Winter	Breeder	Key
Southeastern	C	A	C	U		C Common
Southcoastal	R	R	R	R		U Uncommon
Southwestern	A	–	A	A		R Rare
Central	–	–	–	–		A Casual/Accidental
Western	–	–	A	–		– No Records
Northern	–	–	R	–		

Notes: Some authors consider this species conspecific with Iceland Gull *(L. glaucoides)*.

THAYER'S GULL, *Winter, Adult*

Slaty-backed Gull
(Larus schistisagus)
Length: 27 in.

Identification: Large gull of Herring and Glaucous-winged group of gulls. Entirely dark gray mantle in the adult. No other Bering Sea gull has a dark back, although Western Gull that may occur occasionally in southern Alaska looks virtually identical. Immature similar to dark immature Herring Gull.

Habitat: Asiatic gull seen mostly along the inshore marine waters of western and northern Alaska and in the Aleutian Islands. Not known to breed in Alaska.

Status & Distribution	Spring	Summer	Fall	Winter	Breeder	Key
Southeastern	–	–	–	–		C Common
Southcoastal	A	A	A	A		U Uncommon
Southwestern	R	R	R	A		R Rare
Central	–	–	–	–		A Casual/Accidental
Western	R	R	R	–		– No Records
Northern	R	R	R	–		

Notes: A dark-backed *(L. a. vegia)* form of the Herring Gull found in the northern Bering Sea may be confused with the Slaty-backed Gull.

SLATY-BACKED GULL, *Breeding*

Glaucous-winged Gull

(Larus glaucescens)
Length: 26 in.

Identification: Much like Glaucous Gull, adult has gray wing tips with white spots, visible from above or below. Eyes are usually brown, but may vary to much paler, although never clear pale yellow. First-year immature is buffy, somewhat darker than young Glaucous Gull, and with all-black bill. Second- and third-year immatures become increasingly like adults, which mature in the fourth or fifth year. Intermediate-plumaged birds vary widely and can be difficult to identify. In addition, species of larger gulls hybridize, which also makes identification difficult.

Status & Distribution	Spring	Summer	Fall	Winter	Breeder	Key
Southeastern	C	C	C	C	•	C Common
Southcoastal	C	C	C	C	•	U Uncommon
Southwestern	C	C	C	C	•	R Rare
Central	–	R	R	–		A Casual/Accidental
Western	C	C	C	–	•	– No Records
Northern	–	–	–	–		

Habitat: Breeding — tidal flats and beaches, inshore marine waters, islands and cliffs. Nests in colonies on flat, low islands, cliff ledges and rocky beaches. In migration and winter — various habitats, including coastal communities, garbage dumps, around canneries, salmon streams, inshore and offshore marine waters, tidal flats and beaches.

GLAUCOUS-WINGED GULL, *Breeding*

Glaucous Gull

(Larus hyperboreus)
Length: 27 in.

Identification: Very large, with pure white primaries and no dark color on the wing tips. Eye is yellow. As in other large gulls, bill is yellow with a red spot, feet pink. Immature at a distance looks uniform pale buff (first year) or white (second year) with flesh color on the basal two-thirds of the bill. At close range immature appears finely barred and spotted with pale markings.

Habitat: Breeding — cliffs near the coast, islands, tundra. Nests in colonies on cliff ledges and on the ground in slightly elevated portions of the tundra, or on islands in tundra lakes. In migration and winter — tidal flats and beaches, inshore marine waters.

Status & Distribution	Spring	Summer	Fall	Winter	Breeder	Key
Southeastern	R	R	R	R		C Common
Southcoastal	R	R	R	R		U Uncommon
Southwestern	U	U	U	U	•	R Rare
Central	R	R	R	–		A Casual/Accidental
Western	C	C	C	A	•	– No Records
Northern	C	C	C	–	•	

Notes: Often preys on eggs and young of other birds. Will mob other birds, forcing them to disgorge food.

GLAUCOUS GULL, *Breeding*

Black-legged Kittiwake

(Rissa tridactyla)
Length: 17 in.

Identification: Adult has black wing tips that look as if they had been dipped in ink, a yellow bill and black legs. First-year bird is white below, with a dark band across the back of the neck (shared by winter adults), a dark ear spot, dark tail tip, black bill and legs, and an M-shaped mark across the mantle. Wingbeats are short and choppy.

Habitat: Breeding — sea cliffs, inshore marine waters. Nests on cliff ledges. In migration and winter — inshore and offshore marine waters, tidal flats, beaches, rocky shores, reefs.

Status & Distribution	Spring	Summer	Fall	Winter	Breeder	Key
Southeastern	U	U	U	U	•	C Common
Southcoastal	C	C	C	U	•	U Uncommon
Southwestern	C	C	C	U	•	R Rare
Central	–	–	A	–		A Casual/Accidental
Western	C	C	C	–	•	– No Records
Northern	–	C	C	–		

Notes: Mostly a bird of the ocean, often far offshore. Rarely ventures inland. Feeds mostly on small fish captured in a ternlike manner by diving while on the wing.

BLACK-LEGGED KITTIWAKE, *Breeding*

Red-legged Kittiwake

(Rissa brevirostris)
Length: 15 in.

Identification: Red legs and feet. Shorter and heavier bill than Black-legged Kittiwake. Mantle is darker above than in Black-legged Kittiwake. Wing linings are conspicuously dark — a good distant field mark. First-year bird lacks dark diagonal bar across the wing coverts and black tip on the tail of immature Black-legged Kittiwake.

Habitat: Breeding — Pribilof Islands, Buldir and Bogoslof islands in the Aleutian Islands. Nests on cliff ledges and cliff points. In migration and winter — inshore and offshore marine waters.

Status & Distribution	Spring	Summer	Fall	Winter	Breeder	Key
Southeastern	–	–	–	–		C Common
Southcoastal	–	A	A	R		U Uncommon
Southwestern	U	C	U	U	•	R Rare
Central	–	A	–	–		A Casual/Accidental
Western	–	R	–	–		– No Records
Northern	–	–	–	–		

Notes: Tends to feed even more offshore than Black-legged Kittiwake.

RED-LEGGED KITTIWAKE, *Breeding*

Ross' Gull

(Rhodostethia rosea)
Length: 13¹/₂ in.

Identification: Small, with a wedge-shaped tail, an entirely gray mantle and darker gray wing linings. Breeding adult has a rosy tinge to the body and a dark neck-ring. Immature has a mantle pattern similar to a young kittiwake.

Status & Distribution	Spring	Summer	Fall	Winter	Breeder	Key
Southeastern	–	–	–	–		C Common
Southcoastal	A	–	–	–		U Uncommon
Southwestern	A	–	A	A		R Rare
Central	–	–	A	–		A Casual/Accidental
Western	R	A	R	–		– No Records
Northern	A	A	C	–		

Habitat: Inshore and offshore marine waters. Best place to see this bird is Point Barrow vicinity in fall. Not known to breed in Alaska.

ROSS' GULL, *Breeding*

Sabine's Gull

(Xema sabini)
Length: 13½ in.

Identification: Only gull with forked tail. Black bill has yellow tip. Adult has dark gray hood and bold black-and-white pattern on spread wings. Black primaries and white wedge on midwing are unique. Immature is brown on back, with the adult's wing pattern.

Habitat: Breeding — wet tundra, lakes, ponds, tidal flats. Nests on the tundra near lakes and ponds. In migration — inshore and offshore marine waters, tidal flats and beaches.

SABINE'S GULL, Breeding

Status & Distribution	Spring	Summer	Fall	Winter	Breeder	Key
Southeastern	R	A	R	–		C Common
Southcoastal	U	R	U	–		U Uncommon
Southwestern	U	U	U	–	•	R Rare
Central	–	A	–	–		A Casual/Accidental
Western	C	C	C	–	•	– No Records
Northern	C	C	C	–	•	

Ivory Gull

(Pagophila eburnea)
Length: 16 in.

Identification: Snowy white, with black legs and dark, yellow-tipped bill. Immature is heavily marked on the wings and tail tip with small black spots and has a dark smudge on the face.

Habitat: Inshore and offshore marine waters, pack and drift ice of Chukchi, Bering and Beaufort seas, coastal areas. Not known to breed in Alaska.

Notes: With the long wings, flight is similar to a tern. Less inclined to land on water than other gulls, although does rest on the ice. Feeds on carrion and offal as much as live food.

IVORY GULL, Adult

Status & Distribution	Spring	Summer	Fall	Winter	Breeder	Key
Southeastern	–	A	A	–		C Common
Southcoastal	A	–	A	–		U Uncommon
Southwestern	R	–	R	U		R Rare
Central	–	–	–	–		A Casual/Accidental
Western	U	–	U	U		– No Records
Northern	U	R	U	–		

Caspian Tern

(Sterna caspia)
Length: 19–23 in.

Identification: Large tern, larger than a Mew Gull, with large red bill, short-crested black cap, slightly forked tail, and black on the undersides of the wing tips. Immatures have white streaking on the cap.

Habitat: Ocean coasts, tidal estuaries, rivers and lakes. Since the early 1980s, has been annual in southeastern and southcoastal Alaska west to Cook Inlet. Probably breeds on the western Copper River delta and Alsek River delta.

Status & Distribution	Spring	Summer	Fall	Winter	Breeder	Key
Southeastern	A	A	–	–		C Common
Southcoastal	R	R	R	–	•	U Uncommon
Southwestern	–	–	–	–		R Rare
Central	–	A	–	–		A Casual/Accidental
Western	–	–	–	–		– No Records
Northern	–	–	–	–		

CASPIAN TERN, *Breeding*

Common Tern

(Sterna hirundo)
Length: 14¹/₂ in.

Identification: The Common Tern
seen in Alaska is a Siberian subspecies
(S. h. longipennis) that has an entirely black
bill and brown or black legs and feet in
breeding plumage. Immature and nonbreeding birds are more difficult to distinguish
from Arctic Tern, but the neck and bill are
longer, giving them a more pointed look in
front, with more of the bird projecting in
front of the wings. Common Tern has more
obvious black posterior borders on each
wing than does Arctic Tern.

Status & Distribution	Spring	Summer	Fall	Winter	Breeder	Key
Southeastern	–	–	–	–		C Common
Southcoastal	–	–	–	–		U Uncommon
Southwestern	R	R	A	–		R Rare
Central	–	–	–	–		A Casual/Accidental
Western	A	A	–	–		– No Records
Northern	–	–	–	–		

Habitat: Seen most frequently in western
and central Aleutian Islands and in Pribilof
Islands during spring and summer. Not
known to breed in Alaska.

COMMON TERN, Breeding

Arctic Tern

(Sterna paradisaea)
Length: 15 in.

(Pictured on right)
Identification: Long, pointed wings, forked
tail, black cap, bright red bill and feet allow
easy identification.

Habitat: Breeding — tidal flats, beaches,
glacial moraines, rivers, lakes, marshes.
Nests in colonies or scattered pairs on sand,
gravel, moss or in rocks. In migration —
inshore and offshore marine waters, tidal
flats, beaches, rivers, lakes.

Status & Distribution	Spring	Summer	Fall	Winter	Breeder	Key
Southeastern	C	C	C	–	•	C Common
Southcoastal	C	C	C	–	•	U Uncommon
Southwestern	C	U	C	–	•	R Rare
Central	U	U	U	–	•	A Casual/Accidental
Western	C	C	C	–	•	– No Records
Northern	U	U	U	–	•	

Notes: May be observed hovering over
water in search of small fish, which probably
make up most of its diet. Has one of the
longest migrations of any species. Some
individuals that breed in the Arctic have
been found wintering in the Antarctic, a
20,000-mile round trip.

Aleutian Tern

(Sterna aleutica)
Length: 15 in.

Identification: Adult darker above and below than Arctic Tern, with a dark bill and feet and white forehead. Gray back and belly contrast strongly with white tail, unlike Arctic Tern, in which the back and tail look about the same. Unique call notes include a loud, ploverlike whistle and loud chirpings, both totally unlike the nasal, bickering *keearr* of Arctic Tern.

Habitat: Breeding — coastal areas, marshes, islands, rivers, lagoons, inshore marine waters. Nests on ground in matted dry grass. In migration — offshore marine waters.

Status & Distribution	Spring	Summer	Fall	Winter	Breeder	Key
Southeastern	A	A	–	–	•	C Common
Southcoastal	U	U	U	–	•	U Uncommon
Southwestern	U	U	U	–	•	R Rare
Central	–	–	–	–		A Casual/Accidental
Western	U	U	U	–	•	– No Records
Northern	–	A	–	–	•	

Notes: In North America this tern only nests in Alaska.

ALEUTIAN TERN, *Breeding*

ARCTIC TERN, *Breeding*

Black Tern

(Chlidonias niger)
Length: 9$^{1}/_{2}$ in.

Identification: In summer head and underparts black and mantle and tail gray. Immature and winter-plumaged adult are much grayer above than Arctic Tern and smaller and shorter tailed than any of the other Alaskan terns. Gray tail is diagnostic.

Habitat: Primarily freshwater marshes. Not known to breed in Alaska.

Status & Distribution	Spring	Summer	Fall	Winter	Breeder	Key
Southeastern	–	–	A	–		C Common
Southcoastal	–	A	–	–		U Uncommon
Southwestern	–	–	–	–		R Rare
Central	A	A	–	–		A Casual/Accidental
Western	–	–	–	–		– No Records
Northern	–	A	–	–		

BLACK TERN, *Breeding*

Family *Alcidae*
ALCIDS
(16)

Members of the alcid family are seabirds that come to shore only to breed. They nest in colonies and lay only 1 or 2 eggs. They have small, narrow wings that are used for swimming underwater and for flight. When on land, alcids stand almost erect and penguinlike. All are short-necked and heavy-bodied, and have webbed feet placed far back on the body to facilitate diving. Most are black and white; some have a brightly colored bill. Alcids feed mostly on small fish, crustaceans and other marine invertebrates.

Dovekie
(Alle alle)
Length: 8 in.

Identification: Sharply black and white with an entirely black head and breast in summer. In winter, white of the throat extends up in a half-collar almost around the neck. Otherwise looks much like a Least Auklet.

DOVEKIE, *Breeding*

Status & Distribution	Spring	Summer	Fall	Winter	Breeder	Key
Southeastern	–	–	–	–		C Common
Southcoastal	–	–	–	–		U Uncommon
Southwestern	A	A	A	A		R Rare
Central	–	–	–	–		A Casual/Accidental
Western	R	R	R	–	•	– No Records
Northern	–	A	–	–		

Habitat: Considered a rare probable breeder on the islands in Bering Strait.

Common Murre
(Uria aalge)
Length: 16½ in.

Identification: Looks black above and white below on the water or in flight. Actually, Common Murre is very dark brown above but this is only distinguishable in good light at medium or close range. In breeding plumage entire head and upper breast are dark; in winter throat and breast are white. Bill is long, pointed, quite slender and lacks the pale bill mark of Thick-billed Murre. Breast and belly coloration meet at an obtuse angle. In winter has white cheeks and a distinct dark line extending behind the eye.

Status & Distribution	Spring	Summer	Fall	Winter	Breeder	Key
Southeastern	C	C	C	C	•	C Common
Southcoastal	C	C	C	C	•	U Uncommon
Southwestern	C	C	C	C	•	R Rare
Central	–	–	–	A		A Casual/Accidental
Western	C	C	C	C	•	– No Records
Northern	–	A	–	–		

COMMON MURRE, Winter

Habitat: Breeding — coastal sea cliffs and islands, inshore marine waters. Nests in colonies on the ground on cliff ledges and on the flat tops of cliffs. In winter — inshore and offshore marine waters.

COMMON MURRE, Breeding

Thick-billed Murre

(Uria lomvia)
Length: 18 in.

Identification: Black above, white below.
In breeding plumage entire head and upper
breast are black; in winter throat and breast
are white. Bill is shorter and more curved
than in Common Murre and has a pale line
along the upper mandible visible only at
close range. White of the belly in summer
penetrates forward at an acute angle into
the black breast. In winter the dark cap
extends below eye level both before and
behind the eye.

THICK-BILLED MURRE, *Breeding*

Status & Distribution	Spring	Summer	Fall	Winter	Breeder	Key
Southeastern	R	R	R	R	•	C Common
Southcoastal	R	R	R	R	•	U Uncommon
Southwestern	C	C	C	C	•	R Rare
Central	–	–	–	–		A Casual/Accidental
Western	C	C	C	C	•	– No Records
Northern	R	R	R	–		

Habitat: Breeding — coastal sea cliffs and
islands, inshore marine waters. Nests in
colonies on the ground on cliff ledges and
on the flat tops of cliffs. In winter — inshore
and offshore marine waters.

Black Guillemot

(Cepphus grylle)
Length: 13 in.

Identification: Both Black Guillemot and
Pigeon Guillemot are black, plump-bodied
and pigeon-billed. Mouth lining and feet
are bright red, and a conspicuous white
shoulder patch covers much of the wing
base. Much larger White-winged Scoter has
a smaller white patch on the rear edge of
the wing. Black Guillemot has an immaculate shoulder patch; Pigeon Guillemot's has
a black wedge. Black Guillemot has white
wing linings, an excellent field mark in
flight. Winter adult is pale, very whitish
at a distance, with the same distinguishing
marks. Immature of both species, commonly
seen in late summer, has dark bars across
white wing patches and may be much darker
than winter adult.

Status & Distribution	Spring	Summer	Fall	Winter	Breeder	Key
Southeastern	–	–	–	–		C Common
Southcoastal	–	–	–	–		U Uncommon
Southwestern	R	–	–	R		R Rare
Central	–	–	A	A		A Casual/Accidental
Western	U	U	U	U	•	– No Records
Northern	U	U	U	U	•	

Habitat: Breeding — Chukchi and Beaufort
sea coasts. Nests in burrows and beach
flotsam. In winter — inshore and offshore
marine waters, leads and edge of the
ice pack.

Notes: Distribution of the 2 guillemot
species overlaps in the Bering Strait area.

BLACK GUILLEMOT, *Breeding*

Pigeon Guillemot

(Cepphus columba)
Length: 13 in.

Identification: See Black Guillemot.

Status & Distribution	Spring	Summer	Fall	Winter	Breeder	Key
Southeastern	C	C	C	C	•	C Common
Southcoastal	C	C	C	C	•	U Uncommon
Southwestern	C	C	C	C	•	R Rare
Central	–	–	–	–		A Casual/Accidental
Western	C	C	C	–	•	– No Records
Northern	–	–	–	–		

Habitat: Breeding — inshore marine waters, cliffs, islands. Nests in cliff crevices and between boulders above high tide line. In winter — inshore and offshore marine waters.

PIGEON GUILLEMOT, *Winter*

PIGEON GUILLEMOT, *Breeding*

Marbled Murrelet
(Brachyramphus marmoratus)
Length 9¹/₂ in.

Status & Distribution	Spring	Summer	Fall	Winter	Breeder	Key
Southeastern	C	C	C	C	•	C Common
Southcoastal	C	C	C	C	•	U Uncommon
Southwestern	U	U	U	U	•	R Rare
Central	–	–	–	–		A Casual/Accidental
Western	A	A	A	–	•	– No Records
Northern	–	–	–	–		

Identification: Marbled and Kittlitz's
murrelets are smallest of the common alcids
along Alaska's southern coast. In summer
brown mottled with white (Marbled
Murrelet somewhat darker than Kittlitz's
Murrelet) because of the need for camou-
flage at inland nesting sites. In winter both
murrelets black above and white below, like
tiny murres but with a white stripe on either
side of the back. Black cap of Marbled
Murrelet extends below the eyes; entire
face of Kittlitz's Murrelet is white to above
the eyes. Marbled Murrelet has a longer
bill than Kittlitz's Murrelet. Small size,
slender appearance for an alcid, and distinct
rocking from side to side while in buzzy
flight are distinctive of both murrelets.
Flight is very rapid, wings long and pointed.
Almost always seen in pairs and probably
stay mated for life.

Habitat: Breeding — inshore marine
waters. Nests on the ground along the
steep tundra-edged coasts of southwestern
Alaska or in the thick moss on branches of
old-growth coniferous trees in southeastern
and southcoastal Alaska. In winter —
inshore and offshore marine waters.

MARBLED MURRELET, Breeding

MARBLED MURRELET, Winter

Kittlitz's Murrelet

(Brachyramphus brevirostris)
Length: 9 in.

Status & Distribution	Spring	Summer	Fall	Winter	Breeder	Key
Southeastern	U	U	U	U	•	C Common
Southcoastal	C	C	C	U	•	U Uncommon
Southwestern	U	U	U	R	•	R Rare
Central	–	–	–	–		A Casual/Accidental
Western	U	U	U	–	•	– No Records
Northern	R	R	R	–		

Identification: Difficult to distinguish from Marbled Murrelet. Best distinguished when flushed from water; Kittlitz's has a white tail, Marbled has dark tail. Call is deep squawk; Marbled's call is soft whistle. See Marbled Murrelet.

Habitat: Breeding — inshore marine waters and adjacent mountains, sea cliffs. Little is known about the nesting habits, but 1 egg is usually laid on bare rock above timberline and/or on unvegetated glacial moraines and on grassy ledges of island sea cliffs. In winter — inshore and offshore marine waters.

KITTLITZ'S MURRELET, *Breeding*

Ancient Murrelet

(Synthliboramphus antiquus)
Length: 10 in.

Identification: Breeding bird has a white stripe over the eye and a black throat patch. In all plumages black cap contrasts with gray back, and there is no white scapular line as in Marbled and Kittlitz's murrelets. Has broader wings and lacks the very fast, rocking flight of other murrelets.

Habitat: Breeding — inshore marine waters and islands including Aleutian Islands, Shumagin Islands, Semidi Islands and Forrester Island. Nests in colonies and lays eggs in crevices or burrows. In winter — inshore and offshore marine waters.

Notes: In migration often occurs in flocks rather than pairs. Young leave the nest from 1 to 4 nights after hatching. In response to parents' calls, they scramble down to the sea and are led offshore. Prefers the open ocean and is usually not found in sheltered inshore waters inhabited by other murrelets.

Status & Distribution	Spring	Summer	Fall	Winter	Breeder	Key
Southeastern	U	U	U	U	•	C Common
Southcoastal	U	U	U	U	•	U Uncommon
Southwestern	C	C	C	C	•	R Rare
Central	–	–	–	–		A Casual/Accidental
Western	–	R	R	–		– No Records
Northern	–	–	–	–		

ANCIENT MURRELET, Breeding

Cassin's Auklet

(Ptychoramphus aleuticus)
Length: 7¹⁄₂ in.

Identification: Small, stocky, looking entirely gray-brown at a distance but with a white center on the belly. On the water appears all dark. At close range a tiny white spot over the eye and a pale area at base of the lower mandible are visible.

Habitat: Breeding — inshore coastal waters and islands. Breeds in scattered colonies from Buldir Island in the western Aleutian Islands to Forrester Island in southeastern Alaska. Largest colonies are found in the Sandman Reefs and Shumagin Islands, south of the Alaska Peninsula, and at Forrester Island. Nests are similar to Ancient Murrelets' but the burrows tend to be deeper. In winter — inshore and offshore marine waters.

Status & Distribution	Spring	Summer	Fall	Winter	Breeder	Key
Southeastern	U	U	U	U	•	C Common
Southcoastal	R	R	R	–		U Uncommon
Southwestern	C	C	C	C	•	R Rare
Central	–	–	–	–		A Casual/Accidental
Western	–	–	–	–		– No Records
Northern	–	–	–	–		

CASSIN'S AUKLET

Parakeet Auklet

(Cyclorrhynchus psittacula)
Length: 10 in.

Identification: Chunkier than a murrelet; looks black and white at a distance. Head and throat are black in summer; throat is white in winter. At close range the enlarged bright-red bill is obvious.

Status & Distribution	Spring	Summer	Fall	Winter	Breeder	Key
Southeastern	R	A	–	A		C Common
Southcoastal	U	U	U	A	•	U Uncommon
Southwestern	C	C	C	U	•	R Rare
Central	–	–	–	–		A Casual/Accidental
Western	C	C	C	–	•	– No Records
Northern	–	–	A	–		

Habitat: Breeding — inshore marine waters and islands, especially in Aleutian, Shumagin and Pribilof islands. Nests under loose boulders and in crevices in sea cliffs. In winter — inshore and offshore marine waters.

Notes: Less colonial in nesting habits than other auklets. Tends to occur in scattered pairs. On occasion gathers in flocks.

PARAKEET AUKLET, *Breeding*

Least Auklet

(Aethia pusilla)
Length: 6 in.

Identification: Black above and white below, with an extremely stubby bill. In summer has a wide, dusky band across white of the upper breast; in winter has a white stripe above the folded wing.

Habitat: Breeding — inshore marine water, islands. Nests in cliff crevices, among boulders above high tide line and on talus slopes. In winter — inshore and offshore marine waters.

Status & Distribution	Spring	Summer	Fall	Winter	Breeder	Key
Southeastern	–	–	–	–		C Common
Southcoastal	A	A	A	–		U Uncommon
Southwestern	C	C	C	C	•	R Rare
Central	–	–	–	–		A Casual/Accidental
Western	C	C	C	–	•	– No Records
Northern	–	A	–	–		

Notes: Most abundant of the auklets in some breeding colonies. Parents take turns incubating, and the change occurs in the evening.

LEAST AUKLET, *Breeding*

Whiskered Auklet

(Aethia pygmaea)
Length: 7 in.

Identification: Adult has quail-like crest and 3 white plumes on each side of the face. Immature is difficult to distinguish from young Crested Auklets, although traces of 3 white head stripes are sometimes visible.

Status & Distribution	Spring	Summer	Fall	Winter	Breeder	Key
Southeastern	–	–	–	–		C Common
Southcoastal	–	–	–	–		U Uncommon
Southwestern	U	U	U	A	•	R Rare
Central	–	–	–	–		A Casual/Accidental
Western	–	A	–	–		– No Records
Northern	–	–	–	–		

Habitat: Breeding — inshore marine waters, islands. Nests in cliff crevices, on talus slopes, between boulders above high tide. In winter — inshore and offshore marine waters.

WHISKERED AUKLET, *Breeding*

Crested Auklet

(Aethia cristatella)
Length 9¹/₂ in.

(Pictured on right)
Identification: All dark appearance with stubby orange bill and crest that curves forward over it. Immature is difficult to distinguish from Cassin's Auklet.

Habitat: Breeding— inshore marine waters, island cliffs and beaches. Nests in crevices of talus slopes, cliffs and among beach boulders. In winter — inshore and offshore marine waters.

Notes: Spectacular aerial displays occur at colonies, with birds spiraling high above the colony, then swooshing down to the sea where they alight together, dive in unison and take to the air again.

Status & Distribution	Spring	Summer	Fall	Winter	Breeder	Key
Southeastern	–	–	–	–		C Common
Southcoastal	–	–	–	U		U Uncommon
Southwestern	C	C	C	C	•	R Rare
Central	–	–	A	–		A Casual/Accidental
Western	C	C	C	–	•	– No Records
Northern	–	R	–	–		

Rhinoceros Auklet

(Cerorhinca monocerata)
Length: 15 in.

Status & Distribution	Spring	Summer	Fall	Winter	Breeder	Key
Southeastern	U	U	U	A	•	C Common
Southcoastal	R	R	R	–	•	U Uncommon
Southwestern	R	R	R	R	•	R Rare
Central	–	–	–	–		A Casual/Accidental
Western	–	–	–	–		– No Records
Northern	–	–	–	–		

Identification: Appears all dark on the water; white center of the belly is visible in flight. Much larger and longer billed than Cassin's Auklet, with which it occurs. In summer bill becomes brighter, yellowish-orange to pink, and a short upright horn appears at its base. Two white head plumes also appear at this time, and if the upper plume is not clear, this bright-billed bird might be mistaken for a Parakeet or Crested auklet, which have even a brighter, shorter bill.

Habitat: Breeding — inshore marine waters, islands. Nests in deep burrows on sea islands. In migration — inshore and offshore marine waters. Breeds mainly in southeastern Alaska, primarily on Saint Lazaria and Forrester islands. Sizeable colonies also exist in the Barren and Chiswell islands and on Middleton Island in the Gulf of Alaska.

RHINOCEROS AUKLET, *Breeding*

CRESTED AUKLET, *Breeding*

Tufted Puffin

(Fratercula cirrhata)
Length: 15 in.

Identification: Breeding adult has long, curved, yellowish tufts that hang behind the eyes and an entirely dark body. In winter distinguished from Horned Puffin by dusky rather than white sides. Smaller Rhinoceros Auklet has a considerably narrower bill.

Status & Distribution	Spring	Summer	Fall	Winter	Breeder	Key
Southeastern	U	U	U	R	•	C Common
Southcoastal	C	C	C	R	•	U Uncommon
Southwestern	C	C	C	U	•	R Rare
Central	–	–	–	–		A Casual/Accidental
Western	C	C	C	–	•	– No Records
Northern	–	A	–	–		

Habitat: Breeding — inshore marine waters, islands. Nests principally in burrows in the soil, but rock crevices are also used. In winter — inshore and offshore marine waters.

TUFTED PUFFIN, *Breeding*

Horned Puffin

(Fratercula corniculata)
Length: 14¹/₂ in.

Identification: Large, triangular orange-red and yellow bill, clear white underparts and broad black collar are diagnostic. In summer cheeks are white and a small dark fleshy appendage appears above each eye. In winter face and bill are darker. Juvenile has even darker face and narrow darkish bill. In all plumages the contrasting white belly distinguishes it from Tufted Puffin. Horned Puffin is chunkier than a murre, which it often accompanies in flying flocks.

Status & Distribution	Spring	Summer	Fall	Winter	Breeder	Key
Southeastern	R	R	R	R	•	C Common
Southcoastal	U	U	U	R	•	U Uncommon
Southwestern	C	C	C	U	•	R Rare
Central	–	–	–	–		A Casual/Accidental
Western	C	C	C	–	•	– No Records
Northern	–	R	–	–		

Habitat: Breeding — inshore marine waters, islands. Nests on sea islands in rock crevices or in burrows among boulders, on sea cliffs, and on grassy slopes. In winter — inshore and offshore marine waters.

HORNED PUFFIN, *Breeding*

Family *Columbidae*
PIGEONS, DOVES
(3 + 2)

Pigeons and doves are short-legged birds with pointed wings and a small, rounded head that they bob when walking.

Rock Dove

(Columba livia)

Length: 13 in.

Identification: Color of individual birds may vary considerably from mostly white to browns and blacks. Most common color is a blue- or ash-gray with a white rump, dark head and black bars across the wing. Distinguished from less common Band-tailed Pigeon and Mourning Dove by 2 dark wing bars, reddish legs and dark bill. Rock Dove is never plain brown or brownish-gray, as are Band-tailed Pigeon and Mourning Dove. At a distance flocks of pigeons will be Rock Doves if variably colored, pointed-winged and shorter tailed, and especially if they perch on human-made objects or cliffs or glide with the wings up in a "V."

Habitat: Cities, towns. Nests on building ledges.

Notes: Only feral Alaska bird that occurs in human communities, having been introduced locally.

ROCK DOVE

Status & Distribution	Spring	Summer	Fall	Winter	Breeder	Key
Southeastern	C	C	C	C	•	C Common
Southcoastal	C	C	C	C	•	U Uncommon
Southwestern	–	–	–	–		R Rare
Central	C	C	C	C	•	A Casual/Accidental
Western	–	–	–	–		– No Records
Northern	–	–	–	–		

Band-tailed Pigeon

(Columba fasciata)
Length: 14¹/₂ in.

Identification: More rounded wings and longer tail than a Rock Dove. Flocks at a distance appear all gray-brown, lacking color variation of Rock Dove flocks. At close range the yellow, black-tipped bill, yellow feet and white ring on hind neck are visible. In flight the tail shows a wide, pale-gray band at its tip. Call is a deep owl-like hooting.

Habitat: Open woodlands, forest edges. Nests in conifers or deciduous trees.

Status & Distribution	Spring	Summer	Fall	Winter	Breeder	Key
Southeastern	R	R	R	–	•	C Common
Southcoastal	–	–	A	–		U Uncommon
Southwestern	–	–	–	–		R Rare
Central	–	–	–	–		A Casual/Accidental
Western	–	–	A	–		– No Records
Northern	–	A	–	–		

Notes: Always perches in trees, although it will feed on the ground.

BAND-TAILED PIGEON

Mourning Dove
(Zenaida macroura)
Length: 12 in.

Identification: Smaller and slimmer than pigeons. Entirely brown with a pointed tail bordered extensively with white. Call is a mournful *coo-a-coo, coo, coo.*

Status & Distribution	Spring	Summer	Fall	Winter	Breeder	Key
Southeastern	R	R	R	–		C Common
Southcoastal	R	R	R	A		U Uncommon
Southwestern	–	–	A	–		R Rare
Central	R	R	R	–		A Casual/Accidental
Western	–	–	A	–		– No Records
Northern	–	–	–	–		

Habitat: Open woodlands, commonly perches in trees. Not known to breed in Alaska.

MOURNING DOVE

Family *Cuculidae*
CUCKOOS
(2)

Cuckoos are slender, long-tailed birds with 2 toes forward and 2 behind. The 2 species that have occurred in Alaska are casual visitors from Asia.

Common Cuckoo

(Cuculus canorus)
Length: 13 in.

Identification: Long and slender with a long tail and pointed wings, almost falcon-like. In the adult the upperparts, head and breast are gray, the underparts barred gray and white. Tail is spotted rather than barred, as in most hawks. Bill is slender and not hawklike. Young and some females (brown phase) are rufous, extensively barred with brown, including the tail. Thinner, lighter bars on the underparts than in Oriental Cuckoo. The 2 species of cuckoos are very difficult to identify in the field. Brown phase distinguished from similar Oriental Cuckoo by unbarred rump and upper tail coverts.

Status & Distribution	Spring	Summer	Fall	Winter	Breeder	Key
Southeastern	–	–	–	–		C Common
Southcoastal	–	–	–	–		U Uncommon
Southwestern	A	A	–	–		R Rare
Central	–	–	–	–		A Casual/Accidental
Western	–	A	–	–		– No Records
Northern	–	–	–	–		

Habitat: Has occurred in the western and central Aleutian Islands; on Saint Paul Island, Pribilofs; in Nome area; and on the Yukon-Kuskokwim river delta. Not known to breed in Alaska.

COMMON CUCKOO, *Gray and Brown Phases*

Oriental Cuckoo

(Cuculus saturatus)
Length: 13 in.

Identification: See Common Cuckoo. Bars
on the underparts are broader and darker
than in Common Cuckoo. Generally smaller
and more buffy below than Common
Cuckoo. Has immaculate white alula (wrist
at front of wing).

Status & Distribution	Spring	Summer	Fall	Winter	Breeder	Key
Southeastern	–	–	–	–		C Common
Southcoastal	–	–	–	–		U Uncommon
Southwestern	A	A	–	–		R Rare
Central	–	–	–	–		A Casual/Accidental
Western	–	A	–	–		– No Records
Northern	–	–	–	–		

Habitat: Has occurred on Saint Lawrence
Island, Attu and Rat Island in the Aleutians
group; the Pribilof Islands; and near Cape
Prince of Wales on the Seward Peninsula.

ORIENTAL CUCKOO

Family *Strigidae*
TYPICAL OWLS
(11 + 1)

Typical owls are large-headed and short-necked birds of prey. Many are nocturnal and more often heard than seen. Large forward-facing eyes are immovable, so the entire head must move to look in another direction. Owls excel at hunting; they approach prey silently because the modified downy edges of the primaries eliminate sound caused by the straight-edged primaries of other birds.

Western Screech-Owl
(Otus kennicottii)
Length: 8$^{1}/_{2}$ in.

Identification: Smaller than a Boreal Owl, with conspicuous ear tufts. Voice is a series of short notes accelerating toward the end of the series.

Habitat: Coniferous forests. Nests in holes in trees.

Status & Distribution	Spring	Summer	Fall	Winter	Breeder	Key
Southeastern	R	R	R	R	•	C Common
Southcoastal	–	A	A	–		U Uncommon
Southwestern	–	–	–	–		R Rare
Central	–	–	–	–		A Casual/Accidental
Western	–	–	–	–		– No Records
Northern	–	–	–	–		

WESTERN SCREECH-OWL

Great Horned Owl

(Bubo virginianus)
Length: 18–25 in.

Identification: Large, with prominent ear tufts. Voice is a series of deeply resonant *hoo* notes, often 5 in males and 8 in females. Also has a scream.

Habitat: Coniferous and deciduous forests. Nests in abandoned hawk nests or cliff crevices.

Status & Distribution	Spring	Summer	Fall	Winter	Breeder	Key
Southeastern	U	U	U	U	•	C Common
Southcoastal	C	C	C	C	•	U Uncommon
Southwestern	U	U	U	U	•	R Rare
Central	C	C	C	C	•	A Casual/Accidental
Western	U	U	U	U	•	– No Records
Northern	–	–	A	–		

Notes: Primarily night hunters. They prey on living mammals and birds such as rabbits, squirrels, minks, weasels, porcupines, mice, domestic cats, ducks, geese, domestic poultry, shorebirds and songbirds. Very aggressive. Will attack humans in defense of nest.

GREAT HORNED OWL, *Immature*

Snowy Owl

(Nyctea scandiaca)
Length: 22–25 in.

Identification: White, with a round head and no ear tufts. Adult male is almost immaculate white; adult female usually has at least scattered brown spots and bars. Immature may be heavily marked with brown. Face of the brownish birds is usually white. Silent except on breeding grounds, when it utters loud croaking and whistling sounds.

Habitat: Open country. Breeding — tundra. In winter — marshes and beaches. Nests on the ground in dry areas of tundra or on rocky ledges or cliffs.

Status & Distribution	Spring	Summer	Fall	Winter	Breeder	Key
Southeastern	A	–	A	R		C Common
Southcoastal	R	A	R	U		U Uncommon
Southwestern	R	R	R	U	•	R Rare
Central	R	–	A	R		A Casual/Accidental
Western	U	U	U	U	•	– No Records
Northern	U	U	U	A	•	

Notes: Perches on the ground or fence posts, even on buildings, and does most hunting during the day or at dusk. Chief prey is lemmings.

SNOWY OWL

Northern Hawk Owl

(Surnia ulula)
Length: 16 in.

Identification: Slender, long-tailed with barred underparts and without ear tufts. At rest and in flight similar to a hawk because of the long tail. Voice is a hawklike cry sounding like *ki-ki-ki-ki*.

Status & Distribution	Spring	Summer	Fall	Winter	Breeder	Key
Southeastern	R	A	R	R	•	C Common
Southcoastal	U	U	U	C	•	U Uncommon
Southwestern	R	R	R	U	•	R Rare
Central	C	C	C	C	•	A Casual/Accidental
Western	U	U	U	U	•	– No Records
Northern	A	–	–	–		

Habitat: Open coniferous and deciduous forests. Nests in tree cavities, on the tops of tree stubs and occasionally cliffs or among limbs of a conifer.

Notes: When perching, often flicks its tail.

NORTHERN HAWK OWL

Northern Pygmy-Owl

(Glaucidium gnoma)
Length: 7 in.

Identification: Lacks ear tufts. Coloration similar to the Boreal and Northern Saw-whet owls but has a smaller head, obviously longer tail and a pair of black patches on the hind neck that look like eyes at a distance. Call is a single, short whistle repeated at intervals of about 1 second.

Status & Distribution	Spring	Summer	Fall	Winter	Breeder	Key
Southeastern	R	R	R	R	•	C Common
Southcoastal	–	–	A	–		U Uncommon
Southwestern	–	–	–	–		R Rare
Central	–	–	–	–		A Casual/Accidental
Western	–	–	–	–		– No Records
Northern	–	–	–	–		

Habitat: Open coniferous forests and forest edges.

Notes: Daytime activity is a diagnostic feature.

NORTHERN PYGMY-OWL

Barred Owl

(Strix varia)
Length: 17–24 in.

Identification: Large owl. Brown eyes, barring across chest and lengthwise streaks on belly distinguish Barred Owl in Alaska. Call, as recorded in Juneau, had very emphatic hoots that gradually rose in intensity in the pattern *hoo hoo hoo hoo hoo hoo ho hooo.*

Status & Distribution	Spring	Summer	Fall	Winter	Breeder	Key
Southeastern	R	R	R	R	•	C Common
Southcoastal	–	–	–	–		U Uncommon
Southwestern	–	–	–	–		R Rare
Central	–	–	–	–		A Casual/Accidental
Western	–	–	–	–		– No Records
Northern	–	–	–	–		

Habitat: Has been seen or heard several times in coniferous forests around Juneau, Petersburg, Wrangell and Ketchikan. Nesting has been noted near Ketchikan.

Great Gray Owl

(Strix nebulosa)
Length: 24–33 in.

Identification: Appears to be the largest owl in Alaska, although both Great Horned and Snowy owls are heavier and stronger. Lacks ear tufts. Dusky gray with streaked underparts. Has a very large facial disk with concentric gray circles, overall gray appearance and relatively long tail. Voice is a deep *hooo* note at irregular intervals.

Status & Distribution	Spring	Summer	Fall	Winter	Breeder	Key
Southeastern	R	R	R	R	•	C Common
Southcoastal	R	R	R	R	•	U Uncommon
Southwestern	–	–	–	–		R Rare
Central	R	R	R	R	•	A Casual/Accidental
Western	–	–	–	–		– No Records
Northern	–	–	–	–		

Habitat: Coniferous and deciduous forests and forest edges. Nests on tops of broken-off trees and in raven nests.

BARRED OWL, Immature

GREAT GRAY OWL

Long-eared Owl

(Asio otus)

Length: 15 in.

Identification: A slender owl with long, closely set ear tufts. Facial disk is rusty. At rest, wings extend to or beyond tail. Lacks the white throat patch of the much larger Great Horned Owl and has vertical chest markings rather than horizontal. Voice is a hooted *hoooo*, repeated at intervals; also gives catlike calls.

Notes: This owl is nocturnal in its habits and very secretive during the day, hence seldom seen.

LONG-EARED OWL

Status & Distribution	Spring	Summer	Fall	Winter	Breeder	Key
Southeastern	A	–	A	–		C Common
Southcoastal	–	–	–	–		U Uncommon
Southwestern	–	–	–	–		R Rare
Central	–	–	–	–		A Casual/Accidental
Western	–	–	–	–		– No Records
Northern	–	–	–	–		

Habitat: Entering from the woodlands of British Columbia, this owl has been recorded at Skagway, the Taku River and the Stikine River.

Short-eared Owl

(Asio flammeus)

Length: 15 in.

(Pictured on right)

Identification: Buffy-brownish color and mothlike flapping flight, with very deep wing strokes, are diagnostic. Has light facial disks, yellow eyes, buffy patches on the upper side of the wing and black wrist marks on the lower side of the wing. Northern Harrier inhabits similar open areas but has a conspicuous white rump patch and different flight. Voice is a sharp bark *kyow!*

Status & Distribution	Spring	Summer	Fall	Winter	Breeder	Key
Southeastern	C	R	C	R		C Common
Southcoastal	C	C	C	R	•	U Uncommon
Southwestern	C	C	C	R	•	R Rare
Central	C	C	C	–	•	A Casual/Accidental
Western	C	C	C	–	•	– No Records
Northern	C	C	C	–	•	

Habitat: Open country. Lowland tundra, tidal flats, muskegs, freshwater marshes. Nests on ground in grass-lined depressions.

Boreal Owl

(Aegolius funereus)
Length: 10 in.

Identification: Dark brown and white with a short tail, no ear tufts and a striped belly. Black framing of the facial disks, yellow bill and white forehead spotting are diagnostic. Voice sounds like the ringing of a soft bell. Also emits a high-pitched whistle.

Status & Distribution	Spring	Summer	Fall	Winter	Breeder	Key
Southeastern	A	A	–	R		C Common
Southcoastal	U	U	U	U	•	U Uncommon
Southwestern	U	U	U	U	•	R Rare
Central	C	C	C	C	•	A Casual/Accidental
Western	R	R	R	R	•	– No Records
Northern	–	–	–	–		

Habitat: Coniferous and mixed coniferous-deciduous forests. Nests in holes in trees.

Notes: Seems quite tame and is easily approached. Feeds on mice when available and on small birds and insects at other times.

BOREAL OWL

SHORT-EARED OWL

Northern Saw-whet Owl

(Aegolius acadicus)
Length: 7½ in.

Identification: Smaller version of the Boreal Owl with dark bill and streaked forehead. Call is similar in quality to Boreal Owl's, but is of separate notes, not run together in a tremolo.

Habitat: Coniferous and deciduous forests. Nests in holes in trees.

Status & Distribution	Spring	Summer	Fall	Winter	Breeder	Key
Southeastern	R	R	R	R	•	C Common
Southcoastal	R	R	R	R	•	U Uncommon
Southwestern	–	–	A	–		R Rare
Central	A	–	–	–		A Casual/Accidental
Western	–	–	A	–		– No Records
Northern	–	–	–	–		

Notes: Only active at night. May be discovered roosting in a dense thicket during the day.

NORTHERN SAW-WHET OWL

Family *Caprimulgidae*
GOATSUCKERS
(1 + 2)

Members of the goatsucker family are typically nocturnal birds. The Common Nighthawk, however, the 1 species most likely to be seen in Alaska, often feeds on flying insects during the day.

Common Nighthawk

(Chordeiles minor)
Length: 9 in.

Identification: Mottled and barred brown. May be seen perched flat on the ground or lengthwise on a branch where the large head, very tiny bill, long, pointed wings, and manner of resting are distinctive. In flight, at times high in the air, appears very long- and narrow-winged, with a conspicuous white spot halfway between the bend of the wing and the wing tip. Male has conspicuous white throat and a white band across the tail. Call is loud, buzzy *peent*.

Status & Distribution	Spring	Summer	Fall	Winter	Breeder	Key
Southeastern	A	A	R	–		C Common
Southcoastal	–	A	A	–		U Uncommon
Southwestern	–	–	–	–		R Rare
Central	A	A	A	–		A Casual/Accidental
Western	–	–	–	–		– No Records
Northern	–	A	–	–		

Habitat: Open woodlands. Mostly seen near the mouths of mainland rivers in southeastern Alaska from mid-August through mid-September. Not known to breed in Alaska.

COMMON NIGHTHAWK, *Female*

Family *Apodidae*
SWIFTS
(4 + 2)

Swifts resemble swallows, but the wings are narrow, slightly decurved and held very stiffly. They appear to beat the wings alternately but this is an illusion. They feed exclusively on insects while flying.

Black Swift

(Cypseloides niger)
Length: 7 in.

Identification: Appears entirely black. Has a deeply notched tail, and is considerably larger than Vaux's Swift or any swallow in Alaska except casual Purple Martin. In flight has faster wingbeats than swallows, and glides less than they do. See Vaux's Swift.

Habitat: Mountains, open woodlands. Nests on cliffs in niches or cavities.

Status & Distribution	Spring	Summer	Fall	Winter	Breeder	Key
Southeastern	R	R	R	–	•	C Common
Southcoastal	–	A	–	–		U Uncommon
Southwestern	–	–	–	–		R Rare
Central	–	–	–	–		A Casual/Accidental
Western	–	–	–	–		– No Records
Northern	–	–	–	–		

Notes: Usually flies fairly high, but sometimes, especially in rainy weather, will fly low over water or open ground.

BLACK SWIFT

Vaux's Swift
(Chaetura vauxi)
Length: 4 in.

Identification: Smaller than any of Alaska's swallows with no apparent tail and pale brown underparts. See Black Swift.

Status & Distribution	Spring	Summer	Fall	Winter	Breeder	Key
Southeastern	U	U	U	–	•	C Common
Southcoastal	–	–	A	–		U Uncommon
Southwestern	–	–	–	–		R Rare
Central	–	–	–	–		A Casual/Accidental
Western	–	–	–	–		– No Records
Northern	–	–	–	–		

Habitat: Mountains, open woodland. Nests on the inner walls of hollow trees.

Notes: Usually flies fairly high, but sometimes, especially in rainy weather, will fly low over water or open ground.

VAUX'S SWIFT

White-throated Needletail
(Hirundapus caudacutus)
Length: 8¹/₄ in.

Identification: Large swift distinguished from others in Alaska by white throat, pale back, and white "V" on undersides near square-cut tail.

Status & Distribution	Spring	Summer	Fall	Winter	Breeder	Key
Southeastern	–	–	–	–		C Common
Southcoastal	–	–	–	–		U Uncommon
Southwestern	A	–	–	–		R Rare
Central	–	–	–	–		A Casual/Accidental
Western	–	–	–	–		– No Records
Northern	–	–	–	–		

Habitat: Has been seen in western Aleutians on Shemya and Attu islands.

WHITE-THROATED NEEDLETAIL

Fork-tailed Swift

(Apus pacificus)
Length: 7 in.

Identification: Large like a Black Swift, but much longer winged and has a conspicuous white rump and a much more deeply forked tail.

FORK-TAILED SWIFT

Status & Distribution	Spring	Summer	Fall	Winter	Breeder	Key
Southeastern	–	–	–	–		C Common
Southcoastal	–	–	A	–		U Uncommon
Southwestern	A	A	A	–		R Rare
Central	–	–	–	–		A Casual/Accidental
Western	–	–	–	–		– No Records
Northern	–	–	–	–		

Habitat: Mostly found in the Pribilof Islands and western Aleutian Islands. Not known to breed in Alaska.

Family *Trochilidae*
HUMMINGBIRDS
(2 + 2)

Hummingbirds are the smallest birds found in Alaska. They are known for the ability to hover and fly backward while rapidly beating their wings. The long slender bill and extensile tongue are especially adapted for sipping nectar from flowers.

Anna's Hummingbird

(Calypte anna)
Length: 4 in.

Identification: Male has green back, whitish underparts and rose-red crown and throat. Female is similar but lacks the red. Neither sex has any rufous on the back, belly or tail.

Habitat: Forest edges and openings wherever flowers occur. Most often seen at sugar-water feeders. Spring and summer observations indicate possible breeding in Alaska.

Status & Distribution	Spring	Summer	Fall	Winter	Breeder	Key
Southeastern	R	R	R	A		C Common
Southcoastal	A	A	A	A		U Uncommon
Southwestern	–	A	A	–		R Rare
Central	–	–	–	–		A Casual/Accidental
Western	–	–	–	–		– No Records
Northern	–	–	–	–		

ANNA'S HUMMINGBIRD, *Male*

ANNA'S HUMMINGBIRD, *Female*

Rufous Hummingbird

(Selasphorus rufus)
Length: 3 1/2 in.

Identification: Adult male distinguished from all other birds by rufous color and extensive flaming orange-red throat patch. Adult female lacks throat patch and has a green back, dull rufous sides and considerable rufous at base of the tail. Immatures are similar to females.

Status & Distribution	Spring	Summer	Fall	Winter	Breeder	Key
Southeastern	C	C	C	A	•	C Common
Southcoastal	C	C	C	–	•	U Uncommon
Southwestern	–	–	–	–		R Rare
Central	–	R	–	–		A Casual/Accidental
Western	–	–	–	–		– No Records
Northern	–	–	–	–		

Habitat: Forest edges and openings from sea level to the mountains, wherever flowers are available. Nests in various trees and bushes.

Notes: Feeds on flower and blossom nectar with a preference for red flowers; also feeds on tiny insects.

RUFOUS HUMMINGBIRD, *Female*

RUFOUS HUMMINGBIRD, *Male*

Family *Alcedinidae*
KINGFISHERS
(1)

In Alaska the kingfisher family is represented by only 1 species, the Belted Kingfisher.

Belted Kingfisher
(Ceryle alcyon)
Length: 13 in.

Identification: Large head and bill, which look out of proportion to body size, short tail and tiny feet are distinctive. Blue-gray above and white below, with a white collar. In flight has jerky wingbeats and rattling call. Both sexes have a gray breast band; female has an additional rufous band, one of the rare instances in which the female appears more brightly colored than the male. The kingfisher has a tuft of longer feathers on its head, called a crest. This crest may be lowered or raised.

Habitat: Rivers, streams, lakes, ponds, sloughs, inshore marine waters. Nests in burrows that it excavates in sandy, clay or gravelly banks.

Status & Distribution	Spring	Summer	Fall	Winter	Breeder	Key
Southeastern	C	C	C	C	•	C Common
Southcoastal	U	U	U	U	•	U Uncommon
Southwestern	U	U	U	U	•	R Rare
Central	C	C	C	–	•	A Casual/Accidental
Western	U	U	U	–	•	– No Records
Northern	–	–	A	–		

Notes: Catches small fish by diving straight into the water, sometimes completely submerging. When fish are scarce, feeds on insects, mice and berries.

BELTED KINGFISHER, *Female*

Family *Picidae*
WOODPECKERS
(7 + 2)

Woodpeckers are highly specialized for climbing the trunks and branches of trees and for digging out wood-boring insects. The bill is hard, straight and chisel-like; the tongue is slender and fitted with a horny spear at the tip for impaling insect larvae. Legs are short. Feet have 4 toes (rarely 3), 2 in front and 2 behind, that have sharp claws for climbing. Stiff, pointed tail feathers serve as a brace against tree trunks.

Yellow-bellied Sapsucker

(Sphyrapicus varius)
Length: 9 in.

Identification: Yellow-bellied Sapsucker is separated from Red-breasted Sapsucker by the red forehead, 2 white horizontal stripes across face, black bib across upper breast and straw-yellow underparts. Throat is red in male and white in female.

Status & Distribution	Spring	Summer	Fall	Winter	Breeder	Key
Southeastern	–	–	–	A		C Common
Southcoastal	–	A	–	–		U Uncommon
Southwestern	–	–	–	–		R Rare
Central	A	A	–	–	•	A Casual/Accidental
Western	–	–	–	–		– No Records
Northern	–	–	–	–		

Habitat: Mixed deciduous-coniferous forests, especially those with aspen trees. Has been recorded nesting near Northway in eastern-central Alaska.

YELLOW-BELLIED SAPSUCKER, *Male*

Red-breasted Sapsucker

(Sphyrapicus ruber)
Length: 9 in.

Identification: Red hood covering the head, neck and breast and a long, white stripe down the folded wing are diagnostic. Flight is undulating, but the wings appear to be held closed for a slightly longer interval than in other woodpeckers. Sexes are alike. Call is a squealing *chee-ar*, most often heard during breeding season.

Habitat: Coniferous and mixed deciduous-coniferous forests. Nests in holes in trees.

Status & Distribution	Spring	Summer	Fall	Winter	Breeder	Key
Southeastern	C	C	C	R	•	C Common
Southcoastal	A	A	A	A		U Uncommon
Southwestern	–	–	–	–		R Rare
Central	A	–	–	–		A Casual/Accidental
Western	–	–	–	–		– No Records
Northern	–	–	–	–		

Notes: Is responsible for the horizontal rows of squarish holes frequently found on tree trunks. Drinks sap from these holes and also may obtain insects that are attracted by the sap.

RED-BREASTED SAPSUCKER

Downy Woodpecker

(Picoides pubescens)
Length: 6¹/₂ in.

Identification: Smaller version of Hairy
Woodpecker, with stubby bill that is
obviously shorter than the head. Barred
outer tail feathers. Call is similar to
but much softer than that of Hairy
Woodpecker.

Status & Distribution	Spring	Summer	Fall	Winter	Breeder	Key
Southeastern	U	U	U	U	•	C Common
Southcoastal	U	U	U	U	•	U Uncommon
Southwestern	R	R	R	R	•	R Rare
Central	U	U	U	U	•	A Casual/Accidental
Western	R	R	R	R	•	– No Records
Northern	–	–	–	–		

Habitat: Coniferous and deciduous forests,
shrub thickets. Nests in holes in trees.

Notes: Often will come to feed on suet in
winter.

DOWNY WOODPECKER, *Male*

Hairy Woodpecker

(Picoides villosus)
Length: 9 in.

Habitat: Coniferous and deciduous forests.
Nests in holes in trees.

HAIRY WOODPECKER

Identification: Vivid black-and-white
markings, white back and large bill.
Immaculate white outer tail feathers.
Bill is nearly as long as the head. Downy
Woodpecker's bill is more stubby and
obviously shorter than the head. Adult
males of both species have a bright red
patch, which may be divided into 2 spots,
on the nape. Young males of both species
just out of the nest usually have a red crown.
Call is a far-carrying *pick*.

Status & Distribution	Spring	Summer	Fall	Winter	Breeder	Key
Southeastern	U	U	U	U	•	C Common
Southcoastal	U	U	U	U	•	U Uncommon
Southwestern	–	–	–	–		R Rare
Central	U	U	U	U	•	A Casual/Accidental
Western	–	–	–	–		– No Records
Northern	–	–	–	–		

Three-toed Woodpecker

(Picoides tridactylus)
Length: 8½ in.

Identification: Appears darker than the
Hairy Woodpecker, with a dull black-and-
white-barred back and barred sides. Adult
male has a yellow cap. Call is a sharp *pik* or
kik, uttered much less frequently than that
of Hairy Woodpecker.

Status & Distribution	Spring	Summer	Fall	Winter	Breeder	Key
Southeastern	U	U	U	U	•	C Common
Southcoastal	R	R	R	R	•	U Uncommon
Southwestern	U	U	U	U	•	R Rare
Central	U	U	U	U	•	A Casual/Accidental
Western	U	U	U	U	•	– No Records
Northern	–	–	–	–		

Habitat: Coniferous and mixed deciduous-
coniferous forests. Nests in tree cavities,
usually of conifers.

THREE-TOED WOODPECKER, *Male*

Black-backed Woodpecker

(Picoides arcticus)
Length: 9½ in.

Identification: Larger and darker than
Three-toed Woodpecker. Has solid, glossy
black back. Sides are barred. Adult male has
yellow cap.

Status & Distribution	Spring	Summer	Fall	Winter	Breeder	Key
Southeastern	R	A	R	–		C Common
Southcoastal	A	A	A	A	•	U Uncommon
Southwestern	A	–	–	–		R Rare
Central	R	R	R	R	•	A Casual/Accidental
Western	–	–	–	–		– No Records
Northern	–	–	–	–		

Habitat: Coniferous and mixed deciduous-
coniferous forests. Nests in tree cavities,
usually of conifers.

BLACK-BACKED WOODPECKER, *Male*

Northern Flicker

(Colaptes auratus)
Length: 12¹/₂ in.

Identification: Has conspicuous white rump patch and yellow or reddish wing and tail linings. Males have a black (yellow-shafted) or red (red-shafted) mustache. Voice is a loud, far-carrying series of rapid *wucks* or a deliberate *wicka-wicka-wicka*.

Habitat: Coniferous and deciduous forests. Nests in holes in trees or stumps.

Status & Distribution	Spring	Summer	Fall	Winter	Breeder	Key
Southeastern	U	U	U	A	•	C Common
Southcoastal	A	R	U	A		U Uncommon
Southwestern	–	–	A	–		R Rare
Central	C	C	C	A	•	A Casual/Accidental
Western	–	–	A	–		– No Records
Northern	–	–	A	–		

Notes: Essentially a forest bird, but may feed on insects on the ground, especially in cleared areas along the highway. Also eats wild berries such as dwarf dogwood, mountain ash and blueberries. Two subspecies found in Alaska: red-shafted is most numerous in southeastern Alaska; yellow-shafted occurs throughout forested regions of the state.

NORTHERN FLICKER, *Male*

Family *Tyrannidae*
TYRANT FLYCATCHERS
(11 + 1)

Flycatchers typically perch in an upright position on bare branches and make frequent short flights after flying insects, usually returning to the same perch. They have broad, flat bills especially adapted for catching insects.

Olive-sided Flycatcher

(Contopus borealis)
Length: 7¹/₂ in.

Identification: Stout, with a large bill and dark chest patches separated by narrow white stripe. Song is emphatic whistled *whip-three-beers*, with the middle note the highest in pitch. Call is incessant *pilt, pilt.*

Status & Distribution	Spring	Summer	Fall	Winter	Breeder	Key
Southeastern	U	U	U	–	•	C Common
Southcoastal	R	R	R	–	•	U Uncommon
Southwestern	R	R	R	–	•	R Rare
Central	U	U	U	–	•	A Casual/Accidental
Western	R	R	R	–	•	– No Records
Northern	–	A	–	–		

Habitat: Coniferous forests. Nests in conifers.

OLIVE-SIDED FLYCATCHER

Western Wood-Pewee

(Contopus sordidulus)
Length: 6¹/₄ in.

Identification: Slightly larger and even
duller than *Empidonax* flycatchers. Lacks
their white eye-ring. Voice is nasal *pee-wee*.

Status & Distribution	Spring	Summer	Fall	Winter	Breeder	Key
Southeastern	U	U	U	–	•	C Common
Southcoastal	–	R	R	–	•	U Uncommon
Southwestern	–	–	–	–		R Rare
Central	U	U	U	–	•	A Casual/Accidental
Western	A	A	–	–		– No Records
Northern	A	A	–	–		

Habitat: Open coniferous and deciduous
forests, forest edges. Nests on horizontal
limbs and occasionally in upright crotches
of deciduous or coniferous trees.

WESTERN WOOD-PEWEE

Yellow-bellied Flycatcher

(Empidonax flaviventris)
Length: 5¹/₂ in.

Identification: Much like Pacific-slope
Flycatcher but with slightly more yellowish
underparts. Adult has olive back, wings and
head, broad yellow eye-ring, yellow throat
and belly separated by an olive wash on
breast. Voice is an abrupt *killik* or *chilink*
and a whistled *chu-wee* rising in pitch.

Status & Distribution	Spring	Summer	Fall	Winter	Breeder	Key
Southeastern	–	A	–	–		C Common
Southcoastal	–	–	–	–		U Uncommon
Southwestern	–	–	–	–		R Rare
Central	–	A	–	–		A Casual/Accidental
Western	–	–	–	–		– No Records
Northern	–	–	–	–		

Habitat: Deciduous and mixed woodlands.
Has occurred at Hyder in southeastern
Alaska. Singing males have been reported
from Kenny Lake and Ester in central
Alaska.

YELLOW-BELLIED FLYCATCHER

Alder Flycatcher

(Empidonax alnorum)
Length: 6 in.

Identification: Eye-ring faint, brownish-olive above, very pale yellow belly and whitish throat. Alder Flycatcher is much like Hammond's Flycatcher and might also be mistaken for Pacific-slope Flycatcher. Song is a *fee-bee-o* and call is a short, sharp *whit* or *wee-o*.

Status & Distribution	Spring	Summer	Fall	Winter	Breeder	Key
Southeastern	U	U	U	–	•	C Common
Southcoastal	U	U	U	–	•	U Uncommon
Southwestern	U	U	U	–	•	R Rare
Central	C	C	C	–	•	A Casual/Accidental
Western	U	U	U	–	•	– No Records
Northern	A	A	–	–		

Habitat: Alder and willow thickets, usually in moist areas. Nests in upright crotches of shrubs.

Least Flycatcher

(Empidonax minimus)
Length: 5¼ in.

Identification: Strongly marked eye-ring and 2 white wing bars, olive-gray above with white throat and gray breast, and faint yellow on belly. Has habit of flicking its tail upward. Song is an explosive *Che-bek*, with emphasis on the second syllable, while singing from a high perch. Call note is a clear *whit* or *wit*.

Status & Distribution	Spring	Summer	Fall	Winter	Breeder	Key
Southeastern	A	A	–	–		C Common
Southcoastal	–	A	A	–		U Uncommon
Southwestern	–	–	–	–		R Rare
Central	A	A	–	–		A Casual/Accidental
Western	–	–	–	–		– No Records
Northern	–	–	–	–		

Habitat: Deciduous woodlands. Singing males have been recorded at numerous localities in recent years. Breeding is possible at Kenny Lake and Hyder, where territorial males have recurred.

ALDER FLYCATCHER

LEAST FLYCATCHER

Hammond's Flycatcher

(Empidonax hammondii)
Length: 5 in.

Identification: Very similar to Alder
Flycatcher and Yellow-bellied Flycatcher.
Clear white eye-ring, grayish-olive back,
throat generally grayish-white, very pale
yellow belly. Typical 3-part song begins
and ends with a double note and has a short
or slightly rolling middle part described as
seedick, prrt, pewit. Call note is lower pitched
and quite different from that of the Alder
Flycatcher.

Notes: Hammond's Flycatcher is an early
migrant arriving in central Alaska about the
first of May; Alder Flycatcher is a late
migrant arriving near the end of May.

HAMMOND'S FLYCATCHER

Status & Distribution	Spring	Summer	Fall	Winter	Breeder	Key
Southeastern	U	U	U	–	•	C Common
Southcoastal	–	–	–	–		U Uncommon
Southwestern	–	–	–	–		R Rare
Central	C	C	C	–	•	A Casual/Accidental
Western	–	–	–	–		– No Records
Northern	–	A	–	–		

Habitat: Riparian deciduous forests. Also
dry upland mixed or deciduous forests with
closed canopy.

Dusky Flycatcher

(Empidonax oberholseri)
Length: 5³/₄ in.

Identification: Very similar to Hammond's
Flycatcher. Gray back with a tinge of olive;
buffy breast, light throat and pale yellow
belly. White eye-ring and wing bars. Song
is similar to that of Hammond's Flycatcher
and sounds like a staccato series of chirps,
transcribed as *se-lip, churp, treep.* Call is a
sharp *wit.*

Habitat: Breeds in open woodlands in
interior British Columbia, and has occurred
in fall migration along the Stikine River in
southeastern Alaska, and was accidental at
Icy Cape in northern Alaska.

DUSKY FLYCATCHER

Status & Distribution	Spring	Summer	Fall	Winter	Breeder	Key
Southeastern	–	–	A	–		C Common
Southcoastal	–	–	–	–		U Uncommon
Southwestern	–	–	–	–		R Rare
Central	–	–	–	–		A Casual/Accidental
Western	–	–	–	–		– No Records
Northern	–	A	–	–		

Pacific-slope Flycatcher

(Empidonax difficilis)
Length: 5¹/₂ in.

Identification: Has extensive yellowish underparts, including the throat. Song is 3 thin notes, *pseet-ptsick-seet;* call is a sharp, lisping *ps-seet.*

Status & Distribution	Spring	Summer	Fall	Winter	Breeder	Key
Southeastern	C	C	C	–	•	C Common
Southcoastal	–	A	–	–		U Uncommon
Southwestern	–	–	–	–		R Rare
Central	–	–	–	–		A Casual/Accidental
Western	–	–	–	–		– No Records
Northern	–	–	–	–		

Habitat: Open coniferous forests. Nests on rock ledges near streams, in the roots of upturned trees and on stumps or buildings.

PACIFIC-SLOPE FLYCATCHER

Say's Phoebe

(Sayornis saya)
Length: 7¹/₂ in.

Identification: Gray-brown on back and breast, light cinnamon on belly and a black tail. Voice is mellow, whistled *pee-ur.*

Habitat: Open areas and cliffs in mountains and uplands. Nests on shelves or in crevices of cliffs and on buildings.

SAY'S PHOEBE

Status & Distribution	Spring	Summer	Fall	Winter	Breeder	Key
Southeastern	R	R	R	–	•	C Common
Southcoastal	R	R	R	–	•	U Uncommon
Southwestern	–	A	A	–		R Rare
Central	U	U	U	–	•	A Casual/Accidental
Western	U	U	U	–	•	– No Records
Northern	U	U	U	–	•	

Notes: Sits in the open on dead limbs, electrical wires or posts, and makes short flights after insects.

Western Kingbird

(Tyrannus verticalis)
Length: 8¹/₂ in.

Identification: Olive-gray above, with
light-gray breast and yellow belly. Tail is
black with white edges. Call is a sharp *wit*
or *wik*.

Status & Distribution	Spring	Summer	Fall	Winter	Breeder	Key
Southeastern	A	A	A	–		C Common
Southcoastal	–	–	A	–		U Uncommon
Southwestern	–	–	–	–		R Rare
Central	–	A	–	–		A Casual/Accidental
Western	–	–	–	–		– No Records
Northern	–	–	–	–		

Habitat: Open areas with trees, shrubs and
posts for perching. Not known to breed in
Alaska.

WESTERN KINGBIRD

EASTERN KINGBIRD

Eastern Kingbird

(Tyrannus tyrannus)
Length: 8¹/₂ in.

Identification: Dark gray above and white
below, with a white band at tip of the black
tail. Call is a loud, harsh *dzeeb*, at times
uttered in rapid progression.

Status & Distribution	Spring	Summer	Fall	Winter	Breeder	Key
Southeastern	–	R	R	–		C Common
Southcoastal	–	A	A	–		U Uncommon
Southwestern	–	A	–	–		R Rare
Central	–	A	A	–		A Casual/Accidental
Western	–	A	–	–		– No Records
Northern	–	A	A	–		

Habitat: Open areas with trees, shrubs or
posts for perching. Not known to breed in
Alaska.

Notes: Usually perches on fences or utility
wires, and flies out substantial distances
after insects.

Family *Alaudidae*
LARKS
(2)

Larks are sparrow-sized ground birds that rarely perch in trees or bushes.

Eurasian Skylark

(Alauda arvensis)
Length: 7 in.

Identification: Brown, streaked above and on the breast, with a slight crest. Bill is thinner than that of a longspur or sparrow. Larger than a pipit and does not wag its tail. Extremely elongated, straight hind claw. Lacks indistinct head markings of an immature Horned Lark. Call is liquid *chirrup*.

Status & Distribution	Spring	Summer	Fall	Winter	Breeder	Key
Southeastern	–	–	–	–		C Common
Southcoastal	–	–	–	–		U Uncommon
Southwestern	R	A	A	–	•	R Rare
Central	–	–	–	–		A Casual/Accidental
Western	A	–	–	–		– No Records
Northern	–	–	–	–		

Habitat: Asiatic lark. Occurs in the western Aleutian Islands and has occurred in the Pribilof Islands.

Notes: Ground bird that prefers open country.

EURASIAN SKYLARK, *Fall*

Horned Lark

(Eremophila alpestris)
Length: 7¹/₂ in.

Identification: Has a black shield below a light throat and a black face patch curving downward from the bill to below the eye. "Horns" are not always visible. In flight black tail is conspicuous against sandy brown back or white belly. Immature is streaky brown, with a typical lark shape and behavior, and often is vaguely marked with the adult head pattern. Song is a series of tinkling notes given from high in the air.

Status & Distribution	Spring	Summer	Fall	Winter	Breeder	Key
Southeastern	U	R	U	–		C Common
Southcoastal	R	R	R	–		U Uncommon
Southwestern	R	R	R	–	•	R Rare
Central	C	C	C	–	•	A Casual/Accidental
Western	U	U	U	–	•	– No Records
Northern	U	U	U	–	•	

Habitat: Breeding — alpine tundra. Nests on the ground in the tundra. In migration — drier grassy areas of tidal flats, alpine meadows.

HORNED LARK

Family *Hirundinidae*
SWALLOWS
(8)

Swallows are excellent flyers that capture insects on the wing. They have long, pointed wings, a flattish head, a small, flat bill, wide mouth and most have notched or forked tails. They commonly perch on wires.

Purple Martin

(Progne subis)
Length: 8 in.

Identification: Male is entirely blue-black; female is brownish-black above and gray below. Soars much more than the smaller swallows.

Habitat: Open areas of forests, water, marshes. Not known to breed in Alaska.

Status & Distribution	Spring	Summer	Fall	Winter	Breeder	Key
Southeastern	–	–	–	–		C Common
Southcoastal	A	–	–	–		U Uncommon
Southwestern	–	A	A	–		R Rare
Central	A	A	–	–		A Casual/Accidental
Western	–	A	–	–		– No Records
Northern	–	A	–	–		

PURPLE MARTIN, *Male*

Tree Swallow

(Tachycineta bicolor)
Length: 5 1/2 in.

Identification: Steely-blue on back and white on belly. May be confused with Violet-green Swallow, but lacks white patches that almost meet over the base of the tail of that species. Dark cap extends down over the eyes, presenting a very different appearance from Violet-green Swallow. First-year female is much duller; mature female and all males are fully colored.

Status & Distribution	Spring	Summer	Fall	Winter	Breeder	Key
Southeastern	C	C	C	–	•	C Common
Southcoastal	C	C	C	–	•	U Uncommon
Southwestern	C	C	C	–	•	R Rare
Central	C	C	C	–	•	A Casual/Accidental
Western	C	C	C	–	•	– No Records
Northern	A	A	A	–		

Habitat: Forages for insects over water or moist ground. Lakes, larger streams, marshes and wet muskegs. Nests in tree cavities and sometimes in buildings and bird boxes. Closely tied to human settlements in tundra areas.

TREE SWALLOW

Violet-green Swallow

(Tachycineta thalassina)
Length: 5 1/2 in.

(Pictured on right)
Identification: One of 2 swallow species that, from a distance, look dark above and entirely white below. White patch on either side of the rump shows from above in flight, and green and violet upperparts are visible at close range. White of the face extends around the eye, which distinguishes this species from similar Tree Swallow. Female is considerably duller, especially around the head.

Status & Distribution	Spring	Summer	Fall	Winter	Breeder	Key
Southeastern	U	U	U	–	•	C Common
Southcoastal	C	C	C	–	•	U Uncommon
Southwestern	U	U	U	–	•	R Rare
Central	C	C	C	–	•	A Casual/Accidental
Western	A	–	–	–		– No Records
Northern	–	A	–	–		

Habitat: Forages for insects in open areas, over water, above tree tops. Nests in holes, cavities and crevices in trees, cliffs, buildings.

Northern Rough-winged Swallow

(Stelgidopteryx serripennis)
Length: 5¹/₂ in.

Identification: All brown above, with an entirely brown throat. Flight is batlike.

Status & Distribution	Spring	Summer	Fall	Winter	Breeder	Key
Southeastern	R	R	A	–	•	C Common
Southcoastal	A	A	–	–		U Uncommon
Southwestern	–	A	–	–		R Rare
Central	–	–	–	–		A Casual/Accidental
Western	–	–	–	–		– No Records
Northern	–	A	–	–		

Habitat: Forages over water and open land. Nests in burrows in sand, gravel or clay and in other cavities.

Notes: Usually occurs in single pairs; not colonial like the Bank Swallow.

NORTHERN ROUGH-WINGED SWALLOW

VIOLET-GREEN SWALLOW

Bank Swallow

(Riparia riparia)
Length: 5 in.

Identification: Brown back, white throat
and clearly defined dark breast band.
Smallest and dullest swallow found in
Alaska.

Status & Distribution	Spring	Summer	Fall	Winter	Breeder	Key
Southeastern	U	U	U	–	•	C Common
Southcoastal	U	U	U	–	•	U Uncommon
Southwestern	U	U	U	–	•	R Rare
Central	C	C	C	–	•	A Casual/Accidental
Western	U	U	U	–	•	– No Records
Northern	A	A	A	–		

Habitat: Usually near water. Nests in holes
in clay and sand banks near rivers, creeks
and lakes and along highways.

BANK SWALLOW

Cliff Swallow

(Hirundo pyrrhonota)
Length: 5¹/₂ in.

Identification: Appears plump because of
short, almost square tail. Blue-black above
and white below, with a dark chestnut
throat, whitish forehead and conspicuous
buffy rump patch. More likely to soar than
other small swallows.

Status & Distribution	Spring	Summer	Fall	Winter	Breeder	Key
Southeastern	R	R	R	–	•	C Common
Southcoastal	U	U	U	–	•	U Uncommon
Southwestern	U	U	U	–	•	R Rare
Central	C	C	C	–	•	A Casual/Accidental
Western	U	U	U	–	•	– No Records
Northern	U	U	U	–	•	

Habitat: Forages over water and open land.
Nests on buildings and under bridges.

CLIFF SWALLOW

Barn Swallow
(Hirundo rustica)
Length: 6 in.

Identification: Has deeply forked tail; steely, iridescent blue back and light-orange belly. Immature has much shorter tail and paler belly. Easily recognized at great distances by leisurely flight with relatively slow wingbeats for a swallow.

BARN SWALLOW, Immature

Status & Distribution	Spring	Summer	Fall	Winter	Breeder	Key
Southeastern	C	C	C	–	•	C Common
Southcoastal	C	C	C	–	•	U Uncommon
Southwestern	A	A	–	–		R Rare
Central	A	A	A	–		A Casual/Accidental
Western	A	A	A	–		– No Records
Northern	–	A	–	–		

Habitat: Forages over marshes, open land and water. Nests in buildings and under bridges.

Common House-Martin
(Delichon urbica)
Length: 5¹/₄ in.

Identification: Similar to Tree Swallow, with its pure white underparts and glossy bluish-black upperparts, but distinguished by large white rump patch.

COMMON HOUSE-MARTIN

Status & Distribution	Spring	Summer	Fall	Winter	Breeder	Key
Southeastern	–	–	–	–		C Common
Southcoastal	–	–	–	–		U Uncommon
Southwestern	A	–	–	–		R Rare
Central	–	–	–	–		A Casual/Accidental
Western	A	–	A	–		– No Records
Northern	A	–	–	–		

Habitat: Open country. Has been seen at Nome, Saint Paul Island, Pribilof Islands and at the mouth of the Colville River.

Family *Corvidae*
JAYS, MAGPIES, CROWS
(7)

Members of this family are medium to large, gregarious birds with heavy bills. They will feed on meat (including carrion), eggs and young of other birds, insects, fruits and seeds.

Gray Jay
(Perisoreus canadensis)
Length: 11 in.

Identification: Adults are long-tailed, primarily gray, with darker back and crown and rather short bill. Immature — from fledging to September — is very dark gray, almost black, all over. Utters a variety of shrill, high-pitched notes and whistles, including a soft *whee-oh* and a harsh, scolding *cla, cla, cla, cla.*

Habitat: Openings in coniferous and deciduous forests. Campgrounds. Nests in conifers.

GRAY JAY, *Immature*

Status & Distribution	Spring	Summer	Fall	Winter	Breeder	Key
Southeastern	A	–	R	R		C Common
Southcoastal	R	R	R	R	•	U Uncommon
Southwestern	U	U	U	U	•	R Rare
Central	C	C	C	C	•	A Casual/Accidental
Western	U	U	U	U	•	– No Records
Northern	A	A	A	A	•	

GRAY JAY, *Adult*

Steller's Jay

(Cyanocitta stelleri)
Length: 13 in.

Identification: Dark blue to black, with a conspicuous crest. Flight is series of wing-flappings interspersed with long, straight glides. Voice is a harsh *shack-shack-shack-shack* or *chook-chook-chook*. Also mimics the screams of hawks.

Status & Distribution	Spring	Summer	Fall	Winter	Breeder	Key
Southeastern	C	C	C	C	•	C Common
Southcoastal	C	C	C	C	•	U Uncommon
Southwestern	–	–	–	–		R Rare
Central	–	–	A	–		A Casual/Accidental
Western	–	–	–	–		– No Records
Northern	–	–	–	–		

Habitat: Coniferous and mixed coniferous-deciduous forests. Nests 10 feet or more above the ground in conifers.

STELLER'S JAY

Clark's Nutcracker

(Nucifraga columbiana)
Length: 12¹/₂ in.

Identification: Gray, wings and tail black with large white patches. Bill is much longer and tail much shorter than Gray Jay. Call is loud, harsh *kraaa*.

Status & Distribution	Spring	Summer	Fall	Winter	Breeder	Key
Southeastern	A	A	A	A		C Common
Southcoastal	–	–	–	–		U Uncommon
Southwestern	–	–	A	–		R Rare
Central	–	–	A	A		A Casual/Accidental
Western	–	–	A	–		– No Records
Northern	–	–	–	–		

Habitat: Open coniferous forests. Not known to breed in Alaska.

CLARK'S NUTCRACKER

Black-billed Magpie
(Pica pica)
Length: 20 in.

Identification: Very long tail and black-and-white color at rest or in flight are diagnostic. Young share the adult color pattern but have a much shorter tail. Voice is a rapid, nasal *mag? mag? mag?* or *yak yak yak.*

Status & Distribution	Spring	Summer	Fall	Winter	Breeder	Key
Southeastern	U	R	U	C	•	C Common
Southcoastal	C	C	C	C	•	U Uncommon
Southwestern	C	C	C	C	•	R Rare
Central	C	C	C	C	•	A Casual/Accidental
Western	–	–	–	R		– No Records
Northern	–	A	–	–		

Habitat: Shrub thickets, open woodlands, forest edges along saltwater beaches. Nests in tall bushes.

BLACK-BILLED MAGPIE

American Crow
(Corvus brachyrhynchos)
Length: 17–21 in.

Identification: All black, with a slight purplish gloss. Slightly larger and more robust than the similar-looking Northwestern Crow. Most common call is a distinctive *caw* that is not as hoarse as the *kaah* call of the Northwestern Crow.

Habitat: Meadows, fields and woodlands; an extension of interior British Columbia population occurs at Hyder and in the adjacent Salmon River valley at the end of the Portland Canal.

AMERICAN CROW

Status & Distribution	Spring	Summer	Fall	Winter	Breeder	Key
Southeastern	A	A	A	–	•	C Common
Southcoastal	–	–	–	–		U Uncommon
Southwestern	–	–	–	–		R Rare
Central	–	–	–	–		A Casual/Accidental
Western	–	–	–	–		– No Records
Northern	–	–	–	–		

Northwestern Crow

(Corvus caurinus)
Length: 17 in.

Identification: All black. Sometimes, when silent and in dim light, may be confused with Common Raven, but the square-cut tail and shorter bill are distinguishing. Voice is a raucous *kaah*, sometimes repeated endlessly. Imitates a variety of sounds.

Habitat: Marine shores; rarely ventures inland. Coniferous forests, beaches and tidal flats, rocky shores and reefs. Nests in conifers or sometimes under boulders or windfalls close to shore.

Status & Distribution	Spring	Summer	Fall	Winter	Breeder	Key
Southeastern	C	C	C	C	•	C Common
Southcoastal	C	C	C	C	•	U Uncommon
Southwestern	R	R	–	–	•	R Rare
Central	–	–	–	–		A Casual/Accidental
Western	–	–	–	–		– No Records
Northern	–	–	–	–		

Notes: Diet consists chiefly of dead fish, clams, mussels, small crabs; elderberries, salmonberries and some insects in summer. Opens clams and mussels by carrying them aloft and dropping them on the rocks below.

NORTHWESTERN CROW

Common Raven

(Corvus corax)
Length: 22–27 in.

Identification: Can be confused only with
Northwestern Crow, but is much larger,
with a proportionately larger bill and
wedge-shaped tail. Soars like a buteo. From
the ground Common Raven often takes 2
or 3 hops to become airborne; crow jumps
directly into the air. Most common call is
hoarse, croaking *kraaak*. Utters a variety of
other sounds including a hollow, knocking
sound and a melodious *kloo-klok*, usually
in flight.

COMMON RAVEN

Status & Distribution	Spring	Summer	Fall	Winter	Breeder	Key
Southeastern	C	C	C	C	•	C Common
Southcoastal	C	C	C	C	•	U Uncommon
Southwestern	C	C	C	C	•	R Rare
Central	C	C	C	C	•	A Casual/Accidental
Western	C	C	C	C	•	– No Records
Northern	C	C	C	U	•	

Habitat: Marine shores to mountain ridges
and glaciers. Garbage dumps. Nests in trees
or on cliffs.

Family *Paridae*
CHICKADEES
(5 + 1)

Chickadees are small, dull-colored, acrobatic birds with black bibs and dark caps. They are quite tame and readily come to feeders. They typically inhabit the forested regions of Alaska.

Black-capped Chickadee

(Parus atricapillus)
Length: 5 in.

Identification: Solid black cap, gray back and pale buffy sides are diagnostic. Most common call is clear *tsick-a-dee-dee-dee*. Male in spring sings clear, 2-noted whistle *fee-bee*.

Habitat: Prefers deciduous woods; secondarily, coniferous forests, particularly the edges. In southeastern Alaska, most often found in cottonwoods and alders along the mainland river systems. Nests in holes in the dead wood of trees or tree stubs.

Status & Distribution	Spring	Summer	Fall	Winter	Breeder	Key
Southeastern	U	U	U	U	•	C Common
Southcoastal	U	U	U	U	•	U Uncommon
Southwestern	U	U	U	U	•	R Rare
Central	C	C	C	C	•	A Casual/Accidental
Western	U	U	U	U	•	– No Records
Northern	–	–	A	–		

Notes: Easily attracted to feeders.

BLACK-CAPPED CHICKADEE

Mountain Chickadee

(Parus gambeli)
Length: 5¹/₂ in.

Identification: Very similar to Black-capped Chickadee but has a conspicuous white line over the eye separated from white of the cheek. Sides are gray, lacking the buffy wash of Black-capped Chickadee. Song is 4-note whistle, and the *chick-a-dee* call is buzzier than that of Black-capped Chickadee, more like *chick-a-zhee-zhee-zhee*. Not known to breed in Alaska.

Status & Distribution	Spring	Summer	Fall	Winter	Breeder	Key
Southeastern	A	A	A	A		C Common
Southcoastal	–	–	–	–		U Uncommon
Southwestern	–	–	–	–		R Rare
Central	–	–	–	–		A Casual/Accidental
Western	–	–	–	–		– No Records
Northern	–	–	–	–		

Habitat: Open coniferous forests, deciduous woods and thickets. Nests in tree holes. Has been found at sea level near Juneau and in the mountains near Skagway.

MOUNTAIN CHICKADEE

Siberian Tit

(Parus cinctus)
Length: 5 1/2 in.

Identification: Larger, longer tailed, washed-out version of more frequently encountered Boreal Chickadee. Gray-brown cap, very little brown on the sides, and white on the cheek extends onto sides of the neck.

Status & Distribution	Spring	Summer	Fall	Winter	Breeder	Key
Southeastern	–	–	–	–		C Common
Southcoastal	–	–	–	–		U Uncommon
Southwestern	–	A	–	–		R Rare
Central	R	R	R	R	•	A Casual/Accidental
Western	R	R	R	R	•	– No Records
Northern	–	–	–	–		

Habitat: Breeding — spruce forests at or near timberline. In winter — willow and alder thickets along valley floors. Nests in the holes of dead trees.

Notes: Locally distributed and rarely seen.

SIBERIAN TIT

Boreal Chickadee

(Parus hudsonicus)
Length: 5 in.

Identification: Has brown cap, brown back and reddish-brown flanks; generally duller and paler than Chestnut-backed Chickadee. Voice is somewhat similar to Chestnut-backed Chickadee.

Status & Distribution	Spring	Summer	Fall	Winter	Breeder	Key
Southeastern	–	–	A	A		C Common
Southcoastal	R	R	R	R	•	U Uncommon
Southwestern	U	U	U	U	•	R Rare
Central	C	C	C	C	•	A Casual/Accidental
Western	U	U	U	U	•	– No Records
Northern	–	–	–	–		

Habitat: Coniferous forests, deciduous-coniferous woodlands. Nests in holes in trees.

BOREAL CHICKADEE

Chestnut-backed Chickadee

(Parus rufescens)
Length: 5 in.

Identification: Chestnut back and sides and very dark brown cap. Darkest appearing chickadee. Voice is *tsida-tsida-see*.

Habitat: Coniferous forests, deciduous trees and thickets. Nests in holes in trees.

Status & Distribution	Spring	Summer	Fall	Winter	Breeder	Key
Southeastern	C	C	C	C	•	C Common
Southcoastal	C	C	C	C	•	U Uncommon
Southwestern	–	–	–	–		R Rare
Central	–	–	–	–		A Casual/Accidental
Western	–	–	–	–		– No Records
Northern	–	–	–	–		

Notes: Readily comes to feeders with sunflower seeds and suet.

CHESTNUT-BACKED CHICKADEE

Family *Sittidae*
NUTHATCHES
(1)

Nuthatches are small, tree-climbing birds with short tails and long, straight bills.

Red-breasted Nuthatch
(Sitta canadensis)
Length: 4 1/2 in.

Identification: Short tail, straight, slender bill, blue-gray back and reddish underparts, and a prominent white eye-stripe are diagnostic. A worn bird may have much paler underparts. More often heard than seen. Call, audible for considerable distances, is a high nasal *yank-yank-yank*.

Habitat: Coniferous and deciduous trees. Nests in tree cavities.

Status & Distribution	Spring	Summer	Fall	Winter	Breeder	Key
Southeastern	U	U	U	R	•	C Common
Southcoastal	R	R	U	R	•	U Uncommon
Southwestern	A	–	A	–		R Rare
Central	A	A	A	A	•	A Casual/Accidental
Western	–	–	A	–		– No Records
Northern	–	–	–	–		

Notes: Expert climber. Runs nimbly up and down tree trunks and on underside of limbs, searching for insects, their eggs, or seeds of pine and spruce. Makes short flights to catch insects on the wing. Name derived from the habit of inserting nuts in bark crevices and hammering them with the bill until the shell is broken.

RED-BREASTED NUTHATCH

Family *Certhiidae*
CREEPERS
(1)

Creepers are small, tree-climbing birds with long, stiff tail feathers and a long, slender bill.

Brown Creeper

(Certhia americana)
Length: 5¹/₂ in.

Identification: Dark-brown, streaked back, white breast, long, slender downcurved bill and long tail are distinguishing. Blends in well with the bark of trees. Best way to detect presence of the creeper is the faint, high-pitched call, *ts-ts.* Golden-crowned Kinglet has similar call but usually with more syllables and not quite so pure.

Habitat: Coniferous forests, mixed deciduous-coniferous woodlands. Nests in trees behind strips of loosened bark.

Status & Distribution	Spring	Summer	Fall	Winter	Breeder	Key
Southeastern	U	U	U	U	•	C Common
Southcoastal	U	U	U	U	•	U Uncommon
Southwestern	U	U	U	U	•	R Rare
Central	R	R	R	R	•	A Casual/Accidental
Western	–	–	–	–		– No Records
Northern	–	–	–	–		

Notes: Searches cracks in tree bark for insects by starting at the bottom of a tree and working upward in a spiral fashion; then flies to the base of the next tree and repeats the pattern. Sometimes forages along the undersides of horizontal branches.

BROWN CREEPER

Family *Troglodytidae*
WRENS
(1)

Wrens are small, restless, brownish birds that hold the tail straight up when not in flight. Represented in Alaska by the Winter Wren.

Winter Wren
(Troglodytes troglodytes)
Length: 4 in.

Identification: All brown, with the tail cocked over the back. Song is a rapid succession of high, tinkling warbles and trills. Call is a loud *chimp-chimp*, easily imitated.

Habitat: The ground or low branches of heavily forested areas. Beaches in the Aleutian Islands and Pribilof Islands, where it feeds among beach rocks and nests in cliffs and talus slopes. Usually nests among the roots of an upturned tree, in old stumps, brush piles, and abandoned buildings.

Status & Distribution	Spring	Summer	Fall	Winter	Breeder	Key
Southeastern	C	C	C	U	•	C Common
Southcoastal	U	U	U	U	•	U Uncommon
Southwestern	C	C	C	C	•	R Rare
Central	–	–	–	–		A Casual/Accidental
Western	–	–	–	–		– No Records
Northern	–	A	–	–		

WINTER WREN

Family *Cinclidae*
DIPPERS
(1)

Dippers are stocky, wrenlike birds with short tails. They are perching birds that have adapted to feeding underwater, with compact plumage, strong toes for holding on to rocks in a current, and special oil glands.

American Dipper
(Cinclus mexicanus)
Length: 7¹/₂ in.

Identification: Is solid gray with a short tail. Call is a loud, sharp *zeet* given singly or repeatedly. The dipper's song is very melodious and sounds like a long rendition of some of the best notes of thrushes and wrens. Both sexes may be heard singing during all months of the year except immediately after the young have left the nest.

Habitat: Fast-moving streams and occasionally ponds, lakeshores, saltwater beaches, especially in winter when streams are frozen. Nests on rock walls or perpendicular banks bordering streams, often behind waterfalls.

Status & Distribution	Spring	Summer	Fall	Winter	Breeder	Key
Southeastern	C	C	C	C	•	C Common
Southcoastal	C	C	C	C	•	U Uncommon
Southwestern	C	C	C	C	•	R Rare
Central	U	U	U	U	•	A Casual/Accidental
Western	U	U	U	U	•	– No Records
Northern	R	R	R	R	•	

Notes: Can walk, completely submerged, along the bottom of a rushing stream by grasping stones or rough places with long toes while probing under stones for aquatic insects, small fish and fish eggs. Dippers can also propel themselves underwater with swimming motions of their wings.

AMERICAN DIPPER

Family *Muscicapidae*
OLD WORLD WARBLERS AND FLYCATCHERS, KINGLETS, THRUSHES
(22 + 6)

The thrush, solitaire and bluebird group consists of songbirds characterized by large eyes and slender bills. Color varies widely among adults of these species, but birds in juvenile plumage all have spotted breasts. This group encompasses some of the finest singers in the bird world. Old World flycatchers and warblers, and kinglets are small, drab perching birds with slender bills. They are very active and flit from branch to branch after insects.

Middendorff's Grasshopper-Warbler

(Locustella ochotensis)

Length: 6 in.

Identification: Rather large Old World warbler with a whitish line over the eye and a white-tipped, fan-shaped tail. Dark olive-brown above; whitish below with an olivaceous wash on the sides. Fall immatures have a buffy yellow throat, indistinctly streaked breast and white-tipped tail. A skulker, this warbler keeps close to ground cover and is difficult to flush.

Status & Distribution	Spring	Summer	Fall	Winter	Breeder	Key
Southeastern	–	–	–	–		C Common
Southcoastal	–	–	–	–		U Uncommon
Southwestern	–	A	A	–		R Rare
Central	–	–	–	–		A Casual/Accidental
Western	A	–	A	–		– No Records
Northern	–	–	–	–		

Habitat: Has been found in western Aleutians, on Saint Paul Island in the Pribilofs, and on Nunivak and Saint Lawrence islands in western Alaska. Breeds in northeast Asia.

MIDDENDORFF'S GRASSHOPPER-WARBLER

Dusky Warbler
(Phylloscopus fuscatus)
Length: 4¹/₂ in.

Identification: Small, drab Old World warbler best identified by absence of greenish or yellowish colors. Also identified by fine bill, buffy line above eye, rounded tail tip, and by distinctive, harsh call *tsack* that it utters frequently. This species skulks and is difficult to observe.

Status & Distribution	Spring	Summer	Fall	Winter	Breeder	Key
Southeastern	–	–	–	–		C Common
Southcoastal	–	–	–	–		U Uncommon
Southwestern	–	–	A	–		R Rare
Central	–	–	–	–		A Casual/Accidental
Western	A	–	–	–		– No Records
Northern	–	–	–	–		

Habitat: Has been found on Shemya Island in western Aleutians and at Gambell on Saint Lawrence Island. Breeds in northern Asia.

DUSKY WARBLER

Arctic Warbler

(Phylloscopus borealis)
Length: 4³/₄ in.

Identification: Plain, rather like a Warbling
Vireo although the 2 species do not occur
together. Has dark line through the eye
and light greenish-yellow stripe over the
eye. Has pale legs. Of the species with
which Arctic Warbler occurs, perhaps
it is most similar to Orange-crowned
Warbler, but Arctic is brown above and
white below rather than greenish. Song is a
trill introduced by a note sounding like *zick*
or *zick-zick-zick*; call is also *zick* or *zirrup*.

Status & Distribution	Spring	Summer	Fall	Winter	Breeder	Key
Southeastern	–	–	–	–		C Common
Southcoastal	–	–	–	–		U Uncommon
Southwestern	U	U	U	–	•	R Rare
Central	C	C	C	–	•	A Casual/Accidental
Western	C	C	C	–	•	– No Records
Northern	C	C	C	–	•	

Habitat: Willow thickets. Nests on the
ground in grass or moss in willow thickets.

ARCTIC WARBLER

Golden-crowned Kinglet
(Regulus satrapa)
Length: 3 1/2 in.

Identification: Olive-green and gray, with a white eyebrow stripe that distinguishes this species from Ruby-crowned Kinglet and any other small species. Male has yellow and orange crown with black border; female has a yellow crown with black border. Voice is thin *see-see-see*, so high-pitched that some people cannot hear it.

Status & Distribution	Spring	Summer	Fall	Winter	Breeder	Key
Southeastern	C	C	C	U	•	C Common
Southcoastal	U	U	U	U	•	U Uncommon
Southwestern	U	U	U	U	•	R Rare
Central	–	R	R	A		A Casual/Accidental
Western	–	–	–	–		– No Records
Northern	–	–	–	–		

Habitat: Coniferous forests. Nests in branches of conifers.

Notes: Flicks its wings almost constantly. Feeds mostly on insects and their eggs and larvae found on conifer branches.

GOLDEN-CROWNED KINGLET, Female

Ruby-crowned Kinglet
(Regulus calendula)
Length: 4 in.

Identification: Olive above and gray below. Conspicuous white eye-ring and lack of head stripes separate this species from Golden-crowned Kinglet. Ruby crown of male usually concealed. Song is usually in 3 parts: *tee tee tee, chur chur chur, teedadee teedadee teedadee.* First notes are high, like those of the Golden-crowned Kinglet, but the rest is a loud, finchlike warble. Call is a harsh, usually 2-syllabled chatter.

Habitat: Coniferous forests, mixed coniferous-deciduous woodlands, shrub thickets. Widespread in Alaska; occurring wherever spruce forests exist. Nests in conifers usually 20 to 60 feet from the ground.

Notes: Characteristically flicks its wings nervously.

RUBY-CROWNED KINGLET, Male

Status & Distribution	Spring	Summer	Fall	Winter	Breeder	Key
Southeastern	C	C	C	A	•	C Common
Southcoastal	C	C	C	A	•	U Uncommon
Southwestern	R	R	R	–	•	R Rare
Central	U	U	U		•	A Casual/Accidental
Western	U	U	U		•	– No Records
Northern	A	–	A	–		

Red-breasted Flycatcher

(Ficedula parva)
Length: 4¹/₂ in.

Identification: Small Old World flycatcher best distinguished by black tail and white patches at base of outer tail feathers. Frequently flicks tail upward. Adult male has orange throat, grayish head, back and upper breast, white belly and under tail coverts. Females are grayish-brown above, white below, with a creamy wash on the throat and breast.

Status & Distribution	Spring	Summer	Fall	Winter	Breeder	Key
Southeastern	–	–	–	–		C Common
Southcoastal	–	–	–	–		U Uncommon
Southwestern	A	A	–	–		R Rare
Central	–	–	–	–		A Casual/Accidental
Western	A	–	–	–		– No Records
Northern	–	–	–	–		

Habitat: Has been found in western Aleutians on Shemya and Attu islands and at Gambell on Saint Lawrence Island. Breeds in northern Eurasia.

RED-BREASTED FLYCATCHER; *Female, left; Male, right*

Siberian Flycatcher

(*Muscicapa sibirica*)
Length: 5 1/2 in.

Identification: A small Old World flycatcher with a short tail. Upperparts dull
sooty-brown. Adult has white throat that
extends onto the neck as a half-collar, a
fused band of sooty streaks and smudges
across the breast, and a pale wing bar. Fall
immature has spotted wings and dingy,
streaked underparts.

Status & Distribution	Spring	Summer	Fall	Winter	Breeder	Key
Southeastern	–	–	–	–		C Common
Southcoastal	–	–	–	–		U Uncommon
Southwestern	A	–	A	–		R Rare
Central	–	–	–	–		A Casual/Accidental
Western	–	–	–	–		– No Records
Northern	–	–	–	–		

Habitat: Prefers open woodlands. Breeds in
East Asia. Has been found on Attu and
Shemya islands in the Aleutians.

SIBERIAN FLYCATCHER

Gray-spotted Flycatcher

(*Muscicapa griseisticta*)
Length: 4 1/2 in.

Identification: Drab, about the size of an
Empidonax. Perches upright like Tyrant
Flycatcher, but has streaked underparts and
white spectacles.

Status & Distribution	Spring	Summer	Fall	Winter	Breeder	Key
Southeastern	–	–	–	–		C Common
Southcoastal	–	–	–	–		U Uncommon
Southwestern	R	–	–	–		R Rare
Central	–	–	–	–		A Casual/Accidental
Western	–	–	–	–		– No Records
Northern	–	–	–	–		

Habitat: Asiatic flycatcher that has occurred
in the western Aleutian Islands. Not known
to breed in Alaska.

GRAY-SPOTTED FLYCATCHER

Siberian Rubythroat
(Luscinia calliope)
Length: 6 in.

Identification: Much like Bluethroat in appearance, habits and habitat, but larger. Male has bright-red throat and black-and-white moustaches. Female has white throat, not bordered on chest by dark as in female Bluethroat, and both sexes have white lines both over and under the eye.

Status & Distribution	Spring	Summer	Fall	Winter	Breeder	Key
Southeastern	–	–	–	–		C Common
Southcoastal	–	–	–	–		U Uncommon
Southwestern	R	A	A	–		R Rare
Central	–	–	–	–		A Casual/Accidental
Western	A	–	–	–		– No Records
Northern	–	–	–	–		

Habitat: Asiatic species that has been found in the western Aleutian Islands, Pribilof Islands and at Gambell on Saint Lawrence Island. Summer observations at Attu Island indicate possible breeding.

SIBERIAN RUBYTHROAT, *Male*

Bluethroat
(Luscinia svecica)
Length: 5 1/2 in.

Identification: Summer male has bright-blue throat patch with a chestnut-colored spot in the center. Both sexes are plain brown above, with rusty patches at the base of the tail that are conspicuous in flight. Female has a white throat bordered by black and a white eye-stripe. No other plain brown thicket-inhabiting bird with these characteristics occurs in Alaska. Musical song is introduced by notes sounding like *dip, dip, dip*; alarm call is *buyt-tock*.

Status & Distribution	Spring	Summer	Fall	Winter	Breeder	Key
Southeastern	–	–	–	–		C Common
Southcoastal	–	–	–	–		U Uncommon
Southwestern	A	–	A	–		R Rare
Central	–	–	–	–		A Casual/Accidental
Western	R	R	R	–	•	– No Records
Northern	R	R	R	–	•	

Habitat: Shrub thickets in the uplands and foothills of western and northern Alaska. Nests on the ground.

BLUETHROAT, *Male*

Red-flanked Bluetail
(Tarsiger cyanurus)
Length: 5¹/₂ in.

Identification: Adult male has bright-blue eyebrow, forehead, shoulder and rump; bright-orange flanks. Adult female has olive-brown upperparts, bluish rump and tail, whitish throat, dingy breast and pale rufous flanks. Immature male similar to female, but with varying amounts of blue.

Status & Distribution	Spring	Summer	Fall	Winter	Breeder	Key
Southeastern	–	–	–	–		C Common
Southcoastal	–	–	–	–		U Uncommon
Southwestern	A	–	–	–		R Rare
Central	–	–	–	–		A Casual/Accidental
Western	–	–	–	–		– No Records
Northern	–	–	–	–		

Habitat: Breeds in northern Japan, the far eastern Soviet Union, and the Kamchatka Peninsula. Has been found on Attu Island in the Aleutians and on Saint Paul Island in the Pribilofs.

RED-FLANKED BLUETAIL, *Male, Adult*

RED-FLANKED BLUETAIL, *Female*

Northern Wheatear
(Oenanthe oenanthe)
Length: 6 in.

Identification: In all plumages shows a white rump patch and black-and-white tail pattern like an inverted "T." Breeding male has black wings, black face patch and gray back. Young are buffy-brown, paler below. Song is short, abrupt twitter, sounding like an ungreased door hinge; alarm call is *tuck, tuck.*

Status & Distribution	Spring	Summer	Fall	Winter	Breeder	Key
Southeastern	–	–	A	–		C Common
Southcoastal	R	R	R	–	•	U Uncommon
Southwestern	R	A	R	–		R Rare
Central	U	U	U	–	•	A Casual/Accidental
Western	C	U	C	–	•	– No Records
Northern	U	U	U	–	•	

Habitat: Above timberline, rock fields in the tundra and rocky mountain ridges. Nests in crevices under rocks or in rubble.

Notes: Has a habit of frequently bobbing, spreading its tail feathers and moving its tail up and down.

NORTHERN WHEATEAR, *Male*

Mountain Bluebird
(Sialia currucoides)
Length: 7 in.

Identification: Male is bright sky-blue all over. Female is much duller than the male, with an overall brownish appearance but with enough blue wash on the wings and tail to be recognizable.

Status & Distribution	Spring	Summer	Fall	Winter	Breeder	Key
Southeastern	R	–	R	A		C Common
Southcoastal	A	–	A	–		U Uncommon
Southwestern	–	–	–	–		R Rare
Central	R	R	A	–	•	A Casual/Accidental
Western	–	–	A	–		– No Records
Northern	A	–	–	–		

Habitat: Open woodlands. Perches conspicuously on dead limbs, tree tops, fences, utility wires. Nests in tree holes, rock crevices and in buildings.

MOUNTAIN BLUEBIRD, *Male*

Townsend's Solitaire
(Myadestes townsendi)
Length: 8¹/₂ in.

Identification: Slim, gray bird with short bill, long tail and white eye-ring. In flight shows a conspicuous buffy wing patch and white tail edges. Song of fluted rising and falling phrases is loud and melodious; call is a bell-like *heep*.

Status & Distribution	Spring	Summer	Fall	Winter	Breeder	Key
Southeastern	R	R	R	A	•	C Common
Southcoastal	R	R	R	A	•	U Uncommon
Southwestern	–	–	–	–		R Rare
Central	R	R	R	A	•	A Casual/Accidental
Western	–	–	–	–		– No Records
Northern	–	–	–	–		

Habitat: Open forests usually near the timberline, especially during breeding season. Nests on the ground under overhanging banks, rocks, tree roots.

Notes: Solitary bird not often observed, probably because of its retiring habits and rather sparse distribution.

TOWNSEND'S SOLITAIRE

Gray-cheeked Thrush

(Catharus minimus)
Length: 7¹/₂ in.

Identification: All brown above, with grayish cheeks; lacking the conspicuous buffy eye-ring of Swainson's Thrush. Song is a thin, nasal *wee-oh, chee, chee, wee-oh* that usually rises abruptly at the end. Call is *wee-a* and, when alarmed, *chuck*.

Status & Distribution	Spring	Summer	Fall	Winter	Breeder	Key
Southeastern	U	U	U	–	•	C Common
Southcoastal	U	U	U	–	•	U Uncommon
Southwestern	C	C	C	–	•	R Rare
Central	C	C	C	–	•	A Casual/Accidental
Western	C	C	C	–	•	– No Records
Northern	C	C	C	–	•	

Habitat: Mixed deciduous-coniferous woodlands, shrub thickets, coniferous forests. Forages for food in open areas near thickets and on the tundra. Nests in bushes or low trees.

GRAY-CHEEKED THRUSH

Swainson's Thrush

(Catharus ustulatus)
Length: 7 in.

Identification: Distinguished from other spotted Alaskan thrushes by entirely brown back and tail and buffy eye-ring and face. Sings almost continuously in the morning and evening and often throughout the night. Song is breezy, flutelike phrases starting with a clear, long note on 1 pitch, then spiraling up the scale, becoming fainter until the last notes fade out. Call is a *whit*.

Habitat: Mixed deciduous-coniferous woodlands, shrub thickets, coniferous forests. Nests low in trees or bushes close to the trunk.

SWAINSON'S THRUSH

Status & Distribution	Spring	Summer	Fall	Winter	Breeder	Key
Southeastern	C	C	C	–	•	C Common
Southcoastal	U	U	U	–	•	U Uncommon
Southwestern	U	U	U	–	•	R Rare
Central	C	C	C	–	•	A Casual/Accidental
Western	R	R	R	–	•	– No Records
Northern	–	A	–	–		

Hermit Thrush
(Catharus guttatus)
Length: 7 in.

Identification: Three brown, spotted-breasted thrushes occur in Alaska (Hermit, Gray-cheeked, and Swainson's). Hermit Thrush is distinguished by reddish tail that is often slowly raised and lowered. Song is loud, slow, repetitive phrases spiraling down the scale. Call is a soft *cheep* or *chup-chup*, or catlike mew.

Habitat: Edges of coniferous forests, mixed deciduous-coniferous woodlands, shrub thickets. Nests usually on the ground; sometimes in trees.

Status & Distribution	Spring	Summer	Fall	Winter	Breeder	Key
Southeastern	C	C	C	A	•	C Common
Southcoastal	C	C	C	–	•	U Uncommon
Southwestern	C	C	C	–	•	R Rare
Central	U	U	U	–	•	A Casual/Accidental
Western	R	R	R	–	•	– No Records
Northern	A	A	–	–		

HERMIT THRUSH

Eyebrowed Thrush

(Turdus obscurus)
Length: 7 1/2 in.

Identification: Warm olive-brown above, with a distinct white eye-line, gray head and throat; orange breast and sides and white belly. Built like, but smaller than, an American Robin.

Habitat: Asiatic thrush that has occurred in the western and central Aleutian Islands, in the Pribilof Islands, at Wales and at Barrow. Not known to breed in Alaska.

Status & Distribution	Spring	Summer	Fall	Winter	Breeder	Key
Southeastern	–	–	–	–		C Common
Southcoastal	–	–	–	–		U Uncommon
Southwestern	R	–	A	–		R Rare
Central	–	–	–	–		A Casual/Accidental
Western	A	–	–	–		– No Records
Northern	A	–	–	–		

EYEBROWED THRUSH

Dusky Thrush

(Turdus naumanni)
Length: 9 in.

Identification: Mottled blackish-brown above, with a bold white eye-line and throat, dark breast band and spotted sides. Wings are washed with bright cinnamon color. Very distinctive bird. Not known to breed in Alaska.

Status & Distribution	Spring	Summer	Fall	Winter	Breeder	Key
Southeastern	–	–	–	–		C Common
Southcoastal	–	–	–	–		U Uncommon
Southwestern	A	–	A	–		R Rare
Central	–	–	–	–		A Casual/Accidental
Western	A	–	–	–		– No Records
Northern	A	–	–	–		

Habitat: Asiatic thrush that has been found in the Aleutian Islands, on Saint Lawrence Island and at Barrow.

DUSKY THRUSH

Fieldfare

(Turdus pilaris)
Length: 10 in.

Identification: Large thrush with gray head and rump that contrast with its red-brown back and wing coverts and blackish tail. Arrowheadlike spots adorn the buffy breast and sides. Black legs and yellowish bill also useful for identification. In flight, look for flashing white wing linings.

Status & Distribution	Spring	Summer	Fall	Winter	Breeder	Key
Southeastern	–	–	–	–		C Common
Southcoastal	–	–	–	–		U Uncommon
Southwestern	–	–	–	–		R Rare
Central	–	–	–	–		A Casual/Accidental
Western	A	–	–	–		– No Records
Northern	A	A	–	–		

Habitat: Open country. Has been found at Point Barrow and in the Gates of the Arctic National Park and at Gambell on Saint Lawrence Island. Breeds from Greenland to Siberia.

FIELDFARE

American Robin

(Turdus migratorius)
Length: 10 in.

Identification: Brick-red breast, dark-gray
back and yellow bill are distinguishing. Male
has blackish head and brighter underparts
than female. The spotted-breasted young,
very common in middle to late summer, are
usually associated with adults. Song is a
procession of 2- or 3-syllable phrases that
suggest *cheer-up* or *cheerily* with variations in
pitch. Common calls are the alarm *pip, pip*
and the sibilant flight call *swee-weep*.

Habitat: From above timberline to forest
edges, muskegs, tundra and saltwater
beaches and tidal flats. Nests in crotches of
trees, less commonly on horizontal limbs or
ledges of buildings or bridges.

AMERICAN ROBIN, Male

Status & Distribution	Spring	Summer	Fall	Winter	Breeder	Key
Southeastern	C	C	C	R	•	C Common
Southcoastal	C	C	C	R	•	U Uncommon
Southwestern	C	C	C	–	•	R Rare
Central	C	C	C	A	•	A Casual/Accidental
Western	C	C	C	–	•	– No Records
Northern	R	R	R	–	•	

Varied Thrush

(Ixoreus naevius)
Length: 9$^1/_2$ in.

Identification: Resembles robin in size,
shape and orange-brown breast. Is slightly
smaller and shorter tailed than robin and
has a broad, black breast band (gray in the
female), orange-buff line above and behind
the eye, and orange-brown wing bars and
wing patches. Light markings on wing
are conspicuous in flight. Song, which is
penetrating and has a ventriloquial quality,
is a long, somewhat burry, whistled note,
followed after a pause by another note on a
lower or higher pitch.

Habitat: Forests from sea level to alpine;
prefers shady, damp forests. Usually nests
in conifers, from 5 to 15 feet above the
ground. Forages on the tundra, muskegs,
tidal flats and beaches.

VARIED THRUSH, Male

Status & Distribution	Spring	Summer	Fall	Winter	Breeder	Key
Southeastern	C	C	C	R	•	C Common
Southcoastal	C	C	C	R	•	U Uncommon
Southwestern	C	C	C	R	•	R Rare
Central	C	C	C	–	•	A Casual/Accidental
Western	C	C	C	–	•	– No Records
Northern	A	–	–	–		

Family *Mimidae*
MIMIC THRUSHES
(1 + 1)

Mimic Thrushes are excellent singing birds. They often mimic the songs of other birds and other sounds.

Northern Mockingbird

(Mimus polyglottos)
Length: 10 in.

Identification: A robin-sized bird that is gray above and white below. Best distinguished in flight when the striking white borders of the black tail and the white wing patches can be easily seen.

Habitat: Open country. Has been seen at Juneau, Petersburg, Middleton Island and Fairbanks.

Status & Distribution	Spring	Summer	Fall	Winter	Breeder	Key
Southeastern	–	A	A	–		C Common
Southcoastal	–	–	A	–		U Uncommon
Southwestern	–	–	–	–		R Rare
Central	–	–	A	–		A Casual/Accidental
Western	–	–	–	–		– No Records
Northern	–	–	–	–		

NORTHERN MOCKINGBIRD

Family *Prunellidae*
ACCENTORS
(1)

This Old World family of songbirds is usually found in alpine and sparsely vegetated habitat. Accentors resemble sparrows but have more slender pointed bills.

Siberian Accentor
(Prunella montanella)
Length: 6 in.

Identification: Ground-dwelling bird with a thin bill. Dark reddish-brown above, grayer at the rump and tail, and warm buffy to whitish below with streaked sides. Has distinct buffy eye-stripe and black mask through the eyes.

Status & Distribution	Spring	Summer	Fall	Winter	Breeder	Key
Southeastern	–	–	A	–		C Common
Southcoastal	–	–	A	–		U Uncommon
Southwestern	–	–	–	–		R Rare
Central	A	–	–	–		A Casual/Accidental
Western	–	–	A	–		– No Records
Northern	–	–	A	–		

Habitat: Asiatic species that has occurred on Saint Lawrence Island, at Point Barrow, Fairbanks and Juneau. Breeds in northeastern Asia.

SIBERIAN ACCENTOR, *Immature*

Family *Motacillidae*
WAGTAILS, PIPITS
(8 + 1)

Wagtails and pipits are sparrow-sized ground birds with slender bills. They walk instead of hop, and wag their tails almost constantly. All have dark tails and white outer tail feathers. They feed mostly on insects.

Yellow Wagtail

(Motacilla flava)
Length: 6¹/₂ in.

Identification: Olive-gray back, white eye-line and yellow underparts are diagnostic. Call, a loud single note, *tzeep*, is often heard as the bird flies overhead.

Status & Distribution	Spring	Summer	Fall	Winter	Breeder	Key
Southeastern	–	–	–	–		C Common
Southcoastal	–	A	A	–		U Uncommon
Southwestern	R	R	R	–	•	R Rare
Central	A	A	A	–		A Casual/Accidental
Western	C	C	C	–	•	– No Records
Northern	U	U	U	–	•	

Habitat: Willow thickets on the tundra. Nests on open tundra under grass, overhanging banks.

Notes: Tail is constantly in motion.

YELLOW WAGTAIL

Gray Wagtail

(Motacilla cinerea)
Length: 7 in.

Identification: Has pale rump and white wing bars conspicuous only in flight. Summer male is distinguished from Yellow Wagtail by black throat. Females and winter birds have a white throat but differ from Yellow Wagtail in the gray rather than olive back. Call is sharper and more metallic than those of Yellow and White wagtails, but is double-noted like that of White Wagtail.

Status & Distribution	Spring	Summer	Fall	Winter	Breeder	Key
Southeastern	–	–	–	–		C Common
Southcoastal	–	–	–	–		U Uncommon
Southwestern	A	–	A	–		R Rare
Central	–	–	–	–		A Casual/Accidental
Western	A	–	–	–		– No Records
Northern	–	–	–	–		

Habitat: Asiatic species that has occurred in the Aleutian Islands, Pribilof Islands and on Saint Lawrence Island. Not known to breed in Alaska.

GRAY WAGTAIL, *Male, Breeding*

White Wagtail

(Motacilla alba)
Length: 7 in.

Identification: Gray above, white below, with a black crown and throat vaguely like a chickadee; the female has less black. When disturbed, flies up in great undulating arcs uttering a loud *tizzick*.

Habitat: Open areas with short vegetation usually along the coast. Nests near or on the ground in crevices or niches in old buildings.

Status & Distribution	Spring	Summer	Fall	Winter	Breeder	Key
Southeastern	–	–	–	–		C Common
Southcoastal	–	–	–	–		U Uncommon
Southwestern	A	A	–	–		R Rare
Central	A	–	–	–		A Casual/Accidental
Western	R	R	R	–	•	– No Records
Northern	R	–	R	–		

Notes: Slender, hyperactive ground bird that wags its very long tail constantly. Wary. Recent taxonomic splitting of White and Black-backed wagtails has resulted in records of "White" Wagtails in southeastern, southcoastal and southwestern Alaska that cannot now be assigned to species.

WHITE WAGTAIL

Black-backed Wagtail
(Motacilla lugens)
Length: 7 in.

Status & Distribution	Spring	Summer	Fall	Winter	Breeder	Key
Southeastern	–	A	–	–		C Common
Southcoastal	–	–	–	–		U Uncommon
Southwestern	R	A	A	–	•	R Rare
Central	–	–	–	–		A Casual/Accidental
Western	A	A	–	–	•	– No Records
Northern	–	–	–	–		

Identification: Adult male differs from White Wagtail by having an all-black or mostly black back and more black on the nape, and may have some dark shading on the face. Adult female has a white chin, whereas almost all White Wagtails have a black chin. Adult black-backed of both sexes has a much larger white wing patch than White Wagtail. After the fall molt, males and females of both species are gray-backed, with a white throat that makes identification very difficult. Juveniles of both species are virtually identical.

Habitat: Much less common than White Wagtail. Most sightings have been in spring on western Aleutian Islands. Nests have been found under a bridge on Attu Island and in an old building in Nome.

BLACK-BACKED WAGTAIL, *Female*

BLACK-BACKED WAGTAIL, *Male*

Olive Tree-Pipit

(Anthus hodgsoni)
Length: 6¹/₂ in.

Identification: Only pipit with an obscurely streaked olive back and strongly streaked breast. Prominent eye-stripe ends just behind the eye. Call is similar to but thinner than that of the Red-throated Pipit.

Status & Distribution	Spring	Summer	Fall	Winter	Breeder	Key
Southeastern	–	–	–	–		C Common
Southcoastal	–	–	–	–		U Uncommon
Southwestern	A	–	A	–		R Rare
Central	–	–	–	–		A Casual/Accidental
Western	A	–	–	–		– No Records
Northern	–	–	–	–		

Habitat: Asiatic species that has occurred in the western Aleutian Islands and on Saint Lawrence Island. Not known to breed in Alaska.

OLIVE TREE-PIPIT

Pechora Pipit

(Anthus gustavi)
Length: 5³/₄ in.

Identification: Diagnostic features are
heavily striped breast and back, with 2
distinctive whitish streaks on the back, and
buff rather than white outer tail feathers.
Call is a hard 1- or 2-noted *pwit*, given 2 to
3 times in series.

Status & Distribution	Spring	Summer	Fall	Winter	Breeder	Key
Southeastern	–	–	–	–		C Common
Southcoastal	–	–	–	–		U Uncommon
Southwestern	A	–	–	–		R Rare
Central	–	–	–	–		A Casual/Accidental
Western	A	–	–	–		– No Records
Northern	–	–	–	–		

Habitat: Asiatic pipit that has occurred at
Gambell on Saint Lawrence Island, and on
Attu Island in the Aleutians. Not known to
breed in Alaska.

PECHORA PIPIT

Red-throated Pipit

(Anthus cervinus)
Length: 6 in.

Identification: In summer can be distinguished from the American Pipit by the
reddish or pinkish color on the face, throat
and breast, especially in the male, and the
heavily striped back. Call is *teez*, similar to a
Yellow Wagtail.

Status & Distribution	Spring	Summer	Fall	Winter	Breeder	Key
Southeastern	–	–	–	–		C Common
Southcoastal	–	–	R	–		U Uncommon
Southwestern	R	–	R	–		R Rare
Central	–	–	–	–		A Casual/Accidental
Western	U	U	U	–	•	– No Records
Northern	–	–	A	–		

Habitat: Shrubby areas on the tundra.
Nests on the ground in tussock-sheltered
areas.

RED-THROATED PIPIT

American Pipit

(Anthus rubescens)
Length: 6 1/2 in.

Identification: Resembles a sparrow because of the brown, streaked color, but is slender and longer tailed than a sparrow, walks instead of hops and has a very slender bill. In flight the white outer tail feathers are conspicuous. Has a plain back unlike the other, much rarer, Alaskan pipits. Song is a series of simple notes, given in flight; call is a soft *tsi-tsip*, hence "pipit."

Habitat: Tundra, tidal flats and beaches, fields, alpine meadows, lakeshores, ponds, rivers and streams. Nests on the ground on drier ridges and foothills and above timberline.

Status & Distribution	Spring	Summer	Fall	Winter	Breeder	Key
Southeastern	C	C	C	A	•	C Common
Southcoastal	C	C	C	A	•	U Uncommon
Southwestern	C	C	C	A	•	R Rare
Central	C	C	C	–	•	A Casual/Accidental
Western	C	C	C	–	•	– No Records
Northern	C	C	C	–	•	

Notes: One of the most common and widely distributed birds in Alaska. Tail is wagged frequently but not continuously.

AMERICAN PIPIT

Family *Bombycillidae*
WAXWINGS
(2)

Waxwings are crested birds with black masks and yellow tips to the tails. The red, waxlike spots on the wings of the adult give the birds their name.

Bohemian Waxwing
(Bombycilla garrulus)
Length: 8 in.

Identification: Brownish, with a black eye patch, yellow tail tip and a crest. Larger than Cedar Waxwing, with chestnut rather than whitish under tail coverts and with small white wing patches. Belly is very gray in Bohemian Waxwing, yellowish buffy in Cedar Waxwing. Call is a high and sibilant rattle, often given in flight.

Habitat: Breeding — wet muskegs. Nests in conifers. In winter — usually any habitat where there are trees or shrubs with berries.

Status & Distribution	Spring	Summer	Fall	Winter	Breeder	Key
Southeastern	U	R	U	U	•	C Common
Southcoastal	U	U	U	R	•	U Uncommon
Southwestern	R	R	R	–	•	R Rare
Central	C	C	C	R	•	A Casual/Accidental
Western	R	R	R	–	•	– No Records
Northern	–	–	–	–		

Notes: Feeds on fruits and insects. Is an expert flycatcher; takes most of its prey on the wing like flycatchers or circles high in the air like swallows. In winter often gathers in flocks in the towns of southeastern Alaska wherever there are cultivated shrubs with fruit.

BOHEMIAN WAXWING

Cedar Waxwing
(Bombycilla cedrorum)
Length: 7 in.

Identification: Smaller than the Bohemian Waxwing, with a dull, pale yellowish belly and undertail and no white in the wings. Call is similar to the Bohemian Waxwing, but higher pitched and even more sibilant.

Status & Distribution	Spring	Summer	Fall	Winter	Breeder	Key
Southeastern	R	R	R	A	•	C Common
Southcoastal	–	–	A	–		U Uncommon
Southwestern	–	–	–	–		R Rare
Central	–	–	A	–		A Casual/Accidental
Western	–	–	–	–		– No Records
Northern	–	A	–	–		

Habitat: Openings and edges of coniferous forests. Nests in trees, usually in isolated trees in open areas.

CEDAR WAXWING

Family *Laniidae*
SHRIKES
(2)

Shrikes are songbirds with hook-tipped bills that prey on smaller birds and rodents.

Brown Shrike
(Lanius cristatus)
Length: 8 in.

Identification: Much smaller than Northern Shrike. Reddish-brown with black mask and buffy sides. Females and immatures have narrow, dark wavy bars on the sides and across the breast.

Status & Distribution	Spring	Summer	Fall	Winter	Breeder	Key
Southeastern	–	–	–	–		C Common
Southcoastal	–	–	A	–		U Uncommon
Southwestern	A	–	A	–		R Rare
Central	–	–	–	–		A Casual/Accidental
Western	A	–	–	–		– No Records
Northern	–	–	–	–		

Habitat: Has been found at Gambell on Saint Lawrence Island, on Shemya and Attu islands in the western Aleutians, and in Anchorage. Breeds in eastern Asia.

BROWN SHRIKE

Northern Shrike

(Lanius excubitor)
Length: 10 in.

Identification: Robin-sized gray bird
with a black mask and black wings and tail.
Normally perches at tops of trees or posts.
Has a hooked bill and the habits of a bird
of prey. Song is variable, and has been
described as similar to a canary, parakeet,
crow and robin.

Habitat: Openings and edges of coniferous
forests and mixed deciduous-coniferous
woodlands, shrub thickets on the tundra,
trees near freshwater and saltwater marshes.
Usually nests in small deciduous trees. May
be found singly or in pairs in spruce forests
over much of Alaska.

Status & Distribution	Spring	Summer	Fall	Winter	Breeder	Key
Southeastern	U	–	U	U		C Common
Southcoastal	U	U	U	U	•	U Uncommon
Southwestern	U	U	U	U	•	R Rare
Central	U	U	U	R	•	A Casual/Accidental
Western	U	U	U	U	•	– No Records
Northern	U	U	U	A	•	

Notes: Feeds on small rodents and birds.
Impales prey on thorns, broken twigs, barbs
of barbed-wire fences, or suspends prey
from the crotch of a tree. When hunting is
good, kills and hangs up more than can be
eaten at once, hence the nickname "butcher
bird."

NORTHERN SHRIKE

Family *Sturnidae*
STARLINGS
(1)

Starlings, related to crows, are Old World equivalents of North American blackbirds. One, the European Starling, was introduced into the United States in the late–19th century and is now well established in Alaska. Starlings feed on insects, seeds, berries and refuse.

European Starling
(Sturnus vulgaris)
Length: 8 in.

(Pictured below and at right)
Identification: Resembles a blackbird, but has a short, stubby tail. From midwinter to midsummer a yellow bill separates it from any blackbird. Plumage is highly iridescent, with flashes of green and violet. In late summer bill turns dusky and plumage becomes white-spotted, unlike any blackbird. In flight short tail is obvious and wings are more pointed than those of blackbirds. Flight is also more rapid and direct, reminiscent of a Bohemian Waxwing.

Habitat: Open woodlands, fields, beaches and tidal flats, garbage dumps. Nests in natural cavities such as woodpecker holes, Bank Swallow holes, and in buildings.

Status & Distribution	Spring	Summer	Fall	Winter	Breeder	Key
Southeastern	U	U	U	U	•	C Common
Southcoastal	R	R	R	R	•	U Uncommon
Southwestern	–	–	–	–		R Rare
Central	R	R	R	A	•	A Casual/Accidental
Western	A	A	A	–		– No Records
Northern	–	A	–	–		

Notes: European Starling was considered hypothetical in Alaska by Gabrielson and Lincoln (1959). They stated that its phenomenal spread was almost certain to eventually include parts of Alaska. Their prediction has come true, and the species is now well established in several parts of the state (Kessel and Gibson, 1978).

EUROPEAN STARLING, *Winter*

Family *Vireonidae*
VIREOS
(3 + 1)

Vireos look like rather plain warblers but have heavier bills. They eat mostly insects and some berries.

Warbling Vireo
(Vireo gilvus)
Length: 5 in.

Habitat: Deciduous trees mostly along the mainland rivers of southeastern Alaska. Nests in forked branches of trees.

WARBLING VIREO

Identification: Dull brownish-olive above and whitish below, with a white eye-line and no other distinctive marks. Drabness alone aids identification. The dullest Yellow Warblers are still obviously yellowish, Orange-crowned Warblers are greenish, and neither has a white line over the eye. Song is a short warble, with a characteristic up-and-down pattern.

Status & Distribution	Spring	Summer	Fall	Winter	Breeder	Key
Southeastern	U	U	U	–	•	C Common
Southcoastal	A	A	A	–		U Uncommon
Southwestern	–	–	–	–		R Rare
Central	–	–	–	–		A Casual/Accidental
Western	–	–	–	–		– No Records
Northern	–	–	–	–		

EUROPEAN STARLING (wet bird), *Breeding*

Philadelphia Vireo

(Vireo philadelphicus)
Length: 4³/₄ in.

Identification: Similar in size and shape to Warbling Vireo. Has yellowish throat and breast; Warbling Vireo is always whitish on throat and on center of breast. Philadelphia has a black eye-line that extends to the bill; Warbling Vireo lacks this line. Song is series of 2- or 3-syllable whistles like for the Red-eyed Vireo but higher pitched and slower.

Status & Distribution	Spring	Summer	Fall	Winter	Breeder	Key
Southeastern	–	–	–	–		C Common
Southcoastal	–	–	A	–		U Uncommon
Southwestern	–	–	–	–		R Rare
Central	–	A	–	–		A Casual/Accidental
Western	–	–	–	–		– No Records
Northern	–	–	–	–		

Habitat: Has been found at Eagle in central Alaska and on Middleton Island in the southcoastal region. Breeds in western and southern Canada and the northeastern United States.

PHILADELPHIA VIREO

Red-eyed Vireo

(Vireo olivaceus)
Length: 6 in.

Identification: A typical vireo, plain and slow-moving, when compared with the active warblers. Olive-green above and white below, with a distinctly gray cap and black-and-white eye-stripes. Song is a series of 2- or 3-syllable whistles, given monotonously for hours.

Status & Distribution	Spring	Summer	Fall	Winter	Breeder	Key
Southeastern	R	R	R	–	•	C Common
Southcoastal	–	A	A	–		U Uncommon
Southwestern	–	–	–	–		R Rare
Central	–	A	–	–		A Casual/Accidental
Western	–	–	–	–		– No Records
Northern	–	–	–	–		

Habitat: Deciduous trees mostly along the mainland rivers of southeastern Alaska. Nests in forked branches of trees.

RED-EYED VIREO

Family *Emberizidae*

WOOD WARBLERS, TANAGERS, SPARROWS, BUNTINGS, BLACKBIRDS
(43 + 17)

This bird family is the largest in the world. More than 150 species occur in North America, and of these 60 have been found in Alaska.

Tennessee Warbler

(Vermivora peregrina)
Length: 5 in.

Identification: Bright olive-green above and white below, with a gray head and white eye-line. Red-eyed Vireo is much larger with more distinct head stripes. In fall the breast is suffused with yellowish color and the head becomes greenish, rather like an Orange-crowned Warbler, but yellower and with a more distinct eye-line. The undertail is always white; it is greenish-yellow in the Orange-crowned Warbler. Song begins with buzzy paired notes in series and ends in a dry trill.

Status & Distribution	Spring	Summer	Fall	Winter	Breeder	Key
Southeastern	R	R	R	–	•	C Common
Southcoastal	A	–	A	–		U Uncommon
Southwestern	–	–	–	–		R Rare
Central	A	A	A	–		A Casual/Accidental
Western	–	–	–	–		– No Records
Northern	–	–	–	–		

Habitat: Deciduous and mixed deciduous-coniferous woodlands. Nests on or near the ground, often in a muskeg.

TENNESSEE WARBLER, *Male, Breeding*

Orange-crowned Warbler

(Vermivora celata)
Length: 5 in.

Identification: Only dingy, greenish-yellow warbler with no distinct markings. Crown patch is rarely visible. Only a dull female Yellow Warbler might be confused with an Orange-crowned Warbler, but the Yellow Warbler is always more yellow on the breast and has yellow tail patches. Song is a simple trill going up or down the scale toward the end. Call is a sharp *stick*.

Status & Distribution	Spring	Summer	Fall	Winter	Breeder	Key
Southeastern	C	C	C	A	•	C Common
Southcoastal	C	C	C	–	•	U Uncommon
Southwestern	C	C	C	–	•	R Rare
Central	C	C	C	–	•	A Casual/Accidental
Western	U	U	U	–	•	– No Records
Northern	A	A	A	–		

Habitat: Deciduous woodlands, shrub thickets, coniferous forest edges where low deciduous growth is present. Nests on the ground or in low shrubs.

ORANGE-CROWNED WARBLER

Yellow Warbler

(Dendroica petechia)
Length: 5 in.

Identification: Only clear-yellow bird with yellow markings in the outer tail feathers found in Alaska. Adult male has reddish streaks on the breast, but in female and young the streaks are faint or absent. Has a lively, cheerful song of single and double whistles, *sweet-sweet-sweet-sweet-setta-see-see-whew!* Call is loud, down-slurred *cheep*.

Status & Distribution	Spring	Summer	Fall	Winter	Breeder	Key
Southeastern	C	C	C	–	•	C Common
Southcoastal	U	U	U	–	•	U Uncommon
Southwestern	C	C	C	–	•	R Rare
Central	C	C	C	–	•	A Casual/Accidental
Western	C	C	C	–	•	– No Records
Northern	R	R	R	–	•	

Habitat: Deciduous woodlands and shrub thickets. Nests in shrubs or trees, usually near the ground.

YELLOW WARBLER, *Male*

Magnolia Warbler

(Dendroica magnolia)
Length: 5 in.

Identification: Male is gray and black above, with a gray head and black cheek patch; bright yellow below, heavily striped with black. Rump is yellow and wings have an extensive white patch. Tail crossed by a band of white is diagnostic in any plumage. Female and fall immatures are much duller, with reduced striping beneath. Usually has a distinct eye-ring. Song is a rising *wisha-wisha-wisha-witsy* or *pretty-pretty-Rachel*.

Status & Distribution	Spring	Summer	Fall	Winter	Breeder	Key
Southeastern	A	A	A	–	•	C Common
Southcoastal	–	A	A	–		U Uncommon
Southwestern	–	–	–	–		R Rare
Central	–	A	–	–		A Casual/Accidental
Western	–	–	A	–		– No Records
Northern	–	–	A	–		

Habitat: Coniferous forests and mixed deciduous-coniferous woodlands. Nests are usually placed in small conifers less than 14 feet from the ground.

MAGNOLIA WARBLER, *Male, Breeding*

Cape May Warbler

(Dendroica tigrina)
Length: 5 in.

Identification: Summer male is distinguished by chestnut cheek patches, olive back and bright-yellow underparts heavily striped with black. Female and fall birds are very dull, olive above with a vague yellowish rump patch, lightly but extensively streaked below and with a distinctive yellow patch around the ear area.

Status & Distribution	Spring	Summer	Fall	Winter	Breeder	Key
Southeastern	–	–	A	–		C Common
Southcoastal	–	–	–	–		U Uncommon
Southwestern	–	–	–	–		R Rare
Central	–	–	A	–		A Casual/Accidental
Western	–	–	–	–		– No Records
Northern	A	–	–	–		

Habitat: Has occurred at Fairbanks, Haines and Point Barrow. Not known to breed in Alaska.

CAPE MAY WARBLER, *Male, Breeding*

Yellow-rumped Warbler
(Dendroica coronata)
Length: 5 ¹/₂ in.

Identification: Brightly marked with black streaks on an overall gray background above. Throat and belly are white, breast is black. Crown, a patch at either side of the breast and the rump are bright yellow; these 4 yellow patches are unique to this species. Female is duller, and young in the fall are very drab brownish-gray, with scattered streaks and the obvious yellow rump. Song is a tinkling trill that either rises or falls in pitch at the end.

Status & Distribution	Spring	Summer	Fall	Winter	Breeder	Key
Southeastern	C	C	C	A	•	C Common
Southcoastal	U	U	U	A	•	U Uncommon
Southwestern	U	U	U	–	•	R Rare
Central	C	C	C	–	•	A Casual/Accidental
Western	C	C	C	–	•	– No Records
Northern	A	A	–	–		

Habitat: Coniferous forests, mixed deciduous-coniferous woodlands, shrub thickets. Nests in conifers, usually 4 to 10 feet above the ground.

YELLOW-RUMPED WARBLER

Townsend's Warbler
(Dendroica townsendi)
Length: 5 in.

(Pictured on right)
Identification: Only regularly occurring Alaska warbler that is olive above and yellow below with dark streaks. Male has a black throat, cheek patch and cap. Female has an olive cap and cheek and yellow throat. Song is *weazy weazy weazy twea* or *dee dee dee-de de*; call is soft *chip*.

Status & Distribution	Spring	Summer	Fall	Winter	Breeder	Key
Southeastern	C	C	C	A	•	C Common
Southcoastal	U	U	U	–	•	U Uncommon
Southwestern	–	–	A	–		R Rare
Central	C	C	C	–	•	A Casual/Accidental
Western	–	–	–	–		– No Records
Northern	–	–	A	–		

Habitat: Coniferous forests, mixed deciduous-coniferous woodlands. Nests in conifers.

Palm Warbler

(Dendroica palmarum)
Length: 5 1/2 in.

Identification: Adult in breeding plumage
has a rufous cap and yellow eyebrow. The
throat, upper breast and under tail coverts
are yellow; otherwise mostly grayish below
and brown above. The fall adult and the
immature have a white eyebrow and yellow
only on the under tail coverts. A ground-
dwelling warbler that constantly wags its
tail while feeding. Song is a trill given on
1 pitch.

Habitat: Open brushy areas, meadows and
marshes. Has been found at Juneau, Kodiak
and Dot Lake.

PALM WARBLER, *Breeding*

Status & Distribution	Spring	Summer	Fall	Winter	Breeder	Key
Southeastern	–	–	A	–		C Common
Southcoastal	–	–	A	–		U Uncommon
Southwestern	–	–	–	–		R Rare
Central	–	–	A	–		A Casual/Accidental
Western	–	–	–	–		– No Records
Northern	–	–	–	–		

TOWNSEND'S WARBLER

Blackpoll Warbler

(Dendroica striata)
Length: 5¹/₂ in.

Identification: Breeding male is olive above and white below, with black streaks. Has a black cap and white cheeks. Female and fall male are drab olive-green with white wing bars; liberally streaked on back and sides. Lacks the distinctive head pattern of female Townsend's Warbler and the yellow patches of fall Yellow-rumped Warbler. Only streaked warbler with pale legs. Song is a high-pitched *zi-zi-zi* repeated 6 to 12 times; call is low *chip* and thin *zeep*.

Habitat: Coniferous forests, mixed deciduous-coniferous woodlands, shrub thickets. Nests in small conifers or on the ground near conifers.

BLACKPOLL WARBLER, *Male, Breeding*

Status & Distribution	Spring	Summer	Fall	Winter	Breeder	Key
Southeastern	R	–	R	–		C Common
Southcoastal	R	R	R	–	•	U Uncommon
Southwestern	C	C	C	–	•	R Rare
Central	U	U	U	–	•	A Casual/Accidental
Western	C	C	C	–	•	– No Records
Northern	A	A	A	–		

American Redstart

(Setophaga ruticilla)
Length: 5 in.

(Pictured right and far right)
Identification: Males are black, with a white belly and bright-orange patches on the wings and tail. Female and immatures are olive-brown above and white below, with yellow patches on the wings and tail. Song is similar to that of the much more common Yellow Warbler but less variable, more on 1 pitch.

Habitat: Has occurred mostly in the deciduous forests along the mainland rivers of southeastern Alaska. Nests in deciduous trees usually 5 to 20 feet up.

Notes: Flits about, droops the wings and spreads the tail feathers almost constantly.

AMERICAN REDSTART, *Male*

Status & Distribution	Spring	Summer	Fall	Winter	Breeder	Key
Southeastern	U	U	U	–	•	C Common
Southcoastal	–	A	A	–		U Uncommon
Southwestern	–	–	–	–		R Rare
Central	A	A	–	–		A Casual/Accidental
Western	–	–	–	–		– No Records
Northern	–	–	A	–		

Northern Waterthrush

(Seiurus noveboracensis)
Length: 6 in.

Identification: Dark brown above and heavily streaked below, with a prominent buffy eyebrow stripe. Much more vividly marked than a pipit, and teeters more like a Spotted Sandpiper. Song is a sequence of quickly uttered, identical, short, chattering phrases repeated many times and speeded toward the end. Call is a loud, sharp *chink*.

Habitat: Deciduous trees bordering streams, lakes, ponds and swamps. Nests on the ground beneath logs, roots, stumps or in mossy banks.

Notes: A difficult bird to see because it frequents dense underbrush. Best found by listening for the song during breeding season.

NORTHERN WATERTHRUSH

Status & Distribution	Spring	Summer	Fall	Winter	Breeder	Key
Southeastern	U	U	U	–	•	C Common
Southcoastal	R	R	R	–	•	U Uncommon
Southwestern	C	C	C	–	•	R Rare
Central	C	C	C	–	•	A Casual/Accidental
Western	C	C	C	–	•	– No Records
Northern	A	–	–	–		

AMERICAN REDSTART, *Female*

MacGillivray's Warbler

(Oporornis tolmiei)
Length: 5 in.

Identification: Olive above and yellow below, with a slate-gray hood and conspicuous white eye-ring. Female is duller than the male. No other plain olive-and-yellow Alaska warbler has gray throat and breast. Song is chanting *tree tree tree tree sweet sweet*; call is a loud *tik*, sharper than the calls of most other western warblers.

Status & Distribution	Spring	Summer	Fall	Winter	Breeder	Key
Southeastern	U	U	U	–	•	C Common
Southcoastal	A	–	A	–		U Uncommon
Southwestern	–	–	–	–		R Rare
Central	–	–	–	–		A Casual/Accidental
Western	–	–	–	–		– No Records
Northern	–	A	A	–		

Habitat: Shrub thickets. Nests near the ground in shrubs or weed clumps.

MacGILLIVRAY'S WARBLER, Male

Common Yellowthroat
(Geothlypis trichas)
Length: 5 in.

Identification: Olive above and yellow below, like several other Alaska species, but both sexes have an obvious white belly and the male has a black face mask. Other warblers of this general appearance have the undersides yellow all the way to the tail. Song is a well-enunciated *witchity-witchity-witchity-witch*; call is a low *djip*.

Status & Distribution	Spring	Summer	Fall	Winter	Breeder	Key
Southeastern	U	U	U	–	•	C Common
Southcoastal	–	A	A	–		U Uncommon
Southwestern	–	–	–	–		R Rare
Central	–	A	–	–		A Casual/Accidental
Western	–	A	–	–		– No Records
Northern	–	–	–	–		

Habitat: Freshwater marshes and estuarine meadows along mainland rivers of southeastern Alaska and on islands near the mouths of these rivers. Nests on or near the ground in grasses and weeds.

COMMON YELLOWTHROAT, *Male*

Wilson's Warbler
(Wilsonia pusilla)
Length: 4 1/2 in.

Identification: Olive above and entirely bright yellow below. Male has a glossy black cap. Female has an olive cap, with the yellow of the face extending above the eye. Yellow Warbler has very plain head and yellow tail patches. Song is an evenly spaced series of notes, *chip chip chip chip chip*; call is soft *timp*.

Status & Distribution	Spring	Summer	Fall	Winter	Breeder	Key
Southeastern	C	C	C	–	•	C Common
Southcoastal	C	C	C	–	•	U Uncommon
Southwestern	C	C	C	–	•	R Rare
Central	C	C	C	–	•	A Casual/Accidental
Western	U	U	U	–	•	– No Records
Northern	A	A	A	–	•	

Habitat: Shrub thickets, mixed deciduous-coniferous woodlands. Nests on or near the ground in shrub thickets.

Notes: Typically holds the tail cocked up like a wren.

WILSON'S WARBLER, *Male*

Western Tanager

(Piranga ludoviciana)
Length: 7 in.

Identification: Male is bright yellow
with a red face and black wings and tail.
Female has a dull greenish back, dull yellow
underparts and 2 white or yellowish wing
bars. Female Evening Grosbeak is browner,
with much heavier bill, and female Pine
Grosbeak is considerably larger, with a gray
body and yellow only on the head and rump.
Song is robinlike but harsh and burry; call is
per-dick.

Status & Distribution	Spring	Summer	Fall	Winter	Breeder	Key
Southeastern	U	U	U	–	•	C Common
Southcoastal	A	–	–	–		U Uncommon
Southwestern	–	–	–	–		R Rare
Central	–	A	A	–		A Casual/Accidental
Western	–	–	–	–		– No Records
Northern	A	–	–	–		

Habitat: Open coniferous forests. Edge
of Western Hemlock/Sitka Spruce forests
of mainland rivers of southeastern Alaska.
Nests in forked conifer branches.

WESTERN TANAGER, *Male*

American Tree Sparrow

(Spizella arborea)
Length: 6 in.

Identification: Slender sparrow with red cap, single dusky spot in the middle of an unstreaked breast and 2 white wing bars. After young leave the nest, American Tree Sparrows form large flocks and, when feeding, utter a twittering *teedle-eet*. Song usually begins with several *seet* notes followed by a variable, rapid warble. Call is a *tseet*.

Status & Distribution	Spring	Summer	Fall	Winter	Breeder	Key
Southeastern	U	–	U	R		C Common
Southcoastal	U	R	U	R	•	U Uncommon
Southwestern	U	U	U	R	•	R Rare
Central	C	C	C	A	•	A Casual/Accidental
Western	C	C	C	–	•	– No Records
Northern	U	U	U	–	•	

Habitat: Shrub thickets. Near timberline to sea level, on the tundra wherever willows occur. Nests on the ground or in low bushes.

AMERICAN TREE SPARROW

Chipping Sparrow

(Spizella passerina)
Length: 5 ½ in.

Identification: Slightly smaller than an American Tree Sparrow with the same overall appearance. Clean gray, not beige, underparts. Has a broad white stripe over the eye and a black stripe through the eye. Lacks the breast spot of the Tree Sparrow. Fall immatures have a streaked crown, less distinct eye-stripe and brown cheek patch. Song is an even trill, drier and less musical than that of the junco.

Status & Distribution	Spring	Summer	Fall	Winter	Breeder	Key
Southeastern	R	R	R	A	•	C Common
Southcoastal	A	A	A	–		U Uncommon
Southwestern	–	–	–	–		R Rare
Central	U	U	U	–	•	A Casual/Accidental
Western	A	–	–	–		– No Records
Northern	–	–	A	–		

Habitat: Openings and edges of woodlands. Nests in deciduous or coniferous trees.

Notes: Found mostly along the mainland rivers of southeastern Alaska and the upper Tanana River valley of eastern central Alaska.

CHIPPING SPARROW

Savannah Sparrow
(Passerculus sandwichensis)
Length: 5 1/2 in.

Identification: Streaked sparrow that resembles but is paler than most Song Sparrows. Usually has a yellowish line over the eye and a much shorter, slightly notched tail. Often has breast spot like that of Song Sparrow. Song is quiet buzzing *tsit-tsit-tsit-tseee-tseee*.

Status & Distribution	Spring	Summer	Fall	Winter	Breeder	Key
Southeastern	C	C	C	–	•	C Common
Southcoastal	C	C	C	–	•	U Uncommon
Southwestern	C	C	C	A	•	R Rare
Central	C	C	C	A	•	A Casual/Accidental
Western	C	C	C	–	•	– No Records
Northern	C	C	C	–	•	

Habitat: Open places, especially grassy fields. Widespread in Alaska from seashore to mountain ridges. Nests on the ground, usually in open grassy areas.

SAVANNAH SPARROW

Fox Sparrow
(Passerella iliaca)
Length: 7 in.

Identification: Has brown or grayish-brown back and very heavily spotted-to-streaked underparts. Northern and Interior subspecies have bright, reddish-brown tail that contrasts sharply with the back; striped back; and partially striped head. Coastal forms are much darker and browner, without the strong contrast between the back color and the tail and with no stripes on the head or back. Darkest and smallest Fox Sparrows are found in lower southeastern Alaska. Subspecies to the north are grayer and larger. Southern birds are distinguished from Song Sparrows by the plain head and back, and all Fox Sparrows are recognizable by the light lower mandible. Song opens with 1 or more clear whistles and follows with several short *trills* or *churrs*; call is a sharp *chink*.

Habitat: Shrub thickets. Nests on the ground under shrubs or low in trees or shrubs.

FOX SPARROW

Status & Distribution	Spring	Summer	Fall	Winter	Breeder	Key
Southeastern	C	C	C	R	•	C Common
Southcoastal	C	C	C	R	•	U Uncommon
Southwestern	C	C	C	–	•	R Rare
Central	C	C	C	A	•	A Casual/Accidental
Western	C	C	C	–	•	– No Records
Northern	U	U	U	–	•	

Song Sparrow
(Melospiza melodia)
Length: 6–7¹/₂ in.

Identification: Brownish back, heavy streaks on the breast, usually a prominent spot in the center of the breast streaks. Head and back are streaked, bill is dark. Song Sparrow in the Aleutian Islands is huge, as big as the biggest Fox Sparrow, and very long billed; Song Sparrow from southern Alaska is obviously smaller than a Fox Sparrow. Song is staccato but musical, usually beginning with 2 or 3 loud notes that sound like *sweet, sweet, sweet,* followed by a trill, then several short notes; call is harsh single note.

Habitat: Marine beaches, only occasionally ventures inland. Beach rocks, shrub thickets. Nests on ground in grass clumps.

SONG SPARROW

Status & Distribution	Spring	Summer	Fall	Winter	Breeder	Key
Southeastern	C	C	C	C	•	C Common
Southcoastal	C	C	C	C	•	U Uncommon
Southwestern	C	C	C	C	•	R Rare
Central	–	–	–	–		A Casual/Accidental
Western	–	–	–	–		– No Records
Northern	–	–	–	–		

Lincoln's Sparrow
(Melospiza lincolnii)
Length: 5¹/₂ in.

Identification: Small, trim, finely streaked. Paler than a Song Sparrow with fine streaks, seldom massed into a central spot, across a buffy band on the breast and sides. Side of the head looks gray. Song is a low, gurgling stanza that ends after some rising phrases; calls are *tik* and buzzy *tzeee*.

Habitat: Shrubs, saltwater and freshwater marshes. Nests on the ground in marshy places.

LINCOLN'S SPARROW

Status & Distribution	Spring	Summer	Fall	Winter	Breeder	Key
Southeastern	C	C	C	A	•	C Common
Southcoastal	C	C	C	A	•	U Uncommon
Southwestern	U	U	U	–	•	R Rare
Central	C	C	C	–	•	A Casual/Accidental
Western	U	U	U	–	•	– No Records
Northern	–	A	–	–		

Swamp Sparrow
(Melospiza georgiana)
Length: 5³/₄ in.

Identification: Adult has chestnut-colored crown, gray face, white throat and reddish wings (without wing bars) and tail. Immature has blackish stripes on its head, a gray central stripe and reddish wings.

Habitat: Dense brushy vegetation at and near springs, seeps and swampy ground. Has been found at Saxman and near Petersburg in southeastern Alaska, Middleton Island and Anchorage.

SWAMP SPARROW

Status & Distribution	Spring	Summer	Fall	Winter	Breeder	Key
Southeastern	–	–	A	–		C Common
Southcoastal	A	–	A	–		U Uncommon
Southwestern	–	–	–	–		R Rare
Central	–	–	–	–		A Casual/Accidental
Western	–	–	–	–		– No Records
Northern	–	–	–	–		

White-throated Sparrow
(Zonotrichia albicollis)
Length: 6¹/₂ in.

Identification: Superficially like the White-crowned Sparrow, but in all plumages the throat is white, sharply distinct from the gray breast. Bill is darker, head is rounder, never angular-looking as it often is in the White-crowned Sparrow.

Status & Distribution	Spring	Summer	Fall	Winter	Breeder	Key
Southeastern	A	–	A	A		C Common
Southcoastal	A	–	A	A		U Uncommon
Southwestern	–	–	–	–		R Rare
Central	–	A	A	–		A Casual/Accidental
Western	–	–	–	–		– No Records
Northern	A	–	A	–		

Habitat: Has occurred in a variety of places including Colville River delta, Fairbanks, Cordova, Kodiak, Juneau, Sitka and Ketchikan. Not known to breed in Alaska.

WHITE-THROATED SPARROW

Golden-crowned Sparrow

(Zonotrichia atricapilla)
Length: 6¹/₂ in.

Identification: Slightly larger than White-crowned Sparrow. Has a golden crown bordered by a wide black stripe on either side. First winter bird is very dull, darker than a young White-crowned Sparrow with a dark bill. Top of the head is finely streaked, lacking prominent stripes of the White-crowned and White-throated sparrows. Song is normally 3 high, whistled notes of minor tone quality, running down the scale like 3 blind mice.

GOLDEN-CROWNED SPARROW

Status & Distribution	Spring	Summer	Fall	Winter	Breeder	Key
Southeastern	C	U	C	R	•	C Common
Southcoastal	C	C	C	R	•	U Uncommon
Southwestern	C	C	C	–	•	R Rare
Central	U	U	U	A	•	A Casual/Accidental
Western	C	C	C	–	•	– No Records
Northern	R	R	R	–		

Habitat: Willow and alder thickets usually near timberline. Nests on the ground under shrubs. Favors brushy areas in migration.

Notes: In migration travels in flocks often with White-crowned Sparrows. Readily comes to feeders.

White-crowned Sparrow
(Zonotrichia leucophrys)
Length: 6 in.

Status & Distribution	Spring	Summer	Fall	Winter	Breeder	Key
Southeastern	C	–	U	R		C Common
Southcoastal	U	R	U	R	•	U Uncommon
Southwestern	C	C	C	–	•	R Rare
Central	C	C	C	A	•	A Casual/Accidental
Western	C	C	C	–	•	– No Records
Northern	U	U	U	–	•	

Identification: Streaked above, plain gray below; slender; long-tailed and larger than Tree and Chipping sparrows. Adult has conspicuously black-and-white-striped head. Throat is the same color as the rest of the underparts. Fledgling has finely streaked crown and streaked breast; it will usually be with an adult. First winter bird has plain breast, head is striped with rusty-brown and gray instead of black and white. Bill of all birds is flesh-colored. Song is a series of 6 whistled notes, sounding lazy and wheezy, which rises on the second and third notes and falls on the last 3 notes.

Habitat: Forest edges and brush patches. Nests on the ground in grass clumps or low shrubs.

Notes: Often travels with Golden-crowned Sparrows in migration. Readily comes to feeders.

WHITE-CROWNED SPARROW

Harris' Sparrow

(Zonotrichia querula)
Length: 7¹/₂ in.

Identification: Large, long-tailed; easily
recognized by black crown, face and throat,
streaked sides, and otherwise white underparts. Immature and winter birds have much
less black, often restricted to a dark blotch
on the upper breast. Only other large,
streaked sparrows are the Song Sparrow
and Fox Sparrow, both of which are much
more heavily streaked below.

Status & Distribution	Spring	Summer	Fall	Winter	Breeder	Key
Southeastern	R	–	R	R		C Common
Southcoastal	A	–	A	A		U Uncommon
Southwestern	–	–	–	–		R Rare
Central	–	–	–	–		A Casual/Accidental
Western	–	–	–	–		– No Records
Northern	A	A	–	–		

Habitat: Has occurred mostly at feeders in
southeastern Alaska. Not known to breed in
Alaska.

HARRIS' SPARROW

Dark-eyed Junco
(Junco hyemalis)
Length: 5 1/2 in.

Identification: Adult has no streaks, wing bars or head markings. Has flashy white outer tail feathers especially conspicuous in flight. Juncos breeding north of Yakutat Bay are all slate gray with a white belly; those from Yakutat Bay south have a black (male) or gray (female) hood, reddish-brown back and buffy-pink sides. The 2 subspecies have been called Slate-colored and Oregon respectively. Fledgling is colored like an adult but is heavily streaked. Song is a loud, musical trill all on 1 pitch.

Habitat: Breeding — coniferous forests and forest edges, clearings, muskegs. Nests on the ground. In winter — easily attracted to feeders. Both Slate-colored and Oregon subspecies occur together in southeastern Alaska when not breeding.

DARK-EYED JUNCO, *Slate-colored Subspecies*

Status & Distribution	Spring	Summer	Fall	Winter	Breeder	Key
Southeastern	C	C	C	U	•	C Common
Southcoastal	U	U	U	U	•	U Uncommon
Southwestern	U	U	U	R	•	R Rare
Central	C	C	C	R	•	A Casual/Accidental
Western	U	U	U	–	•	– No Records
Northern	A	R	R	–	•	

DARK-EYED JUNCO, *Oregon Subspecies, Male*

Lapland Longspur
(Calcarius lapponicus)
Length: 6 ½ in.

Identification: Breeding male has black crown, face and breast and chestnut hind neck. Female is more nondescript, like many sparrows, but usually is accompanied by a male. Savannah Sparrow might be mistaken for a longspur, but the sparrow is smaller, with heavily streaked breast and no white in the tail. Autumn male is colored like a female. In flight appears bulkier and shorter tailed than a lark or pipit and flies in tighter, faster flocks. Song is beautiful series of tinkling notes given in flight. Call on the breeding grounds is a liquid *teew*; migrants utter a dry rattle.

Status & Distribution	Spring	Summer	Fall	Winter	Breeder	Key
Southeastern	C	–	C	A		C Common
Southcoastal	U	R	U	A	•	U Uncommon
Southwestern	C	C	C	A	•	R Rare
Central	C	C	C	–	•	A Casual/Accidental
Western	C	C	C	–	•	– No Records
Northern	C	C	C	–	•	

Habitat: Breeding — tundra. Nests on small clumps of grass or dry knolls. In migration — grassy fields, wetlands, alpine meadows and ridges.

Notes: One of the most common and widespread breeding land birds on the tundra. In migration often associated with Horned Larks and Snow Buntings. All longspurs spend much time on the ground and usually run or walk instead of hopping.

LAPLAND LONGSPUR, *Male, Breeding*

Smith's Longspur

(Calcarius pictus)
Length: 6 in.

Identification: Distinguished from the Lapland Longspur and other open-country birds by buffy underparts, brighter in summer. Breeding male has conspicuous black-and-white head pattern. Song is warblerlike, with sweet notes. Call on breeding grounds is distinct 2-note rattle.

Status & Distribution	Spring	Summer	Fall	Winter	Breeder	Key
Southeastern	A	–	A	–		C Common
Southcoastal	–	–	–	–		U Uncommon
Southwestern	–	–	–	–		R Rare
Central	R	R	R	–	•	A Casual/Accidental
Western	–	–	–	–		– No Records
Northern	U	U	U	–	•	

Habitat: Brooks Range — damp tussock meadow, usually on wide alpine valley floors, often on flat meadows surrounding lakes. Central Alaska — dry ridgetop tundra. Nests on the ground.

Notes: Far less abundant in Alaska than Lapland Longspur. Sings from the ground, rather than from the air like Lapland Longspur.

SMITH'S LONGSPUR, *Male, Breeding*

Little Bunting

(Emberiza pusilla)
Length: 4³/₄ in.

Identification: Breeding-plumaged male has a rufous medium stripe on its crown, rufous eyebrow and cheek outlined with black. Females and immatures also have the rufous coloration, but the head pattern is duller.

Status & Distribution	Spring	Summer	Fall	Winter	Breeder	Key
Southeastern	–	–	–	–		C Common
Southcoastal	–	–	–	–		U Uncommon
Southwestern	–	–	A	–		R Rare
Central	–	–	–	–		A Casual/Accidental
Western	–	–	–	–		– No Records
Northern	–	–	A	–		

Habitat: Prefers shrubs bordering open tundra. This bunting is native to northern Eurasia. Has been seen at Chukchi Sea and at Attu and Shemya islands in the Aleutian Islands.

LITTLE BUNTING, *Winter*

LITTLE BUNTING, *Summer*

Rustic Bunting

(Emberiza rustica)
Length: 5 ³/₄ in.

Identification: An Old World bunting, more brightly marked about the head than New World sparrows. Summer male has black top and sides of the head, a white eye-stripe behind the eye, white throat and underparts and narrow rusty breast band. Female and winter male are similarly rusty, with a band of rusty streaks on the breast and sides. Female and winter male Lapland Longspur have darker streaks and never show the slight crest of Rustic Bunting. Call is sharp *tsip, tsip, tsip.*

Status & Distribution	Spring	Summer	Fall	Winter	Breeder	Key
Southeastern	–	–	–	–		C Common
Southcoastal	A	–	–	–		U Uncommon
Southwestern	R	–	R	–		R Rare
Central	–	–	–	–		A Casual/Accidental
Western	A	–	–	–		– No Records
Northern	–	–	–	–		

Habitat: Asiatic bunting that has occurred in the western and central Aleutian Islands and at Gambell on Saint Lawrence Island. Not known to breed in Alaska.

Notes: Buntings, like sparrows, hop; long-spurs walk or run.

RUSTIC BUNTING, *Male, Breeding*

Gray Bunting
(Emberiza variabilis)
Length: 6 in.

Identification: Breeding-plumaged males distinctive dark slate gray. Winter males have dark brown back with black streaks. Females are dark brown above, paler below; very similar to other female buntings but lack the white in the tail of other species. In flight, females and immature males best distinguished by chestnut-colored rump.

Status & Distribution	Spring	Summer	Fall	Winter	Breeder	Key
Southeastern	–	–	–	–		C Common
Southcoastal	–	–	–	–		U Uncommon
Southwestern	A	–	–	–		R Rare
Central	–	–	–	–		A Casual/Accidental
Western	–	–	–	–		– No Records
Northern	–	–	–	–		

Habitat: Has been found in western Aleutians on Attu and Shemya islands. Breeds in northeast Asia.

GRAY BUNTING, *Male, Breeding*

Pallas' Reed-Bunting

(Emberiza pallasi)
Length: 5¹/₂ in.

Identification: Very similar to Common Reed-Bunting but smaller. Male has a more extensive black throat and a pale yellow rather than white nape. Female has less rusty edges to the wing and back feathers. Bill is more slender and pointed than in the Common Reed-Bunting.

Status & Distribution	Spring	Summer	Fall	Winter	Breeder	Key
Southeastern	–	–	–	–		C Common
Southcoastal	–	–	–	–		U Uncommon
Southwestern	–	–	–	–		R Rare
Central	–	–	–	–		A Casual/Accidental
Western	A	–	–	–		– No Records
Northern	A	–	–	–		

Habitat: Asiatic bunting that has been found at Barrow and at Gambell on Saint Lawrence Island. Not known to breed in Alaska.

PALLAS' REED-BUNTING, *Male, Breeding*

Common Reed-Bunting

(Emberiza schoeniclus)
Length: 6 in.

Identification: Entire head and throat are black except for a white line extending back and down from the bill and a white hind neck. Female and winter male are heavily streaked, longer tailed than longspurs and lack the reddish nape patch and pale crown stripe of the Lapland Longspur. Call is loud *tseek,* somewhat like that of the Yellow Wagtail.

Status & Distribution	Spring	Summer	Fall	Winter	Breeder	Key
Southeastern	–	–	–	–		C Common
Southcoastal	–	–	–	–		U Uncommon
Southwestern	A	–	–	–		R Rare
Central	–	–	–	–		A Casual/Accidental
Western	–	–	–	–		– No Records
Northern	–	–	–	–		

Habitat: Asiatic bunting that has occurred in the western Aleutian Islands. Not known to breed in Alaska.

COMMON REED-BUNTING, *Male, Breeding*

Snow Bunting
(Plectrophenax nivalis)
Length: 6 1/2 in.

Identification: Whitest small bird found in Alaska except for McKay's Bunting. Striking black-and-white plumage of breeding male is unmistakable. Breeding female and all winter birds have more brown, but in flight show extensive white in the wings and tail. Song is short musical warble, often with some phrases repeated, and is given on the ground or in flight.

Habitat: Breeding — tundra. Coastline of northern, western and southwestern Alaska. Nests in various locations including buildings, empty gas drums and bird houses. In mountains — nests beneath rocks or in rock crevices. In migration and winter — prefers open fields, shoreline, roadsides.

SNOW BUNTING, *Male, Breeding*

Status & Distribution	Spring	Summer	Fall	Winter	Breeder	Key
Southeastern	U	R	U	U	•	C Common
Southcoastal	U	R	U	R	•	U Uncommon
Southwestern	C	C	C	C	•	R Rare
Central	C	U	U	R	•	A Casual/Accidental
Western	C	C	C	U	•	– No Records
Northern	C	C	C	–	•	

McKay's Bunting
(Plectrophenax hyperboreus)
Length: 7 in.

Identification: Breeding male is mostly white except for black wing tips and black on the tip of the central tail feathers. Female and winter birds show some brown on the back; more black in the wings but much less than the Snow Bunting. Song is loud and warbling. Call is a musical rattle.

Habitat: Breeding — islands of the Bering Sea, where nests in small depressions on the ground or in rock crevices. In migration and winter — mainland bordering the Bering Sea.

McKAY'S BUNTING, *Male, Breeding*

Status & Distribution	Spring	Summer	Fall	Winter	Breeder	Key
Southeastern	–	–	–	–		C Common
Southcoastal	–	–	–	A		U Uncommon
Southwestern	U	R	U	U	•	R Rare
Central	–	–	–	–		A Casual/Accidental
Western	R	R	R	R	•	– No Records
Northern	–	–	–	–		

Red-winged Blackbird

(Agelaius phoeniceus)
Length: 8 in.

Identification: Has red shoulder patch. When perched, the red may be concealed, but the buffy rear border of the patch is usually visible. Female is dark above and light below; heavily streaked all over. Pointed bill distinguishes the female from vaguely similar sparrows. Young male is the size of an adult (considerably larger than a female), but mottled with brown and with duller shoulder patches. Song is loud, liquid, ringing *ok-a-lee*; common call is *chuck* and a thin *teeyee*.

Habitat: Freshwater marshes and water edges with thick vegetation. Nests in shoreline vegetation or bushes.

Notes: This species is either increasing in Alaska or more observations make it seem to be. Gabrielson and Lincoln (1959) list only 3 specimens for Alaska. However, in recent years many sightings have been made, and they have been reported from all but the southwestern region (Kessel and Gibson, 1978).

RED-WINGED BLACKBIRD, *Female*

Status & Distribution	Spring	Summer	Fall	Winter	Breeder	Key
Southeastern	U	U	U	R	•	C Common
Southcoastal	R	R	R	–	•	U Uncommon
Southwestern	–	–	–	–		R Rare
Central	U	U	U	A	•	A Casual/Accidental
Western	–	A	A	–		– No Records
Northern	A	A	–	–		

RED-WINGED BLACKBIRD, *Male*

Western Meadowlark

(Sturnella neglecta)
Length: 10 in.

Identification: Shaped like a Starling, streaked brown and white above, with a short tail bearing conspicuous white edges. Mostly yellow below, with a conspicuous black "V" on the breast.

Habitat: Has occurred at Craig, Juneau and Ketchikan in southeastern Alaska and in the Brooks Range at Anaktuvuk Pass. An open-country ground bird. Not known to breed in Alaska.

Status & Distribution	Spring	Summer	Fall	Winter	Breeder	Key
Southeastern	–	–	A	A		C Common
Southcoastal	–	–	A	–		U Uncommon
Southwestern	–	–	–	–		R Rare
Central	–	–	–	–		A Casual/Accidental
Western	–	–	–	–		– No Records
Northern	–	–	A	–		

WESTERN MEADOWLARK, *Breeding*

Yellow-headed Blackbird

(Xanthocephalus xanthocephalus)
Length: 10¹/₂ in.

Identification: Male has entirely yellow head and neck, and white wing patch conspicuous in flight. Female is considerably smaller; brown with a yellow throat and breast.

Status & Distribution	Spring	Summer	Fall	Winter	Breeder	Key
Southeastern	A	–	A	–		C Common
Southcoastal	–	A	A	–		U Uncommon
Southwestern	–	–	–	–		R Rare
Central	–	A	A	–		A Casual/Accidental
Western	–	–	A	–		– No Records
Northern	–	A	–	–		

Habitat: Has been found at Fairbanks, Barrow, Juneau and near Cordova. Not known to breed in Alaska.

YELLOW-HEADED BLACKBIRD, *Male*

YELLOW-HEADED BLACKBIRD, *Female*

Rusty Blackbird

(Euphagus carolinus)
Length: 9 in.

Identification: Has conspicuous yellow
eyes. Adult male is black, without iridescence. Adult female is slate-colored. Adult
and young in winter have close, rust-colored
bars, especially on the undersides. Song is
short and ends with a note sounding like a
squeaky hinge; call is a harsh *chack*.

RUSTY BLACKBIRD, *Female*

Status & Distribution	Spring	Summer	Fall	Winter	Breeder	Key
Southeastern	U	R	U	R	•	C Common
Southcoastal	U	R	U	R	•	U Uncommon
Southwestern	U	U	U	–	•	R Rare
Central	U	U	U	R	•	A Casual/Accidental
Western	U	U	U	–	•	– No Records
Northern	R	R	R	–	•	

Habitat: Willow thickets near rivers in
coastal areas. Swampy areas inland. Nests in
conifers, willows or alders near water. After
nesting season may frequent garbage dumps.

RUSTY BLACKBIRD, *Male*

Brewer's Blackbird

(Euphagus cyanocephalus)
Length: 9 in.

Identification: Male is black with whitish eye; female is brownish-gray with dark eye. Female Brewer's and Rusty blackbirds are best distinguished from one another by eye color; dark in Brewer's, yellow in Rusty. Male Brewer's may show purplish reflection on the head; male Rusty may show dull greenish reflections, but these are hard to see. In winter, Brewer's lacks extensive rusty color of Rusty Blackbird.

Status & Distribution	Spring	Summer	Fall	Winter	Breeder	Key
Southeastern	A	–	A	A		C Common
Southcoastal	–	–	–	–		U Uncommon
Southwestern	–	–	–	–		R Rare
Central	–	–	–	–		A Casual/Accidental
Western	–	–	–	–		– No Records
Northern	–	A	–	–		

Habitat: Has been found at Point Barrow in northern Alaska and in southeastern Alaska.

BREWER'S BLACKBIRD, *Male*

BREWER'S BLACKBIRD, *Female*

Common Grackle
(Quiscalus quiscula)
Length: 12 in.

Identification: Has a yellow eye. Both sexes are conspicuously iridescent like the male Brewer's Blackbird. Larger size, much longer and heavier bill, and long, wedge-shaped tail, which is noticeably lengthened in males, are distinctive.

Status & Distribution	Spring	Summer	Fall	Winter	Breeder	Key
Southeastern	–	–	A	–		C Common
Southcoastal	–	–	A	–		U Uncommon
Southwestern	–	–	–	–		R Rare
Central	A	A	–	–		A Casual/Accidental
Western	–	A	–	–		– No Records
Northern	–	A	–	–		

Habitat: Open places, fields, marshes, shores, wet woodlands. Not known to breed in Alaska.

COMMON GRACKLE

Brown-headed Cowbird
(Molothrus ater)
Length: 7 in.

Identification: Has finchlike bill. Male is shiny black with a brown head. Female is entirely brownish-gray. Only a young rosy finch is as plain, and it has wing bars. Young are light brown, obscurely streaked. Song of male is a variety of high, squeaking whistles and gurgling notes. Female gives a rattling call and soft *tsip*.

Status & Distribution	Spring	Summer	Fall	Winter	Breeder	Key
Southeastern	R	R	R	A	•	C Common
Southcoastal	–	A	A	A		U Uncommon
Southwestern	–	–	A	–		R Rare
Central	A	A	A	–		A Casual/Accidental
Western	–	A	A	–		– No Records
Northern	–	A	A	–		

Habitat: Open woodlands, fields, pastures. Often associated with horses and cows; cowbird feeds upon insects stirred up by the hoofed animals. Lays eggs in nests of other small birds.

BROWN-HEADED COWBIRD, *Female*

BROWN-HEADED COWBIRD, *Male*

Family *Fringillidae*
FINCHES
(14 + 2)

Members of the finch family have a short, heavy, conical beak, which is used for cracking seeds, their main food. They also eat insects and berries.

Brambling
(Fringilla montifringilla)
Length: 5³/₄ in.

Identification: Small finch with a conspicuous white rump, rusty or orange breast and white wing bars in any plumage. Summer male is contrastingly marked with black head, back, wings and tail. Winter male and all females are duller, with gray to brown streaked head and back. Flight call is *tchuck, tchuck*; another common call is a harsh *tsweep*.

Status & Distribution	Spring	Summer	Fall	Winter	Breeder	Key
Southeastern	A	–	A	A		C Common
Southcoastal	A	–	A	A		U Uncommon
Southwestern	R	–	R	–		R Rare
Central	–	–	–	–		A Casual/Accidental
Western	A	–	–	–		– No Records
Northern	A	–	A	–		

Habitat: Asiatic finch that has been found mostly in the western and central Aleutian Islands. Other sightings have occurred in the Pribilof Islands and at many communities in coastal Alaska. Not known to breed in Alaska.

BRAMBLING, *Winter*

Rosy Finch

(Leucosticte arctoa)
Length: 6 in.

Identification: Dark brown with rosy wash on wings, belly and rump. Head is mostly gray in male from southern Alaska; an interior bird has gray only bordering the crown from behind. Female is duller, with much less gray on head than male. In late summer immatures, entirely dull brown with buffy wing bars, can be confusing. Song is canarylike warble. Flying flocks give harsh *cheep, cheep* notes.

Status & Distribution	Spring	Summer	Fall	Winter	Breeder	Key
Southeastern	U	U	U	R	•	C Common
Southcoastal	U	U	U	R	•	U Uncommon
Southwestern	C	C	C	C	•	R Rare
Central	U	U	U	A	•	A Casual/Accidental
Western	U	U	U	–	•	– No Records
Northern	R	R	R	–	•	

ROSY FINCH

Habitat: Alpine tundra, mountain ridges above timberline, near snowfields. Beaches in the Aleutian Islands and Bering Sea islands. Nests in cliff crevices or rock slides. In winter — lower elevations, often seen in flocks near towns.

Pine Grosbeak
(Pinicola enucleator)
Length: 9 in.

Identification: Plump, stocky, about the size of a robin, appearing slim and long-tailed in flight overhead. Male is rosy red with gray belly and 2 conspicuous white wing bars. Female is gray with white wing bars, but head and rump are tinged with yellow instead of the red found in adult male. Song is a 3-note whistle similar to that of the Greater Yellowlegs.

Status & Distribution	Spring	Summer	Fall	Winter	Breeder	Key
Southeastern	U	U	C	C	•	C Common
Southcoastal	U	U	U	U	•	U Uncommon
Southwestern	U	U	U	U	•	R Rare
Central	U	U	U	U	•	A Casual/Accidental
Western	U	U	U	U	•	– No Records
Northern	R	R	R	–		

Habitat: Coniferous forests. Nests in conifers, usually not more than 10 to 15 feet above ground. In winter travels in flocks and feeds on buds and fruits of trees. Fond of Mountain Ash berries.

PINE GROSBEAK, *Female*

PINE GROSBEAK, *Male*

Common Rosefinch
(Carpodacus erythrinus)
Length: 5 ³/₄ in.

Identification: Males are rosy below and brown above. Female is brown above, obscurely streaked with brown below. Both sexes have 2 obscure wing bars. Call is soft and 2-syllabled, rising at the end to a squeak.

Status & Distribution	Spring	Summer	Fall	Winter	Breeder	Key
Southeastern	–	–	–	–		C Common
Southcoastal	–	–	–	–		U Uncommon
Southwestern	R	A	A	–		R Rare
Central	–	–	–	–		A Casual/Accidental
Western	R	–	–	–		– No Records
Northern	–	–	–	–		

Habitat: Asiatic finch that has been found mostly on Saint Lawrence Island and in Aleutian Islands. Not known to breed in Alaska.

COMMON ROSEFINCH, *Male*

Purple Finch

(Carpodacus purpureus)
Length: 6 in.

Identification: Similar to Common
Rosefinch, but male is more distinctly
streaked above, and female is more distinctly
streaked all over with a conspicuous white
eye-line. The 2 finches are unlikely to occur
in the same regions. Flight call is sharp *tip*.

Status & Distribution	Spring	Summer	Fall	Winter	Breeder	Key
Southeastern	A	A	A	A		C Common
Southcoastal	A	–	A	A		U Uncommon
Southwestern	–	–	–	–		R Rare
Central	–	–	–	–		A Casual/Accidental
Western	–	–	–	–		– No Records
Northern	–	–	–	–		

PURPLE FINCH, *Female*

Habitat: Has occurred in Homer, Middleton Island, Juneau and Ketchikan. Not
known to breed in Alaska.

PURPLE FINCH, *Male*

Red Crossbill

(Loxia curvirostra)
Length: 6 in.

Identification: Large-headed and heavy-billed, with crossed mandibles and stubby tail. Male is brick red and female dull olive-gray with a yellowish rump. Immature is striped above and below. Call is repeated *kip-kip* or *jeep-jeep* and whistled notes sometimes interspersed with warbled passages.

Status & Distribution	Spring	Summer	Fall	Winter	Breeder	Key
Southeastern	C	C	C	C	•	C Common
Southcoastal	R	R	R	R	•	U Uncommon
Southwestern	–	R	A	–		R Rare
Central	–	–	A	–		A Casual/Accidental
Western	–	–	A	–		– No Records
Northern	–	–	–	–		

Habitat: Coniferous forests. Nests in conifers, usually well out on branches. May nest almost any time of the year.

Notes: Often hangs upside down on conifer cones. Flies in flocks and feeds on seeds of conifers that are extracted by the specialized bill and tongue. Number of birds varies with abundance of the cone crop. Often feeds quietly in tree tops or flies high in the air between trees, so presence can only be detected by call.

RED CROSSBILL, Female

RED CROSSBILL, Male

White-winged Crossbill

(Loxia leucoptera)
Length: 6 in.

Identification: Similar to Red Crossbill, but both sexes have conspicuous white wing bars. Male is a much pinker red than male Red Crossbill, more like color of a Pine Grosbeak. Song is variable, melodious, with warbling trilling; flight call is soft *twee* or a loud, harsh *cheet, cheet.*

Habitat: Coniferous forests. Nests in conifers from 5 to 80 feet up. May nest almost any time of the year.

Status & Distribution	Spring	Summer	Fall	Winter	Breeder	Key
Southeastern	C	C	C	C	•	C Common
Southcoastal	U	U	U	U	•	U Uncommon
Southwestern	U	U	U	U	•	R Rare
Central	U	U	U	U	•	A Casual/Accidental
Western	U	U	U	U	•	– No Records
Northern	–	–	A	–		

Notes: Usually seen in small flocks feeding near the tops of spruce trees. Numbers may fluctuate considerably from one year to the next, depending on the cone crop.

WHITE-WINGED CROSSBILL, *Female*

Common Redpoll

(Carduelis flammea)
Length: 5 in.

Identification: Stubby-billed finch with bright red cap, blackish chin and dark streaks on the sides. Adult male often has pinkish wash on the breast. Larger bill than the Hoary Redpoll. Song is a trill, followed by a rattling *chit-chit-chit-chit;* call is loud *chit-chit-chit-chit* and a *swee-e-et,* often given in flight.

Habitat: Tundra shrub thickets, mixed deciduous-coniferous woodlands, open fields and grasslands, near cities and towns especially in winter. Nests on the ground or in lower branches of bushes. May be found with Hoary Redpoll at any time of the year.

Notes: In most of Alaska outnumbers the Hoary Redpoll, but in some Arctic localities the reverse may be true. Redpolls have an enlarged esophagus that acts similar to a crop, a feature that birds of this family do not normally have. This allows them to take in more food in winter and digest it through the night.

COMMON REDPOLL

Status & Distribution	Spring	Summer	Fall	Winter	Breeder	Key
Southeastern	C	U	C	C	•	C Common
Southcoastal	C	U	U	C	•	U Uncommon
Southwestern	C	C	C	C	•	R Rare
Central	C	C	C	C	•	A Casual/Accidental
Western	C	C	C	C	•	– No Records
Northern	U	U	U	–	•	

Hoary Redpoll

(Carduelis hornemanni)
Length: 5 1/2 in.

Identification: Stubby-billed finch with bright red cap, blackish chin and dark streaks on the sides. Adult male often shows a pinkish suffusion on the breast. Paler than Common Redpoll on the average, but there is much overlap. Has a pure white rump with no streaking, unstreaked under tail coverts. Configuration of head and very short bill make the face look pushed in. Bill is smaller than that of Common Redpoll. Song is a trill, followed by rattling *chit-chit-chit-chit*; call is loud *chit-chit-chit-chit* and a *swee-e-et*, often given in flight.

Habitat: Tundra shrub thickets, mixed deciduous-coniferous woodlands, open fields and grasslands, near cities and villages especially in winter. Nests on the ground or in the lower branches of bushes. May be found with Common Redpoll at any time of the year.

Status & Distribution	Spring	Summer	Fall	Winter	Breeder	Key
Southeastern	–	–	–	R		C Common
Southcoastal	R	–	–	R		U Uncommon
Southwestern	U	–	U	C		R Rare
Central	C	R	U	C	•	A Casual/Accidental
Western	C	C	C	C	•	– No Records
Northern	C	C	C	–	•	

HOARY REDPOLL

Pine Siskin
(Carduelis pinus)
Length: 5 in.

Identification: Streaked finch with a touch of yellow on the wings and tail base. Even if the yellow is not visible, siskin is smaller than any sparrow and more heavily streaked than any redpoll. Presence usually detected by long, buzzy *schhrreeee*; in flight utters a scratchy *shick-shick* and a thin *tseee*.

Habitat: Coniferous forests. Nests in conifers, usually well out on branches. During non-nesting season may be found in deciduous trees and on the ground.

Status & Distribution	Spring	Summer	Fall	Winter	Breeder	Key
Southeastern	C	C	C	C	•	C Common
Southcoastal	C	C	C	U	•	U Uncommon
Southwestern	A	A	A	–		R Rare
Central	R	R	R	A	•	A Casual/Accidental
Western	A	A	–	–		– No Records
Northern	–	A	–	–		

Notes: Unlike sparrows, roams in tight flocks searching for plant seeds. Nesting is erratic and may occur during many months.

PINE SISKIN

Oriental Greenfinch
(Carduelis sinica)
Length: 6 in.

Identification: Has bright-yellow patches on wings and tail. Male has a gray crown and nape with yellowish-green cheeks and throat and a brown body with greenish-yellow rump. Female is light brown, with yellow wing and tail patches. Call is thin, metallic tinkle.

Status & Distribution	Spring	Summer	Fall	Winter	Breeder	Key
Southeastern	–	–	–	–		C Common
Southcoastal	–	–	–	–		U Uncommon
Southwestern	A	–	A	–		R Rare
Central	–	–	–	–		A Casual/Accidental
Western	–	–	–	–		– No Records
Northern	–	–	–	–		

Habitat: Asiatic finch that has occurred in the western Aleutian Islands. Not known to nest in Alaska.

ORIENTAL GREENFINCH, *Male*

Eurasian Bullfinch
(Pyrrhula pyrrhula)
Length: 5³/₄ in.

Identification: Slightly stouter with distinctly shorter, stouter bill than Brambling. Has a black cap and white rump and wing bars in all plumages. Male is gray above, rosy below. Female is dull brownish above, more buffy below. Movements are slow and deliberate. Call is soft, piping whistle.

Status & Distribution	Spring	Summer	Fall	Winter	Breeder	Key
Southeastern	–	–	–	A		C Common
Southcoastal	–	–	A	A		U Uncommon
Southwestern	A	–	A	–		R Rare
Central	–	–	–	A		A Casual/Accidental
Western	A	–	A	A		– No Records
Northern	–	–	–	–		

Habitat: Asiatic finch that has been found mostly on Bering Sea islands and western Aleutian Islands. Has occurred at Nulato, Anchorage and Petersburg. Not known to breed in Alaska.

EURASIAN BULLFINCH, *Male*

Evening Grosbeak
(Coccothraustes vespertinus)
Length: 7 1/2 in.

Identification: Size and shape of the
Hawfinch. Bill is large and pale greenish
to ivory. Male is brown and yellow, with a
conspicuous yellow eye-line and black wings
with large white bases. Female is duller,
gray-brown with less white in the wings.
Loud, ringing call is often a clue to the
presence of these nomadic birds.

Status & Distribution	Spring	Summer	Fall	Winter	Breeder	Key
Southeastern	A	–	A	A		C Common
Southcoastal	–	–	–	–		U Uncommon
Southwestern	–	–	–	–		R Rare
Central	–	–	A	A		A Casual/Accidental
Western	–	–	–	–		– No Records
Northern	–	–	–	–		

Habitat: Has been found at Sitka,
Ketchikan and Juneau in southeastern
Alaska. Not known to breed in Alaska.

EVENING GROSBEAK, *Female*

EVENING GROSBEAK, *Male*

Hawfinch

(Coccothraustes coccothraustes)
Length: 7 in.

Identification: Stocky and short-tailed with a huge, gray bill. Built like Evening Grosbeak, to which it is closely related. Brown with black wings and conspicuous white patches on the shoulder and in the primaries. Tail is brown with a white tip. Call is a loud, metallic *tik*.

Status & Distribution	Spring	Summer	Fall	Winter	Breeder	Key
Southeastern	–	–	–	–		C Common
Southcoastal	–	–	–	–		U Uncommon
Southwestern	A	A	A	–		R Rare
Central	–	–	–	–		A Casual/Accidental
Western	A	–	–	–		– No Records
Northern	–	–	–	–		

Habitat: Asiatic finch found in the western and central Aleutian Islands and in the Pribilof Islands. Not known to breed in Alaska.

HAWFINCH

ACCIDENTALS

ACCIDENTALS

"Accidentals" are species that have been recorded only a time or two in Alaska. These birds are far from their normal range and further observations are unlikely.

Cook's Petrel *(Pterodroma cookii)*. Central Aleutian Islands.

American White Pelican *(Pelecanus erythrorhynchos)*. Petersburg.

Magnificent Frigatebird *(Fregata magnificens)*. Alaska Peninsula; Kodiak Island; Prince William Sound; Gulf of Alaska.

Chinese Little Bittern *(Ixobrychus sinensis)*. Attu Island, Aleutian Islands.

Chinese Egret *(Egretta eulophotes)*. Agattu Island, Aleutian Islands.

Snowy Egret *(Egretta thula)*. Juneau.

Green-backed Heron *(Butorides striatus)*. Juneau.

Spot-billed Duck *(Anas poecilorhyncha)*. Adak Island, Aleutian Islands; Kodiak Island.

Virginia Rail *(Rallus limicola)*. Klawock, Prince of Wales Island, southeastern Alaska.

Eurasian Coot *(Fulica atra)*. Pribilof Islands.

Common Crane *(Grus grus)*. Fairbanks.

Black-winged Stilt *(Himantopus himantopus)*. Nizki Island, Aleutian Islands.

American Avocet *(Recurvirostra americana)*. Valdez.

Oriental Pratincole *(Glareola maldivarum)*. Attu Island, Aleutian Islands; Gambell, Saint Lawrence Island.

Marsh Sandpiper *(Tringa stagnatilis)*. Buldir Island, Aleutian Islands.

Willet *(Catoptrophorus semipalmatus)*. Minto Lakes west of Fairbanks.

Eskimo Curlew *(Numenius borealis)*. Formerly western and northern Alaska (not seen since 1886).

Little Curlew *(Numenius minutus)*. Gambell, Saint Lawrence Island.

Jack Snipe *(Lymnocryptes minimus)*. Pribilof Islands.

Black-tailed Gull *(Larus crassirostris)*. Saint Lawrence Island; Attu Island, Aleutian Islands.

Western Gull *(Larus occidentalis)*. Bristol Bay.

Forster's Tern *(Sterna forsteri)*. Yukon Delta.

White-winged Tern *(Chlidonias leucopterus)*. Nizki Island, Aleutian Islands.

Rufous Turtle Dove *(Streptopelia orientalis)*. Attu Island, Aleutian Islands.

White-winged Dove *(Zenaida asiatica)*. Skagway.

Oriental Scops-Owl *(Otus sunia)*. Buldir and Amchitka Islands, Aleutian Islands.

Whip-poor-will *(Caprimulgus vociferus)*. Kupreanof Island, southeastern Alaska.

Jungle Nightjar *(Caprimulgus indicus)*. Buldir Island, Aleutian Islands.

Chimney Swift *(Chaetura pelagica)*. Saint George Island.

Common Swift *(Apus apus)*. Pribilof Islands.

Ruby-throated Hummingbird *(Archilochus colubris)*. Saint Michael.

Costa's Hummingbird *(Calypte costae)*. Anchorage.

Hoopoe *(Upupa epops)*. Old Chevak.

Eurasian Wryneck *(Jynx torquilla)*. Wales.

Great Spotted Woodpecker *(Dendrocopos major)*. Attu Island, Aleutian Islands.

Willow Flycatcher *(Empidonax traillii)*. Hyder; Juneau; Anchorage.

Great Tit *(Paris major)*. Little Diomede Island, Bering Strait.

Lanceolated Warbler *(Locustella lanceolata)*. Attu Island, Aleutian Islands.

Wood Warbler *(Phylloscopus sibilatrix)*. Shemya Island, Aleutian Islands.

Narcissus Flycatcher *(Ficedula narcissina)*. Attu Island, Aleutian Islands.

Asian Brown Flycatcher *(Muscicapa dauurica)*. Attu Island, Aleutian Islands.

Siberian Blue Robin *(Luscinia cyane)*. Attu Island, Aleutian Islands.

Stonechat *(Saxicola torquata)*. Gambell, Saint Lawrence Island.

Brown Thrasher *(Toxostoma rufum)*. Point Barrow; Point Lay.

Brown Tree-Pipit *(Anthus trivialis)*. Wales.

Solitary Vireo *(Vireo solitarius)*. Hyder.

Northern Parula *(Parula americana)*. Middleton Island, southcoastal Alaska.

Black-throated Green Warbler *(Dendroica virens)*. Chichagof Island.

Prairie Warbler *(Dendroica discolor)*. Middleton Island.

Bay-breasted Warbler *(Dendroica castanea)*. Fairbanks.

Black-and-white Warbler *(Mniotilta varia)*. Colville River.

Ovenbird *(Seiurus aurocapillus)*. Prudhoe Bay; Fairbanks.

Kentucky Warbler *(Oporornis formosus)*. Beaufort Lagoon.

Mourning Warbler *(Oporornis philadelphia)*. Middleton Island.

Canada Warbler *(Wilsonia canadensis)*. Point Barrow; Prudhoe Bay.

Scarlet Tanager *(Piranga olivacea)*. Point Barrow.

Rose-breasted Grosbeak *(Pheucticus chrysopeplus)*. Annette Island, southeastern Alaska; Petersburg.

Blue Grosbeak *(Guiraca caerulea)*. Petersburg.

Rufous-sided Towhee *(Pipilo erythrophthalmus)*. Juneau.

Clay-colored Sparrow *(Spizella pallida)*. Stikine River; Arctic Wildlife Refuge.

Yellow-breasted Bunting *(Emberiza aureola)*. Attu Island, Aleutian Islands.

Bobolink *(Dolichonyx oryzivorus)*. Point Barrow.

Northern Oriole *(Icterus galbula)*. Petersburg.

Cassin's Finch *(Carpodacus cassinii)*. Homer.

House Sparrow *(Passer domesticus)*. Petersburg.

ARCTIC TERN

BIBLIOGRAPHY

American Birding Association. *A.B.A. Checklist: Birds of Continental United States and Canada*. 2nd ed., Austin, Texas,1982.

American Ornithologists' Union. *Check-list of North American Birds*. 6th ed., Allen Press, Lawrence, Kansas, 1983.

————. "Thirty-fifth Supplement to the American Ornithologist's Union Check-list of North American Birds." *Auk* 102:680–686, 1985.

————. "Thirty-sixth Supplement to the American Ornithologist's Union Check-list of North American Birds." *Auk* 104:591–596, 1987.

————. "Thirty-seventh Supplement to the American Ornithologist's Union Check-list of North American Birds." *Auk* 106:532–538, 1989.

Anchorage Audubon Society. *Birds of Anchorage, Alaska: A Checklist*. Anchorage, 1978.

Bellrose, F. C. *Ducks, Geese and Swans of North America*. Wildlife Management Institute, Washington, D.C., 1976.

Bent, A. C. *Life Histories of North American Birds*. U.S. National Museum Bulletins 107, 113, 121, 126, 130, 135, 142, 146, 162, 167, 170, 174, 176, 179, 191, 195, 196, 197, 203, 211 and 237. 1919–1958.

Clark, W. S. "The Field Identification of North American Eagles." *American Birds* 37(5):822–826, 1983.

Clements, J. *Birds of the World: A Checklist*. Facts on File, Inc., New York, 1981.

Dement'ev, G. P., and N. A. Gladkov, eds. *Birds of the Soviet Union*. Vol. 6, 1954. Translated by Israel Program for Scientific Translation. U.S. Department of the Interior and National Science Foundation, Washington, D.C., 1968.

Farrand, J., Jr., ed. *The Audubon Society Master Guide to Birding*. Alfred A. Knopf, New York, 1983.

Gabrielson, I. N., and F. C. Lincoln. *The Birds of Alaska*. The Stackpole Company, Harrisburg, Pa.; and Wildlife Management Institute, Washington, D.C., 1959.

Gibson, D. D. *Alaska Region, American Birds*, for the years 1978–1986.

————. *Checklist of Alaska Birds*. University of Alaska Museum, Fairbanks, 1977.

————. *Checklist of Alaska Birds*. University of Alaska Museum, Fairbanks, November 1983.

————. *Checklist of Alaska Birds*. University of Alaska Museum, Fairbanks, 1986.

————. *Master List of Alaska Birds*. University of Alaska Museum, November 4, 1982.

—————. "Migrant Birds at Shemya Island, Aleutian Islands, Alaska." *The Condor* 83 (1):65–77, 1981.

Gibson, D. D., and S. O. MacDonald. *Bird Species and Habitat Inventory, Mainland Southeast Alaska, Summer 1974.* University of Alaska Museum, Contract Report no. 01-248. U.S. Forest Service, 1975.

Gibson, D. D., T. G. Tobish, Jr., and M. E. Isleib. *Alaska Region, American Birds,* for the years 1987–1989.

Godfrey, W. E. *The Birds of Canada.* National Museum of Canada Bulletin no. 203, Biological Series no. 73, 1966.

Harrison, H. H. *A Field Guide to Western Birds' Nests.* Houghton Mifflin Company, Boston, 1979.

Isleib, M. E. *Birds of the Chugach National Forest, Alaska: A Checklist.* U.S. Forest Service, U.S. Department of Agriculture, n.d.

Isleib, M. E., and B. Kessel. *Birds of the North Gulf Coast — Prince William Sound Region, Alaska.* Biological Papers no. 14, University of Alaska, Fairbanks, 1973.

Isleib, P., R. Armstrong, R. Gordon, and F. Glass. *Birds of Southeast Alaska: A Checklist.* Alaska Natural History Association; U.S. Forest Service Alaska Region; Audubon Society Juneau Chapter; and the State of Alaska Department of Fish and Game, 1987.

Johnsgard, P. A. *Waterfowl of North America.* Indiana University Press, Bloomington, Ind., 1975.

Johnson, D. H., D. E. Timm, and P. F. Springer. *"Morphological Characteristics of Canada Geese in the Pacific Flyway."* Typewritten manuscript, 1978.

Juneau Audubon Society, U.S. Forest Service, U.S. Department of Agriculture, Alaska Department of Fish and Game. *Birds of Southeast Alaska: A Checklist,* 1978.

Kertell, K. *Bird Checklist for Denali National Park.* Alaska Natural History Association in cooperation with the National Park Service, 1985.

Kessel, B. *Birds of Interior Alaska.* University of Alaska Museum, Fairbanks, 1980.

—————. *Birds of the Seward Peninsula, Alaska.* University of Alaska Press, Fairbanks, 1989.

Kessel, B., and D. D. Gibson. *Status and Distribution of Alaska Birds.* Studies in Avian Biology no. 1, Cooper Ornithological Society, Los Angeles, 1978.

King, B. F., and E. C. Dickinson. *A Field Guide to the Birds of South-East Asia.* Houghton Mifflin Company, Boston, 1975.

MacIntosh, R., *Kodiak National Wildlife Refuge and Kodiak Island Archipelago: Birdlist.* Kodiak National Wildlife Refuge, Kodiak, 1986.

Marshall, D. B. "The Marbled Murrelet Joins the Old-Growth Forest Conflict." *American Birds* 42(2):202–212, 1988.

Morlan, J. "Status and Identification of Forms of White Wagtail in Western North America." *Continental Birdlife* 2(2):37–50, April 1981.

Murphy, D., and K. Kertell. *Bird Checklist for Denali National Park.* Alaska Natural History Association in cooperation with the National Park Service, 1980.

————. *Birds of Mount McKinley National Park, Alaska: A Checklist,* 1977.

National Geographic Society. *Field Guide to the Birds of North America.* Washington, D.C., 1983.

National Park Service, U.S. Department of the Interior. *Birds of Glacier Bay National Monument: A Checklist,* 1978.

Naveen, R. "Storm-Petrels of the World: An Introductory Guide to Their Field Identification." *Birding* XIV(2):56–62, 1982.

Ogilvie, M. A. *The Winter Birds: Birds of the Arctic.* Praeger Publishers, New York, 1976.

WHISKERED AUKLET

Peterson, R. T. *A Field Guide to Western Birds.* Houghton Mifflin Company, Boston, 1961.

————. *A Field Guide to the Birds East of the Rockies.* Houghton Mifflin Company, Boston, 1980.

Peterson, R. T., G. Mountfort, and P. A. D. Hollum. *A Field Guide to the Birds of Britain and Europe.* Houghton Mifflin Company, Boston, 1974.

Pitelka, F. A. *An Avifaunal Review for the Barrow Region and North Slope of Arctic Alaska.* Arctic and Alpine Research vol. 6:161–184, Barrow, 1974.

Pough, R. H. *Audubon Western Bird Guide.* Doubleday & Co., Garden City, New York, 1957.

Prater, A. J., J. H. Marchant, and J. Vuorinen. *Guide to the Identification and Ageing of Holarctic Waders.* British Trust for Ornithology, Field Guide 17. Beech Grove, Tring, Herts, 1977.

Robbins, C. S., B. Bruun, and H. S. Zim, *A Guide to Field Identification, Birds of North America.* Golden Press, New York, 1966.

Roberson, D. *Rare Birds of the West Coast of North America.* Woodstock Publications, Pacific Grove, California, 1980.

Stromsem, N. E. *A Guide to Alaskan Seabirds.* Alaska Natural History Association in cooperation with the U.S. Fish and Wildlife Service, 1982.

Terres, J. K. *The Audubon Society Encyclopedia of North American Birds.* Alfred A. Knopf, New York, 1980.

Trapp, J. L., M. A. Robus, G. J. Tans, and M. M. Tans. "First Breeding Record of the Sora and American Coot in Alaska—with Comments on Drought Displacement." *American Birds* 35(6):901–902, 1981.

Udvardy, Miklos D. F. *The Audubon Society Field Guide to North American Birds — Western Region.* Alfred A. Knopf, New York, 1977.

Walsh, T. "Identifying Pacific Loons: Some Old and New Problems." *Birding* XX(1):12–28, 1988.

Weeden, R. B., and L. N. Ellison. *Upland Game Birds of Forest and Tundra.* Wildlife Booklet Series no. 3. Alaska Department of Fish and Game, Juneau, 1968.

Whitney, B., and K. Kaufman. "The *Empidonax* Challenge: Looking at *Empidonax*, Part II." *Birding* XVII(6):277–287, 1985.

Wild Bird Society of Japan. *A Field Guide to the Birds of Japan.* Tokyo, 1982.

Williams, R. B. "First Breeding Record of the Redhead in Southeast Alaska." *The Murrelet* 64(1), 1983.

Yamashina, Y. *Birds in Japan: A Field Guide.* Tokyo News Service, Tokyo, 1961.

ABOUT THE AUTHOR

Robert H. Armstrong
(Homo sapiens)
Length: 69 in.

Identification: Bob Armstrong has pursued a career in Alaska as a biologist, naturalist and nature photographer since 1960. He has authored and co-authored more than 100 scientific and popular articles on fish, birds, mammals, plants and insects in Alaska. From 1960 to 1984 he was a fishery biologist and research supervisor for the Alaska Department of Fish and Game and an assistant leader for the Alaska Cooperative Fishery Research Unit and Associate Professor of Fisheries at the University of Alaska in Fairbanks. He retired from the State of Alaska in 1984 to pursue broader interests in the natural history of Alaska and nature photography.

Armstrong has led bird walks in Denali National Park and Preserve and for the Juneau Audubon Society, and he has given numerous lectures and workshops throughout Alaska on bird identification and techniques for photographing birds.

Habitat: Armstrong lives outside of Juneau with his family.

Notes: In recognition of his contributions to Alaska he received an Honorary Doctorate of Science from the University of Alaska in Juneau and the Wallace H. Noerenberg award for fishery excellence from the Alaska chapter of the American Fisheries Society.

BOB ARMSTRONG, in Australia, with a Crimson Rosella on his camera lens.

ABOUT THE ILLUSTRATOR

John C. Pitcher
(Homo sapiens)
Length: 72 in.

Identification: John Pitcher's national recognition as an artist/naturalist had its start in Alaska. A member of the distinguished Society of Animal Artists, his paintings hang in the permanent collections of the Anchorage Museum of History and Art, University of Alaska Museum, Leigh Yawkey Woodson Art Museum, National Wildlife Federation, and private and corporate collections throughout the United States. Pitcher has had numerous one-man shows and has co-exhibited with the author at the Alaska State Museum in Juneau. Individual works have toured abroad at the British Museum of Natural History, the Royal Scottish Academy, and the Beijing Museum of Natural History.

In addition to this guide and a limited edition of prints published by Mill Pond Press, Pitcher's illustrations have been published in the 1981 *World Book Encyclopedia*, National Geographic Society's *Field Guide to the Birds of North America*, and Brina Kessel's *Birds of the Seward Peninsula, Alaska*, 1989.

Habitat: Pitcher and his family now reside in the beautiful Gifford Pinchot National Forest in western Washington state.

Notes: Pitcher is listed in *Who's Who in American Art* and *Contemporary Western Artists*.

JOHN PITCHER, *on Tongue Mountain near Randle, Washington.*

PHOTO CREDITS

Photos were provided by photographers and agencies. Photo position on pages is indicated after page number by t (top), b (bottom), m (middle), l (left), r (right).

Bob Armstrong: 4, 38, 47, 65, 71, 74t, 74b, 75, 76, 77t, 77b, 78t, 78b, 81t, 81b, 86t, 95b, 103l, 103r, 111t, 111b, 112b, 115, 121t, 124, 128b, 129b, 135m, 135b, 137b, 140t, 140b, 141b, 142t, 142b, 148t, 149, 152t, 152b, 157b, 158b, 161l, 161r, 170, 172, 175, 190t, 190b, 198, 204, 207t, 216b, 217, 219, 220b, 221t, 224t, 225t, 226t, 227b, 234t, 234b, 236t, 239t, 240, 242, 243, 245, 248, 249, 253b, 258b, 259b, 260, 264t, 273, 274, 277, 278, 279b, 284, 287t, 292t, 292b, 293t, 293b, 295, 298b, 314t, 314b, 318t, 318b, 319, 320, 322t, 327.
Paul Arneson: 105b, 197.
Rick Austin: 129t, 157t.
Cheryl Boise: 134b.
Fred Bruemmer: 100, 185, 188.
Henry Bunker: 93t.
Ed Burroughs: 200, 220t, 247, 294b, 311t, 311b.
G. V. Byrd: 45b, 194, 330.
R. J. Chandler: 123, 144t.
Don Cornelius: 17t, 103t, 118.
Betty Cottrille, Cornell Laboratory of Ornithology: 280t.
H. Cruickshank, VIREO: 239b.
Don Cunningham: 94, 108, 238.
A. J. Davis: 41, 339.
R. H. Day: 29, 150, 156t, 192t, 195b.
Bill Donaldson: 189b.
G. Dremeaux, VIREO: 265.
Bill Dyer, Cornell Laboratory of Ornithology: 309t, 309b.
Jim Erckmann: 148b, 151b, 162, 163b, 269, 304t.
Lynn Erckmann: 105t, 141t.
Kenneth Fink: 14b, 42b, 55m, 60, 64b, 92t, 121b, 127, 128t, 135t, 139, 256b.
Doug Forsell: 174.
Daniel Gibson: 207b.
Robert Gill: 209b.
Michael Gordon: 86b.
Skip Gray: 299.
Ed Greaves: 87.
C. H. Greenwalt, VIREO: 294t.
Martin Grosnick: 257b.
Jack Gustafson: 102l.
Craig Harrison: 20, 22, 23b.
V. Hasselblad, VIREO: 235b, 263.
David Hatler: 32, 306.
Jim Hawkings: 68b, 120, 136b, 147b, 165t, 180b.
John Helle: 237.
Doug Herr: 97b, 233b.
Merrick Hersey: 14t, 73, 116b, 215l, 215r, 221b, 289b, 307b, 316t, 316b.
Sue Hills: 59t.
Michael Hopiak, Cornell Laboratory of Ornithology: 43, 109, 228b, 246, 275, 305t, 322b.
Jerry Hout: 67b, 69t, 72b, 136t, 186r.
Frank Jackson: 97t.
Loyal Johnson: 102r.
Edgar Jones: 16b, 67t, 93l, 99, 106, 210, 223, 279t, 281, 282t, 282b, 287b, 291b, 308b.
Gary Jones: 90, 147t, 164, 280b, 317t.
Jo Keller: 178.
Lee Kuhn, Cornell Laboratory of Ornithology: 84.

Henry Kyllingstad: 69b, 131, 267.
Peter M. LaTourrette: 227t.
Stephan Lang: 286b.
Cal Lensink: 304b.
Mike Lettis: 56b, 165b.
E. Lieske: 18b, 114, 117, 176.
Richard MacIntosh: 28, 195t.
James Mackovjak: 193b.
Steve Maslowski, Photo Researchers: 225b.
Ted & Lois Matthews: 199.
Mark McDermott: 107.
Rick McIntyre: 104t.
I. Mellinger, VIREO: 116t.
Dave Menke: 34.
S. S. Menon, Bruce Coleman, Inc.: 276.
Brian Milne: 35.
Doug Murphy: 19, 21b, 36, 44t, 44b, 53t, 59b, 61t, 61b, 63b, 66t, 66b, 89, 110, 112t, 137t, 158t, 160t, 160b, 166, 169, 171t, 205, 206b, 232, 235t, 236b, 241, 252, 259t, 286t, 291t, 296, 298t, 305b, 310, 313.
J. P. Myers, VIREO: 144b.
Jerrold Olson: 159, 203.
W. A. Paff, Cornell Laboratory of Ornithology: 285t.
Dennis Paulson: 16t, 17b, 18t, 21t, 23t, 24l, 24r, 26t, 26b, 27t, 27b, 33, 40, 45t, 46, 50, 52t, 52b, 53b, 54b, 55t, 55b, 56t, 57, 58t, 58b, 63t, 64t, 68t, 70t, 70b, 79a, 79b, 80t, 80b, 82t, 82b, 85, 92b, 125t, 134t, 145t, 154, 161b, 163t, 167, 168b, 171b, 173, 211, 233t, 253t, 283b, 289t, 317b.
O. S. Pettingill, Jr., Cornell Laboratory of Ornithology: 218, 307t.
John C. Pitcher: 122, 300t.
Lee Post: 183b, 186l.
Lee Post/Mike Lettis: 31.
B. Randall, VIREO: 226b.
Nancy Ratner: 95t.
Mark Rauzon: 187
Hans Reinhard, Bruce Coleman, Inc.: 96, 254.
Pete Robinson: 244b.
David G. Roseneau: 191.
Len Rue, Jr.: 51b, 54t.
Leonard Lee Rue III.: 30.
W. E. Ruth: 91.
John Sarvis: 151t, 189t.
Robert Schulmeister: 256t.
R. Shallenberger, VIREO: 37b.
James Simmen: 101l.
Heinrich Springer: 93r, 130, 308t.
Gilbert Staender: 125b, 206t, 209t.
Tokio Sugiyama: 15b, 300r.
J. Surman, Cornell Laboratory of Ornithology: 181.
Anton Szabados: 230.
W. E. Townsend: 192b, 196.
Will Troyer: 101r.
Tom Ulrich: 42t, 49t, 49b, 51t, 83, 216t, 222, 258t, 290.
Jack VanHoesen: 264b.
R. Villani, VIREO: 37t.
Tom Walker: 62, 104b, 177, 193t.
R. T. Wallen: 183t.
Wild Bird Society of Japan: 15t, 98t, 98b, 213b, 250, 255t, 257l, 257r, 270t, 270b, 300l, 302.
Dick Wood: 156b, 180t.
D. & M. Zimmerman, VIREO: 208.

Field guides beautiful enough for browsing, like this one, are a specialty of Alaska Northwest Books™. Here is a sample of the books available:

Under Alaskan Seas, by Lou and Nancy Barr.
Color photographs, drawings, and clear, descriptive text. Useful for scuba divers, students, and anyone wanting to know more about marine invertebrates.
208 pages/paperback/$14.95   ISBN 0-88240-235-8

The Alaska-Yukon Wild Flowers Guide
Large color photographs and detailed line drawings. It's perfect for visitors to the Far North, and residents will enjoy it too.
218 pages/paperback/$16.95   ISBN 0-88240-032-0

Alaska Wild Berry Guide and Cookbook
Will delight the eye and palate. Photographs and drawings help you identify the berries, and the recipes show you how to turn your harvest into scrumptious treats. A great gift for the whole family.
201 pages/paperback/$14.95   ISBN 0-88240-229-3

A recent release for plant lovers:
Discovering Wild Plants: Alaska, Western Canada, the Northwest, by Janice J. Schofield, illustrated by Richard W. Tyler.
This beautiful book profiles 149 wild plants, with definitive information on botanical identification, history, harvest and habitat, as well as recipes. Each plant illustrated with color photos and elegant line drawings.
354 pages/paperback/$24.95   ISBN 0-88240-369-9
          hardbound/$34.95   ISBN 0-88240-355-9

Ask for these books at your favorite bookstore, or contact Alaska Northwest Books™ for a catalog of our entire list.

ALASKA NORTHWEST BOOKS™
P.O. Box 3007
Bothell, WA 98041-3007
1-800-331-3510
A division of GTE Discovery Publications, Inc.

Praise for *Old Souls*

"Fascinating . . . This is science. Shroder brings it alive for the reader by emphasizing the human interest of the children's stories and memories themselves. . . . This book explodes the worldview we know and demands that we enlarge our perspective."

—Claire Douglas, *The Washington Post*

"A book worth reading, if only for the many unsettling questions it will raise."

—Patti Thorn, *Rocky Mountain News*

"Whether or not you believe, but especially if you're a born skeptic, you'll be in good company sharing the travels of author Tom Shroder. . . . *Old Souls* is quietly mind-boggling."

—*Chicago Tribune*

"The journalistic objectivity Shroder brings to his material makes this an exceptionally valuable treatment of an often disparaged subject."

—*Publishers Weekly*

"Shroder, whose journalistic background makes him a cleared-eyed observer and brilliant reporter of his surroundings, provides unforgettable descriptions. . . . While true believers will find much here to buttress their notions about the immortality of the human soul, skeptics will enjoy watching a trained scientist in his careful explorations of the inexplicable."

—*Kirkus Reviews*

"Tom Shroder has written a fantastic and unnerving documentation of his investigation of the work of psychiatrist Ian Stevenson, who has devoted decades to the study of thousands of children who seem to remember details of previous lives. *Old Souls* is a fascinating account of Shroder's travels with Stevenson through Lebanon, India, and Virginia in search of verification of the continuity of human conciousness beyond death."

—*New York Press*

"Tom Shroder uses a journalist's craft and style to make this nonfiction book come alive. He has written about Stevenson's findings in a way that will surprise believers and skeptics alike."

—*Florida Times-Union*

Old Souls

The Scientific Evidence
for Past Lives

Tom Shroder

Simon & Schuster Paperbacks
New York   London   Toronto   Sydney

For Lisa

SIMON & SCHUSTER PAPERBACKS
Rockefeller Center
1230 Avenue of the Americas
New York, NY 10020

Copyright © 1999 by Tom Shroder
All rights reserved, including the right of reproduction
in whole or in part in any form.

SIMON & SCHUSTER PAPERBACKS and colophon are
registered trademarks of Simon & Schuster, Inc.

For information about special discounts for bulk purchases,
please contact Simon & Schuster Special Sales:
1-800-456-6798 or business@simonandschuster.com.

Designed by DEIRDRE C. AMTHOR

Manufactured in the United States of America

21 23 25 27 29 30 28 26 24 22 20

The Library of Congress has cataloged the hardcover edition as follows:
Shroder, Tom.
Old souls : the scientific evidence for past lives / Tom Shroder.
p. cm.
Includes bibliographical references.
1. Reincarnation—Case studies. 2. Memory in children—Miscellaneous. I. Title.
BL515.S46 1999   99-12705
133.9'01'35—DC21   CIP
ISBN-13: 978-0-684-85192-1
ISBN-10:   0-684-85192-X
ISBN-13: 978-0-684-85193-8 (Pbk)
ISBN-10:   0-684-85193-8 (Pbk)

There are more things in heaven and earth, Horatio,
Than are dreamt of in your philosophy.

—Shakespeare, *Hamlet*, act 1, scene 5

Contents

Part IV: The United States—Children Next Door

PART I:

Prologue
Children Who Remember Previous Lives

1

The Question

It is late, nearly lightless. Smoke from a million dung fires hangs in the headlights as the Maruti microbus bangs along the narrow, cratered hardpack that passes for a paved road in the Indian outback. We are still hours away from the hotel, an island of First World comfort in this simmering Third World ocean, and the possibility that we will never get there looms as large as the oncoming truck, absurdly overloaded and undermaintained, shuddering violently as it hurtles toward us dead in the middle of the road. Using every inch of the rutted dirt shoulder, we barely escape. Through the thin tin of the Maruti, I can feel the truck vibrate, smell death in the exhaust pumping from its tailpipe. In escape, there is no relief. We bounce back onto the road's pitted surface and immediately overtake a wooden cart lumbering to the heavy gait of yoked oxen with immense horns. Our driver leans on his horn as he swerves around the cart into a blind curve that I can only pray is not occupied by a bus loaded to the dented metal ceiling with humans and farm animals. I try not to think about the lack of seat belts or the mere half inch of glass and metal that separates the front seat from whatever we plow into—or the *Lonely Planet* article I read that said fatal accidents were forty times more likely on Indian roads than on American highways. Or the account of a Western traveler who hired a car and driver in northern India, exactly as we have, only to crash head on into a truck, then regain consciousness in agony in a crude hospital, stripped of passport, money belt, and insurance papers. I try not to think about dying ten thousand miles from home, about never seeing my wife and children again, about their lives going on without any trace of me. I try not to think about absolute darkness.

But even within my bubble of fear, I am aware of the irony. Sitting in the backseat, apparently unconcerned about the two-ton mud-splattered torpedoes racing toward us, is a tall, white-haired man, nearly eighty, who insists that he has compiled enough solid, empirical evidence to demonstrate that physical death is not necessarily the end of me or anyone else.

His name is Ian Stevenson, and he is a physician and psychiatrist who has been braving roads like this and worse for thirty-seven years to bring back reports of young children who speak of remembering previous lives and provide detailed and accurate information about people who died before they were born, people they say they once were. While I struggle with my fear of dying, he is wrestling with his own fear of annihilation: that his life's work will end, largely ignored by his peers.

"Why," he asks for the third time since night has fallen, "do mainstream scientists refuse to accept the evidence we have for reincarnation?"

On this day, and for the past six months, Stevenson has shown me what he means by "evidence." He has permitted me to accompany him on field trips, first to the hills surrounding Beirut and now on a wide swath of India. He has responded to my endless questions and even invited me to participate in the interviews that are the heart of his research. The evidence he is referring to does not come from fashionable New Age sources, past-life readings, or hypnotic regressions during which subjects talk about being a Florentine bride in the sixteenth century or a soldier in the Napoleonic Wars, rendering the kind of details one might garner in an hour's time paging through a few romance novels. The details Stevenson's children recall are far more homely and more specific than those. One remembers being a teenager called Sheila who was hit by a car crossing the road to collect grass for cattle feed, another recalls the life of a young man who died of tuberculosis asking for his brother, a third remembers being a woman waiting for heart surgery in Virginia, trying and failing to call her daughter before the operation she would not survive. It goes on and on: These children supply names of towns and relatives, occupations and relationships, attitudes and emotions that, in hundreds of cases around the world, are unique to a single dead individual, often apparently unknown to their present families. But the fact is, the people the children remember did exist, the memories that the children claim can be checked against real lives and their alleged feats of identification verified—or contradicted—by a variety of witnesses.

This is what Stevenson has been doing for almost forty years; it is what we have been doing in Lebanon and India: examining records, interviewing witnesses, and measuring the results against possible alternative explanations. I have seen close up, as few others have, how compelling some of these cases can be—and not just factually, but in the emotion visible in the eyes and the voices of the subjects, their families, and the families of the people they claim to have been. I have seen and heard astonishing things, things for which I have no easy explanation.

Now we are near the end of our last trip together, perhaps the last trip of Stevenson's career. It dawns on me in the noisy chill of the microbus, droning and rattling through the night, that Stevenson's question is not rhetorical. He is asking *me,* the outsider, the skeptical journalist who has seen what he has to show, to explain. How can scientists, professed to hold no dogma that reasonable evidence cannot overturn, ignore the volumes of reasonable evidence that he has provided?

I begin to go into some long riff about how, in the absence of any knowledge about the mechanism of the transfer—the means by which personality, identity, and memory can be reassigned from one body to another—it is hard to talk about proof. But then I stop cold. I hear myself rambling, and realize what he is really asking: After all I have seen and heard, do I, at least, believe?

I, who have always felt mortality in my marrow, who have stared inward but never seen a ripple nor heard a whisper of any life but my own, who have seen people near to me disappear into death with an awesome and unappealable finality and learned in my flesh, where it counts, that the only thing abiding is an unyielding sense of diminishment. What do I think?

He wants to know. He is asking me. He deserves an answer.

2

You Only Live Once

It's a long answer, and it begins ten years before he asks the question, in a small, surprisingly comfy doctor's office just blocks from my home in Miami Beach. The room is dimly lit. Dr. Brian Weiss, chief of psychiatry for Mount Sinai Hospital, is speaking softly in a remarkable voice, a voice that rustles like wind chimes, rises like the smoke from a joss stick—a perfect voice for hypnosis. He is wearing a white coat and spectacles; his great, graying, blow-dried mane engulfs an earnest, open face. He is telling a story:

In 1982, he hypnotized a young woman. She lay on her back on the couch, eyes closed, hands lightly at her sides, eased into a trance by the doctor's voice and the willingness of her mind, swaddled in a blanket of imaginary white light. He ordered her back to her earliest memories, back to the root of the anxiety that plagued her life.

Weiss had been treating the woman for acute phobias once or twice a week for eighteen months, but this was only the second attempt at hypnosis. The first session uncovered a significant memory from the age of three—a disturbing sexual encounter with her drunken father—but there had been no improvement in her condition. Weiss found it extraordinary that such a breakthrough would not be accompanied by some alleviation of symptoms. Could there be a memory even further back, buried even deeper in her mind?

Weiss decided to give her an open suggestion. He made his voice firm and commanding: "Go back to the time from which your symptoms arise."

In her deep trance she spoke in a hoarse whisper. There were long pauses between her words, as if it were difficult or painful to speak. "I see white steps leading up to a building, a big white building with pillars. . . . I am wearing a long dress, a sack made of rough material. My name is Aronda. I am eighteen. . . ."

Weiss, uncertain what was happening, scribbled notes. The whisper went on: "I see a marketplace. There are baskets. You carry the baskets on your shoulder. We live in a valley. There is no water. The year is 1863 B.C."

Before the end of the session, Aronda died, terrified, gasping and choking in a flood.

This was the turning point for the woman on the couch, Weiss said. Her fears—of choking, of drowning, of the dark—would fall away after that. In the ensuing months, her hoarse whisper ranged through centuries. She would become Johan, who had his throat slit in the Netherlands in 1473; Abby, a servant in nineteenth-century Virginia; Christian, a Welsh sailor; Eric, a German aviator; a boy in the Ukraine of 1758 whose father was executed in prison. In between lives, floating in a shining void, she would become the host for disembodied spirits who revealed the mysteries of eternity. And, said Weiss, she also became well.

Weiss would write a book about the anonymous woman he called Catherine. *Many Lives, Many Masters* became an international bestseller and is considered a New Age classic.

In 1988, with the book buoyantly topping local paperback bestseller lists, I decided to write a story about Weiss for *Tropic*, the *Miami Herald*'s Sunday magazine, of which I was then editor. What interested me was Weiss himself: He was no New Age flake. At forty-four, he was a Yale Med School graduate and a nationally recognized expert in psychopharmacology, brain chemistry, substance abuse, and Alzheimer's disease. He said that he had waited four years to write his book for fear that his professional peers would ostracize him. Two years after he finally summoned the courage to publish his account, though, his fears had not been realized, at least not publicly.

Before going to interview him, I called the president of his hospital for comment and got only gushing praise: "Brian Weiss is highly respected, a competent leader in his field." When I asked him if Weiss's reputation had been tainted by the book, he responded with a sharp "No."

Others concurred. "If anyone else had written the book, I would not have believed it," said a colleague. "But I do because I know Brian Weiss as an astute clinician, researcher, and diagnostician."

The fact that normally conservative medical people were taking Weiss's ostensibly extravagant claim of evidence for previous lives seriously intrigued me. It didn't persuade me of anything, but it made for a better story.

When I read his book, the first thing I noticed was a surprising lack of skepticism. Okay, so one of his psychiatric patients had imagined herself to be an Egyptian named Aronda. That, in itself, did not seem to me to merit any further assumption than that she was expressing a fantasy. And yet Weiss was absolutely persuaded. I didn't get it.

In that first meeting in his office, I made no secret of my puzzlement. I told Weiss that I wanted the opportunity to satisfy my curiosity about his story, and that meant that I would be asking a lot of pointed questions. Weiss responded with a shrug and a self-effacing smile. "The whole field is new," he said. "There are a lot of possible loose ends."

Sitting behind his desk, his voice hoarse from a round of talk shows in Pittsburgh, where he had spent a sleepless night in an overheated hotel room, Weiss patiently worked through his logic: He had been treating Catherine, a lab technician in his own hospital, for eighteen months. During that time, he had used conventional therapy, and Catherine had never mentioned any belief in the occult or tried to manipulate him in any way. The only unusual thing about her therapy was her lack of progress. So, if Catherine were a con artist, Weiss reasoned, she was an incredibly patient one, for such a fraud would require her faking psychological problems for eighteen months, waiting for Weiss to suggest hypnosis, faking an emotional reexperience of an early childhood trauma in the first session, and only then slipping back into the phony past lives.

Weiss said that he had had thousands of hours to observe an endless array of patients, to hone his diagnostic ability, his BS meter. With Catherine, he felt sure that he had a patient with symptoms she genuinely wanted to alleviate. She was a simple, honest woman with a commitment to the Roman Catholic faith of her childhood; here was not a schizophrenic or psychotic, no manic-depressive or multiple personality. Her thinking was not delusional.

Then there was the way Catherine responded to the past lives herself. She seemed uncomfortable with them. They did not square with Catholicism, and she found them somewhat embarrassing. But she was thrilled with the rapid improvement in her condition, so she continued the sessions until she felt that she was cured. There was nothing about her that suggested any interest in using the past-life experiences for anything other than a therapeutic purpose. She hesitantly agreed to sign a release for the book, but she had no monetary stake in it. Even now, he said, when he bumped into her at Mount Sinai, she showed little interest in the metaphysical implications of her experience.

For those reasons, Weiss believed that Catherine was not crazy or a con artist. What convinced him that she was remembering actual past lives was that the lives themselves were strikingly mundane—a fact that Weiss felt lent credibility that would have instantly evaporated had Catherine appeared as, say, Cleopatra in one life and Madame Curie in another. She was a servant, a leper, a laborer. In her deep trance, she focused on things like the scent of flowers and the glamour of a wedding she was not permitted to attend—everyday things, real-life things. Her memories were at times fairly detailed—in one life, she described the process of churning butter, in another, the preparation of a body for embalming. To Weiss, the descriptions—though far from technically complex—seemed to be beyond Catherine's normal range of knowledge. Once, recently returned from a trip to Chicago, Catherine told him that she had stunned herself on a visit to a museum by spontaneously blurting out corrections to the guide's description of four-thousand-year-old Egyptian artifacts.

I was impressed with Weiss's sincerity, but not by his evidence. Had he located the museum guide and the guide confirmed Catherine's account, admitting that he had later researched the artifacts in question and found himself wrong and Catherine correct, I might have been impressed. But none of that had happened. And in none of Catherine's past-life memories did she come up with the kind of details that any fan of historical fiction couldn't have manufactured. Catherine did not speak in archaic languages or scribble madly in Sanskrit or even mention the name of a single person who could be proven to have existed.

"I was so overwhelmed by what was coming out that I didn't really probe for that kind of thing," Weiss responded. "When I did try to steer her, she would often ignore me. This is the kind of thing that would be interesting to investigate. I've only made a small beginning. Catherine is just one case history."

And not a very convincing one, I decided, the more I considered it. In the session when Catherine remembered the life of Aronda the Egyptian, she used the term "1863 B.C."—"before Christ"—a term that no ancient Egyptian would know, and a translation of the ancient dating system that would require painstaking calculation by an Egyptologist. Furthermore, despite this eerie omniscience displayed as an eighteen-year-old Egyptian, in another lifetime Catherine could not come up with the date because she "can't see a newspaper." I also noticed that according to Weiss's account, Catherine said she was living as a Ukrainian boy at precisely the same date that she later claimed to be a Spanish prostitute.

None of that shook Weiss's faith: "The totality of the experience," Weiss said, "was such that these inconsistencies only add to its complexity. There is so much we don't know."

Way *too* much, I thought.

While interviewing Weiss, I met one of his patients. A therapist herself, she was a clinical social worker who worked with multiple-personality cases and also did past-life regressions with some of her own clients. She saw Weiss because she believed that dimly remembered traumas from her past were haunting her. Under hypnosis in a session with him, she had taken the elevator of her mind into the basement of the past—and kept going:

"I saw a lot of darkness—blackness—and I realized that I was blindfolded. Then I saw myself from outside. I was standing on top of a tower, one of those castle towers made of stone. My hands were tied behind my back. I was in my early twenties, and I knew that I was on the side that had lost the battle. Then I felt an excruciating pain in my back. I could feel my teeth gritting and my arms stiff and fists clenching. I was being lanced, I could feel the lance in my back, but I was defiant, I wasn't going to scream. Then I felt myself falling, and felt the water of the moat closing around me. I've always been terrified of heights and drowning. When I came out of it I was still shaken, and I spent a couple days in agony—I couldn't even touch the bones of my face, the pain was so great—but the next morning when I woke up I thought, 'Something's different. Something's very different.' "

Now she was willing to undergo another hypnotic regression while I watched. She lay down on the carpet in Weiss's office and, under his suggestions, drifted back to another lifetime in which she saw herself hanged in public.

Once again, the descriptions that she offered of her experience struck me as unremarkable in detail, devoid of archaic vocabulary or knowledge beyond what any contemporary college graduate could produce without research or even hesitation. Watching the woman on the carpet, listening to her speak, what I was witnessing seemed self-evident: a contemporary American free-associating on a medieval theme.

Maybe, though, I was missing something that could only be found in the subjective experience. I asked Weiss to recommend a hypnotist to guide me through my own regression. I found the process to be relaxing, soothing, and oddly narcissistic, but completely devoid of any sense that forgotten past lives were opening to memory. Instead, I had the clear perception that I was attempting to supply the hypnotist with what she wanted, scenes from a time before I was born. I waited for an image to pop into my mind, and then attempted to embellish it into an appropriate life situation—exactly what I did when I was trying to write a piece of fiction or drifting off to sleep. When I became even more relaxed, more deeply "into" a slightly altered state of consciousness, the images began to come without any conscious effort. But even then, they never carried with them any more weight of authenticity than a garden-variety daydream.

When I saw the therapist/public-hanging victim again, I related my impressions. Without meaning to, she revealed what I took to be an ulterior motive for believing in her past-life memories:

"It never made sense to me that we could be here for such a short time, and then . . . nothing," she told me.

And who hasn't felt that, felt it with the deepest instinct in their soul? Being into nothingness; light into dark. Current on, current off—it just doesn't seem right. Or, maybe more accurately, it doesn't seem fair.

Also on Weiss's recommendation, I visited a psychic who specialized in "reading" past lives. Even in the context of reporting the story, I did it as a lark.

The psychic worked out of an office on the second floor of a Miami Beach shopping center across Route A1A from the Atlantic Ocean. She sat opposite me at her desk, animated, excited still, after all the years, with the prospect of her work. Speaking in a charming delirium, she pointed out signs and portents on astrological charts. "I'm warming up my right brain," she told me. "I'm waiting until I see it."

And soon she did see, past lives by the handful—I was an alcoholic, drinking away the last of an old Southern family's money after the Civil War; an aging Japanese sage with arthritic hands and students at his feet, a black Jamaican sorceress, an Australian rancher, a German physician. As she talked, the lives filled with lovers and children, struggle and success, landscapes and lifescapes ranging through history, around the globe. My wife, my daughter, I've known them all before, she told me. And I'll know them all again. And again.

It was wonderful to imagine: never having to say good-bye; the soul unfettered from this claustrophobic constriction of time and circumstance that is our single life, our only life.

Unfortunately, nothing this woman told me had any resonance whatsoever, no echo, no fading scent of jasmine or sting of gin on the back of my tongue. The lives she sketched belonged to a stranger, or a stranger's imagination. The only thing clear to me was how powerful the urge is to believe, how strong the motivation for self-delusion. I filed the thought away, thinking I might need to refer to it in the future.

Though I was a little shocked that Weiss had recommended this woman—apparently taking such a parlor game seriously—and thought it might reflect an inadequacy in his BS-detection system after all, I realized that his hypnotic regressions still begged some alternative explanation. Other psychiatrists I interviewed, while not ready to make the conclusions Weiss had made, were still intrigued as well.

"Those of us who do hypnosis are not all that shocked by Dr. Weiss's book," one told me. "Many have had patients who have gone back to something. I'm not prepared to say it was a previous life. I think we are very interested and very afraid to talk about it."

A psychologist widely considered an expert in hypnotherapy and multiple-personality disorders said, "I have had a number of patients who have had vivid, emotionally laden experiences that have taken place in the past and had a profound effect in the present. I can't say that these experiences were actual memories of past lives. It is possible that they were fantasy material similar to screen memory—an indirect way of describing a problem. For example, a person who talks about being raped in a previous life may actually be discussing a childhood memory of incest. But there is a purposefulness to the unconscious. Whatever is happening with these past-life memories, I don't believe they are a sham."

Just recently, this man told me, he had a patient who awoke at 2 A.M. "famished" and very disturbed. She couldn't get back to sleep. When he hypnotized her, he asked her to drift back to the cause of her upset. Suddenly there was a big smile on her face. "Of course," she said. "I was there!"

She was talking about Kristallnacht—the beginning of the Holocaust in Germany. There had been a lot of news coverage the preceding week on the fiftieth anniversary of the Nazi thugs' night of terror against Jewish homes and businesses.

"What struck me was that she kept using the word famished, which seemed an unusual word for her. Interestingly, *fa-misht* is a Yiddish word meaning something like 'all mixed up, bewildered'—a good description of the chaos of Kristallnacht. When I asked her about it, she said she didn't know why she chose that word, that it wasn't in her normal vocabulary. I have to say that I am open to explore this subject. It's my responsibility as a scientist to be open."

There is an old skeptics' saying: "If you're too open-minded, your brains will fall out." That was the position of some doctors I spoke to, and I tended to agree with them. Dr. Jack Kapchan, a clinical psychologist at the University of Miami with a special interest in parapsychology, for instance was troubled by Weiss's claim to being scientific. Where was the concrete evidence? Where's the thorough background check on the patient?

"What Weiss has in the book can be explained in naturalistic terms," he said, citing suggestion, fantasy, multiple personalities. In such a case, Kapchan said, it is improper to offer explanations that involve "the paranormal process." What sense does it make to "explain" a relatively simple set of facts—a woman describing a scene from the

historical past under hypnosis—by conjuring up a vast array of phenomena, such as a soul, an afterlife, a reintroduction of an old soul into
a new body, that have never been detected by any objective measure?
That kind of explanation, clearly, should be a last resort, to be used
when all other simpler, less-demanding explanations have been ruled
out.

I decided to find the expert's expert, the man who wrote the *Encyclopedia Britannica* entry on hypnotic past-life regression. This turned
out to be Dr. Martin Orne, then a professor of psychiatry at the University of Pennsylvania Medical School, a senior attending psychiatrist
at the hospital there, and the editor of *The Journal of Clinical and Experimental Hypnosis*. He had plenty to say:

"I always feel like I'm the Grinch who says there is no Christmas,
no Santa Claus. The people who promote these things are not malevo-
lent, but they want very badly to believe. People think that if something
comes out under hypnosis it is more likely to be true, when in fact the
opposite is the case. Hypnosis can create pseudomemories. Reincarnation memories are no different than the cases of people who under hypnosis relate being captured by UFO space aliens and examined aboard
the mother ship. These are what I call 'honest liars.' Therapists ask
their patient to go back to the cause of a problem. This is something
many people find very difficult, and if they can't find a good cause in
this lifetime, they'll go back to a previous one—fantasy, of course."

I remember hanging up the phone in my office feeling that my curiosity had been satisfied. Once again, as I had seen so many times in
my career as a journalist, a story that at first appeared to have some
fantastic explanation had, under closer examination, been relegated to
the realm of the mundane.

Only recently a classic example of that occurred: the "face" on
Mars. For years, after an early flyby of the planet in the 1970s produced a photograph of an area on the surface that appeared to mimic
the physiognomy of the human face, an enormous number of pages and
Internet computer bytes had been devoted to promoting the idea that
this was some kind of monumental architecture that proved the existence of ancient intelligence on Mars. Some saw more than intelligence—they saw divinity.

Most scientists insisted that the image was a geologic formation and the face nothing more than a trick of shadowing and the human imagination. Others, though, maintained that the scientists throwing cold water on the face idea were thickheaded, biased against anything that upset status-quo concepts of the universe, or part of an immense conspiracy to keep evidence of alien civilization from the public.

Then, one spring morning, the front page of my newspaper carried the intriguing news that another NASA craft had been directed to fly directly over the "face" and take high-resolution photographs of the area. By midday, the report concluded, we would be able to tap in to the Internet and see for ourselves if the close-up photos revealed clear evidence of alien intelligence.

I knew the pattern. And I knew that the photographs, when published, would show exactly what they did show: an obviously natural geologic formation, fascinating in its own right as possible evidence of a billion-years-past Martian environment that was surprisingly earth-like, but bitterly disappointing for people longing to see the face of God.

I saw a similarity in the Weiss story line: "Accomplished psychiatrist and objective scientist supplies convincing proof of reincarnation" was just too easy a way out of the dilemma of mortality. I was now completely satisfied that Weiss had become enchanted with an interesting phenomenon and assumed too quickly that it proved something supernatural when all it truly showed was the amazing richness of the human imagination. (In fact, when I interviewed Weiss again, years after *Many Lives, Many Masters,* he distanced himself from the idea that regressions proved the reality of reincarnation. What he cared about, he declared, was that whatever these regressions tapped into, even if only the patient's subconscious, had proved to be tremendously helpful in therapy. He had seen problems resistant to all other kinds of treatment clear up almost instantaneously after dramatic regressions. I asked him if he had done any clinical studies to verify his impression that regression therapy got such dramatic results. He hadn't, he said, but he wished that somebody would.)

Meanwhile, until another Catherine surfaced who could decode the Egyptian hieroglyphics without benefit of even a high school diploma, say, or perhaps tell what a Boston widow whispered in her son's ear on her deathbed in 1947—and have that son confirm its accuracy and swear that he had never told a living soul—I was willing to call it a day on the evidence for the reincarnation front.

Except . . .

I came across an article about a Dr. Ian Stevenson, identified as the Carlson Professor of Psychiatry at the University of Virginia Medical School, who had been investigating reports of past-life memories from a very different source: spontaneous, waking memories experienced by very small children, no hypnosis involved. These accounts often included names, addresses, and intimate details from lives that the children had no apparent way of knowing about. Surviving family members could be located and the child's purported memories checked against reality. In many cases, according to Stevenson's analysis, the memories passed the reality test fairly persuasively.

What astonished me was that Stevenson wasn't claiming to have investigated just a handful of such cases, but hundreds of them—more than two thousand, in fact, from all over the world. My first thought, I confess, was that perhaps this was some kind of delusional wacko who also had a drawer full of fragments of the true cross as well as a radio that communicated directly with a race of blood-red dwarves on Io, the fifth moon of Jupiter. But upon reading further, I saw that this was clearly not the case. I found a quote from a 1975 article in no less than *The Journal of the American Medical Association* stating that Stevenson "had collected cases in which the evidence is difficult to explain on any other grounds [besides reincarnation]."

The JAMA article also cited a book in which Stevenson had compiled his cases. But although I visited a couple of bookstores and found many books on hypnotic regression and other related topics, I encountered nothing from Stevenson. And while the public library listed several volumes by Stevenson, I could locate only one. I took it home and read it. Its academic style made it difficult to follow, reminding me of the eye-crossing effort it took to read some of my graduate-level college anthropology texts. It proved worth the effort: The cases were compelling, even astonishing, and I was impressed by the apparent evenhandedness and thoughtfulness of Stevenson's investigation. He was after precisely the kind of details that Weiss's case sorely lacked; he sought statements that were concrete, specific, and verifiable about a previous life, things that the subject could not have had any way of knowing normally.

Time and again, according to his reports, he had found them.

How in the world, I wondered, could I have never before heard of this man's work? How was it possible that a rather flimsy case of hypnotic regression was the basis for a best-seller, while hundreds of cases of the spontaneous production of verifiable memories took a day at the library to discover?

And, finally, I wondered this: Why was I writing about Brian Weiss and not Ian Stevenson?

It would take a decade to set that last one right.

3

The Man Behind the Curtain

Over the next few years, the idea of tracking down Stevenson and writing about his research continued to reassert itself. From time to time, I would find myself in the New Age section of bookstores looking through the indexes of books on reincarnation, always finding a number of pages devoted to Stevenson. From these books, I learned the basics of his biography: He earned his medical degree from McGill University in Montreal in 1943, graduating at the top of his class. He trained in internal medicine and did some work in biochemistry, but ultimately specialized in psychiatry. In 1957, at the age of thirty-nine, Stevenson became the head of the department of psychiatry at the University of Virginia Medical School, and it was from there that he began his research into reports of children who remembered past lives. Eventually, he gave up his administrative duties to become a full-time researcher of paranormal phenomena, his professorial chair endowed by Chester Carlson, the man who invented xerography.

Beyond general, usually positive, often uncritical mentions of his work, there was very little in the way of serious discussion of the meaning of his cases to be found in popular literature. And apart from that early, positive review of Stevenson's research in *The Journal of the American Medical Association,* mainstream science had all but ignored him. I began to look through the indexes of more-obscure journals, notably *The Journal of the American Society for Psychical Research* and *The Journal of Scientific Exploration.*

These journals, of whose existence I had been ignorant, were a revelation. They were filled with discussions of fright-night subjects—

apparitions, possessions, UFOs, psychokinesis, anomalies in the space-time continuum—but not in the wide-eyed, semihysterical, and altogether too-credulous tones I was used to seeing in the New Age aisles. These reports, for the most part, were as serious as cancer research. In each, the methodology was laid out, the observations carefully itemized, the discussion sober and impressively detached, and the conclusions cautious.

They were, in fact, clones of Stevenson's case reports—which would turn out to be no coincidence. Time and again, writers acknowledged their debt to Stevenson for his opening to investigation by scientific technique subjects taboo in the orthodoxy of mainstream science. One writer even compared him to Galileo. And here, at last, were articles that critically assessed Stevenson's work, including some by researchers who had investigated similar cases themselves.

These researchers produced case reports almost identical to Stevenson's cases, although, as a group, their conclusions tended to be slightly more cautious than his: They saw their investigations only presenting the high probability that some of these children could have had no normal way of obtaining intimate details of a deceased person's life. Usually, they observed that while their findings could possibly be interpreted as evidence that the children were actually reincarnated, it wasn't necessarily so: there could be some other, paranormal explanation.

This reticence dovetailed with another group of articles by researchers who had not studied cases themselves, but on the basis of logic and theory were arguing against Stevenson's research as evidence for reincarnation. It made more sense, these writers argued, to see it as evidence of some sort of super psychic ability.

I remember reading one of these articles late one night and laughing aloud, not because what I was reading was ridiculous, but because it was so astounding: Here was someone essentially debunking Stevenson by arguing for the existence of extrasensory perception so powerful that it was akin to omniscience.

The tone of these articles, too, was fascinating. For one thing, these folks were really, really *smart*. This wasn't pseudo-erudition—it was the actual, palpable item. Here are four paragraphs from an article by Stephen E. Braude, of the University of Maryland philosophy department, published in *The Journal of Scientific Exploration* in 1992:

Many have wondered if the very concept of survival [life after death] is intelligible. And as the reader may realize, some have decided that it is not, and have therefore argued that we should reject the survival hypothesis a priori.

Now I am by no means opposed to a priori arguments against scientific claims. In many cases, ostensibly empirical claims rest on thoroughly indefensible philosophical presuppositions, and those presuppositions often blind researchers to alternative ways of interpreting the data. . . . Nevertheless, some a priori arguments are more persuasive and profound than others, and I consider the usual arguments against the intelligibility of survival to be quite shallow.

What really matters is that it is relatively easy to construct hypothetically ideal cases so coercive that we would have no choice but to admit (or at least entertain seriously) that survival of some sort is a fact, no matter how much of a challenge that poses for our familiar conceptual framework. Our ability to formulate such ideal cases shows that the evidence for survival cannot be rejected for facile reasons. The more pressing question is to what extent actual cases approach the theoretical ideal.

But even the best real cases—and possibly also the best ideal cases—face certain purely conceptual obstacles. . . . As I see it, the most serious obstacle to taking even the best evidence for survival at face value is the possibility that the data can be explained in terms of highly refined psi [psychic ability] among the living.

In other words, faced with Stevenson's research, some intensely intelligent, highly respected scholars were saying, *You got two choices: reincarnation or clairvoyance.*

That did it. In the spring of 1996, I found the number that I had used to call Stevenson at the University of Virginia in 1988, when I was seeking a comment on Brian Weiss. I dialed, fully expecting to discover that he had long since retired.

To my surprise, Stevenson was in, and took my call. I reminded him that I had interviewed him years earlier, and explained my continued interest. We talked at some length. He mentioned that he was very involved in finishing a new volume of his series and that he couldn't afford to be distracted from that work. "Besides," he said, "I'm afraid I'm all interviewed out."

After we hung up, I wrote him a letter asking him to reconsider. I told him that I was more interested in observing him than in interviewing him (which I realized might be even more bothersome, from his point of view), but my major point was that his work deserved not to be obscured by hypnotic regression—and worse—in the public discussion of reincarnation, as it in fact had been.

If you type "reincarnation research" into the search field of an Internet search engine, one of the hits comes up like this:

Thanks to "New Age Technology" (NAT), the unthinkable has become not only thinkable but doable as well. Would you like to relieve yourself of the fear that has everyone in its grip? Would you like to move about with the confidence and assurance that all is well? If the answer is yes, here is what you can do: send for your very own "Fountain of Youth Reincarnation Systems" kit. It comes with detailed instructions on what you need to do to put together your or a loved one's "Happy Ever After Return Package" (HARP). It's that easy. But please don't wait until it's too late because now you can truly "rest in peace."

Frequently Asked Questions

Q. How soon after death does the reincarnation process begin?
A. Immediately.
Q. Why do I need to purchase a Fountain of Youth Reincarnation Systems kit?
A. The kit will guide your soul safely from the "other side" back to the world as we know it to exist. Without it, your soul might otherwise wander aimlessly, finally seeking refuge in heaven or hell. This is referred to as "crossing over."

Hey, friend, let's be honest. When a person's number is up, it's a little too late in the game to ask for our reincarnation kit then. When your whole life flashes before you, you can't press a pause button and stop everything. Who can predict the next hour, the next day, or the next week. Better to err on the side of caution, don't you think? Don't lose your soul. Recapture it with our Fountain of Youth Reincarnation Systems kit.

Just send us a personal check, cashier's check, or money order for $399 payable to:
Fountain of Youth Reincarnation Systems

And there's this, from a *Los Angeles Times* column written after two Arkansas teenagers opened fire on their classmates in early 1998:

The reincarnated souls of Jack the Ripper and the Boston Strangler are responsible for the recent spate of schoolyard shootings, says a Laguna Beach, California, homeopathic expert. In an interview with Wireless Flash News Service, Frederick Bell claims such tragedies are the work of long-dead serial killers who reincarnate before the spirit world can rehabilitate them. Bell says the solution is to require all kindergartners to undergo a hypnotic past-life regression to see if they were homicidal maniacs in a previous life. He also suggests that kids wear pyramid hats to "detoxify negative energies."

ᕲ

Once again, Stevenson surprised me by responding to my letter, saying that I should raise the proposal at the end of the year when things weren't quite so hectic for him. I wrote again in December. This time, Stevenson invited me to Charlottesville so he could consider my request in person.

In January 1997, I met Stevenson in his office at the Division of Personality Studies, not far from the Rotunda designed by Thomas Jefferson on the University of Virginia's regal campus. The DOPS building turned out to be an ancient two-story frame house sandwiched between apartments and a high-rise parking garage. I parked in what had once been the backyard and entered through a porch attached to a small kitchen. Something about the door slamming behind me reminded me of dropping in on a neighborhood friend in my grammar-school days. I waited in the house's front parlor, which had been converted into a reception area. Behind the secretary's desk was an interior room, lined with filing cabinets containing all the typed notes and transcripts from more than 2,500 investigations that Stevenson had conducted over the years. On one wall, a large-scale map of the United States was unfurled. It was peppered with hat pins of red, black, and white; on one margin was the key: RED—REBIRTH CASES; BLACK—NEAR DEATH EXPERIENCES; WHITE—GHOST/POLTERGEIST CASES.

Upstairs, some of Stevenson's associates were gathered around a big wood table in a conference room, eating takeout. All were researchers working on various projects funded by DOPS. One of them was a cardiologist who, on his rounds at the university health center, was identifying and studying heart patients who had reported having near-death experiences—mystical or out-of-body experiences supposedly triggered by severe medical crises, presumed by some to be evidence of consciousness after death. Upon being introduced to him, and told what he was working on, I asked, "What are you trying to accomplish?"

He swallowed down the remnants of his ham sandwich. "World peace," he said, then let the silence that followed linger before adding, "I'm quite serious. If you removed the fear of death, the world would be stood on its head. There would be no reason for war."

Perhaps this isn't quite as sober an enterprise as I had imagined, I was thinking as I was shown into Stevenson's ground-floor office.

The man himself was tall and lean, with a full head of silvering, slightly mussed hair. His blue suit and white dress shirt were well pressed, and he had a somewhat formal air about him. I asked him about the terminology: "Division of Personality Studies." He laughed and said, "That's just a benign-sounding front for the real gambling that goes on in the back room."

When I asked if he thought that his research had "proven" reincarnation, he said, "I don't think there is any proof in science outside of mathematics." However, he said, "Of the cases we know now—at least for some—reincarnation is the best explanation we have been able to come up with. There is an impressive body of evidence, and I think it is getting stronger all the time. I think a rational person, if he wants, can believe in reincarnation on the basis of evidence."

I loved the circumspection of that, the cool precision, the essential humility. World peace was nowhere in the equation. I decided to prod him a bit, just to make sure there wasn't a New Age ideologue lurking beneath the surface.

"One thing that bothers me about reincarnation as an explanation for anything," I said, "is the obvious problem of the population explosion. It's likely that more people have lived in this century than in all of prior human existence. Do only some people have reincarnated souls? Where do the new souls come from?"

We were seated in armchairs facing each other. There was a sense of the past in the old house, in his dress and manner, and the way we were sitting there like gentlemen taking after-dinner brandy. He didn't say anything right away, but seemed to look inward. He was clearly *thinking* about the question I had asked, and I realized how rarely I ever saw someone do that.

"This is not a problem which should be taken lightly," he said finally. "Some people have suggested that souls might come from other planets—the current thinking is that there are billions of terrestrial planets in the universe. Others say creation of souls is ongoing. But, of course, for any of those assertions, I have no evidence whatsoever."

Once again, I was charmed. But I didn't need to be sold on the idea of spending time with Stevenson: He was the one who needed persuasion. I explained that I wanted to accompany him on his field research. I told him that as an outside observer, bringing a journalist's eye for detail and context, I could re-create for readers the experience of the rigorous detective work only suggested between the lines of his scholarly accounts. I could report on the demeanor of his informants, the subtle qualities of interaction that added up to a sense of credibility or the lack of it. I said I believed that, although subjective, the experience of witnessing this was nonetheless a kind of information with which one could evaluate the data he had collected. In fact, I said, it was impossible to completely assess his research *without* that experience.

He nodded. He appreciated my point, he told me. But there were problems: He was nearing retirement and nearing the end of his traveling days. He did have plans for two final field trips, but they were tentative, and, in any case, he was concerned that the logistics of research in exotic locales—difficult to begin with—might be hopelessly confused if he had to worry about bringing me along.

What he didn't say, but I knew he must have been thinking, was that he had no way of knowing exactly what kind of reception I would give his work or what kind of biases I might bring to it. Talk about gambling: Inviting me along with him must have seemed like a particularly high-stakes crap shoot.

He didn't say yes, but he didn't say no, either.

∽

In the following months, as I waited for Stevenson to set the date for his next field trip and either invite me or deny my request, I came across a just-published volume by another philosophy professor, a man named Paul Edwards from the New School for Social Research in New York. Here, finally, was an extensive discussion of Stevenson's work in a book meant for a mass audience. As it so happened, the book, *Reincarnation: A Critical Examination,* was an energetic debunking of reincarnation from A to Z. Of Stevenson, Edwards had this to say in his introduction:

The writer most frequently criticized in this book is Professor Ian Stevenson of the University of Virginia. I should like to make it clear that there is nothing the least bit personal in these comments. I have never met Professor Stevenson. I have occasionally corresponded with him and he has always courteously responded to requests for reprints of his publications. He has written more fully and more intelligently in defense of reincarnation than anybody else and this is the only reason he features so prominently in my discussions.

Edwards provided me a great service by collecting and elaborating on an encyclopedic listing of objections to reincarnation. However, on the way to raising some important questions, he also exhibited some clear biases. One example comes in his discussion of Virginia Tighe—the woman at the center of the famous Bridey Murphy case that became a national sensation in the 1950s. While under hypnosis, Tighe had recalled being an Irish woman named Bridey Murphy and supplied many details of nineteenth-century Irish customs. Later in her life, Tighe expressed doubt that her memories were authentic. Noting this recantation, Edwards writes, completely gratuitously, "Virginia sounds like a basically sensible down-to-earth middle American, quite different from most of the insane or semi-insane persons who are attracted to the occult."

He also says that the possibility of reincarnation may be dismissed simply because the notion is "ridiculous": "Reincarnationists are committed to the absurd notion of an astral or 'spiritual' body and the even more absurd view that such a body invades the prospective mother's womb at the conception or at some stage during gestation."

This is clearly the kind of "*a priori* objection" that Stephen Braude was talking about, but Edwards isn't willing to accept Braude's argument that it is easy to imagine evidence "so coercive that we would have no choice but to admit (or at least entertain seriously) that survival of some sort is a fact."

After all, that would be insane. Or semi-insane.

Even this degree of bias, though, doesn't make Edwards's objections worthless. One thing he pointed out, which I didn't yet know, concerned the replication studies that I had come across—the research reports of independent scientists who had investigated cases similar to Stevenson's and arrived at similar conclusions: Every one of them was authored by a researcher who had been encouraged, and funded by, Stevenson.

In general, Edwards writes, Stevenson's cases may look good in aggregate, but on close inspection are revealed to be "fatally flawed," and he quotes a former associate criticizing Stevenson for asking leading questions, conducting superficial investigations, not taking into sufficient account the "human fallibility" of the witnesses he interviews, and reporting the cases in a way that makes them sound more impressive than they actually are.

He laid out the case against Stevenson's evidence succinctly:

—————————

Which is more likely—that there are astral bodies, that they invade the womb of prospective mothers, and that the children can remember events from a previous life although the brains of the previous persons have long been dead? Or that Stevenson's children, their parents, or some other witnesses and informants are, intentionally or unintentionally, not telling the truth: that they are lying, or that their very fallible memories and powers of observation have led them to make false statements and bogus identifications?

—————————

Edwards's evident intent is to make Stevenson look absurd for even raising the possibility that he may have uncovered evidence for reincarnation. Yet what caught my attention was the opposite: even Edwards was admitting, without meaning to, that if Stevenson's cases were *not* the product of lies, bogus identifications, and fallible observations—if somehow they could be demonstrated to be honest and accurate accounts of what happened—then they would constitute legitimate evidence for reincarnation.

Edwards tries to dig himself out of that admission a few pages later when he writes that "Stevenson will no doubt claim, that he and some of his associates have much better cases now. . . . Better, perhaps, but not good enough. They do not even begin to overthrow what I called the formidable initial presumption against reincarnation."

What Edwards was really saying was this: Because something challenges the accepted understanding of the world, it obviously cannot be true, and therefore is unworthy of consideration.

That is the position of dogma, not science.

Could any presumption against reincarnation be so great, I wondered, that it wasn't even worth the effort for a skeptic, someone independent of Stevenson's funding, someone thoroughly sane, to check the evidence out for himself? I had no idea how Stevenson's cases would hold up under close scrutiny. But given what was at stake—nothing less than possible concrete evidence of life after death—weren't they at least worth a visit?

Part II:

Beirut

Children of War

4

The Book of Daniel

Lebanon. Wasn't that what Stevenson had said when I'd seen him in January? He was planning a trip in the fall. To Lebanon.

I vaguely remembered registering slight puzzlement, as if I were sure that I couldn't have heard him correctly. The last time I had given that tragic corner of the world any sustained thought, Lebanon and its capital, Beirut, had been synonymous with hell on earth—a total urban war zone in which there were no noncombatants. Massacres, kidnappings, assassinations, indiscriminate shelling of residential neighborhoods, car bombs, kamikaze terrorists . . . Lebanon was a place that sent even the U.S. Marines and the Israeli army fleeing in horror.

But back in January, the prospect of actually accompanying Stevenson anywhere was a gauzy abstraction. Now there was no abstraction: here was the book contract in front of me; here was a pen in my hand. My hand was moving across the bottom line, signing my name.

Had he really said . . . *Lebanon?*

I remembered that Stevenson had put his plans in written form in an e-mail message sent to me several months before. I signed on to the computer, clicked on my mail archives, and there it was.

"I am anticipating two field trips in the coming months; to India in early 1998, and to Lebanon this fall."

I clicked on to the Internet and found this on the State Department's travel-advisory Web page:

Lebanon—Travel Warning
July 30, 1997

The United States Department of State warns all U.S. citizens of the dangers of travel to Lebanon. Therefore, the Department recommends that only those Americans with compelling reasons should consider traveling to Lebanon. Americans have in the past been targets of numerous terrorist attacks in Lebanon. The perpetrators of these attacks are still present in Lebanon and retain the ability to act. Due to limited staff and the local security environment inhibiting movement of U.S. officials in much of the country, the U.S. Embassy in Beirut cannot perform routine consular functions and may not be able to provide timely assistance to Americans traveling in Lebanon. In addition, Americans working at the U.S. Embassy do not normally use Beirut International Airport (BIA) due to the concern about security of passengers and aircraft. The recent expiration of the passport restriction should not in any way be construed as a determination by the Department of State that it is safe for Americans to travel to Lebanon.

I remembered that in our talk that spring Stevenson had chuckled about outlasting "bandits and despots" in his various travels over the years. As the departure date drew close, though, events arose that made even Stevenson raise an eyebrow. In Jerusalem, only 150 miles to the south, brutal acts of terrorism and reprisals had turned the Israeli-Palestinian peace process into a death march. In Iraq, only 200 miles to the east, Saddam Hussein was preparing to expel the American members of a UN inspection team charged with certifying that that country had eliminated its biological and chemical weapons of mass destruction. An American retaliation was possible at any time. And then, who knew what could happen?

But for the moment, at least, Lebanon was upwind of the trouble, and Stevenson, who knew his traveling days to be numbered, wasn't about to postpone this trip: he hadn't been to Lebanon for sixteen years, his research trips derailed by the civil war and its aftermath. I would soon learn why he was so eager to return.

From those earlier visits, Stevenson had friends and supporters in

Beirut for whom the current troubles were barely a blip on the screen. Chief among them was the woman who would serve as his interpreter and research assistant, Majd Abu-Izzedin. The name appeared more difficult to pronounce than it actually was, I discovered. The trick was to say three syllables as if there were only one—like *Ma-je-duh* all slurred together: *Majd*. Stevenson had known Majd for more than twenty years, ever since a professor at the American University in Beirut, who knew Majd as an able student, had recommended to Stevenson that he enlist her in his local efforts. After the war blocked Stevenson's research, Majd stayed on in Lebanon, living through some of the most intense years of war, huddling in apartment-building basements while her city was smashed to rubble. In 1985, she finally left for America, settling in Virginia, not far from Stevenson in Charlottesville. There, raising organic vegetables for gourmet shops and restaurants on the farm she owned with her husband, Faisal, she lived a life as pacific as her life in Beirut had been bellicose. But they had returned to Lebanon the previous summer so that Faisal, an expert horticulturist, could take a post in the Lebanese environmental ministry. Their ten-year-old son traded a life in the semirural Virginia—the only one he had known—for the uncertainties of a Beirut high-rise.

Having Majd in Beirut was an incredible boon for Stevenson. She appeared to know everyone, and she was absolutely fearless. She and Faisal were both from very prominent families in the Druse community. The Druses practice a variation of Shi'ite Islam, though they consider theirs to be an entirely different religion. For generations, their religious practices had been semisecret, but one of the main differences between the Druse and orthodox Moslem sects was the Druse firm belief in reincarnation—a belief, it turned out, that was reinforced by the scores of Druse children who spoke of remembering previous lives.

∽

I met Stevenson in Paris, in the departure lounge of Charles de Gaulle Airport. Our Air France flight was already boarding. Stevenson was flying business class, and I was flying coach, but he waited for me nonetheless, tall and distinguished looking as I remembered. In one hand, he held an overstuffed briefcase with a brass combination lock;

his overcoat was folded over the other arm. His white hair was slightly tousled, just like it had been in Charlottesville, as if ruffled by an unseen wind, and his shoulders stooped as if he were preparing to walk through a low doorway. We barely had a chance to shake hands before going our separate ways in the cabin.

I wondered again if he harbored any second thoughts about what he had gotten himself into by inviting a journalist he had met only once to scrutinize his work at point-blank range. I hoped that his willingness to allow me to accompany him represented not abject foolhardiness but a well-founded confidence that the trip would bear up under skeptical examination.

The flight was three-fourths full and comfortably appointed with excellent food and service. My fellow passengers, most of them Lebanese, were international businessmen in Italian suits and women in designer dresses and tasteful jewelry. This was my first taste of the resurgent Lebanon, the country that, before the fifteen years of war, had been the Paris of the Middle East and appeared now to be in a hurry to regain that mantle.

Night fell over the Mediterranean, and Beirut eventually announced itself as a web of shimmering light against the black water. The web, though, had big, jagged holes in it. I wouldn't realize until daylight what they were: vast sections of the city laid to waste, still in rubble or flattened for reconstruction.

On the ground, the steel frame of a new airport rose just beyond the exhausted, dun-colored terminal that had seen such horror during the years of war. Before I'd ever met Majd, she told me in musically accented English over an international phone line, embarrassed, I think, that "The airport is very bad, horrible ree-lee. It's because of all the construction."

She'd also told me, to the consternation and concern of my travel agent, that I needn't worry about sending to the Lebanese embassy for a visa in advance because I could easily get one upon arrival. Right again—we strolled into the bare, basic terminal, paid $17 in American bills for a visa stamp, and walked out. Elapsed time: ten minutes.

Mahmoud, Majd's driver, stood waving in the thick crowd, a throng really, gathered just outside the terminal doors. His round belly strained against the buttons of his dress shirt, which was open at the neck to reveal a cotton undershirt. His face was pleasantly fleshy, framed by graying hair and punctuated by a mustache and dark, bushy eyebrows. He hadn't seen Stevenson for the better part of two decades and seemed genuinely happy to do so now.

Mahmoud commandeered the luggage cart and steered us through the mild airport chaos to a dark Mercedes. Majd, a small, pretty woman with sharp features, quick eyes, and short black hair, emerged from the backseat. She hugged Stevenson and shook my hand.

The luggage loaded, Stevenson awkwardly folded his lanky frame into the backseat with Majd, and I hopped in the front. Mahmoud (the way Majd said his name sounded halfway between a Southerner drawling "my mood" and a German saying "*mach* mood") steered past the guard gates, waved solicitously at a gauntlet of armed soldiers—I could see that he made sure to look them directly in the eye—and headed toward central Beirut.

As Majd shuffled through her notes, Stevenson asked her about her readjustment to life in Lebanon.

"It's been hard moving from a country—" she started to say "that was civilized," then stopped herself and reloaded: "—where things are easy, to one where they are always difficult. And all those years of the war changed people. That's the worst part."

Then, clearly changing the subject, she said brightly, "Good news. All the subjects you wanted to look up are still living at the same addresses they were living at sixteen years ago. That's something of a miracle, ree-lee, don't you think? And they are all willing to see you."

Stevenson had a number of goals for that visit. He wanted to log follow-up visits on cases that he had originally investigated years earlier but only now intended to publish for the first time. He also was looking for new cases in which the subjects were still children, not to study himself, but to prepare the way for a researcher from Iceland named Erlendur Haraldsson, who had conducted psychological testing of children in Stevenson's cases in Sri Lanka and wanted to expand his study to Lebanese children. Finally, Stevenson planned to revisit some subjects he'd first met more than thirty years earlier, to add to his understanding of how previous-life memories, and some of the behaviors associated with them, played out over a lifetime.

I think he also wanted to say good-bye to them. A number of times before, he'd vowed that he was making his final field trip. This time, I think that he really believed it.

The car turned and headed up a long slope. From a surrounding void, a tall, narrow tower rose blankly into the darkness.

"This is what used to be downtown," Majd said. "It was basically flattened in the war."

"Is that new?" Stevenson asked, pointing at the lone skyscraper now dead ahead of us.

"No, that was the tallest building in the city before the war. They thought they could save it, but it was too badly damaged." As we approached, Majd seemed to wince. "During the fighting, snipers would shoot from the upper floors. It was very, very dangerous."

We rolled out of the emptiness into a web of narrow streets clogged with honking cars and hemmed in by storefronts, most barred with steel security gates. The Cavalier Hotel was down a narrow tributary, opposite a bombed-out building in slow-motion reconstruction and half a block from Rue Hamra, one of West Beirut's main shopping areas. The lobby was small and unprepossessing, just a sofa and a couple of overstuffed chairs around a coffee table in a narrow space between front desk and elevator. Stevenson, I discovered, was not one to acknowledge jet lag or much else in the way of personal discomfort. It was well past midnight when we checked in. We agreed to meet in the lobby at 8:30 A.M.

∽

I appeared at the appointed hour. Stevenson was in the chair where I had left him the night before, now paging through the manila folders bulging with field notes and case summaries.

Majd had not yet arrived. "It's a sign of better times that she's driving the Mercedes," Stevenson observed. "When I was here before, she left the Mercedes at home and drove an old bullet-riddled car because soldiers manning the checkpoints would just take the keys of cars they liked and drive off with them." If the occupants were lucky, they would be left stranded. If they were unlucky, or had the wrong name or wrong accent, they might never be seen again.

One of the cases that Stevenson wanted to revisit on this trip was that of Daniel Jirdi, who, as a small child, claimed to remember the life of Rashid Khaddege, a mechanic who had been killed in a car wreck at the age of twenty-five. Stevenson and Majd had last interviewed Daniel eighteen years ago, when he was nine years old.

As I read the outline of the case in Stevenson's notes, I was gratified: it had a number of important features, which, if they held up under scrutiny, would be very impressive. To begin with—and this is a common feature of Stevenson's cases—the life Daniel remembered was excruciatingly ordinary, virtually glamourless: a single, working-class man, childless, unmarried, unrenowned, killed in a completely routine accident—hardly a likely subject for a youngster's fantasies. More important, each family involved denied any prior knowledge of the other. If true, it would be difficult to explain how a small child was able to come by accurate information about an obscure stranger who lived in a different community and died more than a year before he was born. Furthermore, Daniel began making statements as soon as he could speak, and that extraordinarily young age made the idea of some form of fraud almost unthinkable. Things change rapidly as the child gets older, becomes more aware of his surroundings, more adept verbally, and enters into much wider contact with the world outside his home. As a father myself, I can attest to the fact that by the time they are five, children are picking up all sorts of stray information and repeating it, constantly prompting amused and amazed comments from parents such as, "Where did they come up with *that?*"

But believing that a child could learn and repeat complex, accurate biographies at an age when his peers are struggling to learn the names of colors is almost an absurdity.

Daniel's case, however, also had one key weakness, one shared by all but a rare few of Stevenson's cases: the two families had found each other and met before Stevenson interviewed either. He had no opportunity to see for himself the child's reaction upon first meeting the family he claimed to remember from a previous life, no chance to personally hear the child make statements about his previous personality ("his PP," in Stevenson and Majd's shorthand) before the statements were either supported or disputed by the previous personality's family. In these cases, verifying that the child made statements and that the statements turned out to be accurate, depended on comparing accounts of first-hand witnesses and evaluating the credibility of those witnesses.

It was one thing to read Stevenson's own evaluation of these factors in his case reports, where they seemed, for the most part, sober, cautious, and relatively thorough—but also maddeningly skeletal. It would be quite another thing, I knew, to evaluate it all for myself, eye to eye with the subjects and the witnesses, listening to the tenor of their voices, watching the expressions on their faces, observing the surroundings and circumstances.

∾

When Majd arrived, she and Stevenson sat in the lobby discussing logistics. I looked through her file on the Jirdi case and came across a transcript of a conversation she had had with Daniel in 1979, when the boy was nine. She asked him about the circumstances surrounding Rashid Khaddege's death in an automobile accident, which Daniel claimed to remember happening to him:

> MAJD: *How many were you in that car?*
> DANIEL: *Six.*
> MAJD: *Who was driving?*
> DANIEL: *Ibrahim.*
> MAJD: *Is he older than you?*
> DANIEL: *Older by four years.*
> MAJD: *Do you see him?*
> DANIEL: *No. And if I see him, I'll kill him.*
> MAJD: *How is school?*
> DANIEL: *Very good. I am excellent in math.*
> MAJD: *Which company did you work with?*
> DANIEL: *Datsun? No, Fiat!*
> MAJD: *Where did you work?*
> DANIEL: *In Beirut.*
> MAJD: *How did the accident happen?*
> DANIEL: *While we were in the car, another car passed us and scolded us, so Ibrahim turned the car to go back and scold them, but the car spun and we crashed. They picked up my friend, who was near me, and left me. Everybody who was in the car was found outside after the crash. I also remember I was dropped from a balcony. That is all that I remember.*

I read the transcript over several times. It fascinated me for a variety of reasons that I tried to sort out. For one thing, this kind of source material is alluded to, but not reproduced, in Stevenson's books—this was the first time I actually could see a child responding question by question, talking of himself in the first person, in the personality of a dead man. The matter-of-fact tone was riveting, with the victim of a fatal accident talking in one breath about being thrown from a car and in the next about being a good math student as a little boy in another existence.

I also noticed something else: Some of the statements that Daniel made in the interview contradicted statements from other sources recorded elsewhere in the file. For instance, Rashid's mother said that there were four people in the car, not six. Also, when asked what company he (meaning Rashid) had worked for, Daniel first says Datsun, then quickly changes it to Fiat, the correct answer, as if he had memorized answers to a history quiz and gotten momentarily confused. Some of the claims Daniel made in that interview—most notably that he remembered falling from a balcony—had apparently never been followed up. I couldn't find another reference to such a fall anywhere in the notes.

∽

I had been warned that November in Beirut could be cold, but it was warm and sunny as we loaded back into the Mercedes for the day's journey. I asked Stevenson about Daniel's balcony statement. He said that while it would be worth inquiring about, he had not seriously pursued it or the discrepancies I had noticed, because that interview with Daniel had been conducted long after the families had met and formed a long-term relationship. By then, Daniel might easily have been repeating things—accurate or otherwise—that he'd heard being discussed by his or Rashid's family or any number of other people discussing the case. Stevenson considered any statements made by subjects after they had met or communicated with their "PP families" to be tainted, and gave first priority to verifying those statements made by a child and confirmed by firsthand witnesses before any contact. Also, he noted, no subject's "memory" was ever flawless, which could merely reflect that memory in general is flawed, even in the space of a *single* lifetime.

Looking through the file, I could see that the basic statements

Daniel's parents said he made to them before ever meeting the Khaddeges were limited. One of his earliest words was the name "Ibrahim," which he said frequently. In the beginning, his parents say, they were unable to figure out why Daniel mentioned the name. But as he grew more articulate, it became clear that the name was associated in Daniel's mind with a serious car accident. When Daniel was two and a half years old, at a family picnic, an adult tried to say "Kfarmatta" (it sounds to the American ear like "fur-mat-ta," only with a subtle glottal sound before the "f"), which is the name of a small town some distance from where the Jirdis lived. Daniel's parents, unaware that their toddler had even been listening to the conversation, were flabbergasted when Daniel—who had never been anywhere near the town—quite clearly said, "That's not how you say it," then proceeded to pronounce the name accurately. When they got home, his father asked Daniel how he knew the town. "I am from Kfarmatta," the boy replied.

Some time later, when Daniel and his mother were driving in Beirut, they passed a place on the ocean called Military Beach. Daniel shut his eyes, hiding them with his hands, and started crying, screaming, "This is where I died."

Later, Daniel said that he had been a mechanic, and he described the accident in more complete detail, saying that the car had been speeding and that he had flown out of it and injured his head.

Daniel's father portrayed himself as skeptical about reincarnation, a stance not uncommon for an urbanized Druse. Still, his son's behavior impressed him. The family sent an acquaintance familiar with Kfarmatta to inquire as to whether anyone in the town might fit Daniel's statements, as he had not yet used the name Rashid or the family name Khaddege. But there were enough details—the name Ibrahim, the location and nature of the accident, and the occupation of the deceased—for those with even passing familiarity with Rashid's family to make a connection. Word got back to the Khaddeges, who then came, unannounced, to pay Daniel a visit.

In Stevenson's 1979 interviews, the Jirdis and the Khaddeges both said that Daniel instantly recognized Rashid's sister Najla and called her by name.

It was an impressive account. Nonetheless, I was still struck by the inconsistencies in the interview of nine-year-old Daniel, which, at least, underline the difficulty of dealing with testimony of any kind. And I wasn't inclined to dismiss the "dropped from the balcony" statement so quickly. I decided that if I got a chance, I'd ask about it.

∽

With that thought echoing in my mind, we headed into Beirut for the first time in daylight. It didn't take me long to notice that there are no stoplights in Beirut and no expressways. The entire city is characterized by a massive gridlock of cars and trucks and military vehicles, all of it bathed in exhaust and electrified by a driving ethic that relies almost exclusively on aggression and the theory that possession of the road is considerably more than nine-tenths of the law.

The mayhem on the roads, though, could hold my attention only fitfully, for as we plunged more deeply into the city, it became clear that there was nowhere to look that excluded ruin. Everywhere were shrapnel-pocked walls, windowless buildings with upper floors torn away and concrete balconies hanging by steel threads, piles of rubble spilling across broken sidewalks into the street. But as my eyes, and heart, adjusted, I began to see movement within the desolation. The ruins were alive. Rubble-choked streets were filled with pedestrians, sharply dressed and striding with purpose. Shops were open and well stocked, restaurants and cafés bustled, stores selling expensive toys and electronics roiled with customers. Time and again, on the street level of a building whose top floors had been ripped open, a posh boutique operated, apparently unconcerned for the tons of concrete hanging perilously askew overhead.

At one point, our progress stopped dead in a clot of fuming traffic, bright color caught my eye. On the corner, a vendor had set up an impromptu market. Abundant fruit—ripe yellow bananas still hanging on their stalks, bright red apples spilling out of baskets, green melons lined up like bowling balls, dates and figs overflowing cardboard boxes—called to passersby.

I did a double-take: This produce—so handsomely displayed—was arrayed in the rubble of a collapsed building, beside a trash pile. Boxes were stacked on slabs of shattered concrete, bananas were hung on rusted steel rods twisting out of the wreckage. People stood calmly in the ruins poking fruit, shaking melons, paying the vendor. Meanwhile, the rubble rose all around them, above their heads, and then merged with a bombed-out shell of another building.

I stared at the adjoining ruin. It was sprouting—moss, weeds, even shrubbery and small trees thrust from the cracks, crevices, and raw ravines that had been ripped away by some long-ago explosion. Looking more closely, I noticed motion through the naked portals that had once been windows: laundry! Shorts, slips, pants, dresses, all hung on lines and flapping in the breeze. On the jagged stumps of terraces, potted herbs and tomato plants thrived. Electric cables rose up the pocked exterior from the street, snaking this way and that into the black openings. Here and there, I could see lightbulbs burning. In the cavelike opening on the ground floor, a mechanic was bent under the hood of a car.

I would have expected to feel buoyed by the idea that life had found a way to continue, that commerce and normalcy had taken root in the rocky stubble of destruction. Instead, I felt saddened. Part of me longed for this to be a silent tomb, a memorial with the words "Too Much" and "Never Again" chiseled in the broken concrete. Instead, it was testament to the fact that though we could do our worst, the world would just go on, as if nothing had happened.

The Mercedes descended to the waterfront. Here and there, the stone ruins of ancient mosques, cut into lace by innumerable bombardments, stood behind scaffolding that looked as if it had been erected years before and would remain there years hence. Otherwise, the city center was mowed flat, scraped and plowed hard as a parking lot, its vast emptiness punctuated with immense rectangular pits where the foundations of new buildings would rise, eventually, maybe. On this morning, there was no sign of ongoing construction, save for a pile of ancient marble columns—Ionic, Doric, Corinthian, all those styles I had once been forced to memorize in history class—that had been dug up and stacked like Lincoln Logs beside one of the deeper excavation pits. In the harbor, a few hundred yards distant, an island rose from the water, an odd, naked hump snaking one hundred feet above the Mediterranean: it was composed of cleared debris—literally, a mountain of rubble.

At the outskirts of ground zero, a new white six-story building stood beside an electric guitar three stories tall. The Beirut Hard Rock Café. Could a city where it is safe to worship Jim Morrison's alleged leather pants be all that dangerous?

We left downtown and headed south on the coastal highway, then turned east into the mountains. I was waiting for the country landscape to begin. Instead, we got the same combination of ruined buildings, buildings under construction, and buildings whose construction or repair appeared permanently stalled interspersed among army checkpoints, both Lebanese and Syrian, with tanks and armored cars lined up on the side of the road or backed into the cement-and-steel shells of what once were ground floors. Mahmoud accelerated as we began to climb, charging up the steep grade into the foothills past heavy trucks, military transports, and private cars on what would have been the pocked road's center lane, if it had lanes. Meanwhile, his counterparts charged down the mountain using the same strategy, and the same phantom lane, taking the precaution to beep heartily at each blind corner in hopes that whoever was coming would back down before colliding head on. It seemed to me a drastic and foolish hope.

As we climbed to Kfarmatta, the war damage only increased. These hills, the center of Druse population in Lebanon, had been shelled heavily for years. Concrete and quarried-stone buildings gutted by blast and fire studded the steep slopes, oddly mirroring the new stone buildings that had begun to go up, then stalled in midconstruction.

∾

Nearly two hours out of Beirut, the pavement, pitted as it was, gave way to a dirt road at the village of Kfarmatta. There was not much to speak of, just a line of small shops on the ground floors of two- and three-story buildings, some crumbling, all of them scarred by shrapnel. At the foot of a rise, the road simply disappeared, swallowed by a massive trench. Whether it was unrepaired war damage or stalled construction was unclear. Mahmoud steered around the abyss, driving up on the dirt curb and almost scraping the dusty storefronts with the miraculously unscratched side panels of the Mercedes.

This town was the site of some terrible massacres of Druse civilians by Christian militias. The massacres went both ways in the war, but the

Druse suffered at least as much as anyone. Now children, born since the shooting stopped, watched with idle curiosity as our Mercedes churned the dust.

At the top of the main street, the road zigged right, then climbed again. We drove until we ran out of village, then Mahmoud braked and called out the window to a man bent over a bicycle on the side of the road. We were looking for Najla Khaddege, the older sister of Rashid, the man Daniel claimed to have been in his previous life, but we would never find her by her own name. "You have to know the father's name, then you can always find the house," Majd explained. "Even if the father has been dead for more than forty years, that's the name they know."

That was true in this case. Naim Khaddege, Rashid's father, went off to fight in the war against Israel in 1948 and never came back. The family never learned what became of him. But as soon as Majd mentioned his name, the man pointed, gesturing back the way we came. The house turned out to be right where the trench had swallowed the road.

It was a three-story building, constructed of bare concrete block with an exterior stairway. Another similar building, at one time attached, was now collapsed in on itself. Majd stepped out of the car, over the narrow end of the trench, and disappeared inside for a long time. When she returned, she told us that Najla was in Beirut, but Rashid's younger sister, Muna, was there.

"The reason I was gone so long is that she was telling me about a new case," Majd said. It seemed that Muna's twenty-one-year-old daughter, Ulfat, had memories of being one of the young women killed by Christians during the civil war.

Stevenson was disappointed to hear that the girl was so old, but the news of a brand-new case stunned and slightly alarmed me. Our first day out, our first contact with anyone, and a new case popped up. It seemed a little too good to be true. We followed Majd back into the ground-floor apartment.

Muna, a short, middle-aged woman wearing a navy midcalf-length sheath skirt, a black T-shirt advertising Juniors glasses, and a *mandeel*—a white head scarf that signifies religious devotion—welcomed us enthusiastically. I had been forewarned not to offer my hand to women wearing mandeels: Religious, married Druse women could not physically touch any man outside of their immediate family.

Majd explained that this was the Khaddege family's "summer house"—the place up in the mountains that they, like many families, moved to in the summer months in order to flee the heat and pollution of Beirut. Since large extended families shared inherited houses, a second home didn't carry the same connotation of wealth that it might in America.

Despite the outward ruin, the apartment's interior was spacious, sparsely furnished but comfortable, with high ceilings—at least fifteen feet—bare bulbs dangling from them at the ends of long wires. In the corner of the far room, a television and VCR sat on a small table.

Muna invited us to sit on a worn couch in the front room, then disappeared into the kitchen. She returned shortly, carrying a smudged silver serving tray with three individual cans of pineapple drink and three straws. She set the drinks on TV trays at our knees. While we sipped juice, Muna spoke animatedly to Majd about her daughter's vivid recollection of a previous life; terrible memories of being stabbed in the chest, then slit open in the pattern of a cross. She remembered enormous suffering before her death.

As a child, Muna said, Ulfat had a severe phobia of knives. She said that the girl also remembered that as the men tortured her, she saw a friend named Ida through the window and screamed for her, but Ida, who was a Christian, did not come. As Muna related this to Majd, tears welled in her eyes. Muna said that the victims of these massacres often were abandoned by neighbors too frightened for their own safety to come to their aid. Often, the bodies were left to rot where they fell, and weren't recovered and buried until after the Christians left town.

From what Ulfat said as a small child, Muna's family had been able to match her statements with a girl killed in a massacre in a town called Salina.

Had they known of the family before? I asked. Majd translated. Muna shook her head.

Just then, the door opened and a pretty, young woman with long, dark hair falling past her shoulders entered the room. Ulfat. Two teenage boys, who turned out to be her brother and a friend, followed in her wake. Both boys wore jeans, T-shirts, and baseball caps—they slouched into the room like typical American mallrats. Ulfat's brother's T-shirt said POMONA VALLEY CALIFORNIA; his friend's cap, CIA. Ulfat wore a black sweatshirt and black jeans over hiking boots, but, with silver earrings and makeup, was decidedly feminine.

Muna explained why we were there and asked Ulfat if she'd mind us asking her some questions.

Ulfat turned to us and said, "I don't mind. You can ask me in English if you like."

This wasn't what I had imagined. I'd expected villages with dirt-floored huts, people in traditional dress with customs that seemed strange to me. I knew that some of Stevenson's critics questioned his use of translators on the grounds that he couldn't be sure of the accuracy of the translation or make sense of a cultural context alien to his own. But this didn't feel any more alien than, say, the home of my Cuban neighbors in Miami, where the parents speak little English and the kids listen to heavy-metal CDs. Now, here was the subject of a past-life case who owned a VCR and spoke very American-sounding English.

With Ulfat seated in an armchair opposite her mother, we began. She said she was a college student in Beirut. She didn't know what she would do when she finished school.

Did she still remember her previous life?

"Not so much, only names. When I was a child, I used to talk about it, but now I've forgotten. I remember my name and family name. I remember the day I died and how I died."

The name she remembered was Iqbal Saed.

"On the day I died, I remember every single thing that happened."

"Tell us about what you remember," I said.

"It was at night. I was walking. I was afraid to go through an alley, but had no other way to go. There were about four men carrying guns. As soon as they saw me, they shot me on my leg. I bended to catch my leg. They saw the jewels I was hiding." She paused and pointed to the top of her chest—she had been hiding the valuables in her blouse. "They saw, and then they caught me. Before they killed me, they tortured me a lot. I can't remember too much about that. I remember when they killed me. When I close my eyes I can remember. I can see how I was walking, everything about that night."

"How old a woman were you?" Stevenson asked.

"I was twenty-three."

"Do you remember being that age? Or did someone tell you how old Iqbal was when she died?"

"I remember I died young, but they told me I was twenty-three years old."

"Did you go to school in the previous life?"

"I don't think I went to school."

I scribbled in my notebook, spellbound. She was so matter-of-fact—somber, but straightforward.

"How do you feel about these memories?" I asked her.

"They bother me," she blurted. There was a pause before she continued: "When I was young, I always dreamed someone was coming to kill me, but I don't dream about it now."

Stevenson turned to Majd and asked her to ask Muna if she knew anyone in Salina, the town where Iqbal died. Majd obliged. "No," Muna replied. "It is very far from here."

"Do you have any birthmarks?" Stevenson asked Ulfat. This wasn't an idle question, but one of the main focuses of Stevenson's current interest: The work that Stevenson had just completed primarily concerned birthmarks that apparently corresponded to wounds or defects from remembered lives.

Ulfat shook her head. "No."

"Any phantom pain?"

"No."

"Any other physical difficulties?"

I half expected Ulfat to come up with something just to please him. But she kept shaking her head. "Nothing like that," she said finally.

"This next question is for Muna," Stevenson said. "Did Ulfat have any problems learning to walk?"

No, she walked at eleven months.

Muna went on at some length, and then Majd translated: Muna was out of the country during much of Ulfat's early life. Her sister, Najla, saw more of the first signs of Ulfat's memories of a previous life than she had. Much of what Muna told us were things that she had heard secondhand from Najla. In one such incident, Ulfat, still a toddler, heard that Christians were coming to her village. She ran and hid behind the couch saying, "They're going to kill me like this [she traced a cross on her chest], like they did before."

Majd could barely get the translation out before Muna went on, speaking excitedly. In high gear, she leaned close to Majd and gestured as she told tales of reincarnation: She told a story about a Druse man whose intended marriage was prohibited because his fiancée was discovered to have been his sister in a previous life. She'd heard of a woman whose child began speaking a language nobody could understand. Then, one day, they were walking on the street and saw some Indians talking among themselves. The child ran to them and began speaking Hindi fluently and understanding everything that was said to him.

But this was all hearsay, and Muna couldn't tell us how to contact the families involved. I decided to ask my question about Daniel's memory of a fall from the balcony. Not wanting to make the question suggestive of an answer, I asked Majd to inquire if Rashid had had any accidents as a child. Muna looked surprised and responded with a rapid burst of words. She had no memory of Rashid being involved in an accident, but she herself had fallen from a balcony—she had been eleven, and both she and her baby sister had fallen. Her sister, Linda, died in the fall.

Stevenson seemed uncomfortable with my pressing the point of whether Rashid had ever fallen from a balcony. "That's a question for Najla, she'll know."

I wondered if he thought that I was trying to poke holes in Daniel's stories. He'd already told me that he thought that interview was worthless as evidence, one way or the other. But I was intrigued. Falling from the balcony can't be that common an accident for children.

Could Daniel's memory of falling from a balcony have been a confused past-life memory of the pain of losing a baby sister? Or had he heard the Khaddeges telling family stories after he'd met them, and incorporated one of the most traumatic into his own repertoire of Rashid's "memories"?

We climbed back over the trench and resumed our places in the Mercedes. Mahmoud headed further into the mountains. Before, we had gone south along the coast, then east into the hills. Now we were headed northwest, back toward Beirut through the Shouf mountains.

Our destination was Aley, a much bigger town with a wide main street lined by stone buildings housing shops, restaurants, and offices.

On the way, I had a lot to think about. First, I had been impressed with Ulfat's sophistication and her matter-of-factness. Clearly, she hadn't enjoyed telling us about her "memories"—she was obliging us. I could see the sadness in her face and hear it in her voice. Her memories hadn't brought her any apparent status or special attention—they were no big deal in her immediate environment. And even though Stevenson had asked her questions about whether she had any aches or pains that might be related to her previous life—an open invitation to embellish her story if impressing us had been her motivation—she said no, flatly and unhesitatingly.

On the other hand, the horrific details of her memories—the valuables held against her bosom, the Christian friend ignoring her tortured screams for help, the cross carved in her chest—were almost literary in the way they reflected the agony of the communal experience Ulfat was born into. I could imagine a child internalizing the grief and terror around her, only to have it emerge in a personal metaphor. Maybe somewhere she had half-heard someone telling a story about a girl named Iqbal who had been carved up that way in a massacre. Maybe she gave that name to her own fear, dreamed that it had happened to her.

Her claims raised a million questions and pointed in a hundred directions. I realized that I had just witnessed the initial phase of an investigation, the answer to the question of how Stevenson found these people. Apparently, in the Druse hills of Lebanon, it isn't that difficult. In fact, sometimes, they just walk in the front door.

∽

It was nearly 1 P.M. when we left Muna's house. I was jet-lagged and hungry, but no one mentioned lunch. It was becoming obvious, even this early in our trip, that Stevenson believed in making his travel dollars count.

It was ten miles on a straight line to Aley, but we traveled on anything but a straight line. It took nearly an hour to get there. When we did, we drove across Aley and through its downtown. Even compared

to what we'd seen elsewhere, the destruction was horrific: Entire hillside neighborhoods were in ruin. In fact, anything that wasn't crumbling had clearly been recently rebuilt. I asked Majd about it, and she
mumbled something about "the *New Jersey*."

"The what?" I asked.

"The *New Jersey*," she said. "It was an American battleship that sat
offshore and shelled the hills around here. It did a lot of damage."

I expressed disbelief at the idea that the United States military had
intentionally bombarded civilian neighborhoods.

"The Christians misled them about who they were shooting at,"
she explained.

It's amazing what can escape your notice when you're safe and
comfortable on the other side of an ocean or two. When I got back to
the States, I asked a number of friends, professional journalists, if they
remembered reading anything about the battleship *New Jersey* shelling
Lebanon. They hadn't. Curious, I searched the Internet for the conjunction of the words New Jersey and Beirut. What I got was a cryptic bul-
letin-board conversation from former *New Jersey* crew members. One
posting read:

"Who remembers Feb. 8, 1984? There wasn't any dust on the decks
that day!"

The response: "We were rocking and rolling, I'll tell you that!"

I looked up the date in the newspaper archives and came up with
this:

The 16-inch guns of the battleship New Jersey *and the five-inch guns
of the destroyer* Caron *fired more than 550 shells into the hills east of
Beirut, a Pentagon spokesman said in Washington. It was the fiercest
U.S. naval barrage since the Vietnam war. U.S. officials said the bombardment retaliated for shelling of East Beirut and its suburbs by rebel
Druse gunners in the Syrian-occupied mountains that scored direct hits
on the U.S. ambassador's residence and the Lebanese presidential
palace. Syria charged the American bombardment missed its soldiers
but killed "dozens of civilian women, children and old men."*

But I learned all of this later. For the moment, I didn't know what to
make of the *New Jersey*. We passed through the worst of the damage

and parked at the foot of a five-floor apartment building fronted by balconies overlooking the sinuous valley that wound toward the plain of Beirut. Daniel Jirdi, now twenty-seven, lived there with his parents, his young wife, and their newborn baby girl. We climbed the exterior stairway to the top floor and strode onto an open balcony that extended the length of the building, past several connected apartments. A stout young man with a round, pleasant face appeared at the frosted-glass window and opened the double doors. His face lit up. "Dr. Stevenson," he said in English. "You haven't changed."

He led us into a large room with an arrangement of ornate chairs and couches around a Persian carpet. A cylindrical gas heater sat by the couch, attached to the gas line by a red rubber hose, ready for the winter chill.

Daniel was dressed as if he were about to spend an evening line dancing in a country-western bar: a black cowboy shirt embroidered in white topped black jeans, white socks, and black loafers. His jet-black hair featured a gray spot on the right temple.

The apartment was filled with well-tended houseplants, its walls covered with framed family pictures. Daniel's wife of one year, a doll-like woman with auburn-red hair and porcelain skin (a ravishing beauty in their wedding photo, which hung prominently on the wall), greeted each of us in turn, repeating formally in English: "Welcome to our house."

Daniel plopped expansively in an armchair in the corner of the room by the door. His father, a handsome, courtly man with gray hair and darkly tanned skin, took a seat opposite the couch, next to Daniel's wife.

Once again, Stevenson unclasped his heavy case and pulled out the manila folders, shuffling through them until he found his follow-up forms, and began.

Did he still have memories?

"Of course," Daniel shrugged. "A lot of memories. Everything."

He said that he was still visiting his "other family" once or twice a month. ("Me, too," his wife laughed. "I have two mothers-in-law and two fathers-in-law.") Daniel's PP's mother came last month and brought a gift for their two-month-old daughter, he said. He went to stay with his PP's family "even during the civil war" and slept in the room that they keep just for him at their house in Beirut.

Good deal, I thought. In every society throughout history, the support you could count on always came from family. And the more you could extend the concept of "family," the better off you were. The main way to do that has always been through marriage. The Druse apparently had a second option: a claim of previous-life identity that was found plausible by the deceased's relatives.

That didn't mean that the claims were fraudulent, but it did highlight an important advantage inherent in making them, and a possible motivation for, consciously or unconsciously, inventing them.

On the other hand, it also meant that all over Lebanon, apparently, families in a position to know if a child's statements were accurate, and with a reason to be cautious about accepting them as true, had accepted these claims unreservedly enough to enter into lifelong relationships.

∽

There was a moment of silence as Stevenson shuffled through the papers on his lap. He settled on a page in one of his folders that contained notes from years earlier, an interview with an informant who said that Daniel had a phobia of racing cars. This presumably corresponded to Rashid's death in a speeding car.

In many of Stevenson's cases, children seem to display phobias in some way related to their previous-life memories. Stevenson found this intriguing. It also explained why he was skeptical about the assumption behind the idea of past-life hypnotic regression—that by "reliving" past-life traumas under hypnosis, the patient's present-life symptoms disappear.

"Most of the children I have studied recall past life traumas in great detail," he'd told me. "That doesn't stop them from having phobias."

But when he asked about the alleged fear of race cars, Daniel looked at him blankly.

"I love Formula 1 racing," he said.

Stevenson jotted a note and went on: "Who was driving the car in the accident?"

Daniel gave him a look as if to say, *Everyone knows that.*

"Ibrahim," he said, then paused and seemed to smile at some secret knowledge. "I met him five years ago for the first time," he said.

"Ibrahim?"

"Yes. I was in Kfarmatta with Akmoud [Rashid's cousin], about to visit Rashid's grave, which I'd never seen before. I saw Ibrahim and recognized him. I said to Akmoud, 'This is Ibrahim.'"

How did Daniel feel about seeing Ibrahim?

"I don't like him very much."

Stevenson turned to me and said, "Rashid used to say: 'If you want to die, drive with Ibrahim.'"

I thought about the transcript from the interview with Daniel eighteen years ago: He blamed Ibrahim for the wreck, saying that people in a passing car had scolded him for going too fast, and that Ibrahim, apparently enraged at being lectured, had turned the car around and tried to overtake the offenders, then lost control.

"What do you remember about the accident?" I asked.

He didn't wait for a translation: "The car was a convertible," he said. "I was telling Ibrahim, 'Slow down, don't speed.' Then I remember being on the ground."

"You said you saw Rashid's grave. How did that make you feel?"

Silence. A smile. "I thought, 'Death is not a scary thing.'"

I decided that now would be a good time to ask about the memory of being dropped from a balcony that he had mentioned when he was nine. "I didn't mean Rashid [who died a year and a half before Daniel was born]," Daniel said. "It was another life."

"An intermediate life," Stevenson interpreted.

Daniel excused himself and went into the next room. He returned with a photo of a young man—Rashid. In a striped suit and period tie, he is movie-star handsome.

"When you look at this photo," I asked, "do you feel like you are looking at yourself?"

"Yes," he said. "Sure."

Daniel said that he had finished high school and obtained a degree in accounting at Beirut University College. Now he is an accountant.

And how is he with cars?

He laughed. "No good with cars now."

～

The sky was dark when we left the Jirdis. I felt like it had been several full days since breakfast at the hotel. As Mahmoud gunned the Mercedes down the mountain into the oncoming headlights, weary as I was, my mind kept wrestling with the last thing that Daniel had said: He was no good fixing cars.

If this were indeed a case of reincarnation, it raised a question: Exactly what portion of Rashid had come back? Daniel didn't have Rashid's acquired skills, or, possibly, even his native aptitude. His "memories" were fragmentary, mere splinters from twenty-five years of life.

And yet he looked at Rashid's photograph and thought "that's me." He felt familial affection for Rashid's family. He recognized Ibrahim.

That last was a new claim Stevenson had not heard before. The incident was only five years old. And there was a witness—one we might be able to find.

5

Speed Kills

A piece of paper had been sitting in Stevenson's filing cabinet in Charlottesville for years. On it was a list of things remaining to be done in Daniel's case. One item: Check local newspaper records to see if an account of Rashid's death could be found. Neither of the families had such a clipping, and neither was sure if one existed. Obviously, though, a disinterested contemporary account of the accident, if it matched Daniel's alleged memories, would add a certain weight of veracity beyond the emotion-influenced testimony of the two families involved.

First, however, such a clip had to be found, and that was no easy trick: The majority of the newspapers in existence in 1968 had not survived the decades of war that followed, and even the few that had were likely to have archives—known, appropriately, as "morgues"—that were as shrapnel-shredded as most of the city's buildings. Majd arrived at the hotel Tuesday morning with the address of one of the most substantial of the survivors, a morning paper called *Le Jour.* As it turned out, the paper's offices were only a few blocks from the hotel, so we decided to walk. Following a maze of cracked and sometimes-nonexistent sidewalks, we came to a rear entrance of a nondescript building and took a tiny, battered elevator to the fourth floor. The archives were housed in a small, cluttered, smoky office with two men and a woman sitting at mismatched desks buried under stacks of paper. Majd told them what we were looking for: an account of a car accident involving Rashid Khaddege on July 10, 1968, near Military Beach in Beirut. One of the men grudgingly walked to a file cabinet and, after a few minutes of digging, pulled out a cartridge, which he threaded on an antiquated microfilm viewer. He quickly spun through the pages, printed in Arabic for the July 11 issue. Too quickly, I decided.

He turned to Majd and said something that needed no translation. Nothing here about any accident like that. Majd replied at length, in what seemed to be a slightly scolding tone. The man shrugged and went back to the machine, racing even faster through the days following July 11, finally turning and shaking his head.

"I don't think he ree-leee looked," Majd said disgustedly when we were back out on the street. "Did you see how quickly he went through that roll of film?"

She reached into her purse for her cell phone and, flipping it open, made a quick series of calls as we stood beside her. I shifted impatiently, weighing the value of this one document against the high odds of finding it and the hours we could waste trying. Even if archival records had survived, in a city as large and chaotic as Beirut, there must be fatal accidents daily, and there was no guarantee that they would all be reported. But Stevenson showed no concern, as he stood slightly hunched, impassive as a workhorse at a hitching post, looking as if time were of no consequence.

"Good news," Majd said, slipping the phone back in her purse. "AUB has microfilm of all the major papers publishing in 1968, even the ones that no longer exist. I still have my university ID, so we can go there."

Stevenson decided to stay back at the hotel so that he could read through some notes. Mahmoud, meanwhile, drove Majd and me to American University, a breathtaking oasis of terraced, flowering gardens stepping down rocky cliffs to the sea and tree-shaded paths snaking around unscarred buildings filled with the latest computers and bustling with handsome young men and women in designer clothes—Palo Alto in the middle of Beirut. The only visible legacy of the war was a massive construction project dedicated to re-creating the university's oldest building from the ground up, exactly the way it had been before it was destroyed by a bomb. It now neared completion, complete with Moorish columns, arched windows, and a clock tower rematerializing beneath a latticework of scaffolding. The invisible damage: the American president of AUB, Malcolm Kerr, had been assassinated in 1983. As usual, the killers were never caught. And also as usual, it was impossible to know even which group was behind it, thus leaving a rainbow coalition of suspects to choose from: Christians, Shi'ites, Israelis, and Palestinians.

We were directed to the microfilm department, which, housed in a large, almost preternaturally clean room lined with clearly labeled filing cabinets and brand-new viewers, seemed to be located on a different planet than the *Le Jour* archives. A man with the manners, looks, and accent of Anthony Hopkins in *The Remains of the Day* guided us to six papers that had been publishing in 1968, then left us to go through them. I ran the machine while Majd read. I threaded in a roll and cranked through the pages, sending days dancing across the screen in dizzying procession. Nothing. Then another. Nothing. Then I queued up *Al-Jaridah* for July 1968. The lead headline on July 11: ENEMY BOMBS BURN CHILDREN AND KILL MOTHERS IN EGYPT.

I cranked again, wearily. This was hopeless. Then Majd shouted, "I found it!"

I stopped reeling. There it was, a small photo at the bottom of the page: police huddled around a crumpled Fiat with the roof peeled back. Majd translated: "A Car Fatality at Kornich Al-Manara.

"A car accident took place yesterday on Manara Corniche, leading to the death of one of the passengers," the article began. It said Ibrahim was driving the Fiat, "with Rashid Naim Khaddege, the owner of the car, next to him. [Ibrahim] tried overtaking a car at high speed resulting in the car turning over a number of times resulting in the instant death of Rashid Khaddege."

I hadn't expected the impact. There, on the screen, in the obscure interior of a newspaper published eighteen months before Daniel Jirdi was born, three years before he would tell of dying in an auto accident, was an account of a routine fatality that matched the child's story almost exactly: Military Beach, high speed, Ibrahim driving a Fiat, Rashid thrown from the car. He'd said all those things. And then, there was: *"tried overtaking a car at high speed."*

"Majd, it says trying to overtake another car," I said, my voice too loud in the empty room. "That's just what Daniel said."

Majd stared intently at the screen. "No, wait," she said. "I made a mistake. I was translating too fast. It doesn't mention another car. It says 'trying to overtake a *curve* at high speed.' Not another car."

"Maybe they just didn't mention the other car, or even know about it," I replied. "It doesn't mean it wasn't there. But there *are* some things that contradict what Daniel told us. He said it was a convertible. It isn't a very clear photograph, but that car definitely has a roof. It looks like it was almost peeled off, but it's there. And the caption said Rashid was the owner. Daniel said it was Ibrahim's car."

"The paper must have gotten that wrong," Majd said. "Rashid's family told us he never owned a car."

We printed a copy of the story and drove back to the hotel. It was almost noon when we arrived: an entire morning devoted to checking off one item on a to-do list in one file among the thousands of files and the tens of thousands of to-do items still undone. It would take a lifetime to attend to them all. Stevenson didn't have that long.

He looked over the print of the article with a half-smile and listened to Majd's translation without comment.

"I like to have as much written documentation as I can," Stevenson said almost absently as he tucked the story in his overstuffed briefcase. "Even in the best instances, it tends to be spotty."

And with that, he was out the door, into the car: We had an appointment with the Khaddeges, at the home of Muntaha, Rashid's mother, in central Beirut, not far from the flattened downtown.

As we drove, Majd and Stevenson huddled over a hand-drawn map in the backseat. Finally, they directed Mahmoud to pull to the curb. We got out and walked a half block to a narrow alley. Majd started up the alley, map in hand.

"This is it," she said.

Ducking through a low doorway with a wrought-iron gate, we entered a bare concrete courtyard, empty but for plastic bins filled with garden-grown squash and onions, and a gallery of partially filled gallon water jugs.

One of the boys we'd met that first day at the apartment beside the cavernous ditch in Kfarmatta, Muna's teenage son, the nephew of Rashid, opened the door and led us down a step into a sitting room with stained and nail-pocked blue-plaster walls. A bare bulb hung from the ceiling on a four-foot wire. The only touches of decoration were what looked like the lids from cardboard gift boxes, the kind roses might come in, depicting flowers on a black background, hung side by side on the wall. On a table in the center of the room, surrounded by a half dozen chairs and two deep burgundy sofas of crushed velvet, was a coffee table with a framed eight-by-ten-inch photograph: Daniel Jirdi's wedding photo. The son whom they believed they had lost to death and regained through rebirth.

Muna greeted us as old friends. Muntaha was nowhere to be seen, but a slim, handsome, balding young man dressed sharply in a black dress shirt and black jeans, with black sunglasses tucked into the top of his shirt, sat on the edge of a chair opposite us. Majd exchanged greetings with him. I was glad to discover his identity: Akmad, the cousin of Rashid, the alleged witness to Daniel's spontaneous recognition of Ibrahim. I judged that he was eager to speak to us, but as Muna's boy handed out Mr. Juicy fruit drinks, Muna herself spoke. Majd translated:

Muntaha had been knitting a sweater for Rashid before he died. One day, after they had begun to visit Daniel, the little boy said to her, "Did you ever finish that sweater you were knitting for me?" Muntaha immediately found the unfinished sweater where she'd put it away years earlier, after Rashid's death. She unraveled the yarn, then used it to knit the sweater in miniature. She gave it to Daniel.

As this story came to a close, the door to the back room opened as if by itself. Standing framed in the rectangle of space was an ancient woman peering through the slit of a head scarf pulled down to her eyebrows and up to the tip of her nose so that only a small portion of her wizened, shrunken face was visible: Muntaha. Muna took her by the elbow and helped her into the stuffed chair.

Muna then continued: "My sister, my mother, and I were in this house when a neighbor came here and told us Rashid had been in an accident. My mother said, 'Is he dead?' The woman said she didn't know. We rushed to the hospital, but he was already gone."

Muna looked around her, at the old walls, the black-and-white checkerboard tile floor, the worn carpet. "We were all here together in this room," she said, almost dreamily.

One of Daniel's original statements about Rashid was that he had hit his head when he flew from the car after Ibrahim lost control.

"Did the doctors tell you how Rashid was injured?" Stevenson asked.

"No," Muna said. "He was already dead. We didn't ask. But we saw his body. He had a bandage on his head."

A few years later the family heard from an acquaintance that Rashid had been reborn at the Jirdis' house in Beirut. This was around 1972. Muna went with Najla and a friend to meet the boy. "Daniel did not recognize me, probably because I had changed so much," Muna said. But he saw Najla and he called her by name.

"In what way had you changed?" I asked.

She responded and Majd nodded. She leaned toward me. "Before Rashid died, she was not so religious," Majd explained. "She says she dressed like I do—pants, blouses, high heels. But after his death, she began to wear the head scarf and the long dresses. She thinks Daniel wasn't expecting to see a religious woman."

"Did the Jirdis know you were coming?" I asked.

"No, we came without an appointment. We didn't know the family. We just showed up at the door. Daniel was very happy when he saw us. He said to his mother, 'Bring bananas for Najla and make some coffee, my family is here.' We were astonished. Rashid had liked bananas so much that my mother and Najla had stopped eating them after his death because it reminded them of their grief."

Outside, a sudden blast of thunder rumbled through the shuttered windows, then fat drops of rain pelted the glass.

Akmad, who had been sitting politely through all of this, cleared his throat and spoke: he wanted to talk with us, but he had to leave. He was in the army, and would soon be late for duty. So, we turned our attention to him, to hear his story of the meeting between Daniel and Ibrahim, which differed slightly from Daniel's. Where Daniel had said that he saw Ibrahim on the way to Rashid's grave, Akmad stated that Daniel had asked to be taken to Ibrahim's house. The cemetery with Rashid's grave was nearby, but Akmad didn't remember Daniel mentioning it. "We were walking on the street a few blocks from the house when I saw Ibrahim working on a car. I didn't say anything. I wanted to test Daniel."

But right off, Daniel said, "That's Ibrahim." Akmad kept up his ruse, saying that Daniel was mistaken, that it wasn't Ibrahim, "but Daniel insisted that it was." Ibrahim invited the two men to his house, not knowing who Daniel was.

"I didn't introduce them. So Daniel asked Ibrahim, 'Did something happen to you in 1968?' Ibrahim said, 'I don't remember.' Then he said, 'Yes, I remember, I had an accident, and my cousin died.' Then Daniel said, 'I'm your cousin.' Ibrahim cried, stunned, for fifteen minutes. He had heard about Daniel, but never seen him."

"Ibrahim left after the accident. Police never investigated," Muna said, making a sour face and wiping her hands as if getting rid of something unpleasant on them.

Some time after the accident, a policeman did come to see them, unofficially, with a family friend. He said that he wanted to confess something: He and another cop had seen the Fiat speeding by, and he said to his partner, "Let's stop them," but the other said, "No, let them die."

For a long time, Muna said, Muntaha did not speak to Ibrahim. She had always told him, "Drive slowly, Rashid is my only son." They began to see him again sometime during the war when both families had fled Beirut for the mountains.

I asked her about the item in the newspaper article that had contradicted Daniel's claimed memories. Had Rashid been the owner of the car?

"It was Ibrahim's car," she said. "Rashid did not own a car."

Once outside, we huddled under a building overhang, trying to stay out of what was now a steady downpour. Mahmoud, who had parked down the street, was driving around the block to pick us up.

"Muna said something interesting to me while we were leaving," Majd said. "She said that Rashid had been engaged five days before he died."

How strange, I thought. Daniel seemed to have been born with other memories of Rashid's life, but he had apparently never mentioned anything about being engaged. Once again, I was struck by the fragmentary nature of the previous-life memories that we were seeing. It was like a bad carbon copy—here and there you could make out a word, or even a phrase, but it was impossible to get a sense of the whole document.

It made me think of something that Stevenson had said the other day at dinner when I asked him why he thought that even among the Druse, where these cases were relatively common, in absolute terms, past-life memories were still rare.

"Maybe remembering is a defect," he said. "Maybe we're supposed to forget, but sometimes that system malfunctions, and we don't forget completely."

ᑐᑐ

On the way back to Aley the next morning, we rounded the curve ascending from the waterfront and ran into a solid wall of stopped cars. The Beirut-Damascus road had been shut down for the Lebanese Independence Day parade. The parade itself was still three days off, but an endless procession of tanks, armored cars, truck-towed artillery pieces, fire trucks, and even ambulances queued up along the parade route in preparation. These were no shiny, gleaming showpieces, though—thickly layered with grime and dust, they appeared to be fresh from some battle.

We idled, steaming and fuming for a half hour before Mahmoud managed to find an opening to escape to an alternate, roundabout route. Two hours later, we were once again at Daniel's fourth-floor apartment in Aley, overlooking the hazy spread of the Beirut peninsula, pointing toward Europe. We came to see Latifeh, Daniel's mom, who was not at home when we interviewed Daniel. Stevenson wanted to revisit some of the early history of the case: what Daniel had said as a child, how he had first met the Khaddeges.

After exchanging the usual pleasantries, Latifeh and Majd had a brief discussion.

"She says there are lots of Druse in the United States now," Majd translated.

"That's quite right," Stevenson said. "Maybe we should look for cases. Majd could get a notice put in the American Druse newsletter."

When Majd repeated the comment in Arabic, Latifeh said, "That generation doesn't know about these things. All their children are in nurseries. They don't hear the stories the children tell."

"Yes, yes, perhaps not," Stevenson replied, unfolding a map of the city, eager to move on. He asked Latifeh to point out her Beirut residence, the place where Muna and Najla first came to see the boy. She indicated a spot just under two kilometers from the Khaddeges' house, an easy walk. After the visit from Rashid's two sisters, Latifeh had taken Daniel to see Rashid's mother.

"The first time we went there, we only knew the general neighbor-hood," Latifeh said. "We parked the car on the main street and Daniel led us the rest of the way."

They hadn't asked directions from Muna and Najla because they had thought the family's only home was in Kfarmatta. They had only learned of the Khaddege's Beirut home, Latifeh said, from neighbors in Aley—neighbors who also happened to be related to the Khaddeges.

I glanced at Stevenson, wondering if he was thinking the same thing I was. One of the most persuasive features of his best cases was that the two families involved had no contact before the child began making statements. If the families had never met and had no common friends, the most obvious normal ways that a child might learn something about his alleged past personality were eliminated. Thus far, Daniel's case had appeared to fit in that category. But now the distinction was compromised: Here was a link between the Jirdis and the Khaddeges, and a potentially strong one.

Latifeh, who understood we were concerned about possible contam-ination of Daniel's statements, tried to reassure us. The neighbor had been friendly with her mother, she said, but had never visited her own home.

"They rented an apartment near my mother in Aley. But I'm certain that Daniel never saw them before he started speaking about his previ-ous life, because we were in Beirut then."

"Did Daniel ever go to Aley to visit his grandmother when he was small?" I asked.

"Yes, but I was always with him, and he never saw these neigh-bors."

Even if that were true, I thought, any link muddied the waters. It al-lowed at least the possibility of contamination. It wasn't difficult to imagine how that might happen: Suppose that the Khaddege relatives had at some point told Daniel's grandmother the story of their unfortu-nate cousins in Kfarmatta who had lost their only son to a car accident not long before Daniel was born. Then, imagine that when little Daniel was visiting his grandmother in Aley, he was pretending to drive a car, the way toddlers do. Perhaps the grandmother told him that she hoped he was a safe driver when he grew up, that she didn't want to lose her dear Daniel the way that her neighbor's cousins had lost their son when a car sped out of control at Military Beach. She could have easily forgotten ever saying anything like that to the child. But on some level, Daniel might have remembered.

Once again, I did not think that that kind of convoluted contamination was *likely*, only possible. It clearly would be extremely unlikely for a two-year-old to hear and remember as much detail as Daniel was given credit for—the name of the car's driver, that the car had sped out of control and that Rashid had been thrown out of it, that the accident had occurred near the water, that Rashid's mother had been knitting him a sweater. And, in any case, no grandmother's tale could explain the recognitions attributed to Daniel of the way to the Khaddeges' home, of Rashid's sister Najla, of Ibrahim and others.

Stevenson pushed on, inquiring about the first signs that Daniel was in any way unusual. Latifeh said that, in retrospect, she had wondered if the lemon-sized lump on the top of Daniel's head at birth was related to Rashid's fatal head injury. At the time, they were concerned enough about the lump that they took him to a doctor when he was six days old. The doctor told them not to worry, that the lump may have been caused from the pressure of delivery, which had been difficult—contractions lasted for two days. In three months, the lump had disappeared.

"I wouldn't want to take that lump to court as evidence of reincarnation," Stevenson said sotto voce. "The difficult delivery would be a very normal cause for something like that."

When Daniel was about two, Latifeh said, he told her, "I want to go home." A few months later he said, "This is not my house. You are not my mother. I don't have a father. My father died."

"He would not call Yusuf daddy," she stated. "He called him by name, and said, 'My father was Naim.'"

"What did he say about the accident?" I asked.

"He said he was in the house, eating *loubia* [a green-bean dish] and Ibrahim came and took him to the sea. He said Ibrahim was speeding. He told him to slow down, but Ibrahim ignored him, and then lost control. He said, 'I flew out of the car and landed on my head.' After the crash, he said he heard people talking about removing the injured. When they came to him he heard them say, 'Leave this one, he's dead.'"

When Daniel was older, Latifeh said, after he had already met with

Rashid's family, a cousin of Rashid was visiting his grandmother's neighbor. The man's name was Jihad, and he and Rashid had been hunting buddies. Daniel had never met him.

One day during his visit, Jihad stood in a third-floor window with some other people and waited for Daniel to come outside and play. When they saw him, one of the others called down to Daniel to look up. Daniel looked and said, "Jihad, are you here? Do you still have your hunting rifle?"

"I was standing right beside Daniel," Latifeh said. "Nobody warned us what they were going to do."

In nursery school, Daniel told his teachers that his name was Rashid Khaddege. Latifeh said that when the school contacted her and asked about it, she made up some story to avoid having to tell them that her son claimed to remember a previous life. Apparently, even in Lebanon, there is some reluctance to wade into those waters.

Her hand was forced, however, when little Daniel crept up on a particularly beautiful young teacher and pinched her, then made a suggestive comment.

"They called me down to the school," Latifeh told Stevenson, "and this time I didn't know what to say, so I told them the whole story."

I tried to imagine what it would be like to have a child who behaved as she said Daniel had. I wondered how I might feel if, with calm certainty, one of my children said, "You aren't my father."

"When Daniel rejected you, did that make you unhappy?" I asked.

Latifeh considered Majd's translation of my question for a moment before responding.

"She says she wasn't upset, or sad," Majd said. "She used another word, which means annoyed. No, not annoyed—more like disappointed."

Latifeh went on: "When he said those things, I would tell him, 'I am your mom,' and he would say, 'My mom is a *sheikha* [a religious woman who wears the head scarf].' I did not wear a mandeel, but my mother did, and Daniel always liked her because of that. When he was three, he pointed to my mother and said, 'My mother's like her.'

"I knew he was talking about a previous life. I knew about other children who had spoken about previous lives, so for me, it was not so unusual."

"Did you know that Rashid's mother says that when Daniel was little, he asked her about a sweater she'd been knitting for Rashid when he died, and she took the yarn and reknit a tiny sweater for Daniel?"

Latifeh laughed. "I kept that sweater all these years," she said. "But when we had to leave Beirut during the war, we left everything. And when we came back, nothing was left. Nothing."

Latifeh said that she regularly visited the Khaddeges. "I like them," she said. "I feel relieved to know who my son was and who his family was—for Daniel's sake."

∽

After we returned to the hotel, I put on the one white shirt in my suitcase and my only tie, each of which I had brought precisely because Stevenson had warned me there might be occasions such as this evening: a dinner party at Majd's home in his honor. My shirt's top button was chokingly tight around my neck, and my linen jacket was inexcusably wrinkled. Stevenson, on the other hand, looked as if he had been born in his dark suit and had never been uncomfortable for a moment in his life.

Majd lived an upper floor of a high-rise not far from the American University. The apartment belonged to her parents, who were overseas, and Majd, Faisal, and their son were living in it while Majd supervised the renovation of an apartment on a lower floor. It wasn't a bad campsite: a grand, ornately furnished spread of rooms along a wide terrace overlooking the darkened downtown and the Mediterranean. The reserved, impeccable taste of the furnishings, the fine art on the walls, and the floors lent the apartment the flavor of an ambassador's residence, which was perhaps no coincidence: The family was rife with former diplomats, ambassadors, and UN delegates. The guest list at the dinner in honor of Stevenson was in keeping with such pedigree—all the above were present as well as government ministers and AUB professors.

I was most interested in those who had been invited specifically because of their interest in Stevenson's work. Among them was a Christian psychiatrist named Elie Karam, who argued passionately that not enough was being done to follow up on Stevenson's investigations in Lebanon.

All of the guests were seated council style around the circumference of the room, all participating in the same discussion. Elie was asked why he, a Christian, was interested in the Druse cases.

"Mankind may be losing a valuable opportunity to establish proof of reincarnation," he explained. "The Druse are quickly Westernizing and assimilating into secular society. There is plenty of time to prove that reincarnation is a myth, but time may be running out to prove it is true. If this is a reality, mankind must know."

Another Christian, an ecologist named Ricardo Habre who worked with Majd's husband on environmental restoration projects, made a point that had hung naggingly in the background on the whole trip. "I would *love* to believe in reincarnation," he said. "But it defies logic. If there are so many cases among the Druse, why have I never heard of a single case among the Christians?"

"Who knows?" Elie said, throwing his arms up. "Maybe it is genetic!"

Later, at dinner, I asked Stevenson what he thought accounted for the apparent unbalance in the distribution of his cases. "We may be able to talk ourselves into extinction," he said. "Maybe our beliefs determine our fate: If you believe you will come back, but only as a member of your own faith, that's what happens. If you believe you simply die and don't come back, you don't."

He sipped his wine, then said, more to himself than to me, "Everyone wants a case in Iowa. Well, I'll give them a case in Iowa. They aren't as strong as the Lebanese cases, but they exist."

After dinner, I saw Ricardo on the terrace and walked out to join him.

"I was thinking about what you said about the relative lack of Christian cases," I said. "The thing is, if you believe that the power of cultural belief is strong enough to create this mass delusion that children remember specific details about the lives of dead strangers, don't you have to admit that it could work the other way around? That cultural belief could repress real memories of previous lives to the point where they only appear in a sporadic and fragmentary form?"

Ricardo waved dismissively. "Reincarnation just doesn't make sense," he said. "When I was at a world-population conference in Cairo, I asked a Druse, 'If we are all reincarnated from previous incarnations, how do you explain the population explosion?'

"Do you know what he said? He said, 'There *is* no population explosion. The population has always been the same.'"

Ricardo laughed heartily. "How do you deny the population explosion? That is the point where I said, 'Enough!'"

6

The Love of Her Lives

The next day, we headed back toward the southern suburbs of Beirut, with well over an hour of twisting mountain roads before us. As Mahmoud played chicken with the oncoming trucks, I asked Majd about the Arabic vocabulary for reincarnation. I thought I had identified the word that kept coming up in her translations: *takamous.*

"Literally, it means 'changing your shirt,'" Majd said. "The Druse believe that the body is just clothes for the soul, and when you are reincarnated, it is like changing clothes.

"*Takamous* is reincarnation in general, but when you are talking about someone who has been reincarnated, you use a different word: *natiq* for a boy, *nataq* for a girl. It translates to 'one who talks about the previous generation.'"

It took a minute for the importance of that to sink in. The entire concept of reincarnation wasn't expressed in the abstract—souls returned to flesh—as in English. Instead, it was spoken of in terms of people who remembered, and talked about, living in the past. And not the indefinable past, either, but the *previous generation.* One generation back. How different from the Western/hypnotic-regression idea of people remembering lives at Waterloo or in ancient Babylon (Brian Weiss himself maintained that he remembered being a Babylonian holy man atop a ziggurat). If you wanted to be able to claim to remember an earlier life, but make sure it would be difficult, if not impossible, to check your memories against reality, remembering a life a century, or centuries, earlier was definitely the way to go.

And that's what was so stunning about these Lebanese cases—they were all so checkable. The *expectation* was that the claimed memories could and would be tested against the living memories of relatives and friends of the deceased.

The fact that the words carried this meaning led to the inescapable conclusion that the phenomenon of children claiming to remember recent previous lives had been common for generations.

Of course, to many Lebanese, the idea was still news, as novel to them as it would be to most Americans. A July 1977 article in a Beirut English-language weekly called *Monday Morning* gave me a feel for how the wider secular society viewed these cases. The story was head-lined, THE REINCARNATION OF HANAN MANSOUR, and beneath the headline was this blurb: "Five-year-old Suzy Ghanem insists that she is the mother of three adult children, and her children are convinced she is. An intimate look at the strangest set of family relationships in Lebanon today."

Although there are no exclamation points—"screamers," we call them in the trade—you can feel their phantom presence. The story itself doesn't have quite the tabloid feel of the headline, but it certainly deals with the story with the same level of amazement you'd expect in the American media:

Suzanne Ghanem is now five years old.

She insists that she is not Suzanne Ghanem.

She tells her parents that she is Hanan Mansour, that she died after surgery in the United States and that she wants her children and hus-band back.

The Ghanems and the Mansours had never heard of each other be-fore. Suzanne (Hanan?), however, sought out her children and con-tacted them, and her children—all adults—are now convinced that their mother is a five-year-old girl who lives in Shwaifat, a southern suburb of Beirut.

Though Stevenson had been working in Lebanon for a dozen years by the time the Suzanne Ghanem article appeared, neither he nor any of the cases he had published were mentioned in the article. The igno-rance, however, was not mutual: Stevenson, who gets many tips from accounts in the local media, saw the article and visited Suzanne in March 1978, within eight months of the story in *Monday Morning*.

That was twenty years ago. Now the little girl was a twenty-five-year-old woman.

"I think Suzanne might have the record for remembering proper names," Stevenson said as he handed me the file from his briefcase over the front seat. From bond paper yellowed with age, I read the typewritten background material:

Hanan Mansour was born in the Shouf Mountains in the mid-1930s. When she was twenty, she married Farouk Mansour, a distant relative. A year later, her first child, Leila, was born, followed in two years by a daughter, Galareh. By then, Hanan had been diagnosed with a heart condition and was advised not to have another pregnancy. But she failed to follow the advice and in 1962 had another child, a son. In 1963, Hanan's brother Nabih, who had become a prominant figure in Lebanon, died in a plane crash. The crash and Nabih's death were big news in the Druse community. Not long thereafter, Hanan's own health began to deteriorate. When he was interviewed twenty years ago, Farouk told Stevenson that two years before her death, Hanan talked about dying. "She told him she was going to be reincarnated and have lots to say about her previous life," Stevenson told me.

At the age of thirty-six, Hanan went to Richmond, Virginia, to have what she knew was extremely risky heart surgery. Leila had intended to fly to Virginia to be with her mother, but she had lost her passport, and couldn't get a new one in time to make the trip. Hanan tried to call Leila before her surgery, but was unable to get through on the phone. The following day, she died from complications. Her body was flown back to Beirut International Airport, Lebanon.

Ten days after Hanan died, Suzanne Ghanem was born. Munira Ghanem, the girl's mother, told Stevenson that shortly before Suzanne's birth, "I dreamed I was going to have a baby girl. I met a woman and I kissed and hugged her. She said, 'I am going to come to you.' The woman was about forty. Later, when I saw Hanan's picture, I thought it looked like the woman in my dream."

I handed the file back to Stevenson. "Interesting dream," I said.

Stevenson held the folders in his lap and reread his notes. "I'm afraid there's a gap in technique here," he said after a minute. "I usually ask if she told the dream to anyone else so we could confirm it, but I didn't here."

Suzanne's parents told Stevenson that her first words came when she was sixteen months old: She pulled the phone off the hook as if she were trying to talk into it and said, over and over, "Hello, Leila?" When they later heard the story of how Hanan had been trying to phone Leila before she died, they saw a connection. But, at the time, they had no idea who Suzanne might be talking about. As she got older, she said that Leila was one of her children, and that she was not Suzanne, but Hanan.

When they asked, "Hanan what?," she told them, "My head is still small. Wait until it is bigger, and I might tell you." She eventually did, her parents said. And by the time she was two, she had mentioned the names of her other children, her husband, Farouk, and the names of her parents and her brothers—thirteen names in all. She said things like, "My house is larger and prettier than this house." Sometimes she would tell her father, Shaheen, "I love you. You are kind to me, as my father Halim used to be. That is why I accept you."

Halim was Hanan's father.

As with the Jirdi case, the break in this one came when an acquaintance with connections in the mountain town where the Mansours lived made inquiries there and discovered that what Suzanne had been saying matched the life of Hanan Mansour. The Mansours heard the story of the little girl in Shwaifat and came to visit.

Suzanne was five when Stevenson met her; it was not long after the *Monday Morning* article had been published. Even with all he'd seen of other children like her, Suzanne's fierce attachment to her previous-life memories stood out as unusual.

"It got to be something of a problem. She would call Farouk, Hanan's husband, three times a day. When she went to see him, she would sit on his lap and rest her head against his chest. He remarried, to a woman who had been Hanan's friend, but he was so concerned about Suzanne's reaction that he hid it from her. Eventually, she discovered the truth. She said to him, 'But you told me you'd never love anyone but me.' I don't think Farouk ever quite admitted to saying that to Hanan. The closest he came was telling me, 'Well, I may have said something similar.'"

Stevenson chuckled sympathetically. No man ought to be held accountable for promises he never expected to have scrutinized from beyond the grave.

As we continued to descend from the mountains that rimmed the city like the sides of a bowl, we could see the coastal plain in the distance. Shwaifat was built into the slope that descended directly into Beirut proper. The city had essentially swallowed the town, making it more of a neighborhood than a separate entity. As we cruised past a strip of one-story shops, Stevenson uttered the words I had given up on hearing: "Perhaps we should stop for Mahmoud's lunch," he said.

Finally, an opening. I took it: "Twist my arm and I might be able to eat a little something, too," I said.

Majd laughed. "We could pick up some Lebanese pizza in one of these shops. Have you ever had it?"

I hadn't, but I was glad to make its acquaintance. It was a circle of fresh dough, similar to pita, topped with olive oil and herbs, or a cheeselike yogurt, then baked in a cast-iron oven. Each portion was the size of what's called an "individual pizza" in the States. Even Stevenson had one. The entire bill, including canned drinks, came to $5.

It was late afternoon by the time Mahmoud parked the Mercedes on a narrow lane in a steep neighborhood of small apartments. We had to walk down a series of steps to get to the Ghanems.

Suzanne's parents, Munira and Shaheen, answered our knock and led us into a narrow sitting room where Suzanne's older brother, Hassam, greeted us in perfect English and gave us his card: He sold life insurance in Beirut. We all sat down and made small talk until Suzanne walked in minutes later.

Fresh in my mind was the *Monday Morning* article, which had said that Suzanne's family "saw a profound sadness in Suzy and they pitied her." At the end of the article, the writer described leaving the house and "looking back at the girl who was staring at me through the window. Her brown eyes were filled with tears."

Now, in person, Suzanne's brown eyes were still the most striking thing about her, and there did seem to be something sad about them. Dressed in blue jeans and a blue-green sweater, sunglasses pushed up on top of her wavy brown hair, bracelets on both wrists, and a heart-shaped pendant around her neck, she would have fit in perfectly in any of the college classes I sometimes taught at the University of Miami.

Her face was round, with alabaster skin, and wore a slightly pouty expression. She looked us straight in the eye, but as if from a distance. She told us that she had had two years of college in Beirut and now was teaching English to sixth- and seventh-graders, though her own English skills were considerably less fluent than her brother's.

Stevenson opened the interview in the usual way, asking if she still remembered her previous life.

Suzanne hesitated. Perhaps she hadn't picked up the question entirely. But before Majd could translate, Hassam interrupted in English. "She does not confess to us," he said. "Maybe she will confess to you."

Suzanne gave him an unreadable look. Hassam, though, continued talking to us, seemingly by way of explanation. "A boy who said he was Hanan's brother reborn wanted to meet Suzanne. She refused, because she did not want to raise the emotions. Later, when the boy died, she was upset."

Abruptly, Suzanne stood and walked out of the room as if she had suddenly remembered something she urgently needed to do elsewhere. It took a moment for me to realize that she had been crying. Majd and I exchanged uneasy glances. When Suzanne was gone, Hassam continued, apparently unsurprised by his sister's emotion. "When that boy who claimed to be Hanan's brother was a child, he had a stroke, and we think that it was caused at least partly because the Mansours had refused to meet with him. Suzanne is very sensitive about that now. There was another case she knew of in which she acted as mediator between the two families—the previous family, who wanted to see the reincarnated child, and the current family, who didn't want him to see them. She managed to convince them to let the child meet his previous family."

We sat awkwardly for a few minutes until Suzanne returned, still on the verge of tears.

Stevenson asked if she wanted to take a break.

"No," she said in English. "I am all right."

He asked again if she remembered.

"I don't remember incidents, but the feelings are still there."

"When was the last time you saw Farouk?"

"Four years ago. He came here."

Stevenson turned to her parents: "How old was Suzanne when she stopped calling Farouk every day?"

They smiled.

"I didn't stop," Suzanne said. "I still call him."

"How often?

"Whenever I feel like it. Maybe more than once a week." Her face twisted into an ironic smile. "He is scared of his new wife."

Now she was speaking Arabic. Majd translated the answer. For a minute, I thought that I had misunderstood. New wife? And then I realized that "she" referred to the woman whom Farouk had married a quarter of a century ago, not long after Hanan's death.

How did she feel about Nadir, the "new wife"?

She laughed a short, bitter laugh, then in English said, "Nothing."

Have you forgiven her for marrying Farouk?

"Yes," she said, with that same half-smile.

I asked Suzanne's mother how she felt when her little girl began speaking of a previous life, claiming to belong to another family.

Majd translated.

"I was not concerned," Munira responded. "This is very common. But when Suzanne was crying, suffering, picking up the phone receiver and crying into it the name of her little girl, Leila, over and over, I was concerned for my child's pain."

A few minutes later, Stevenson asked Suzanne his standard closer: "Is it a good thing to remember a previous life?"

Given all that went before, I was surprised when Suzanne straightened, looked him straight in the eye and said, almost fiercely, "Yes, it is a good thing. My previous family is relieved to know I am still here, and I am relieved to have seen my previous family again."

I asked Munira and Shaheen about what they remembered of Suzanne's behavior as a little girl that related to memories of her previous life.

Shaheen said that when Suzanne was little, she could recite the funeral oration spoken at Nabih's funeral. "When she started talking about the previous life, I would get my tape recorder. We had a tape of her reciting the funeral oration, but we gave the tape to Hanan's mother, and now she's dead, and nobody knows where the tape is."

"When she was three or four," Hassam added, "she gave my

mother a recipe for *namoura* [a Lebanese dessert], one of Hanan's favorite recipes. And before she had learned to read or write, she scribbled a phone number. We tried calling it, but it didn't work. Later, when we went to Hanan's house, we discovered that her phone number had been right, except that she had reversed the last two digits, a two and an eight.

"It's very funny—when Helene, Hanan's sister, comes to visit Suzanne, she talks to her exactly as if she were Hanan. She'll say things like, 'I was talking to Mira, the girl who was with us in elementary school.'"

According to the *Monday Morning* article, the Mansour family had initially greeted Suzanne's claim skeptically. They were a prominent family, wealthy, and they were concerned that the Ghanems might be angling for some money. But the girl quickly persuaded them, by, among other things, identifying photographs in a family album. She looked through photos in front of the *Monday Morning* reporter, who described it this way:

Suzy picked out all the relatives and named them accurately. "This is my brother Hercule, my brother Jason, my brother Plato, my mother . . . and this is me. I think I'm wearing my black dress here. I recognize the cut. Look how thin I was." She paused, and the memory of pain was obvious in her eyes. "I was very sick."

But the real clincher, according to the article, came when Suzanne turned to Galareh and said, "Did your Uncle Hercule give you your jewels? Did he give Leila hers?"

Only the family knew that Hanan had given her jewelry to her brother Hercule in Virginia and asked him to divide it between her daughters.

Stevenson's notes said Farouk and Galareh had confirmed to him that Suzanne had accurately spoken of Hanan's wish to distribute her jewels. He had also confirmed the story with those who had been at Hanan's bedside when she made the request.

What could I make of all this? An hour with the Ghanems seemed a powerful argument against intentional hoax: The emotion was too genuine, the openness of the family too apparent.

But what about self-deception?

Nabih Mansour was no Jack Kennedy, but was it possible that his fame was significant enough to—nine years after his death—cause a toddler to fantasize that she was his sister? Or for parents to imagine that a child's random mutterings corresponded to the family of a fallen hero, and then to shape those mutterings to fit the facts they somehow learned concerning names and relationships of Nabih's family?

Again, though, as in the case of Daniel and the Khaddeges, even such unlikely possibilities could not explain all the things that Suzanne had said. I couldn't escape the conclusion that only one conceivable "normal" explanation for Suzanne's knowledge remained, however remote: The Ghanems were so enraptured with their belief in reincarnation that they unconsciously elaborated and directed Suzanne's statements, and that the Mansour family was so desperate to believe Hanan had returned that they unconsciously colluded, elaborating even further, putting new statements in Suzanne's mouth through prolific prompting.

Stevenson had said that he had not contacted the Mansours on this trip, though he had interviewed them earlier. There was no guarantee that they would agree to meet us this time. But, I now knew, I desperately wanted to talk to them.

Suzanne had been sitting silently for at least half an hour as her family talked around her. I wondered if she regretted that we had pried into her life, making her feel such sorrow. But then, abruptly, without any prompting, she began telling a story that she said she had never revealed to anyone: She had spoken to that boy who had remembered being Hanan's brother; not only had she spoken to him, but she felt a deep connection to him. Her family listened, open-mouthed.

"I was in the village and a man approached me," Suzanne began. "He recognized me, but not as Suzanne. He recognized me as Hanan. He said he was Nabih reborn. He remembered more than I remembered. His family had suppressed his claims, so maybe his memories stayed fresher in his mind. But he hugged and kissed me. I cried."

It was almost 8 P.M. when we started back to the hotel. On the road from Shwaifat to the southern outskirts of Beirut, in the shadow of the massive refugee camps, a bootleg commercial district had sprung up. Industry and commerce of every imaginable variety overflowed from haphazard structures that are officially condemned, under perpetual threat of clearance, and protected by only the unfathomable weight of everything else that needs clearing in Beirut.

"Do you think her devotion to Farouk is why she hasn't married?" I wondered aloud as we sputtered through the traffic.

"Did you notice, before we left I went over and sat beside her?" Majd said. "I didn't want to embarrass her by saying anything in front of everyone. But I quietly asked her. She said she knew that Hanan's life is past, but she just hasn't met anyone in this one."

Mahmoud dropped Stevenson and me at the hotel. Stevenson had agreed to give a lecture at AUB that night and wanted to change and freshen up. I took advantage of the rare free hour to stroll down El Hamra. Men and women, mostly young and dressed in business suits, strode smartly along both sides of the street. Cabs inched along, hunting for fares, beeping inquiringly at anyone keeping a slower pace. Cafés were beginning to fill up with people getting off from work. Shopkeepers stood in their doorways watching the procession passively, arms folded or clasped behind their backs. I just walked. In Beirut, like anywhere else, you took one step at a time.

I wondered about the events of the past few days and my reaction to them. One thing was very clear in my mind: These people were not all intentionally deceiving us. It was very difficult to see what any could expect to gain from falsely promoting his or her case. Some of the critiques I had read argued that subjects would be motivated to fraud in hopes of achieving special status among their neighbors. Well, in Druse Lebanon, that potential allure was extremely limited, for these cases were commonplace. They sure weren't expecting a call from Oprah.

True, acceptance of their claims might lead to a sort of pseudofamilial relationship, but I'd seen nothing to suggest that anyone had benefited materially from connecting with their previous-life families, and the emotional benefits seemed to be accompanied by an equal weight of complications.

Which left me looking for some kind of unconscious motivations and the obscure mechanisms that could translate them into the kinds of things we had been hearing.

But why was I looking so hard? Why was I so unwilling to accept the most obvious explanation, that these cases were genuine?

In a way, of course, it was my job to be as skeptical as possible about what I was seeing and hearing. The main objections to Stevenson's evidence all centered on the idea that the apparently paranormal aspects of the cases could all be explained through some combination of fraud, self-deception, and unconscious wish fulfillment. But there was more to it than that; there was my own personal version of "the formidable initial presumption against reincarnation" that Paul Edwards talked about in his reincarnation-debunking book. Only my predisposition wasn't so much based on the logical and logistical difficulties inherent in the idea—If there were a soul, why could nobody detect it? How did it move from one body to another? Did it enter at the moment of conception? Of birth? Why did such a tiny percentage of people remember previous lives? Why were those memories so fragmentary? If souls were recycled, how could you explain the population explosion? Evolution?—as it was rooted in my own feelings.

I didn't believe any of the questions raised by Edwards's logic could overwhelm solid evidence of genuine previous life memories. My real problem was intuitive. In my marrow, I could feel no trace, however faint, of a previous life. The universe before me was a void, a nothingness that flared into somethingness only with my earliest memories of *this* life. And my most profound learning about the deaths of the people I had loved the most was this: They had vanished. Their absence had palpable force, a stunning irrevocability. More than ten years after my father's death, I still sometimes picked up the phone and began to dial his number, only to be stung by one inescapable certainty—there was no one to call. He wasn't there. Or anywhere.

If reincarnation were fact, why hadn't it touched *my* life? Why couldn't I at least feel its possibility in my gut?

∾

Stevenson was waiting in the lobby when I returned. Majd's husband Faisal picked us up in his sport-utility vehicle and drove us to the university campus. I had seen the notice for Stevenson's lecture, a desultory one-page handbill, and I had some questions about what kind of turnout could be expected. But when we arrived fifteen minutes before the scheduled time, the large conference room was packed—the seats were filled and a few dozen people stood in the back, maybe 150 feet from the speaker's platform.

In his talk, Stevenson was dignified, intelligent, low-key, thoughtful. He explained the origin of his interest in children's memories of previous lives, and described the scope of his research, summarizing some of the commonalties, and the differences, among cases found all over the world—from the Indian subcontinent and Southeast Asia to South America, Europe, and North America, including a variety of tribal peoples in Canada and Alaska.

When people asked questions, he always appeared to consider them carefully before answering. One man shouted from the back: "Has there ever been a scientific attempt to detect some difference in a body before and after death that could be accounted for by the passing of a soul?"

"In the early part of the century, they conducted some experiments, but never detected anything," Stevenson said. "They placed a dying man on an elaborately balanced bed. The thought was that if the bed became unbalanced at the instant of death, that would be evidence that the soul had a detectable weight. But the man died and the bed remained balanced.

"My own thought is that it is not inconceivable that at some time in the future, it might be possible to scientifically detect what we would call a soul, but that it would consist of something beyond the present understanding of the physical universe."

Another man, dressed in a dress shirt and tie with a gray sweater, stood up not far from where I sat. "Dr. Stevenson," he said, "can you please tell us, what is your message?"

Stevenson proceeded, at some length, to describe the way in which he collected information, interviewed informants, correlated data. When he finished, the man said, "I said MESSAGE, not *method*."

There was a ripple of laughter in the room, but Stevenson remained poker-faced and he answered the question in a way that puzzled me, and probably didn't do much to satisfy the questioner, saying that he wished that more physicians would pay attention to his work because reincarnation might shed light on many phobias, birthmarks, and birth defects that have no known medical explanation. It seemed a hope that was at once unnecessarily humble and tangential, as if proof of reincarnation would be great primarily as an aid to explaining the blotch on Mikhail Gorbachev's forehead.

At the same time, I realized that Stevenson must get this all the time—people who preferred a prophet to a scientist. I remembered that in his autobiographical essay, he had said he wanted no part of that: "My beliefs should make no difference to anyone," he said. "Everyone should examine the evidence and judge it for himself."

After the last question, a knot of people surrounded Stevenson. I was noticing how eager they seemed when a woman approached and said my name with a charming accent. It took a second for it to register who she was: Suzanne. I took her hand, as happy to see her as if she had been an old friend. In her other hand she had an oversized photocopy of the *Monday Morning* article that had featured her case.

"I thought you might want one," she said.

I scanned the pages. The first had a picture of a little curly-haired girl—Suzanne—with a beautiful, smiling young woman standing by her side. The resemblance between the two was marked; the young woman could easily have been Suzanne's mother. It was Galareh Mansour.

"Is there anything in the article the reporter got wrong?" I asked.

"Yes," Suzanne said quickly. "They call my husband the wrong name."

She was speaking about Hanan Mansour's husband, Farouk, whom the writer had called Fayed.

I knew that Suzanne would have followed Stevenson's lecture only with difficulty. Yet she seemed genuinely moved. "It was a wonderful talk, don't you think?" she said, her usually somber eyes sparkling.

Maybe it made her feel less lonely, I thought, to hear Stevenson talk about the hundreds of children around the world who had grown up with the same odd sense of displacement that she had experienced. Or maybe she was looking for validation.

"Would you be kind enough to pose for a photograph with me and Dr. Stevenson?" Suzanne asked, shyly pulling an automatic camera from her purse. I suggested that she might prefer a photo of her and Stevenson alone, but she insisted. We climbed up on the podium, and her brother Hassam snapped a shot with Suzanne's camera, then one with mine. In the photo, Suzanne stands between us, exposed and vulnerable, her dark eyes heavy with mystery.

Six months later, I would be paging through Suzanne's thick file in

Stevenson's Charlottesville office and come upon a photograph of Hanan Mansour at her wedding, when she was just a few years younger than Suzanne is now. I would see there the same eyes, the same heaviness, the same mystery.

∽

As Stevenson and I made our way to the exit of the auditorium, a young man approached, thrusting his card into Stevenson's hand. "We really must talk," the man said. "I'm working on some very intriguing cases myself."

The man said he was associated with the university's psychology department and that he had encountered two rebirth cases with unusual features. One involved a woman's near-death experience: After nearly dying and being revived, she said that she remembered feeling herself leave her body and being reborn in the bedroom of a home she recognized as belonging to a family she knew. But almost immediately, she felt herself drawn back into her own body. After reviving, she told those around her what she had experienced. Later, they discovered that while the woman was undergoing her crisis, the family she had seen in her vision had had a stillborn child.

The second case, he said, was that of an Arab woman who claimed to have been Hindu in a previous life. In fact, she spoke Hindi, though there was no identifiable source for that ability.

Stevenson appeared at least mildly interested. He knew better than anyone that stories told secondhand most often failed to materialize.

"Do you have names and phone numbers for the subjects?" he asked. The man, who had been crowding Stevenson, took a half step back. "I'll call you," he said. Stevenson gave him the hotel number, and we left.

"Think he'll call about those cases?" I asked about fifteen minutes later as walked into the Cavalier's lobby.

"He seemed somewhat possessive of them," Stevenson replied casually. "I have some what I call 'near-death, near-birth' cases myself. One was very similar to what he was describing: A woman was unconscious and thought to be near death. When she revived, she said she had found herself in the presence of a woman who had just given birth and felt compelled to push herself into the baby's body. But just as she was doing it, she thought of her love for her family and pulled back."

"Interesting," I commented, "that in both of those cases the claim was that they were about to enter at the moment of birth, not conception."

"Isn't it?" he said, smiling.

It was after nine. Surprisingly, I wasn't especially hungry, I was, however, grateful when Stevenson invited me to his room for a drink before dinner.

I walked up to my room and grabbed a can of beer, then joined Stevenson next door. He poured himself a minibottle of Scotch. We both sat in chairs by the window.

"I've been thinking about something," I said. "When the subjects speak of being someone in the past life, even if they acknowledge that person, it seems that they might as easily conclude they had mentally tuned into someone else's life—more ESP than a previous life."

Stevenson took a sip of his Scotch. "There's more than memory involved," he said. "When the subjects are young children, they say, 'I have a wife,' or 'I am a doctor,' or 'I have three buffalo and two cows.' They are the previous personality, and they resist the imposition of a new identity. Daniel told Latifeh, 'You aren't my mother, my mother is a sheikha.' I had a case in Thailand of a man who, as a child, remembered having lived the life of his mother's brother. He said that he has a clear memory from his infancy in this life: When he was on his back, he felt he was an adult man and had all the memories of a previous life. But every so often, meddlesome adults would turn him over and he was then nothing but a small little baby, helpless in the cradle. Like a tortoise, he would struggle to get himself flipped over on his back again."

"On the whole, though," I said, "if reincarnation is the explanation for these cases, it's a process that produces very incomplete and imperfect memories. I mean, you don't have people who emerge with intact memories of entire lifetimes."

"Well, yes, we average maybe thirty statements in our Lebanese cases. From that perspective, it's not much. But as you saw with Suzanne, there may be some very strong emotional memories as well."

Outside the open window, seven floors down, the periodic beeps of the trolling taxis were almost soothing—a random percussion section punctuating our sentences.

"I wanted to ask you," I said. "At your lecture, that one question about your 'message'? Your answer about doctors considering reincarnation as an alternative possibility for the cause of birth defects seemed so—I don't know—*small*. We're talking about *reincarnation*, after all. Compared to that, diagnosing birth defects seems kind of a minor point, doesn't it?"

I think I expected him to see my point immediately, confess that he was just trying to avoid the question. Instead, with real feeling, he defended his answer. "Parents whose children are born with deformities suffer considerable distress not knowing what caused them, maybe believing they themselves did something that caused them. Being able to tell them that something entirely beyond their control may be at fault could be a great comfort."

Then, pausing, he settled back and looked at me. He knew what I meant.

"In general, I tend not to claim too much for the spiritual benefits of proving reincarnation," he said. "When I first went to India, I met with a swami there, a member of a monastic order. I told him about my work and how I thought it would be quite important if reincarnation could be proven, because it may help people to lead more moral lives if they knew they would come back after death. There was a long silence, a terrible silence, and finally he said, 'Well, that's very good, but here, reincarnation is a fact, and we have just as many scoundrels and thieves as you do in the West.' I'm afraid that rather deflated my missionary zeal."

I laughed. I was conscious that I was working, that as a journalist I was drawing Stevenson out. But I was also increasingly aware that I enjoyed his company, his reserve, and the precise way he put things.

I decided to tell him frankly about my doubts, my concern that, unintentionally prompted by unconscious motivations, some of these families could be passing on information to the children or embellishing memories of their statements and behavior.

"The thing is," I said, "it's almost impossible to completely rule something like that out."

Stevenson leaned forward in his chair. "That," he uttered softly, "is what haunts me."

∽

We arranged to meet in the dining room in fifteen minutes, and I went up to my room and flipped on CNN, hoping to hear the comforting drone of generic news. Instead, I got a grim-faced correspondent standing in front of boxy ambulances with flashing lights. That morning, while we were sailing through the Druse hills surrounding Beirut, Islamic militants had attacked a group of tourists touring the Valley of Kings in Luxor, Egypt, 250 miles to the west. The terrorists had opened fire with automatic rifles. Those tourists they only wounded in the initial barrage the terrorists finished off with knives. A total of fifty-eight Europeans were slaughtered.

7

The Heretic

Stevenson was waiting for me at a table against the wall in the crisp second-floor dining room. It was a long, narrow room with windows stretching across one side and a blank wall on the other. The tables were covered with freshly ironed white tablecloths, which the staff changed after every meal and sometimes between courses. Waiters in white jackets lurked inconspicuously behind the pillars in the center of the room, always appearing, as if by telepathy, when they were needed. Periodically, the power went off for a minute or two, but nobody missed a beat.

The restaurant service mirrored that of the hotel: efficient and understated. There were no ostentatious flourishes or gilt edges; they simply got the job done without fuss or comment. Given the ongoing chaos all around them, and the difficulty of maintaining service in cities where every other building *wasn't* in ruins, I marveled at the even keel that the place ran on. And I appreciated it. Far more so, it would become increasingly obvious, than Stevenson, who seemed particularly unconcerned about personal comfort, much less relative luxury.

Feeling finally recovered from jet lag and culture shock, I was hoping that I might make the evening productive by drawing Stevenson out about his life. What insight I had into that subject came from a reprint of a lecture Stevenson had given at Southeastern Louisiana University in 1989, in which he explains how he progressed from analyzing rat livers in a medical lab to interviewing children who claimed to remember previous lives.

I had read it early on, right after I met him for the first time in Charlottesville, and it had dispelled any remaining concerns I had about his intellectual seriousness. Whatever you thought of the ideas contained in his speech, there could be no doubt that they were well thought out and eloquently expressed. It read like something from the nineteenth century, a time when scientists could also be writers, historians, and philosophers, when they weren't afraid to think aloud and puzzle over imponderable topics in public. Even the language seemed a lovely relic of the past, blossoming with precise, venerable word choices (he uses, for example, "these researches" rather than "this research") and studded with quotations from a range of sources so impressive that it reminded me of how limited my own perspective was by comparison. In an age when access to knowledge has allegedly exploded, we somehow seem to have absorbed less and less of it.

But I was also intrigued by a subtle, underlying tone of bitterness, or, at least, hurt and puzzlement, apparent in the text. Stevenson clearly felt that his life's work had been scorned, or merely ignored, by those mainstream scientists whom he considered his peers.

He doesn't even wait for the second paragraph to allude to this. "For me," he writes, "everything now believed by scientists is open to question, and I am always dismayed to find that many scientists accept current knowledge as forever fixed."

At another point he adds, only half jokingly, "If heretics were burned alive today, the successors in science of the theologians who, in the sixteenth century, burned anyone who denied the existence of souls, would today burn those who affirm their existence."

Mostly, though, he sticks to tracing his own evolution with surprising frankness. He attributes his initial interest in the relationship between the spiritual and the material to his mother, who was an adherent of a late-nineteenth-century mystical movement called theosophy, which he describes as "a kind of potted Buddhism" for Westerners.

And then he really got my attention. I remember sitting in my family room late at night, reading by the light of a small desk lamp in an otherwise dark house. I didn't really know what I was looking for in this Xeroxed reprint of a speech, and my eyes were beginning to glaze—until I got to the following:

While I was still involved with psychoanalysis, I began experiment-ing with hallucinogenic (perhaps better called psychedelic) drugs. I have taken or had administered to me a number of drugs as part of a search for drugs that would assist psychiatrists in interviewing or in psychotherapy.

With one of my experiences with LSD I also had a mystical experi-ence, by which I mean a sense of unity with all beings, all things. After that experience I passed three days in perfect serenity. I believe that many persons could benefit as much as I did through taking psychedelic drugs under proper medical supervision, which is the only sensible way to take them.

Uh-oh.

The first thing I imagined was what critics like Paul Edwards could do with that one. *The guy's an acid head! His reincarnation cases are just one big hallucination!*

I might have had a similar little shock of concern myself if it weren't for the fact that what I knew of the man and his writings bespoke so-briety and clear thinking. And there was no shortage of respected thinkers and writers who had positive things to say about the psyche-delic experience, from Aldous Huxley in the 1950s to Robert Stone in the '90s. Besides, judging Stevenson harshly would have been hypocrit-ical. When I was a college student twenty-five years ago, I'd seen more than my share of addled druggies. But I'd also discovered for myself that psychedelic drugs, not taken lightly, could and often did have illu-minating effects far beyond temporary euphoria. In fact, in my experi-ence, taking psychedelic drugs was not euphoric at all—it was hard work that sometimes culminated in moments of real and lasting insight. Nobody can reasonably deny the enormous potential for abuse of these powerful drugs, and maybe the risk of physical or psychological dam-age is too great to be worth taking. But neither can I deny that, in my case and in the case of many others I knew then and whose lives I have followed since, these experiences had been useful in precisely the way that Stevenson described.

Stevenson doesn't say it in so many words, but he implies that his LSD experience reinforced his sense that there was something beyond the material in human consciousness, something that left room among the firing of neurons and the twisting strands of DNA for an entity like a soul, which could conceivably survive the physical decay of brain matter. But, interestingly, it did nothing to diminish his faith in science as a way of either proving or disproving that idea.

"However impressive, mystical experiences are incommunicable, whereas scientific observations are and must be communicable; there is no science without public demonstrability. This means independent verification."

Which is exactly what attracted me to Stevenson's work in the first place. He has never said anything like "Believe this because I believe it." What he *is* saying is, "Look at what I've found. Examine it any way you want to examine it. Think of your own questions, find tests of truth that have escaped me, and if you can imagine a more reasonable explanation for all this, please let me know."

That's science—even if it happens to involve questions that most scientists don't take seriously.

Over dinner that evening, tape recorder running, I tried to fill in the blanks in Stevenson's life story and better understand how he had wound up, just shy of his seventy-ninth birthday, sitting ramrod straight above a pressed white tablecloth in Beirut at the end of a long day visiting the reborn. I asked questions from time to time, but, mostly, he just talked, starting from the beginning.

He was born in Montreal in 1918, the son of the Oxford-educated chief correspondent in Ottawa for *The Times of London*.

"That was almost a semiofficial position," Stevenson said, seeming to consider every word carefully before uttering it. "The *Times* had correspondents in all the major capitals of the world."

He paused, gazing toward the window as if trying to see into the far distance. Then he turned back to me. "It's hard to picture the period now, between the two world wars. Perhaps I can best convey it by saying my father's predecessor was knighted. It was considered that important a position to be the *Times*'s chief correspondent in an important capital like Washington or Ottawa. He'd go back to England about once every two years. Often he'd take one of us. I had two brothers and a sister. I was the second child."

Stevenson's father was a distant man, more involved in career than family, and although Stevenson respected him immensely, the boy had a far stronger emotional connection to his mother.

"My mother was a remarkable woman," he said. "She encouraged my reading. I owe to her also my first exposure to what would be called paranormal phenomena today. She had a good library, lots of books on theosophy and Oriental religion and what now would be called New Age, but then was called New Thought. The power of mind over matter, mind over body. She had a little phase of interest in Christian Science, but my mother was too independent to sign on for any one religion."

Stevenson finished high school at sixteen and was sent to a school in England. He won a scholarship to the University of St. Andrews in Scotland and spent two years there.

"I started out to do history," Stevenson recalled. "I had always been fascinated by history. I still read history for pleasure, but I thought that's not really enough of a career. Nor did journalism appeal to me. A lot of my father's writing seemed to be destructive and critical, not contributing much to human welfare, so I decided I was going to go into medicine."

He transferred to McGill University in Montreal in 1939, completed medical school there and began specialized training. "I had been sickly ever since birth, first bronchitis, then it developed into something more substantial I've had all my life. I had pneumonia three times. When I was in training, one of my professors told me I ought to get out of the cold climate in Montreal. He said I would die if I stayed there.

"My professors had some friends in Arizona, and they arranged for me to go there. In those days, there was no effective treatment for my lung problem, and I didn't know quite what was going to happen to me. I worked for a year in Arizona and got to feeling better. I decided to resume my training, but I was still, unreasonably, I think, as it turns out now, afraid of the cold climate. So I took a position in New Orleans at the Ochsner Clinic and Tulane University. I got a fellowship there. I had been at the top of my medical school class in McGill, so I didn't have any difficulty finding a position. I went through a phase of being interested in biochemistry. I liked that—I've always liked almost everything I've done—but then that too didn't seem quite right. I felt a need to be closer to humans—I was working with rats. So I got a position at the

New York Hospital and Cornell Medical College for two years, another fellowship, doing research in psychosomatic medicine, particularly cardiac arrhythmias brought on by emotional disturbances. I would interview patients while they were attached to an electrocardiograph, talk to them about the stresses in their lives, and then observe changes in their heart function. I had one patient who was a professional arsonist—he would split the insurance proceeds with the owner of the building. He would get into cardiac difficulties just before he did a job. And he had a very uneven income, so in between he was dependent on his sister and his brother-in-law, and his brother-in-law used to taunt him for being an inadequate provider, and while he was telling me about this he might have an arrhythmia. His heart rate would go awry. We were interested in understanding why, under stress, one person might develop asthma, another high blood pressure, and a third cardiac problems. Some of my colleagues thought the reaction might have symbolic meaning determined by the needs and personality of the patient, but that never satisfied me. In fact, we never did explain that to my satisfaction, and though many today would think the whole question is absurd, it still fascinates me.

"Physically, I did all right in New York, but I was still uneasy about the climate. One of my teachers at Cornell invited me to join him at Louisiana State University. I went there in 1949 and spent seven years doing further research. I became interested in hallucinogenic drugs. I took some and I gave some and published some papers on that—it would have been in the early fifties.

"There had been some interest in evaluating mescaline as an artificially induced form of schizophrenia. In some ways, this is the beginning of modern biochemical ideas about the mechanisms of mental illness. So I became interested in what those drugs might do in the treatment of patients and the understanding of various mental conditions. I took them myself, and then I enlisted residents and patients to take them.

"We were interested in LSD as a potential 'knife into the psyche,' and for the arousal of memories as a therapeutic tool. I did recover some memories. I recalled being circumcised, not as an infant but later—I must have had some stricture of my foreskin—and my mother took me, without telling me where we were going. I must have been three. I could remember going along the street saying, 'Where are we going?' When we got there I found that I was being held down by four burly men and I was covered with a mask and given ether, and I woke up with a sore penis. I had never forgotten that, but the point is that it came back with extraordinary vividness with LSD. I do think it could be a useful tool, but Timothy Leary really wrecked things. In my view, he was terribly misguided. His misconduct led to the suppression of the use of the drugs.

"My experience taking psychedelic drugs was very good, on the whole. For one thing, it really changed my perspective on physical beauty. My first wife was an artist with extraordinarily good sensory perception. I was shortsighted and never paid much attention to color and form. Mescaline opened up a whole new world to me. I'm not recommending it for everyone, and it certainly shouldn't be used except under strict medical supervision, but I found it beneficial.

"That experience is really ineffable, very difficult to communicate in mere words. But my interest in the paranormal predates my experiences with LSD—I really got that from my mother's interests—but perhaps they were enhanced.

"During those years in New Orleans I had been reading widely in what would be considered paranormal literature. Toward the end of my time there, I tentatively began to write a little, book reviews and articles, in addition to the reports of my conventional research I was publishing in medical journals.

"In 1957, when I was thirty-nine, I went to Charlottesville as head of the department of psychiatry. By that time I had some reputation as a conventional researcher, but I knew that I wanted to do something with paranormal phenomena. When I was interviewed at the University of Virginia I told them of that interest. They didn't seem to blanch. I had other interests, too.

"I guess I had had a special interest in reincarnation since childhood because it was the central teaching of theosophy. What happened was that as I was a very extensive reader, I began to find in books here and there, and in newspapers and magazines, reports of what were usually individual cases of reincarnation memories. In the end, I found forty-four cases here and there. The thing that came out when you got them all together was that they predominantly featured young children, ages two to five, who spoke of previous-life memories for a brief time, until they were about eight. But you had to get them all together first before that was obvious. Many were little more than journalistic anecdotes, but some were considerably more serious. In several cases, cautious adults had seriously inquired into the claims of the children. And in three cases I found, someone had made a written record of what the child claimed before the statements were verified.

"Numbers count in science, and these forty-four cases, when you put them together, it just seemed inescapable to me that there must be something there. They were from different countries, and from different kinds of sources. . . . There was one from Italy where the father was a doctor and he observed his son, one of twins, who remembered an earlier life—that seemed very persuasive. I couldn't see how they could all be faked or they could all be a deception.

"My conclusion was that this might be a promising line of investigation if more cases could be found and studied earlier and more carefully. I don't think it occurred to me that I might be the one to carry out the investigations. But I submitted an essay on the subject for a prize offered by the American Society for Psychical Research, and won. This was in 1960.

"Some time later, the head of the Parapsychology Foundation in New York called me and said she had a report of a case in India similar to those in my essay, and asked if I would be interested in going out to see it. She gave me a small grant and I went on vacation.

"I was very enthusiastic and curious. I thought it would be just a matter of the cognitive aspect of the cases, listing statements and checking them in the place where the child claimed to have lived. I also fairly soon developed the habit of trying to have multiple informants and not just depend on one or two or three. In some cases, I had as many as ten informants just for one side.

"By the time I arrived in India, I had leads on five cases, not just the one. To my surprise, in four weeks I had found twenty-five cases. The same happened in Sri Lanka—I had a lead to one or two there and I ended up with seven. I didn't pay much attention to the behavioral aspects of these cases. There was one where the child claimed that he was a Brahman and he was born in a low-caste family and he wouldn't eat his family's food. He said, 'You're all just a bunch of Jats; I'm a Brahman, I'm not going to eat your food.' He went on a hunger strike at two and a half. They were not using brass vessels, they were using clay pots, and their food was foul from his perspective. They hired a woman from a neighboring village to cook for him so he wouldn't starve. Then they began to deceive him by feeding him food and telling him it was Brahman food. Eventually, as he got older, they told him it was time for him to change, although he really never was happy. One of my colleagues would later try to find him jobs, but he would quit and say this wasn't work for a Brahman.

"I only caught it out of the corner of my eye. I thought, Well, this is interesting, but what really concerns me is how many of his statements can be verified, and what were the chances he could have learned this normally.

"I had a terrible misfortune in the middle of this. I wrote the first book—*Twenty Cases Suggestive of Reincarnation*—in 1964. That was three years after my first visit; the book was in press in the spring of 1964 with the American Society for Psychical Research when the man who had been my interpreter for two or three of the cases was found to be a fraud: He had pretended to be a Ph.D. when he wasn't. He turned out to be a sociopath. He actually published cases that he had invented, and he *might* have contaminated three of mine. Fortunately, after three cases, he got tired of my pace, and I found other interpreters, and in Pondicherry they still spoke French, so I used my French there. So this man really only contaminated two or three of the Indian cases, but when he was accused of fraud, the publications committee of the society said he might have been cheating on the interpreting, so they stopped the publication of my book. Stopped the presses cold.

"The way it came to light this man was a great traveler, funded by a wealthy man in India, and he left India and wound up in Durham with J. B. Rhine, the founder of experimental parapsychology at Duke, who I visited from time to time. The man began calling himself 'doctor,' and one of Rhine's men said, 'How come you're calling yourself doctor now? Did you get a diploma in Moscow?' He said he'd gotten one in Agra. They checked up on him and found he didn't have one at all.

"I was down there on a visit and J. B. Rhine said, 'I hate to tell you, but I think this man is a cheat.' I first stuck with him. He was accused of cheating on card-guessing experiments, and I didn't think he'd done that; it was hard to tell. Anyway, that was an awkward moment for me.

"By this time, I had the support, morally and financially, of Chester Carlson, the inventor of xerography, a marvelous person as well as a great inventor. He and his wife had read my article about the forty-four cases. He had come to me in Charlottesville and offered me some money. He was determined to give his money to something that he felt would benefit humanity after his death. His wife believed she had psychical ability and he had been a very skeptical and materialistic person, but she gradually persuaded him that there was something to be learned by studying paranormal phenomena. So he then began to give money, first to J. B. Rhine, and then he began to think J. B. Rhine had mined out most of the mineral in the ore he had been working, so he began looking around for people with other ideas. He was directed to me. I said I was too busy, loaded with clinical patients and administrative duties and I couldn't take any money. But, in the end, I did take six hundred dollars maybe for a tape recorder. He began to give the university more money, and as he gave more money, I was able to give up some clinical patients and spend more time on research.

"Chester Carlson was supporting me in 1964, so I wrote to him and said I thought that if I went back to India and revisited these cases with new interpreters, they could be saved. I didn't believe the man had been cheating in interpretation, and rechecking them could readily determine that in any case. So Carlson said go ahead and do it. I went back in August '64 and all the cases held up. I also learned from that the value of follow-up interviews. This was three years after the initial interviews.

"I brought the manuscript up to date. In the meantime, I had also been to Brazil, so I had two Brazilian cases, and I added those. The presses rolled again and that book came out in 1966."

By now, the table had long been cleared and we were just sipping water from time to time. I sat there imagining the horrors—the self-doubt, the sleepless nights, the nausea at facing another morning—that were tied up in the phrase, "that was an awkward moment for me."

"What kind of response did you get when the book was published?"

Stevenson said nothing for long enough that, though I had spoken plainly, I began to wonder if he hadn't heard the question.

Just when I was about to ask it again, he said, "The short answer is none—it was just ignored. It was reviewed in the journals of psychical research, and that was about it. I was disappointed, but I couldn't say I was surprised. I was well aware of the isolation of my work."

"Did you get any negative response from the university?"

"Not precisely at this point, that I knew of. I think it was growing, though, because I learned later that the president of the university had received mail and telephone calls from alumni protesting what I was doing. And my wife was very distressed; she said, 'You're just ruining a promising career. Everything is going great for you. Why do you want to do this?' She was herself very materialistic and very oriented toward biochemistry as the answer to disease. So she didn't have sympathy for what I was doing. But that wasn't the worst of her troubles—what was more distressing was that other people, instead of coming to me and saying, 'I'd like to see your data,' would make cracks to her at cocktail parties in my absence, tease her, and I thought that was shameful. Of course, she didn't really believe in it to begin with, so they had the wrong target.

"But by that time, I was convinced that there was really something substantial in what I was seeing, something that should be pursued no matter what the cost. So I devoted more and more time to the cases. And then Chester Carlson endowed a chair for me. He said, 'I'll match fifty-fifty for any money you raise.' Which was incredible, because it meant for every dollar I raised, the endowment would get four dollars—he'd match the dollar, then the state would match the two dollar total. I got a hundred thousand dollars from private donors, then he matched that, and the state matched *that*. Much of the income from that was really for my salary, so I could give up private patients and my teaching and become a full-time researcher. Carlson was then giving quite handsome annual grants that covered expenses, research assistants, secretaries, travel. He would do that year to year; there was no assurance of any continuity. Then he died suddenly and quite unexpectedly.

"He had coronary-artery disease, but wasn't considered gravely ill. He went into a movie theater in New York and was later found dead. I thought, 'The bottom has dropped out of this. I'll have to go back to ordinary research.' And then his will was read and it was found that he'd left the university a million dollars and a little more for my research. A great controversy broke out over whether the university was going to accept it or not.

"I was no longer chairman of the psychiatry department—I had stepped down when we got the endowment for the professorial chair; being chairman was a full-time job in itself.

"I was head of the Division of Personality Studies, which is just a small research unit. That was the name I wanted, because I always wanted to stay close to medicine and biology; I didn't want to be isolated. I thought that most parapsychologists, as they were then called, were too isolated. They were just talking to themselves and not talking enough to other scientists, and far too inattentive to the fact that the rest of the world wasn't listening to them. They were too locked in to a rather narrow laboratory program and they tended to be neglectful, if not contemptuous, of what happened in the field, of spontaneous experiences. Those interested me more. Modern psychologists imitated physicists by only being interested in what happened in a lab, not in things like love and death, and parapsychologists imitated psychologists—that is, you have tight control of conditions. But it seems to me that it's far better to be ninety percent certain of something *important* than one hundred percent certain of something that is trivial. I thought that a lot of the results obtained in the parapsychology lab testing people's abilities to guess the images on cards were just meager.

"Those cards have pretty much faded now. They got people who could guess the images correctly significantly above what pure chance would predict, sometimes astonishingly beyond chance, but often the results were just borderline."

I didn't even bother to look at my watch. I knew it was too late and that my hopes of typing some notes into the computer would have to give way to a desperate need for sleep.

Stevenson, meanwhile, looked no different than he had at 8:30 that morning.

"Don't these trips wear you down?" I asked.

"Well," he replied, "I always find the work very absorbing. But it's really getting to the point where it's not fair to my wife, Margaret, that I'm gone so frequently."

"Has she become any more reconciled to your work over the years?"

"Oh, no, that was my first wife who had the difficulty," he told me. "Margaret is also very skeptical about my research—I think at present she believes there is nothing after death—but unlike my first wife, she is not troubled by my work and is an angel in her encouragement of it.

"I met my first wife, Octavia Reynolds, when I was a fellow at Tulane University, in New Orleans. We were married in 1947, and she died in 1983, of diabetes. It was well controlled for many, many years, but then she developed every complication conceivable. Terrible neuritis, hemorrhages in her eyes. Then her kidneys failed and she went on dialysis. It was very sad to see her decline. Very sad. But it also made me see that in some ways the best thing for a human being is to be forced to be completely focused on caring for someone else. That was a great gift.

"I married Margaret two years after my wife died. I had known her for a long time. She had been my first research assistant in Charlottesville. When the Russians put up *Sputnik,* like many other American scientists I thought, 'Well, if they are ahead of us in space travel, maybe they are ahead of us in medicine.' So I suggested to Margaret, 'You could go and learn Russian; then you could read their journals and we would know what they are doing.' So she took Russian, and the professor fell in love with her and married her. She had a happy marriage, then he had a stroke and she nursed him devotedly. When he died, she was alone for a number of years. I didn't see much of her. After my wife died, I got to know her again and fell in love. We've been happily married ever since. She teaches German and Russian history at Randolph Macon Women's College in Lynchburg, just down the road from Charlottesville. She's been there since she got her Ph.D., twenty-eight, thirty years ago."

"Do you have any children?"

"My first wife and I had one stillborn child, a large baby, as the babies of diabetics are. We thought of adoption, but never pushed it through, so I never had children, one of the few pleasures of life I have missed."

The dining room was empty except for Stevenson and me and the waiters standing steadfastly by the pillars. I didn't know if they were too polite to tell us it was closing time or if they really did stay open until midnight.

I walked up the five flights to my room—despite the exhaustion, I'd done nothing but sit all day. Stevenson bid me good-night at the elevator, but said he might join me climbing the stairs the next day. "These trips are really terrible for my health," he said. "I could use the exercise."

In my room, I plugged my laptop into the phone line and dialed in to my e-mail. There was a message waiting from my wife:

I took the kids to the Middle Eastern place at the mall, where we discussed whether you might, at that very moment, be having a midnight snack of the same kinds of foods. Then we saw Anastasia, *which the kids really enjoyed. It was interesting to me that, on the way home, Sam noted that part of the movie was very sad—the fact that the Czar and the rest of his family died. Disney had really downplayed that in the movie—you just were told the family was cursed by Rasputin, and then you never saw them again, except for Anastasia and the grandmother. In fact, Emily said she didn't really think the family had died. They are such different children, have been different from birth. On the way to the movie, Emily was composing thank-you notes to each of her teachers, telling them what wonderful teachers they are and how they make class so much fun. She also said they had to write a composition in Spanish saying what they were thankful for and she wrote, 'For having such a wonderful family.'*

As I signed off the computer, I could hear Stevenson coughing through the thick wall between our rooms. It was violent and prolonged, and I was about to go knock on his door when it finally stopped. He hadn't coughed once that I could remember all day. I guessed something about lying down must trigger it. I lay awake for a while, wondering about him. He'd related such sad events in his life with such matter-of-fact humility. The sudden order to stop the presses on his book, the cold reception to his work, the stillbirth of his only child, and then his wife's illness and death. Now, as he was approaching eighty, I wondered if he believed that he had lived other lives, would live others in the future. I'd asked him about that early in our conversation—had he had "any personal experiences that reinforced the idea reincarnation occurred" was the way I put it.

He just sat up a little straighter, got that shuttered expression on his face and said, "None that I care to discuss."

8

In the Name of the Family

Stevenson believes in his luck. He will often drive hours in hopes of interviewing someone without an appointment or even exact directions. More often than not, it all works out: he finds the house, the subject is home and hospitable.

He was hoping for a little more luck when we drove to the Mansour family home, twenty miles due east of Beirut, a journey of several hours on narrow twisting roads that took us into an area more remote than I had yet seen.

It was an impressive three-story stone house cut into the side of a steep slope overlooking a terraced valley. Majd hadn't called ahead; she had sensed from some earlier contacts that the Mansours might not be too eager to cooperate. I think that she was hoping that if we just showed up, the Druse compulsion to honor guests would prevail.

Stevenson's luck, however, flagged a little: nobody was home. After some discussion, Majd called Hanan's sister's Beirut number. Helene was there. Majd spoke for a minute, listened, then put her hand over the phone to translate: Helene was very apologetic, but she could not invite us there to talk to her. In fact, she had to take the call in another room because she did not want her family to know she was talking to Majd. They did not believe the girl. Prominent professionals who now lived elsewhere in the Mideast, where belief in reincarnation was sacrilegious, they feared that being associated with a case like Suzanne's could have serious repercussions. The family had been very upset by the *Monday Morning* article and wanted nothing further to do with Suzanne or any discussion of the girl.

Stevenson sat in the backseat, his arms crossed at the wrist, resting on the files that sat upon crossed knees.

"Can we ask her at least whether she can confirm that Hanan's last words were, 'Leila, Leila'?"

Majd relayed the question.

"She said yes," Majd reported after hanging up. "But she wasn't there herself. That is what her brothers told her."

Stevenson tucked his files into his briefcase.

"Very well," he said. "Let's ask Mahmoud to take us back into Beirut. Perhaps we'll try our luck with Farouk."

∽

Farouk Mansour, now in his sixties, lived in a large, luxuriously appointed apartment in a quiet corner of Beirut. In earlier interviews in the late seventies and early eighties, he had told Stevenson that he believed Suzanne's claims to be true, that she was Hanan reborn, despite the fact that her memories had not been perfect: Suzanne maintained that her husband had been in the military, but Farouk had been a career police officer. She said that he had two guns; Farouk said he'd had just one.

But the overwhelming majority of what Suzanne said was accurate, and sufficient, Farouk believed at the time of Stevenson's last discussion with him in 1981, to confirm the claim of reincarnation. For one thing, Farouk said, he had shown her a group photo of one hundred police officers taken when he was a very young man, and she had picked him out of the large group without hesitation. He said that she had accurately recalled scores of names associated with his and Hanan's life together and known many other things that, in his opinion, only Hanan would have known.

Farouk had remarried some time after Hanan's death, to a woman who had been a close friend of Hanan's. He was so convinced of Suzanne's claim, and so impressed by the little girl's obvious feeling of affection toward him, that he avoided mentioning his remarriage to Suzanne for fear of upsetting her, and lied to her about it when she asked.

When she did find out, she reacted as a spurned lover might, with tears and anger. But she still called Farouk on the phone frequently, some might say obsessively. And Farouk had dealt with her quite tenderly. As far as I knew, Stevenson had never interviewed Farouk's present wife, but she could not have been too thrilled with the situation.

All that was sixteen years ago, though, and Stevenson had not heard from Farouk since.

⤳

Mahmoud dropped us off on the sidewalk. The address we sought was in a five-story building opposite an ancient two-story stucco house with green shutters and a laundry-hung back porch that could easily have fit in a French provincial town. Farouk lived on the second floor, up an unimposing flight of stairs lined with earthen planters. He answered the door himself. I didn't expect him to look so elderly, more seventy-five than sixty. He looked shrunken in his brown jacket, a tie pulled tight around his wrinkled neck, his bald head projecting forward from shoulders. What hair he had came in wisps of white, and he had a white mustache.

Majd announced us and explained who Stevenson was ("an American doctor"). Halfway through her speech, Farouk's face lit up and he grasped Stevenson's hand. "You've barely changed in all these years," he said, beaming. We were ushered into a grand living room, seated, and offered coffee. Despite the unimpressive exterior, the apartment itself was elegant, filled with fine art and antiques and draped with breathtaking silk carpets. It reminded me of some of the fine old apartments on the Upper East Side of Manhattan. After we got settled, Stevenson asked Farouk if he'd stayed in touch with Suzanne.

Not much, Farouk began. He felt that Suzanne was living in two generations, and that he needed to withdraw somewhat—

Before Majd could finish translating, a tall, striking woman emerged from the kitchen. The decisive way she entered the room in midconversation, as if she were unconcerned about the possibility of interrupting, suggested something less than cordiality, and the grim set to her mouth as she turned brusquely to face us removed any doubt. She nodded curtly. "I am Galareh Mansour," she said in perfect American English. Immediately, I could see the glamorous young woman in the twenty-year-old *Monday Morning* article. In her mid-forties now, Galareh was still beautiful, and undoubtedly far more commanding than she had been in her twenties.

"We do not want to talk about this any further," she said, looking us dead in the eyes, one at a time. "The story caused many problems in my family." She looked down, and her voice lowered as if she were talking half to us and half to herself. "It's a true story," she added, almost regretfully. "I lived through it, I believe it one hundred percent, but there are some delicate issues, especially in Lebanon. That article went on and on. It made my life miserable, and my relatives will not accept any more publication."

The three of us sunk deep into the sofa, lamely holding our coffee cups on our laps. For the first time since I had arrived in Lebanon, I could think of nothing to say. The silence was an irresistible force, into which now plunged an unstoppable object: Galareh's husband. He was a large, intense man in black slacks, a blue shirt, and a light-blue cardigan, with bold, almost American Indian features. He reminded me of the American movie star Joe Mantegna. As impressive as Galareh's entrance had been, it paled in comparison to his. Her husband plunged right in, smiling proprietarily, as if he were the host on a talk show and this his set.

"I was regressed to find out about my past lives," were the first words out of his mouth. "I cannot tell you the method," he went on, his eyebrows raising conspiratorially. "It was very spiritual. I was a priest six hundred years ago in Alexandria."

Great, I was thinking. An Alexandrian priest. Maybe he knew Brian Weiss, in his Babylonian priest phase. He must have read my mind.

"Do you know the book by Brian Weiss?" he asked, cocking his head and looking straight at me. "The third book? A very beautiful story about lovers separated by death. He was regressing both separately. Very beautiful story . . ." He trailed off as if feeling the poignancy all over again. Then he suddenly snapped back. "My father remembered a previous life," he rambled on. "I study the Koran for verses related to reincarnation—of course, I speak the language—I've got it on CD-ROM. The Moslems don't believe it, but I've already found five verses."

I looked over at Galareh, who had settled into a chair across the room, still grim-faced but apparently resigned to her husband's monologue. "We're from Virginia. We're just visiting in Lebanon," he continued. "I read an article in *The Washington Post* the other day that said twenty-nine percent of Americans now believe in reincarnation." A professor running through the high points of his curriculum, he turned to Stevenson. "Basically, people who remember previous lives died through a shock—accident, violence, a shock. But most don't remember. But as you know and as I know, all the lifetimes are retained in the subconscious."

I looked at Stevenson to see if the pedantry would force him to respond. I should have known better. He sat back in his rest state, arms crossed on knees, his half-smile unfurled.

I turned again to Galareh, who was sitting uncomfortably in her chair. "Have you had a regression?" I asked her.

A look crossed her face that answered my question more thoroughly than words ever could. "Oh, no. . . . *No,*" she said.

"We were together six hundred years ago," her husband said, as if Galareh had momentarily forgotten that fact. And then, without transition: "I believe the twenty-first century is going to be the spiritual center."

He continued on like this, pacing up and down on the Persian carpet.

"I contracted cancer two years ago," he said. "Leukemia. I refused all medications. One of the doctors said I have only three years to live, but I refused any treatment. This was thirteen months ago. I met a spiritual healer—here, in Lebanon—who gives me holy water. I can tell you I have improved eighty to ninety percent. The doctors are stunned. My first diagnosis was in April '96. All my test results are on my PC."

The holy man apparently had "a channel with St. George," and did spiritual surgeries—operating with telepathy rather than scalpel.

"As Dr. Weiss said in his book," Galareh's husband continued, "every human is supposed to acquire virtues in every lifetime. In my case, everyone says I am courageous. It's not me. I brought it with me from another lifetime. Everyone says I have a strong will. I brought that from another life as well.

"When people have some . . ." He paused in midgesture.

"Disease?" Majd offered.

"You call it a disease," he picked up again. "I call it an abnormality. When someone has an abnormality, they are actually blessed because they are tested and have the opportunity to show faith, which gives us all the virtues. I discovered in regression that I served St. George's temple centuries ago, and that's why he is helping me now."

He stopped, swiveled, and then turned back to us.

"I was with Galareh when she first met the girl," he said, dropping his podium voice. "That was really amazing. My mother-in-law asked something very intimate of her that nobody else but Hanan could have known, and she knew it. And my father-in-law asked something very intimate that no one else could know, and she knew that, too. I witnessed this."

"Suzanne was a real turning point for both of us."

Galareh's eyes had lost their distant gaze. She moved forward in her chair. "It affected me," she said. Her voice caught, and she stopped. Then, after visibly gathering herself, she continued. "It affected me a lot to see this little girl, and she *was* a little girl, not my mother anymore, say those things, treat me like her daughter."

"Was it at all comforting?" I asked. "To think that your mother wasn't simply gone forever?"

Galareh looked pained. "It was my first experience with reincarnation," she said, her voice trailing off. She looked away. "It was very shocking. Very difficult. I'd heard stories, but I'd never encountered anything personally. It was very disturbing. For a long time afterward I didn't want to hear anything about it."

"How did the article come about?"

"I had a friend. A journalist. I told her about Suzanne and she came to the house with me . . ." She looked as if she might be about to cry. "It pulled our family apart," she said and fell back in the chair, silent again.

I noticed out of the corner of my eye that Majd was huddled with Farouk in a whispered conversation. Stevenson was explaining that he intended to publish an account of Suzanne's case.

"My family won't allow it," Galareh said emphatically. "We don't want our name associated with it."

"That might be the solution then," Stevenson said. "I could use pseudonyms, I've done that before."

"We don't want our family's name in any more articles," she reiterated.

As we left, Galareh took my hand and held it for a second. "It tore us apart," she said again, looking into my eyes.

On the street I asked Majd what she and Farouk had been discussing.

"He said he had stopped going to visit Suzanne, not because he didn't want to see her, but for her sake," she said. "He said she visits once or twice a month still, but he's trying to discourage her. He kept saying, 'I just worry about her. This can't be good for her. I still want to go, but I am denying myself for her sake.'"

☙

I'm denying myself for her sake. The words kept echoing on the short ride back to the Cavalier. I felt like I had arrived somewhere. I was no longer poking around on the fringes of these incredible stories; I had gotten sucked up in the middle of one. Galareh's distress, her emotion and ambivalence, had filled the room. *She was a* little girl, *not my mother anymore.*

I knew that in our meeting with the Mansours (which is the pseudonym that Stevenson later settled on) we had stumbled onto something valuable—the confirmation of a case's crucial details by people who had every reason to want to deny them. Here were people with money and status and a serious stake in denying evidence of reincarnation, especially evidence generated by a little girl from a lower, less-sophisticated class. And Suzanne had made believers of them.

Of course, one of the believers apparently also bought into every New Age theory that flitted past, including the idea that sprinkling himself with holy water would cure his cancer. But it seemed clear that his general credulity was not shared by his wife, who was by far the more important witness. And then there was Farouk: Here was a man who had been put in a very awkward position by the acceptance of Suzanne's claim. He had not been pining for his dead wife; he was re-married and happily going about the rest of his life when this . . . *toddler* surfaced, pestering him with astonishing persistence. Not only was it personally awkward, and undoubtedly a thorn in the side of his marriage, but Suzanne's claim had dragged him into the middle of a bitter dispute among his children and former in-laws—a dispute serious enough to send his daughter packing for the States. Yet he clearly could not help himself. He felt strongly for this girl, and he cared more for her welfare than his own difficulties.

It would have been so easy for all of them to say, "This was all a lie."

But they couldn't bring themselves to do it.

∽

Earlier that afternoon, on the way back into Beirut, we had pulled off the road into a cul-de-sac with a fine view of the valley. Majd pointed out a spectacular Moorish villa deep into the process of reconstruction. It was the family home of Dr. Sami Makarem, the professor of Arabic studies at the American University who had first introduced her to Stevenson. The house had been almost completely destroyed during the war, ruined and looted. Now, bit by bit, year by year, it was coming back together.

Makarem's name was first on the list of acknowledgments in Stevenson's 384-page volume on his cases in Lebanon and Turkey. He had assisted Stevenson on early cases, acting as interpreter and cultural guide, and Stevenson credited him with being the only Druse to have written an authoritative text on the religion in a Western language.

I had met Makarem at Stevenson's lecture the previous evening. He was a magnetic, almost cherubic man who spoke precisely, parceling out his words as if each had been forged separately, after great consideration. I had asked him whether he thought the Druse would welcome scientific proof of reincarnation.

"The Druse accept reincarnation as true," he said. "But in the Druse religion, the highest goal is to achieve a oneness with God, the ultimate reality, in *this* life."

Makarem had invited Stevenson and me to dinner, which is where we headed after leaving Farouk.

Makarem's apartment wasn't far from Majd's, in the part of Beirut where many of the embassies were (or had been before the war) and not far from the university campus. It was smaller than Majd's place, but stocked like a museum with art and antiques, including sabers, en-dueling pistols, and old photographs of the city and his father.

Makarem's father had been a famous artist, renowned for his exquisite calligraphy. Much of the framed art on the walls were his father's elaborate renditions of Arabic script, most of them quotations from the Koran. The calligraphy became an abstraction, beautiful in its own right. In addition to this work, the elder Makarem had been known for his ability to inscribe entire passages in gold leaf on a grain of rice. Beautifully bound books of photographs of his father's work included magnifications of microcalligraphy that were staggering to consider. The man became well enough known in the West that his work was exhibited at international expositions—an example of the inscrutable obsessions of the Orient.

Soon after we had been seated in the front parlor, Elie Karam, the Christian psychiatrist who at Majd's party had argued so passionately for the importance of investigating Druse reincarnation cases, arrived with his psychologist wife, a striking woman in a short, black evening dress.

"I have a story to tell you," Karam said to Stevenson as he took off his coat and sat down. "My assistant went to your lecture last night. Afterward, she went home and told her twenty-five-year-old brother about it—they're Christian Maronites—and he said: 'I had a previous life.' Just like that. It was the first she had ever heard about it. He told her, 'All I remember is that I was a tall man living in the suburbs of Vienna and I died in a car crash.' She said, 'Why didn't you ever say anything?' He said, 'I did when I was four, but our parents never listened to me.'

"So she calls her mom and asks her about it. The mom says she didn't remember him talking about a previous life, but he had exhibited a terrible phobia. He screamed bloody murder every time they went in a car, to the point where they often had to leave him behind."

Makarem issued a rich chuckle. "I have a story of my own," he said. "I know a Druse family who tell me that when their son was small, he spoke a strange language, which turned out to be Japanese. They only discovered what language he was babbling when they were out with him and he saw some Japanese standing in the street and heard them speaking. He began shouting that he could understand, and he ran to them before his parents could restrain him. By the time they caught up, he was in deep conversation in Japanese.

"He claimed to remember the life of a Chinese immigrant to Japan.

In fact, he even remembered his previous life address, and wrote to the previous personality's sister, who eventually came to visit him. He spoke about his previous life continually, so much so that his mother was afraid to let him go to Japan for fear that he would never return."

Stevenson was nodding in that considered way of his. When Makarem finished his tale, Stevenson said, "I hope that someone will study the twenty-five cases I have in Burma where children claim to remember lives as Japanese soldiers and exhibit Japanese characteristics."

He had mentioned these cases before. Most had been found in an area along the line of the British advance of 1945, as the Japanese army was about to collapse. These cases were interesting for many reasons, but they certainly provided some insight into the skeptical argument that families and children manufactured such cases to support a belief in reincarnation: The Japanese were hated in Burma, where occupying troops had committed many atrocities. The last thing any Burmese parents would want to suggest was that they were harboring the reincarnation of an Imperial soldier.

"One rather pathetic child was caught by the villagers and burned alive," Stevenson said. "And not only are these children born into Burmese families who want nothing to do with a Japanese child, they frequently long to 'go back to Tokyo,' think the Burmese food is too spicy, the climate too hot. They complain all the time: 'I want raw fish and sweets and want to dress like a Japanese.' Now, that can't be genetic, whatever else it might be."

I found it oddly refreshing to be able to listen to these tales and not have to worry about the ins and outs of trying to determine if they are true. Which reminded me of Galareh's husband. I recounted what he told us that afternoon, about the holy-water cure and the channeling of St. George, who happened to be the namesake of Karam's hospital.

"Do you know this holy man he spoke of?" Stevenson asked.

Karam laughed. "There are hundreds of them," he answered dryly, then went on.

"One night I went to see a faith healer who was getting quite a following. There were ten thousand people there. I had to climb up on a wall to see what was going on. The man said, 'One of you who is watching me has a brain tumor. You will be cured.' Later, I met a friend who had an inoperable brain tumor. I told him about what I had seen, and he said, 'I was the one the healer was talking about.' It turns out he had been watching the healer on television, and he became convinced that the remark was addressed directly to him. Immediately, he said, he began feeling well. He had been so weak he could barely move, and suddenly he felt his old self. Now that he was cured, he was going to go to Italy with his wife for two weeks.

"I knew his wife, too, and I saw her and begged her to have him get an MRI to confirm a cure. 'If not for your husband's sake,' I said, 'then do it for the church—they need that kind of proof.' She said, 'He's fine, but for your sake, I will. But only when we get back from our trip.' They went for two weeks as they planned, had a great time, then he dropped dead.

"I think it's quite possible that part of the immobility he had experienced had nothing to do with the tumor, but was caused by severe depression over his condition, and the pure hope that this faith healer had cured him had lifted the depression. The euphoria of believing he had escaped death could have given him a sudden surge of energy that allowed him to feel normal for two weeks before the tumor killed him."

At least, I thought, the poor man got to enjoy Italy.

9

New Jersey Is a State of Mind

Galareh's husband had at least one thing right: a disproportionate number of children who claim to remember previous lives remember dying violently. The first morning in Lebanon, Stevenson had mentioned a survey of cases he had studied in India showing that 50 to 60 percent involved violent death, even though violence accounted for only 5 to 6 percent of all deaths. I silently registered two possible explanations for that: Either violence tended to imprint itself on a soul, interfering with the usual process of forgetting, or whatever forces created false memories of previous lives had a penchant for the dramatic.

Whichever it might be, at the time I considered it something of an abstract question. But already, after a few days in Lebanon, I was beginning to see the flesh-and-blood (with an emphasis on the blood) side of things. Besides Ulfat, who thought that she remembered being slit open by Christian marauders, and Daniel, who believed that he had died in a car wreck, we'd also fit in interviews with a man who remembered the life of a boy strangled by a demented brother and a woman who believed she had been a washerwoman shot by her drunken husband.

And it was just Friday morning. I didn't yet know it, but we would come across considerably more carnage before the sun went down.

Our first stop was back in Aley, in one of the still-destroyed neighborhoods we had driven past earlier. Following another one of Stevenson's ancient hand-drawn maps, Mahmoud parked the Mercedes in front of what had once been a stone house but was now a windowless, roofless shell with a gaping hole where an entrance hall had been. Weeds were engulfing piles of stone lying about its base, and the brown skeletons of creeping vines covered the rest. We got out as Stevenson tried to orient the map with the surviving landmarks. The ruins stood at the center of a loop of road with other, smaller streets radiating off in four directions. We took the second street from the left, which led down a steep incline past more destroyed buildings and a couple of smashed, abandoned cars, beyond which a hazy Beirut stretched into the sea.

"It's this one to the left," Majd said, looking at the map over Stevenson's shoulder.

Thirty-five years ago, an impoverished young woman named Salma lived on the bottom floor of a two-story plaster-walled building set into the hill where she tended to her many children and her abusive drunk of a husband, taking in laundry from students at the national university in Aley. Now, the faded yellow exterior looked very much like Swiss cheese, filled from top to bottom with holes the size of dinner plates, either from shrapnel impact or persistent machine-gun fire.

The weapon that killed Salma, however, was her husband's hunting rifle.

The woman who said she remembered Salma's dismal life was Itidal Abul-Hisn, a working-class woman we'd interviewed the previous day in the small Beirut apartment where she lived with her sister.

"I still remember some of my kids, I can see them," Itidal had told us as we sat in her living room eating fresh dates that she had put out for us. "I remember my husband shot me twice when I was hanging laundry out to dry. But I only think about these things when someone asks me about it. Although, when I am by myself, I sometimes remember."

She'd made a sound, like clearing her throat and I saw that she was crying. Twice in two days our questions had made a sad young woman cry.

"I'm sorry. Talking about your past life must be painful," Stevenson said when she had regained some composure.

"It's not that," she said. "I'm not crying about my past life. I'm crying about this one."

She said that when she and her husband split up, despite the custom of leaving small children with their mothers for the early years, he took their eleven-month-old son. It was a wound that wouldn't heal. "When I am alone sometimes, I think about how in my first life, my husband killed me, and in my second, he divorced me and took my son."

"Do you feel there's a connection?" Stevenson asked.

"No," she said. "It is just my fate, my destiny."

Itidal's sister, Intisar, was several years older, and had been able to provide testimony about when Itidal first manifested her previous-life memories.

"She began talking about it when she was three, and stopped bringing it up at about ten," Intisar recalled. "Usually, she would mention it whenever she saw younger children. She would take candies and hide them, say she was hiding them for 'her children.' She would also save candies to give to a child in our village who she said had the same name as one of her previous-life children. She would say, 'I want to go to my family in Aley, please take me there.' When we finally went, she showed us where her house had been."

Now we were retracing Itidal's steps. We picked our way over a mound of garbage and junked furniture, ducked through holes in a rusted chain-link fence, and walked around the side of the building, up an incline to a narrow space of weeds between the top floor and a neighboring building. On his map Stevenson had drawn a circle to indicate the large tree where Itidal said she remembered hanging laundry—in her previous incarnation as Salma—when her husband came up the slope we had just climbed and shot her down. Now there was only a stump among some rusted cans and shreds of plastic.

There wasn't much to see, or much in the way of verification of Itidal's memories—except for the stump corresponding to the tree. Yet, standing in the spot stained by murder all those years ago, I felt more strongly than ever the meanness of Salma's life and death. Again I had to wonder: If these memories were manufactured, consciously or subliminally, why in the world would anyone pick this particular life to remember?

But we hadn't really come to see the house. Back up the hill, across the street, lived a man named Chafic Baz. He was a college psychology professor, and, more important for our purposes, a lifetime resident of that address.

Baz's apartment had been burned out, but now was completely rebuilt. It was fronted by sliding glass doors that opened on a patio the size of a large room dominated by a potted citrus tree heavy with green fruit.

Baz and his wife invited us in with the usual Lebanese insistence that, quite literally, their home was ours and we should be certain to treat it exactly as if we lived there. They served us glasses of homemade red wine, from the grapes in their garden, and plates of fresh fruit.

Baz, who came from an upper-middle-class family, said that he had known Salma and her family well. "Her family was quite poor," he said. "She worked at people's homes and took in laundry for students at the national university here."

He had been seventeen when Salma was murdered. He said that he knew—everyone knew—that she had problems with her husband. The couple had seven or eight children and almost no money. "Her husband was a thin, hard man, very hard with Salma. They quarreled all the time—about money, about the children, about everything. Salma worked hard, like everyone else."

I thought back to our interview with Itidal in her tiny Beirut apartment. A few of her statements had puzzled me. For one thing, Itidal had said that she was shot at 3 A.M., but she also said she had been hanging laundry at the time. The middle of the night seemed like a strange time to be hanging laundry.

"Do you remember what time of day she was murdered?" I asked.

"I heard the shots," Baz replied. "It was before dawn, maybe three or four. Of course, I went to look to see what was going wrong. She was on the ground, on her back, the clothes she was hanging were next to her on the ground. There was another neighbor looking to see what was the matter. Salma's husband saw us and tried to pretend he had been shooting birds, aiming up at the trees. Then he took off. I ran out to where she was lying. I was the first one there, but she was already dead, shot from the back."

"Why would she have been hanging laundry at three A.M.?"

"Well, she began work at dawn. If she wanted to do anything for her own family, she needed to get up much earlier. It wasn't an easy life."

Itidal had also said that her husband had shot her twice, though

Stevenson said that he didn't think she had made that statement when he'd interviewed her previously.

"There was only one shot," Baz said. "He shot her from around two meters' range. I only heard one shot, and there was only one wound, I'm quite certain.

"About a year ago," he continued, "I was getting ready to go to the university when I saw people standing around out front watching a girl. When I asked what was going on, they said, 'This is the girl that says she was Salma.' She introduced herself to me. Personally, I believe her. I've seen many cases like this."

"Have you ever encountered a case where you didn't believe the claims?" I asked.

"No," he said. "I think they are true. My wife's brother remembers two lives, but he may not want to talk to you about them. And my eighty-eight-year-old mother remembers a previous life—she definitely wouldn't discuss it.

"But I know of a ten-year-old boy who remembers the life of a neighbor of mine who was killed in the shelling. I haven't talked with the boy, but some of my neighbors say that he was here and they saw him point me out and say my name as I was walking by. I didn't stop, because I had an appointment. But his family lives here in Aley, in the industrial district. It's not far. I can give you directions."

Stevenson, as usual, was poker-faced. In fact, he was ambivalent. Was it worth taking the time to make an initial interview in a case we wouldn't have time to follow up, one he might never revisit?

Still, more and more, Stevenson was thinking about the future of his research. That future, realistically, did not include him, but it might well include Erlendur Haraldsson, the researcher who was conducting psychological tests on some of Stevenson's children. Haraldsson had already done so elsewhere, comparing the children's test results against those of randomly chosen schoolmates. The idea was to see if children claiming to remember previous lives showed any signs of traditional psychological disorders, or unusual tendencies toward fantasy or suggestibility.

The studies that Haraldsson had done so far indicated none of the above. In fact, he had concluded that children subjects tended to be less suggestible than their randomly chosen peers—meaning, among other things, that they weren't as prone to change a memory based on some-thing they were told after the fact. They also had, on the average, a higher score on intelligence tests.

In the end, Stevenson decided, the possibility of finding grist for Haraldsson made the visit worthwhile.

I had my own reasons for wanting to go. So far, all the subjects we had interviewed had grown into adulthood. Their memories were just that—mostly memories. However well witnessed their childhood claims had been, it would be different, I suspected, to hear it all myself from the mouth of a babe.

༄

The "industrial district" turned out to consist of a steep, twisting bro-ken road winding past junked cars, burning trash piles, and cavelike concrete workshops—garages, wood shops, and storage spaces. It didn't seem to be a likely place for anyone to live, but after a few shouted consultations out the Mercedes's window, Mahmoud parked on the dirt in front of a garage with two dismantled cars and some tools scattered around. A stairway led to a second-floor apartment, where a young man in his early twenties answered the door. "We are looking for Bashir Chmeit," Majd said in Arabic. Once again, she explained about the American doctor interested in children's past-life memories.

The man, Bashir's brother, it turned out, showed us in. The apart-ment was a surprise, a plant-filled, carpet-covered oasis popping up at the bleak end of the road. He seated us in a room warmed by an oil stove. The whine of a power tool sliced through the open windows for long seconds. When it stopped, we heard sounds from the adjoining room, feet clomping on tile, water running, furniture scraping. Then, a good ten to fifteen minutes later, the boy emerged, his face glowing. He strode across the room, leaving a wake of cologne-scented air. In both apparel and body language, he conveyed the impression of a miniature adult. He wore black chinos and a purple flower-print shirt buttoned tightly against his neck; his latticed patent-leather loafers shone in the light from the window. The most striking thing about him, however, was the mother-of-pearl sheen to his skin, which seemed to produce a light of its own. He shook our hands in turn, then hopped backward onto the big sofa, crossing his legs crisply at the knee and folding his hands in his lap. He sat, perfectly poised, looking at us directly, waiting for questions.

"We understand you are ten, is that right?" Stevenson began.

"I am eleven," Bashir said. "My birthday was two days ago."

"Do you remember a previous life?"

"I remember that I told my brother, 'I am not Bashir. I am Fadi.' "

The front door opened, and Bashir's parents entered. His father was a compact, swarthy man with a pencil mustache and a head of thick curly hair. He nodded a greeting, but sat beside his son and said nothing further. Bashir barely glanced at him.

"I used to cry a lot until my previous mother came, and I remembered, and I called everybody with their name. And I remember that I was killed at a bunker."

"He's using the word *dishmi*," Majd elaborated on her translation. "It's really just a hole in the ground with sandbags and cement around it."

"It was in Aley west district," the boy continued. "I was going on top, on the cement part of the dishmi. They had just built the concrete top of the bunker and I was going up to check on it. A bomb exploded and a bullet hit me in the throat."

"A bullet hit you?" Majd asked. "Didn't you say a bomb exploded?"

A brief discussion followed. "He said 'bullet' because he couldn't think of the word for a tiny piece of metal from the bomb," Majd said.

"You mean shrapnel?" I asked.

"That's right."

Bashir politely waited for us to finish and continued.

"I fell down. I was unconscious. But I saw my friends removing the injured and I also saw my car parked on the side road—it was a beige Toyota—and I saw a guy going into my car to steal the jewelry I hid in the car. I used to put my jewelry in my car when we were fighting. I saw this guy stealing my jewelry, and I told my friends to take all the injured first and then come get me."

"Didn't you say you were unconscious?" I asked.

"I thought I was unconscious, but I was able to see and talk to my friends. And then I didn't feel anything."

Daniel Jirdi, a twenty-seven-year-old accountant, holds the photograph of a twenty-five-year-old mechanic named Rashid Khaddege who died in 1968 in an auto accident near the Beirut beachfront. At a very early age, Daniel gave details of the accident and made other statements that closely matched Rashid's life and death. Witnesses say he later identified a number of Rashid's relatives, whom he had never met.

Ian Stevenson crossing a river in Burma in 1979, midway through 40 years of research in which he compiled more than 2,000 cases of children who claimed previous life memories. *Courtesy of Ian Stevenson*

3

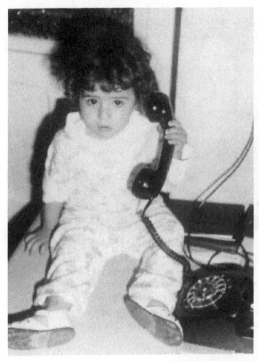

Suzanne Ghanem as an infant, circa 1973. Suzanne spoke of remembering the life of a woman who died after heart surgery in a Virginia hospital. Suzanne's parents say from the time she could utter her first words, she would pick up the phone and urgently call into it the name "Leila." Leila turned out to be the name of the dead woman's daughter. Family members say that the woman had tried and failed to reach Leila by phone shortly before dying. *Courtesy of Ian Stevenson*

4

Suzanne at seven in 1979. By that age, she had met the initially skeptical family of the previous personality and convinced them that what she said was true. The little girl was obsessed with the deceased woman's husband, and was devastated when she discovered he had remarried. *Courtesy of Ian Stevenson*

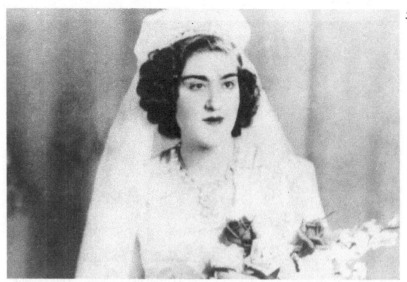

Hanan Mansour, the woman Suzanne claimed to have been, in her wedding photo, age twenty. The bride's face (photo 5) bears a striking resemblance to the photograph of Suzanne Ghanem (photo 6) taken in 1998, at the age of twenty-five. Suzanne, never married, still maintained an intense interest in Hanan's husband, which he reciprocated despite that family's desire to suppress the case. *Courtesy of Ian Stevenson*

*Courtesy of
Ian Stevenson*

This little girl, named Preeti (photo 7, center), told her siblings, "This is your house, not my house. These are your parents, not mine." When punished by her parents for making such statements, she begged a neighbor to take her "home," naming parents in a village miles distant. She said she was a girl named Sheila (photo 8, top row, center) who had been hit by a car and killed shortly before her birth. When Sheila's father came to check out Preeti's story, he says Sheila recognized him, and she clung to him until he agreed to take her home with him.

Stevenson's Indian protégé, Dr. Satwant Pasricha, in 1977. Some skeptics have discounted Pasricha's research because she is a member of the Sikh faith, which accepts the idea of reincarnation. Pasricha points out that the Sikh idea of how reincarnation operates is actually contradicted by the implications of the cases she has studied. *Courtesy of Ian Stevenson*

Villagers crowd into the family's small compound to watch the novel meeting between the American doctor and the parents of a woman whose daughter dramatically changed personalities at eighteen, suddenly claiming to be a stranger to people she had known her whole life, and to remember the details of the life of a woman who died under mysterious circumstances in a town she had never visited. She claimed she had been murdered by her in-laws, and she provided enough accurate information to persuade the girl's father she was telling the truth.

This man, a butcher who lived with his family in a brick shack in the slums of an Indian city, believed his daughter (right) remembered the life of a young cousin who had burned to death in a shack only a few hundred yards distant while slaving over a kerosene-powered candle to manufacture cheap jewelry. The girl's claim to remember such a humble, even miserable life is typical of Stevenson's cases, making it difficult to believe the memories are actually wish-fulfillment fantasies.

This little girl, who lived in the same slum, brought her baby sister for Stevenson's inspection after he revealed his interest in birthmarks and defects. The baby was born without a hand and had a phobia of cats, her grandfather reported. At this, some local hecklers remarked sarcastically, "Maybe a cat ate her hand in a previous life." Throughout India, a general belief in reincarnation does not mean that individual claims are not often considered skeptically.

Eleven-year-old Bashir Chmeit claims to remember the life of Fadi, a teenage militiaman killed by shrapnel in Lebanon's civil war. As soon as Bashir could speak in sentences, he insisted, "I am not Bashir. I am Fadi." When his "previous-life father" died recently, Bashir "stood" and grieved with the man's family at the funeral, accepted as the reincarnation of his son.

The author (left), Lebanese research assistant and interpreter Majd Abu-Izzedin (center), and Stevenson in the hills outside Beirut at the end of their 1997 research trip.

Sunita Chandak (left) spoke of a previous life in an Indian town named Belgaon. Sunita's father enlisted a local journalist to help find a town with the name Belgaon (there were many) that matched her description. When the girl was brought there, witnesses say, she identified a number of people and places accurately, as well as describing things that hadn't existed for years. Her twin sister, Anita (right), had no such memories. Her father says he told her, "Your sister told me where she lived. Why don't you tell me where you lived?" But she never said anything.

Stevenson in 1998, nearly eighty years old, still carrying his "office" sack, still trudging through the chaos of Third World countries (India, in this case) in search of evidence that claimed memories of reincarnation are real.

"Do you have any other memories?" Stevenson asked.

"Yes. I used to go with my friends Mutran and Bassam. I was a member of the Socialist Progressive Party, but I didn't wear a uniform. I wore civilian clothes. I used to go down and help them fight."

Fadi Abdel-Baki, Chafic Baz's neighbor, was only seventeen when he died in the civil war in 1978, eight years before Bashir was born.

Stevenson turned to Bashir's parents. "Did Bashir have any birthmarks?"

"No," the father said. "But when he began to speak, his voice sounded like a young man's. If you heard him from another room, you would think he was a man."

"Was there anything else unusual about him?"

He nodded. "He cried all the time as a baby. We were puzzled because he was healthy and ate well, but he cried constantly until he saw someone from his previous family, and suddenly he was happier. We were living with an uncle near the headquarters of the Socialist Progressive Party. I think he saw one of his friends—one of Fadi's friends—and he saw a Land Rover he—Fadi—had taken from a rival militia."

Bashir started talking at fifteen months, his mother said. "He started speaking in sentences right away. He said, 'I'm not Bashir, I'm Fadi,'" and also gave the names of Fadi's siblings and parents.

"We didn't want to go look for the previous family so quickly," she said. "But after two weeks, my husband's aunt, who knew Fadi's mother, said to her, 'Stop crying, your son may be born again.'"

Two days later, Fadi's family came. Bashir didn't recognize the mother, but when they showed him a photo album, he recognized her there. She was wearing a mandeel when she visited, but she had only begun to wear it after Fadi's death. In the picture, she was bareheaded. Bashir also recognized Fadi's sister and brothers in photos, as well as some of Fadi's friends, his parents said.

"How well did you know Fadi's family?" Stevenson asked.

"When my son first said the name, I knew who he was talking about," the father said. "I knew of the boy who had died. . . . I had met him once . . . and I probably would have gone to the funeral, but I was in Germany on business—I buy used cars for import—when the boy died.

"I didn't know I had met Fadi until his father reminded me. I almost had an accident with him. Fadi was speeding and nearly ran me off the road. I got out of the car and yelled at him. He cursed me, so I grabbed him by the neck—" He laughed, and put his arm around his son, sitting beside him. "When I was grabbing the boy, someone told me whose son he was, so I let him go."

Bashir was sitting quietly, inscrutable as his father told the story. "Do you remember that?" I asked.

He shook his head no.

"Who do you feel like now," I asked, "Bashir or Fadi?"

"Bashir," he said.

"When he was eight or nine," his father added, "he started saying, 'I was Fadi, now I'm Bashir.'"

He turned to Bashir and said something to him in a gentle voice. Bashir jumped off the sofa and left the room.

"I asked him to leave," he said to us in English, "because I don't want to upset him all over again. His previous father died recently. Bashir barely ate, and stood with his previous family from early morning to six P.M., just as he would have if he were Fadi. He was very upset. We were worried about him."

When Bashir came back in, Stevenson asked a last question, designed to determine if the boy displayed any phobias that might relate to the previous life: Did he have any fears?

Bashir smiled, shook his head. He knew what Stevenson was driving at.

"When they are shooting," he said, "I like to go shoot with them. I am a good fighter."

⌒

"He might be a little old for Erlendur," Stevenson commented when we were back on the road. Even if Bashir was fine for Haraldsson, in terms of proving that these cases had no normal explanation, his case had some notable flaws. The families lived in the same town, for instance, had even known each other beforehand, so any accurate information in the child's statements about Fadi's life might have been learned from his parents. Or the parents may have interpreted the nonsensical mutterings of a child in light of what they knew of Fadi.

Nonetheless, I was glad that we had made the visit. These people weren't expecting us, hadn't invited us. They were going about their business when they graciously indulged our intrusion. Clearly, they expected nothing from us or as a result of their son's claims. I liked that about the case, and I also liked the fact that Bashir was still a child. I had seen for myself the precociousness that Stevenson often noted in his case reports—the dressing up, the cologne, the self-possession the boy had demonstrated were all intriguing. And so was his account of a man's death in a child's language, of taking a piece of shrapnel in the throat and, in a brief moment of awareness before dying, of watching his car burglarized and his injured comrades removed, as if from a distance. It reminded me of descriptions of the people Stevenson's colleagues studied, those who recalled rising above themselves in hospital operating rooms or after car wrecks.

I took one more thing away from the Aley industrial district: Despite the different circumstances in each of the cases we had considered, their basic sameness was beginning to thud home—the certainty with which a child, in his first words, insisted: I am not Bashir or Suzanne or Daniel; you are not my parents; this is not my home.

∾

We headed east. The population thinned. The pines thickened. The road climbed.

"I hope Mahmoud has had the brakes adjusted recently," Stevenson said. I knew him well enough by now to recognize a certain dryness of tone, so I waited for the punch line. He twisted in the seat to deliver it. "This little hamlet where we're going is off the main highway, down the steepest grade I've ever been on. When I visited years ago, the whole way down I was imagining what might happen if the brakes should fail."

We were headed to a place deep in the mountains, a place Stevenson had described as "possibly the smallest village in Lebanon." He had last visited in 1971. The hamlet, an apparently barely accessible cul-de-sac, consisted of only about a dozen buildings and a small multiple of a dozen people.

Stevenson had gone there to interview the family of a poor farmer and laborer named Khattar, who collected pine cones and extracted pine nuts that would eventually end up in gourmet shops in Europe and America. It was work that barely kept his six children fed.

Two of those six children, both boys, claimed to have memories of previous lives. Stevenson had concentrated on the elder son, Tali, who was six years old when interviewed in 1971. Tali especially interested Stevenson because he had birthmarks that roughly corresponded to a wound suffered by the man whose life he claimed to remember, a prosperous small businessman, named Said Abul-Hisn (no relation to Itidal Abul-Hisn) who was murdered six weeks before Tali's birth.

On June 22, 1965, Said had been sitting on the patio of his home at 6 A.M. drinking coffee when an acquaintance approached from the street and shot him with a pistol. The bullet entered at the left cheek, traversed the back of his mouth, severing his tongue, and exited the right cheek. He was rushed to the hospital, where he died eleven hours later. The gunman was caught and committed to a psychiatric hospital: the crime appeared to be the result of delusions brought on by Said's physical resemblance to a man against whom the assailant bore a grudge.

Tali did not speak until he was nearly three years old, and then only with difficulty and with an impediment. As soon as he could make himself understood, his parents said that he told them, "Don't call me Tali, my name is Said Abul-Hisn."

He soon began speaking of the shooting. When Stevenson interviewed him at six, he said, "They put me in a car and took me to the hospital. My wife was beside me. One of my teeth fell out of my mouth and my tongue was cut and my clothes were full of blood."

The family said they hadn't noted any birthmarks on Tali, but when Stevenson examined him, he discovered a circle of increased pigmentation, a half inch in diameter, on the right cheek. There was a similar, smaller, fainter mark on the left cheek.

Stevenson measured and photographed the marks, and later compared them to the hospital autopsy report for Said. He found that Tali's birthmarks were slightly more toward the back of the head than the entrance and exit wounds, but decided that the distance could easily be accounted for by the migration of birthmarks that often occurs as a child grows. He also noted that the late speech development and impediment—though more difficult to objectively measure—could be considered a type of functional "birthmark" corresponding to Said's severed tongue.

One question asked by Stevenson in 1971 produced a particularly interesting answer. Tali's last memory of his previous life? Falling out of bed in the hospital.

The hospital record made no mention of it. A postmortem report reports this sequence with bleak minimalism:

Tracheotomy done. At 5 P.M. had respiratory difficulty. Cardiac arrest. Died.

When interviewed, Said's wife said that while she had no proof, she had been told by someone associated with the hospital that Said fell out of bed and died of asphyxiation before attendants could reinsert his breathing tube. That would certainly qualify as "respiratory difficulty." And it would not be the first time an official hospital record omitted significant events that could reflect poorly on the quality of care.

Still, she was skeptical about Tali's claim to be her husband reborn, primarily because Tali had said nothing about one of Said's daughters, whose chronic illness had been a primary concern in Said's life.

Although the town where Said had lived was less than three miles away, Tali's parents told Stevenson that they had never taken Tali there before he began speaking of Said, and had been reluctant to do so afterward because his insistence on being Said was so intense that they were afraid he would refuse to come home. When he finally did visit, he was taken into a room where there were a number of girls sitting at a table, including another of Said's children named Wafa. He was asked, "Do you know your daughter?" Witnesses told Stevenson that Tali sat beside her and said, "Wafa, why don't you come see me?"

All these years later, Stevenson had finally published an account of the case in his most recent book—a two-volume text devoted to birthmarks and birth defects published earlier in the year.

But now, though he wanted to see what had become of Tali's birthmarks, he was more interested in reinterviewing the family about Tali's younger brother, a boy named Mazeed. Mazeed's case—he remembered the life of a well-digger who had been killed at work when a basket of stones had tipped and fallen on his head—had been published only in abbreviated form, and Stevenson wanted to fill in a few blanks before including it in a future volume.

We had been driving for a half hour when we came upon the road. As advertised, it cut off the main highway and proceeded precipitously down the side of the mountain, a dizzying switchback through pines on a slope so steep that nothing could be built on it. Save for a few spots where people above had let their trash spill from the edge of the road and tumble into a scattered heap, it was the most pristine landscape we had seen in Lebanon. But admiration competed with vertigo—I found myself stomping my foot into the floorboard, applying an imaginary brake pedal.

"The road is much improved," Stevenson observed as we hurtled downward. "It seems to have been paved fairly recently."

Nothing, however, had made it less steep. We plunged for nearly five minutes before we came around one last bend into a dead-end road that threaded between a dozen stone houses and outbuildings. Interspersed between the buildings and walled gardens were stone pens piled with pine cones. Grapes hung heavy on the arbors and great clumps of dates dried on porch rafters. It was just after three, but already the sun approached the top of the ridge to the west. Smoke from a variety of small fires drifted into the afternoon air.

Mahmoud stopped halfway to the end of the road, and we stepped out into a surprising chill. The temperature had dropped dramatically and promised to decline further as the sun sank behind the mountains. A handful of people worked unhurriedly in the fields, eyeing us with casual interest. A small man in traditional short black pants and a gray tunic stepped toward us from the farthest house.

"This is Khattar," Stevenson said as the man closed the ground between us and grasped Stevenson's hand, then mine and Majd's. Majd said a few words, the man nodded and smiled, nodded and smiled, then led us the few feet down the road to his stone farmhouse. Inside was a large, dim sitting room lined with worn chairs and sofas. There the two brothers, men now, sat in opposite corners of the room. Mazeed, sitting by the door, watched us blankly. Tali, against the wall to the right, studied us through slitted eyes with something like a smirk. The brothers were wearing jeans, sports shirts, and work boots. Both had cell phones clipped to their hips. Neither stood.

Stevenson did not appear to notice the cool welcome. Seated on the sofa against the far wall, he began unpacking his briefcase. Majd sat beside him, nearer to Tali, and I sat against the wall to the left, beside the old man who, perhaps embarrassed by his sons' manners, patted me on the knee, smiled, and said something in Arabic. I smiled back and looked to Majd for a translation, but she was talking to Tali.

After a minute she turned to Stevenson. "He says he remembers when you came, when he was a child. He remembers that you came and that you gave him a Swiss Army knife. But he says you promised to send him a book and you never did."

Tali began talking again. He spoke for some time, clearly pronouncing the words "New Jersey."

Majd leaned back around and lowered her voice to translate: "He says he is not Tali anymore. He has changed his name to the name of his PP. And something else, too. It seems he is not too eager to cooperate. People here have a grudge against Americans. They have a brother who was killed in the shelling by the *New Jersey*."

"We're really here more to talk with Mazeed," Stevenson said.

From his chair by the door, leaning on one elbow, Mazeed spoke for the first time. Majd responded, and they went back and forth several times, not heatedly, but intently. "We're discussing the Druse religion," she said finally. "He says, 'We know about reincarnation and believe it, so why must we prove it?'"

The mother, wearing a mandeel wrapped just below her nose in the old way, entered with a tray of coffee. I gratefully took a cup. I hoped it would help combat the encroaching cold, but more than that, I hoped that the show of hospitality might balance the simmering resentment I sensed from the brothers. Majd continued to speak with them without consulting or translating, attempting to talk them out of their surliness, wisely leaving Stevenson and me in the background as long as possible.

At least Mazeed appeared to be warming to her, but Tali—now Said—slouched back in the sofa, regarding her with undisguised hostility. He said something clearly unpleasant, but Majd ignored him. Her strategy seemed to be to treat Mazeed as a normal interview, and hope that that would engage the brothers.

"Mazeed owns a business, an employment agency," she said, turning to us at last. "Basically, that means he brings maids in from Sri Lanka and finds them work. He says he's also an insurance broker."

"Ask him if he likes his work," Stevenson suggested. Majd relayed the question.

"If I didn't like it, I wouldn't be doing it," Mazeed shot back. The tone needed no translation.

I began to think about the State Department travel warning, about how long and steep the road out of this place was, about how isolated we were. Stevenson shuffled unhurriedly through his file. He forged ahead with the interview.

Did Mazeed still remember his previous life?

"Just a little." He shrugged. "The war made us forget."

Khattar had appeared in front of me with a tray of hard candies, urging me to take one. I demurred. He insisted. I took one. He said something to Majd.

"The father says Mazeed stopped talking about his previous life at about twenty."

"Let's ask how his health is," Stevenson said.

Mazeed looked up. "I was injured during the war," he said. "Shrapnel from bombs when the *New Jersey* was shelling." He looked at Stevenson and me provocatively and held up his hand to show a jagged scar running from his hand across his wrist. "I was in the hospital for a month and a half." He dropped his hand to the side. "Our brother was killed in the village. The *New Jersey*."

From somewhere, his mother produced a photograph of the dead brother, a thin young man smiling into the camera.

A cell phone trilled loudly. Tali plucked it from his hip and answered.

"Most of the houses in this area were destroyed, and then rebuilt," Khattar said, through Majd. "Come."

"He wants to show you where the house was rebuilt," Majd added.

Khattar led me outside, on a narrow lane by the garden. He pointed to a section of new stone that made up the southern third of the house. He clasped his hands together then flung them apart, making a sound in his throat like an explosion. I looked into his rheumy, brown eyes and he looked back without bitterness.

When we returned, Mazeed was still talking—a good sign, I thought. He said he was engaged to girl from Kfarsalwan, the town where he had lived in his previous life. He still visited his previous-life family. He had stopped seeing them, but began again two years ago when he got engaged. The girl was a relation of his previous family.

"Which life do you prefer?" Stevenson asked from his interview form. "For me, it is the same," Mazeed said. "Life is hard."

Across the room, Tali stirred. "We are Third World," he said disgustedly.

Majd translated, then added, "Earlier, Tali told me he was out of work. He said he drives a cab sometimes. He had some college business courses. But he can't find a job."

Tali leaned forward and said something forcefully. Majd replied at length. Tali shook his head. Majd said something more, and Tali interrupted her.

Majd turned to Stevenson, "He said he doesn't want to be in the book."

Stevenson sat up straight, raised his eyebrows and said, "He already is."

Majd reported back to Tali, who stood up and took a step toward Stevenson, raising his voice just below a shout.

"He says if he is already in the book, he wants compensation," Majd said. "Some money, or help getting a job."

The room was getting steadily colder and the light was beginning to go. I didn't like the way things were headed here at the end of the road in Lebanon. Khattar said something sharply to Tali, who barked back. Majd too got into it with him once again. I leaned close to Stevenson, speaking quietly but forcefully. "I really think we're at the point where we should just try to extricate ourselves as quickly as possible," I said.

Tali had taken another step toward Stevenson and was nearly shouting. Majd spoke quietly. "Since he drives a taxi, maybe he could drive Haraldsson around," she suggested, keeping her eyes on Tali.

Stevenson hesitated. Every cell in my body urged him to make that offer. He shifted in his chair. "Erlendur might not even be coming to Lebanon," he said finally. "But I suppose it wouldn't hurt to ask him for his card."

Majd relayed the request. Tali stood there. She held out her pen. Tali looked at it. Majd said something. He hesitated. Finally, he took the pen, wrote a number on a page from Majd's notes, then, without another word, turned on his heel and walked outside into the cold and dark.

I wasn't convinced that he wouldn't return. I didn't particularly want to be there when he did.

⌒

While I had been riveted on the unfolding conflict, it had barely registered that a woman and a young child of about five or six had entered from another room. The woman sat on the couch beside the mother, while the little girl sat on the floor by the woman's feet. Mazeed's mother caught Majd's eye and spoke.

"They are asking for your medical opinion on a case," Majd said.

"Is it a solved case?" Stevenson asked, using his term for a case in which a past life had been found to match the claimed memories.

I was surprised that Stevenson assumed that they were talking about a reincarnation case. That they wanted his opinion as an MD on some illness or injury seemed more likely.

We were both right. Majd translated Stevenson's question. The younger woman responded at length.

"Yes, it is solved," Majd said. "The PP was a woman shot by her husband in the neck. She was paralyzed and in the hospital for twelve days, then died. The husband went to prison for three years and is out now."

For the first time, I looked closely at the little girl sitting at her mother's feet, clinging to her legs like a kitten clinging to a tree with a dog after it. Slowly, it dawned on me that this child was the subject of the case. There was something lopsided about the girl's smile, and her legs, folded under her, seemed too long and thin for her body. The mother picked the child up by the armpits, holding the girl out for our inspection. Her spindly legs curled beneath her, dangling uselessly in the air. Her head lolled slightly, and her eyes refused to focus.

"This is the child?" Stevenson asked.

"Yes. Please tell us, doctor, what we should do for her," the little girl's mother said.

"Can she walk?"

"No. She moves herself along the floor with her arms, dragging her legs," Majd translated.

"Does she go to school?"

"No, she has never been to school. They have taken her to a number of clinics, but nobody has helped, and doctors are expensive."

"The child needs therapy," Stevenson said. "There are things that can be done to help her. She may never walk unaided, but she can improve her condition considerably, and she should go to school."

The lopsided smile never left the little girl's face. She swung her head and made sing-song sounds. Her mother bent to her and spoke encouragingly, then demandingly.

"They want to demonstrate how she speaks of herself by the name of the murdered woman," Majd said.

The mother was holding the girl's shoulder now, trying to lock in on her lolling head. "What's your name? What's your name?" she repeated. But the girl, overcome, perhaps, by the attention and the presence of strangers, just babbled. She clapped her hands. Her head lolled. She smiled—a big, heartbreaking, lopsided smile.

❧

The Mercedes climbed the hill in silence. Our visit had lasted little more than two hours, but it had seemed an age.

"I'd like to do something for the little girl," I said finally.

"Yes," Stevenson said. "I would say we should give some money directly to the mother so the little girl would be sure to get the benefit, but that might cause problems in the family. Perhaps we should give it to Khattar, then."

"The mother and father were very upset with Tali," Majd said. "There was a lot of arguing among them I didn't translate. He behaved very badly."

Well, maybe. But I was sorry for intruding on him. And sorrier still for the *New Jersey.*

10

To Stop a Train

The next morning, waiting for Majd and Mahmoud to pick us up for our last full day of travel and interviews, Tali and Mazeed were still on our minds. Stevenson was thinking about Mazeed's question: Why, as a Druse and a believer, should he care about proving reincarnation to nonbelievers?

"That's the paradox," Stevenson said. "In the West people say, 'Why are you spending money to study reincarnation when we know it's impossible?' In the East they say, 'Why are you spending money to study reincarnation when we know it's a fact?' "

I was thinking about something else: Ever since we had come to Lebanon, we had been tripping over reincarnation cases wherever we went, from that first day when Ulfat happened to walk in the door with her memories of being stabbed by Christians to last evening, when we thought we were going to interview two brothers who *both* remembered previous lives and wound up examining their niece, crippled in this life and allegedly paralyzed by a murderous husband in her last.

Leaving aside the persuasiveness, or lack thereof, of any individual case, the unchecked proliferation of cases was difficult to accept. I had gone from worrying that we would not find any cases to worrying that we had found too many.

Then Majd arrived. "The reason I was a little late," she announced brightly, "I was talking to the plumber doing the renovations on our apartment, and he gave me two cases, one of an eight-year-old and one ar-old."

Previous-life memories in Lebanon were an epidemic. I remembered Elie Karam's speculation that the ability to remember might be genetic. From a demographer's point of view, that made some sense—the abundance of an otherwise-rare trait in one isolated, intermarrying population, like blond hair in Scandinavia.

But this also just happened to be a population that believed in reincarnation, which brought up yet another chicken-and-egg conundrum: Were false reincarnation memories more or less consciously created to support Druse beliefs? Or did the belief in reincarnation spring from generations of children speaking about previous lives?

Such speculation made our destination that morning all the more interesting, for we were going to visit a family whose little girl was just beginning to make statements that might, or might not, be related to a previous life. It would give me a chance to see the conditions within a family before any previous personality had been identified, and, possibly, to get a sense of how strongly the desire to believe in reincarnation might influence their reporting of events.

The little girl was now three and a half. Her name was Lillian Al-Awar.

The girl's paternal grandmother had become intrigued by the little girl's play: She talked about her husband having "gone," using the Arabic equivalent of "passed away." When playing with her dolls, she seemed to treat them in a precociously maternal way, tucking them tenderly into bed, calling them by name, referring to them feelingly as "my children."

The child lived with her mother and maternal grandparents in an unfinished concrete-block house cut into a steep hillside among pines and raw red earth. Her parents had split up. Since the initial case report had come from the father's side of the family, the mother's family did not know of our visit until we knocked on the door.

A man who we guessed to be Lillian's maternal grandfather listened to Majd's explanation of our interest and invited us in, seating us in a narrow front entrance hall with sofas on either side. A pretty little girl with huge hazel eyes and long, shiny brown hair half hid behind a chair at the end of the hall, watching us intently in her red sweater, which bore the inscription, SNOW BUNNY above an embroidered Mickey Mouse on skis.

Majd spoke with the man, who looked almost young enough to be the girl's father, for some time.

"He says the subject of reincarnation interests him," she reported. "But he hasn't heard Lillian say anything about a previous life. He thinks the case report is based on the fact that she is more hyper, more intelligent than other children."

"Does Lillian show any unusual fears or aversions?" Stevenson asked.

"She doesn't like meat, and doesn't eat it," the grandfather said. "When I take her to the butcher she says, 'Don't put the meat next to me, put it in the backseat.'" He laughed, then spoke at length to Majd, who turned to us:

"It seems that Lillian has two older cousins, twin boys. One of the cousins has an unusual scar-type birthmark on the inside of his elbow. The doctor who delivered him was Christian and the minute he saw it—because he knew they were Druse—said, 'He must have brought it from his previous life.' But the child never made any statements."

On cue, the two boys ran past in the hall. The grandfather beckoned and they stopped, barefoot on the tile. The grandfather said something to the boy nearest us and gestured at Stevenson. Shyly, the child inched toward us and extended his arm, letting Stevenson take it in his large hands, rotating the forearm slowly to reveal a jagged, raised area of depigmented skin about two inches long.

"He wants to know what it looks like to you," Majd said.

Stevenson let go of the arm and smiled at the boy, then looked up calmly.

"A scar from a shrapnel wound."

Now Lillian's mother emerged, wearing a blue jogging suit, hair pinned atop her head. She was clearly unhappy with the intrusion and regarded us with open skepticism.

Majd explained what the paternal grandmother had said about Lillian saying that "her husband" had passed on, and that she spoke to her baby dolls as if they were real children.

"Lilly?" the mother said with great surprise. "I haven't heard anything like that. Maybe when she was playing she would say what she heard older people saying."

We went on for some time, but the answer was always the same:

Lillian had never said anything that could be interpreted as recalling a previous life.

Finally, Stevenson asked if he might take a photograph of the twin's unusual, jagged birthmark.

After some consultation with the boy's parents outside of our hearing—we never saw them—the grandfather declined, with apologies: "Unfortunately, my son and daughter-in-law don't care anything about this. As far as they're concerned, we're born, we live, and that's all that matters."

∾

We drove to Falougha, a town a few miles away, to look for Lillian's paternal grandmother, wondering if she might have other reasons for suspecting that Lillian might remember a previous life. She was not at home, but a neighbor told Majd that we could find her at her shoe store on the small town's main street.

The store was tiny, no bigger than a hospital storage closet, its walls lined with shoes that looked like they'd been there awhile. She was sitting alone, in the front, near an electric space heater plugged into the wall, an attractive woman who looked to still be in her forties, slender with short dark hair. When we explained who we were, she went into the back and retrieved three more plastic chairs and arrayed them around the heater.

"I'm trying every time I see Lillian to ask her questions," she told us. "But she doesn't say much. Maybe when I thought I heard her talking to her children, she was really just playing house. She is very affectionate to babies, very maternal with dolls, but that's not enough to suspect she remembers a previous life. We need to hear things like, 'I was so and so. I lived in such and such a village.'" She paused, as if considering her words, then said, "You know, I didn't even believe in reincarnation until a friend persuaded me there was something to it."

We thanked her and filed out of the store. As I stood on the street of the small Lebanese town, watching the sun set behind the Shouf mountains, it hit me that this was our final interview. In a way, what we had heard was reassuring: Despite a little girl's suggestive remarks about dead husbands and absent children, family members admittedly inter-

ested in and open to the possibility of reincarnation had nonetheless refused to leap to any conclusions or embellish the child's statements. If
anything, they had played them down.

And there was something else I couldn't quite put my finger on,
something both the grandfather and grandmother had said. Then I remembered: They were going to watch the girl and wait for evidence
that was specific and verifiable. The scientific approach.

∽

I said good-bye to Stevenson in Charles de Gaulle airport. He was going on to the United States, and I was going to London to overnight before heading home. On the train from Heathrow into the city, I
watched the quaintly humble suburbs rolling by, rows and rows of
brick houses with their bay windows and peaked roofs, flanked by
identical long, narrow garden fences all backing up on one another.
This gave way to high-rise government buildings, drab and stolid, followed by a manicured golf course shockingly green in the November
gloom. With the last light, just before the train moved into the city
proper, we passed a cemetery, deserted at the end of a gray day, filled
with stones and flowers. One solitary figure, a man in a brown overcoat, stood beside a new grave, the dirt raw at his feet, flowers not yet
wilted against the cold stone, more in his hand. I watched from the
window; first his back, then his profile, then his ruined face fixed on the
scar in the earth. His grief etched his face in brittle lines, its intensity
overwhelming even for a stranger at an ever-lengthening distance, powerful enough, it seemed to me, to stop a train. But not nearly powerful
enough to bring back what he had lost.

11

The Last Easy Answer

As the North American coast slid by beneath the blinding silver wedge of wing, I felt like I was slowly waking from a dream. From 35,000 feet up and an ocean and a half away, Lebanon had been reduced to the battered, black pack at my feet. The pack had never left my side. In it were the five reporter's notebooks I had filled, front to back, with simple descriptions of our encounters, the back and forth of questions and answers that were at once mundane and inconceivable. I had recorded it all diligently, worrying every detail in my mind, turning it this way and that for closer examination. But I hadn't really *looked*. I had been too close, too consumed by the immediacy.

Now I could glimpse the totality for the first time. What I had seen and heard in the previous three weeks had been some kind of monumental deception—or something else far more monumental. I still didn't know what I thought, and I didn't know what to think about not knowing what I thought. Was the evidence still inconclusive? Or was I just unwilling to face the conclusions?

Also in my pack was a stack of research that I had hoped to get through in Lebanon. A foot-high pile of articles copied from obscure scholarly journals, I hadn't even looked at it. I plowed through it now, becoming absorbed in lengthy discussion, complete with frequent footnotes, between skeptics and supporters of Stevenson's research and conclusions. Most of the skeptical arguments had been summarized in the Paul Edwards book that I had read months earlier: The children were fantasizing. The parents fed the children information until the children repeated it. The psychocultural need to believe in reincarnation created the cases in an unconscious conspiracy between parents and children, neighbors and strangers.

To make their point, the skeptics mentioned all the things I had pondered at length: factual inconsistencies that appeared in even the strongest cases, the possibility of connections between present and past-life families, the various incentives for wanting to be thought of as being reborn.

I read through it all as the jet's engines droned on in the empty hours. When I was finished, I felt certain that none of the above came close to explaining all I had witnessed in Lebanon.

But one skeptic, E. B. Brody, took a different tack: "The problem," he wrote, "lies less in the quality of data Stevenson adduces to prove his point, than in the body of knowledge and theory which must be abandoned or radically modified in order to accept it."

In other words, extraordinary claims require extraordinary proof. From the viewpoint of most Western scientists, the idea that living children could embody at least some part of a deceased personality was certainly an extraordinary claim. But who could say that the evidence Stevenson had been collecting for thirty years was not extraordinary? The question is, was it extraordinary *enough?* Maybe that was the question that had been plaguing me.

Another group of writers challenging Stevenson had no problem with his data, and no problem deeming it was sufficient to support an extraordinary claim. Their argument was over *which* extraordinary claim it supported; they preferred to say that the cases were best explained by a combination of a child's suggestibility and extrasensory perception—the ability to telepathically receive some details of a dead person's life. Most of these papers did not explain exactly why the author preferred an ESP explanation to reincarnation, but I intuited (or, who knows, maybe telepathically received) that they were influenced by the fact that laboratory tests had at least offered consistent, though slight, statistical evidence of ESP, whereas nobody had ever managed to measure even the tiniest sliver of a soul.

The arguments against ESP were straightforward: The children weren't saying, "The previous personality had three cows," as they might if they were telepathically gleaning facts about a stranger. Instead, they were saying, "*I* had three cows," and otherwise acting as if they believed that they *were* that person. Also, it was rare that any of these children exhibited any other evidence of psychic ability, which raised this question: Why would a child exhibit intense psychic ability concerning just one specific dead guy?

There was a variation of the ESP argument that I thought of as the "crossed wire" explanation, which proposed that maybe there was some kind of as-yet-unknown energy field associated with human personality that somehow got imprinted on the brain of an infant. I failed to see how this was any different than saying that the explanation for these cases was, well, *reincarnation*. An "as-yet-unknown energy field associated with personality" sounded much like a working definition of "soul." And what was reincarnation if not the transfer of at least some part of a deceased personality to a living person?

At the bottom of my stack, I had grouped a separate category: case investigations—"replication studies," they were called—undertaken by three independent scientists at Stevenson's invitation.

This conclusion by anthropologist Antonia Mills, who studied ten cases in India in 1987, was typical of all of them:

Before undertaking this investigation, I was prepared to find that some, perhaps all, of the cases I would investigate would be hoaxes perpetrated for any number of reasons, such as a desire of the child and/or its family to identify with a higher caste. The investigation did not substantiate these suppositions. . . .

My examination indicates that an independent investigator, using Stevenson's methods of investigation, finds comparable results. Some aspects of some of the cases cannot be explained by normal means. I found no evidence that the cases I studied were the result of fraud or fantasy. . . .

Like Stevenson, I conclude that while none of the cases I studied offer incontrovertible proof of reincarnation or some related paranormal process, they are part of the growing body of cases for which normal explanations do not seem to do justice to the data.

A strong endorsement. Antonia Mills, however, fell into the group of "independent verifiers" claimed by skeptics not to be independent at all, but actually working for Stevenson. This was partly true: These people didn't work for Stevenson, but they did receive some funding from him. In addition, they also had personal relationships with him.

One of them, an Australian psychologist named Jürgen Keil, addressed that problem directly:

> My regard for Ian Stevenson could best be summarized by such terms as professional appreciation and personal friendship. Some readers may question whether this is a good basis for an independent study. However, my high regard for Stevenson leaves me in no doubt that he would welcome any results in his field of interest which are based on sound research, whether they support his point of view or not.

Despite the sincere tone, I could see how someone might reject that assurance. On the other hand, I didn't have to worry too much about Keil's independence or lack of it: I'd seen the cases myself.

∽

I was still trying to digest it all days later when Stevenson sent me an e-mail: He had set the date for his India trip, in all likelihood his final field trip there, and he wanted to know if I intended to accompany him. On many occasions, and in many ways, he had said that doing research in Asia was more trying, more dangerous, and generally more demanding than in Lebanon. That gave me some pause, as did the time and expense it would require, but I never seriously considered not going.

One of the most compelling arguments against looking at Stevenson's compiled cases as evidence of reincarnation was the idea that they were self-reinforcing communal fantasies, proving nothing more than a society's desire to believe. I had thought about that in Lebanon, and now thought about it in the context of India.

I didn't know a tremendous amount about Indian traditional culture and the Hindu belief in reincarnation, but I knew they were as similar to Druse culture and beliefs as those of the Druse were to prevailing attitudes in Miami Beach. I also knew this: If the phenomenon of children remembering previous lives was purely a cultural creation, similarities between cases in Lebanon and India would be superficial at best.

And if they weren't superficial? If the cases had the look and feel of the ones we had seen in Beirut? Then I would know something else: The last easy answer would be gone.

Part III:

India
Children of Poverty

12

The Milkman

As we made our midnight landing in Delhi, the cabin filled with a heavy, acrid smell of smoke. I was relieved to discover the plane hadn't caught fire, but puzzled when the smell followed us throughout the charmless terminal. We emerged into the night to find that the entire airport was blanketed in a fog-like cloud of smoke. Small, fat, bumble-bee-like yellow-and-black taxis buzzed about in the haze just outside the entrance doors, while a throng waited expectantly beyond the security cordon. As Stevenson and I walked outside, a man commandeered our luggage cart without a word, pushing it toward a dark lot a hundred yards distant. He began loading the bags into a small station wagon. I hoped he was a cab driver and not a thief. His wagon was blocked in its spot. He frantically gestured for me to help him push away the two cars that hemmed him in.

Shortly, we found ourselves on the main road to Delhi. Now after 1 A.M., the street was nearly empty. Smoke drifted in the headlights. I kept waiting to emerge from the cloud, but it only got thicker, to the point where I felt I was having difficulty getting oxygen.

"It's a lot worse at night," Stevenson said.

"You mean, it's like this *every* night?" I asked.

"It's from all the dung fires," he explained, calmly staring into the darkness, apparently unconcerned despite his chronic respiratory problems. "It may be a little worse than usual."

India, boggling to most first-time Western visitors, was old hat to Stevenson. It was here that he embarked on his first field investigation. Now, thirty-seven years later, this was most likely his last.

Our hotel was in a dingy, five-story building on Janpath, Delhi's main drag. The rooms were arrayed in three rows along a common, open-air balcony. The room itself was a combination of worn, dirty, and unfinished—the tile work had never been completed when the bathroom was redone, the bathtub had dirt and pebbles in it, the window above the shower was propped open and screenless, the carpet was torn and thick with grime.

I reminded myself that these accommodations were the height of luxury compared to what Stevenson routinely had encountered when he first visited India in the 1960s. And besides, the sheets on the bed were clean and the hot water worked.

I slept fitfully and woke to the raucous cawing of a crow outside the open window. The sky was hazy, but clear, and the smoke scent lingered faintly. We spent the morning waiting for Dr. Satwant Pasricha, the Indian psychologist who had assisted Stevenson on many of his Indian trips and who was conducting her own investigations using Stevenson's methods. She was flying up from Bangalore, three hours by jet to the south, where she worked at the National Institute for Mental Health and Neuro Sciences. At ten minutes before noon, she appeared at the front desk—a short, compact woman in a purple sari, with two large bags slung over her right shoulder, a simple string of pearls about her neck, and a red caste mark just above the bridge of her nose. We met for lunch after she got settled. Satwant paged through notes she'd made on a possible itinerary of cases. She had a gentle manner and an open face: It was interesting to put a real flesh-and-blood image to the Dr. Satwant Pasricha who figured so prominently in the acknowledgments of Stevenson's books and weighed in so heavily in some criticisms of his research.

Satwant was a Sikh, a member of the four-hundred-year-old Indian religion that combined elements of Hinduism with Islam, attempting to fuse the nation's two dominant faiths. One element that the Sikhs had taken from the Hindus was the belief that souls were reborn according to the deeds of the previous life. The virtuous were well-born, while the evil were reborn to misery—or even as animals. Because of this, many skeptics refused to take Satwant's work seriously.

I wasn't too impressed with that criticism. If Satwant should be disqualified from studying these cases because her faith supported the idea of reincarnation, then anyone who personally believed that personality ended with death should be equally disqualified.

When I asked her about it she said, "You're a scientist whether you're a Hindu or not. Besides, what I'm seeing in these cases is completely different from the Hindu belief in reincarnation."

In fact, she said, when an associate told her that Stevenson was looking for an Indian psychologist interested in conducting this type of research, she expressed strong skepticism.

"I didn't think these cases were possible," she said. "I told him that, and he said, 'Wait and see.' So I agreed to go out and look at a case. We first went to the previous personality's village and the brother of the previous personality led us to the village of the subject, who was a little girl. We had to walk all the way across these fields to get there. When we arrived, the little girl just climbed up into the brother's arms and clung to him. It was so moving. And when she talked about her memory of dying—she remembered the life of a girl who had gone to get some water and fallen into the well and drowned—I could see she was really reliving the terror of it. You can't quantify that, but that was the sort of thing that persuaded me these stories might be real."

Lunch stretched on lazily. My eyes blurred by jet lag, I looked forward to an afternoon of collapsing on the bed in my dingy room and only half listened to the scheduling discussion—until Stevenson said, "We thought we'd go and see this case that Satwant came across in the newspaper. It's not far."

Ten minutes later we were in a hired car plunging into urban chaos. Delhi made Beirut look like Boca Raton. Everywhere, people, animals, cars, bicycles, and garbage coexisted in stunning profusion, as if generations of life were all trying to happen at once. Bicyclists pushed by, their scuffed and dented two-wheelers loaded as if they were work trucks, stacked with anything from loads of bricks to bundles of sticks or bales of hay. Trucks overburdened with immense sacks of grain ground through traffic. Buffalo and oxen labored against wooden yokes, pulling wagons wobbling on unsteady wheels. Mules and horses snorted beneath their own burdens. Bike-pulled rickshaws with seats made for two tottered under the weight of entire families. Motorbikes putted past, huge bundles strapped to the rear.

Along the roadside, an endless army of men, women, and children toiled in the mud, breaking stones with sledgehammers and carrying the fragments away in large woven baskets—part of a road-widening project, Satwant explained. They dumped the gravel beside the narrow paved highway until it reached road level, then tramped it down with their feet. Babies played in empty baskets, mothers swung heavy hammers, and dust rose in a brown haze. People wandered along footpaths through immense refuse dumps to ramshackle shacks made of unmortared brick and plastic sheeting, separated by a fetid canal from beautifully tended gardens blooming with vegetables and flowers. Men squatted in high weeds to defecate—a necessity in a country where 700 million of nearly 1 billion people have no access to plumbing. Women strolled past, heavy bundles of every description balanced gracefully atop their heads. Dung patties, each carefully formed into plate-sized disks, dried in the road's narrow median strip. Children played cricket with wickets made of sticks. Barbers snipped and trimmed at the side of the road. A man washed his horse beside an open sewer. Pigs rooted in the black water. Three turbaned shopkeepers shared a hookah by rotating a two-foot-long stem around its base. Crowds gathered over gambling games. Vendors cooked their wares on open flames. Rats sprinted across the road. It all pressed close in on the cab's open windows, a whirlwind sensory overload further enhanced by the scents of food and rot and sweat.

And then, close enough so I could reach out and touch them, huge, heaving dun-colored flanks plodded past my window. I craned my head out and looked up into the foam flecked jowls of a camel, bridled and harnessed to a cart.

Where *was* I? My mind desperately tried to interpret the assault on every one of my senses. Was I seeing a vision of the future? Was Delhi the dystopia that awaited us all when population overwhelmed the planet? It was an uncomfortable feeling—no doubt my own way of perceiving the culture shock I had been warned about.

As we crawled north, the throngs finally gave way to green fields of peas and wheat. On one side of the road, laborers squatted—men and women and children together—picking peas; on the other side, men stood urinating. Beyond them, an overloaded tractor had flipped into a ditch, spilling its load of sugarcane across the road.

An hour and a half from Delhi, we crossed a muddy, foul-smelling river. Crowds of girls and women waded from the banks, slapping wet cloth on the rocks. Another army of ragtag laborers dug an irrigation ditch to the river's edge, laying levels of bricks as they went.

Women carrying clay and brass pots on their heads streamed ahead of us toward a village of brick shacks. This was the village of Juan— our destination. The cobbled road turned to muck as we approached. The driver downshifted. The car shimmied ominously.

"It wouldn't be the first time I had to get out and push," Stevenson observed, not entirely reassuringly. When we regained the brick roadway, we were in the village proper. An open sewer trickled in the center of the street; dirty children in tattered clothes chased around buoyantly. Two boys dropped from the pack to lash a cowering dog with a rope and a stick. The dog broke for cover, and the boys pursued, laughing.

The family we had come to interview lived on a small rise at the top of a narrow dirt lane where some boys had set up a makeshift cricket pitch; to play, they used sticks and a ball made of rags. The house was a two-room brick structure, which, though dirt-floored, had frame doors and windows with screens. It was set at the far corner of a dirt courtyard across from a hand-pumped well and three black water buffalo that stood chained to a stake and twitching with flies.

The subject of the case, a seven-year-old girl named Preeti, small for her age, with a round face and short black hair cut like a boy's, stood shyly to the side, wearing a sweatshirt picturing two American football players beside the slogan THE BEST OF THE WEST. Her parents pulled two wood-frame benches with woven seats from the house into the courtyard and we began the interview.

The father, Tek Ram, was an operator for the phone company in New Delhi. Six days a week, he took a bus from the village to work—a journey of more than two hours each way.

As soon as Preeti could speak clearly, he told us, she said to her brother and sister, "This is your house, not my house. These are your parents, not mine." She told her sister, "You only have one brother, I have four," and said that her name was not Preeti, but Sheila, and gave names for her "real" father and mother. She pleaded to be taken to her "home," a town called Loa-Majra, which was some ten to twelve miles away.

In this end-of-the-road village, so removed in distance and culture from anywhere I had ever been, we were picking up precisely where we had left off in Beirut.

Here, though, the story took an intriguing turn. Preeti's parents, who said that they had never been to Loa-Majra and knew nobody from there, did not send anyone to inquire about their daughter's story. Instead, they told her to stop talking nonsense and ignored her pleas.

The family's early lack of interest in the case made it stronger. If this account were true, then the parents could not be suspected of directing the child or feeding her information with which to manufacture claims.

Preeti's mother brought out a tray with hot tea, salted nuts, and sweets made primarily of cooked milk and sugar. This presented a dilemma I had been warned to expect: If I ignored the offering, I would offend my hosts. But if I drank and ate food prepared in rural India, I was risking serious illness. Stevenson, who once had to spend several days of a field trip here nursing a deathly ill associate, had advised me to sip and nibble minuscule amounts and hope for the best. That is what I did, with some misgiving, as the father continued his story.

"When Preeti was four," he said, "she told the milkman, 'These people won't take me to my village. Will you take me to my village?' "

They have milkmen out here? I thought, but soon realized he wasn't talking about the guy from the dairy who leaves glass bottles at the back door. The milkman here was a neighbor, a laborer, who milked the family's water buffalo in exchange for free milk.

The milkman repeated the girl's story to a woman he knew who had been born in Loa-Majra. Did she know a man named Karna married to a woman named Argoori who had lost a daughter named Sheila?

She said that she knew a man named Karan Singh, nicknamed Karna, whose teenage daughter Sheila had been running across the road when she was hit by a car and killed. Karna's wife was named Argoori.

Word got back to the family in Loa-Majra, and some men, including the dead girl's father, came to see Preeti. Tek Ram said that Preeti recognized the father, and then, when she went back to his village with him, she made more recognitions.

Stevenson and I had often discussed these recognitions that so often figured in his better cases. On the surface, at least, they were among the most spectacular pieces of evidence supporting claims of previous-life memories. But they were almost always problematic, too. Given the nature of these rural, traditional communities, meetings between children and the previous-life families they claimed to belong to often took place before huge crowds of onlookers, who—by blurting something or simply by all turning to look at the person in question—could easily direct a child to make the correct choice.

We probed for details of exactly how this recognition of the PP father took place. Did Preeti see the man approaching?

No, Tek Ram said. When the men from Loa-Majra arrived, Preeti was in school with her sister. The girls returned home to find a crowd, including the visitors, waiting for Preeti.

We asked to interview Preeti's eleven-year-old sister, who was nine when the meeting took place. Wrapped in a green head scarf, like her mother, she sat on the bench beside Satwant and answered our questions in a tiny voice.

"As we were walking toward the house, we saw a crowd," she recalled. "Preeti leaned to me and whispered, 'My father's here.'"

Later, Tek Ram added, when they asked Preeti who her father was, she walked to Karna Singh and hugged him. In the two years since, Tek Ram said, she'd continued to visit the family on special occasions.

Before the visits, he said, she'd been a loner; she didn't play with the other children. "After seeing them four or five times," her father said, "she was much more relaxed. She stopped being unhappy all the time."

"Did she ever say anything about how she died in her previous life?" Stevenson asked.

"All she said was, 'I had fallen from above and died,'" the mother said. "One time I asked her, 'How did you get here?' She said, 'I was sitting at the river and I was crying. I didn't find a mother, so I came with you.'"

Before we left, the father brought out a small stack of clippings about Preeti's case from Indian newspapers. Some of them had been preserved in plastic. He proudly showed me an English philosophy text, inscribed to him from a philosophy professor who came to talk about Preeti. Socrates was quoted on the cover: "The unexamined life is not worth living."

As we walked back down the narrow alley to the car, the driver sidled up to me and said, "You should give them something. Some money."

I reported the comment to Stevenson. "We don't do that," Stevenson said to the driver. "It would taint the information."

Out of the driver's hearing Satwant said, "He might have said something to the family, promised to get them money. I should talk to them."

She walked back to Tek Ram and spoke to him quietly.

When she returned she said, "He says he wasn't expecting anything. He works in a government agency and makes a good wage. I think he was embarrassed the driver said something."

The sun was setting against a clear sky. Despite the open sewer at our feet, the evening smelled of sweet green wheat. As we drove out of the village, a dozen women in long, colorful silk dresses and scarves wrapped around their heads clustered at the village well, filling their water pots.

This one interview had taken most of the day, and we still had a two-hour trip back to Delhi. It made me think of Stevenson's files, more than 2,500 cases from all over the world, each involving multiple interviews. When I was thumbing through the typed pages and handwritten notes stuffed into those manila folders, I hadn't properly appreciated the work, the sheer physical stamina, that they represented.

We bounced along the rutted road as the light faded. Every so often, the driver flashed his lights at oncoming trucks, but he refused to turn them on, as if he felt he needed to conserve his battery. Something that had been rattling around the edges of my apprehension all afternoon finally popped to the fore: This little paved strip of road, circumscribed by irrigation ditches on either side, was barely wide enough for a cab to pass a scooter without the scooter bouncing off the road into the narrow rut beside the canal. It wasn't even close to wide enough to accommodate the trucks and buses hurtling toward us, barely visible shapes approaching against the darkening sky with no intention of slowing down, much less stopping.

"In India, the rule of the road is the bigger vehicle has the right of way," Stevenson volunteered from the backseat. The other rule that soon became apparent, to my acute dismay, was that pulling over to let the bigger vehicle pass was only acceptable if there was no resulting loss of speed.

No wonder Sheila had been run down on the road.

It was interesting to me that despite Sheila's violent mode of death, Preeti had little to say on the subject. And despite her parents' interest in the attention that the case had generated, as witnessed by the carefully saved press clippings, they had resisted the temptation to make up, or persuade themselves that they had heard, Preeti saying something about being hit by a car.

"Falling from above" had nothing to do with being run over—unless . . .

"If we talk to Sheila's family," I said, "we should ask if anyone witnessed the accident. I saw a pedestrian get hit by a car once. He flew about fifteen feet into the air, which would qualify as falling from above, as far as I'm concerned."

∽

It turned out that Satwant's itinerary would take us all over northern India before allowing us a chance to return to the case of the milkman. Our crisscrossing path would take us thousands of miles and include several brief stops back in Delhi, where we remained only long enough to catch yet another train or plane. On one stopover, we attempted the drive north to Loa-Majra only to get hopelessly stuck in what turned out to be the routine peak-hour jam, moving two miles in an hour until we gave up and turned around.

When we finally had a full day in Delhi, we waited until after lunch to make the trip in the brief traffic lull between the morning snarl and the afternoon tie-up. By that time, Satwant had found a description of the fatal accident in a report on Preeti's case from an Indian magazine called *Manohar Kahaniyan*. In the car, I read a translation of the account: Sheila, fifteen, had gone with some other women to gather grass for cattle feed. Sheila had forgotten her sickle and run back across the road to get it.

I read what happened next and stopped short. For one of the few times in my life, the cliché about not being able to believe what I was seeing was literally true for me. I read the next sentence again, slowly: The car hit Sheila and knocked her ten to twelve feet in the air.

I was astonished, then suspicious—maybe the writer had speculated as I had, then attempted to make the account more persuasive by inventing the detail about the girl getting knocked in the air.

But the article contained no mention of Preeti's cryptic comment about "falling from above," and, therefore, no obvious motive for inventing the detail.

⤳

Loa-Majra was a more substantial village than Preeti's had been. As we entered the village proper, we found ourselves passing a line of shops set up in three-walled concrete shelters open to the road. We pulled over to ask directions from a group of men standing in front of a shop. One of them happened to be Sheila's brother. He hopped into the car and directed us through the village and down a dirt road until we bogged down in mud. We walked from there, a field to our left and a brick wall to our right. After what, in the city, would have been about two blocks, we turned right on another dirt road. A few yards down was the entrance to the family compound, a half dozen brick structures surrounding a clay courtyard. Clearly, this family, though the same caste as Preeti's, was more prosperous. Karan Singh was a self-employed tailor and also a farmer. The main house was two stories of well-mortared brick, with an upstairs terrace overlooking the courtyard and the surrounding fields. In addition to wooden benches, some of Karan's sons brought out well-made rattan armchairs and matching footstools for us. Stevenson refused to sit in the comfortable chairs, insisting instead on perching on the edge of the bench, with its hard edge and sagging woven-rope surface.

Word of our presence spread rapidly. In minutes, a small crowd of neighbors materialized in the courtyard to watch the proceedings. While we talked, a teenage boy hand-washed his clothes at the brass water pump.

Sheila's father sat in the afternoon sun in dark aviator-style sunglasses. He had dark hair, but gray stubble showed against his nut-brown skin. He was dressed comfortably in a short-sleeve rayon dress shirt over a cotton T-shirt, thin cotton pants, and rubber thongs. I guessed that he was five-foot-eight or -nine, which was significant, because one of Preeti's statements to Tek Ram had been, "My father is taller than you." However, when we visited Preeti, we had neglected to measure Tek Ram or ask him his height, so we were unable to compare. Both Stevenson and Satwant felt it was clear that Karan was indeed taller, but I could only picture Tek Ram sitting down, so I wasn't sure.

Another of Preeti's first statements to her parents was, "My house is big and yours is small." There was no question that Karan Singh's house was much larger than the one Preeti was born to.

Karan confirmed the story that Preeti's parents had told us: The milkman told Preeti's story to a woman he knew who had been born in Loa-Majra. On her next visit to her birth village, the woman saw Karan Singh's wife and passed along what Preeti had been saying.

The next day, Karan Singh, one of his sons, and four or five other men from Loa-Majra went to see the girl.

"We were curious to see if she was telling the truth, or if there was something wrong with it," he explained.

We asked him to tell us exactly what had happened.

First, he said, they went to the house of the woman who had relayed the news. The woman then led them to Preeti's house. Preeti, her mother, father, brother, and sister were there with one neighbor. But, as word spread, a crowd gathered.

"We wanted to test the girl, so nobody had told them which of us was Sheila's father, but Preeti kept staring at me. After a while, she stopped staring and started playing. Then her mother said to her, 'You used to say you remembered your real father. Which one is he?'

"She pointed at me and said, 'That is my father.' Then one of the neighbors asked her, 'What is your father's name?' She said my name, and also my wife's and the name of our village. Then someone said, 'Don't point to your father from a distance, come put your finger on him.' Preeti walked through the crowd to me and sat on my lap. She hugged my neck tight and wouldn't let go. Then she whispered to me, 'Please take me home with you.'

"I was fully convinced," he said. "On top of everything else, she looked exactly like my daughter."

Stevenson asked if he had a picture of Sheila. One of his sons disappeared into the house and emerged with a photograph. In it, a dozen children posed in two rows. Karan pointed to a girl in the center of the top row: Sheila at the age of ten or eleven. She was a touchingly pretty girl in a blue V-neck sweater staring piercingly into the camera. There did seem to be some physical similarity between this girl and Preeti, though the age difference made comparison difficult. Of course, I presumed that Karan would have remembered how his daughter had looked at Preeti's age. But I also knew that in many of the cases I'd seen, there had been no apparent resemblance between the subject and the previous personality. In any case, I didn't find it to be compelling evidence. But maybe the father was talking about something other than a strictly physical resemblance, some sense of a person that came from more subtle clues than the turn of a nose or length of a chin. Or maybe it was wishful thinking: I could only imagine the emotional pull of this little girl climbing into his lap, clinging to his neck and saying, "Daddy, take me home."

"Did you question Preeti at all? Ask her any details?" I asked.

"The crowd was so big it was difficult," he said. "We stayed until almost midnight, and Preeti was so tired. That was a Friday. I told her I would come back on Sunday, but she just clung to me and said, 'You are my father. I want to go with you.'"

Preeti's parents tried to dissuade her, but she just kept clinging to Karan. "Since the woman who had brought us there was known to them, they decided to let Preeti come with me."

They took a tempo—a three-wheeled taxi—the ten to twelve miles from Preeti's house to Loa-Majra. They stopped in the same spot where we had gotten out of the car and walked through the mud—about a hundred yards from the family compound.

"Preeti led us from there to the house," Karan said. On the way, she saw one of Sheila's brothers heading out to a store. Without prompting, the father said, she pointed and called him by name. When they got to the family compound, it was crowded with friends and relatives. "People were waiting because they had already heard she was coming," Sheila's father said. "Preeti recognized all her brothers and sisters. People would ask her where is so-and-so and she would point. Then she looked around and said, 'Where is Munni? Has she gone to her in-laws?'"

Munni was the sister whom Sheila had been closest to. She had married before Sheila's death, and when Preeti came to visit, she was not there, but at her husband's house. "Munni came to see Preeti the next day and Preeti cried when she saw her," Karan said.

By this time, he went on, he had no doubt that Preeti was Sheila reborn. Besides, he said, in the accident, Sheila had been injured on the thigh, and Preeti had a birthmark there.

Stevenson had examined several marks on Preeti's skin when we had visited her family. He asked Karan Singh to be more specific about the injury to his daughter's leg.

"I didn't see it myself," he said. "Her mother saw it."

Sheila's mother was working in the fields. She was sent for, and appeared a few minutes later. Stevenson asked where Sheila had a visible injury. The mother pointed to the outside of the right thigh. Her husband disputed her. "You said it was here," he said, pointing to the inside of the thigh. The mother grimaced. Stevenson asked her once again, and this time she pointed to the inside of the right thigh. Then she admitted, "I don't remember which leg it was."

"What made you think Preeti was your daughter reborn?" Stevenson asked her.

"When she came, I was standing among so many women, and someone asked her who her mother was, and she pointed to me. When one of my sons pointed to Sheila's younger brother and asked Preeti, 'Is he older or younger than you?' she said, 'He was younger than me. Now he is older.' The next day she was playing in the house and another one of my boys said, 'She looks like my sister.' Preeti looked at him and said, 'You still don't believe that I am her?' My gut feeling is that she's my daughter. One time, when I was taking Preeti in the street, she was afraid. She said, 'Don't, I'll get run over again.'"

I asked if she had witnessed the accident. No, she said. The only one in the family who had was one of Sheila's brothers, who was working in the fields.

"He was very upset for a long time," Argoori said. Two weeks later, she added, he had a dream that Preeti came and sat by him. He was scared, because he knew it was not good to dream of the dead. "In the dream," his mother said, "Sheila told him, 'Don't be afraid, I'm coming back.'"

We waited some time for the brother to return so that we could question him. But after about twenty minutes, we decided that we needed to leave: We still wanted to try to find the milkman, for whom we had only a name and a village. So we said our good-byes and walked back to the car, accompanied by Sheila's father. I tried to imagine how difficult it would have been for Preeti to lead them to the compound. There really weren't many choices to make—she would only have had to know to turn at the first intersecting road, instead of continuing straight, then pick the entrance to the family's compound from other similar entrances. Of course, by the time she got that far, she probably would have heard the voices of the people who had assembled to see her.

As we crossed the muddy area, a boy in a blue-and-white sweatshirt rode up on a bicycle with a large sheaf of green hay lashed to the rear. He stopped and greeted the father.

Satwant listened at Karan's shoulder, then caught up with us at the car. "That's the brother who witnessed the accident," she said. We walked back to where the boy stood and interviewed him at the edge of the mud bog in the street.

He was two years younger than Sheila, twelve or thirteen at the time of the accident. Sheila wasn't knocked in the air, he said. The car hit her and dragged her along the road. She came out on one side of the car, while her shoes came out on the other.

Shoes were so difficult to come by that he was wearing that very same pair of shoes when he dreamed about Preeti two weeks later. He retold the dream as the mother had, with one important difference.

"She didn't say, 'I'm coming back,'" he said. "She sat on my chest and I was terrified. She said, 'Don't be afraid, you won't see my face anymore.'"

∽

We drove through relatively empty countryside down a narrow strip of asphalt hemmed in on both sides by irrigation ditches. Our plan was to drive into a village called Kharkhoda. We knew that the milkman lived there somewhere, but it was a fairly substantial village, and we had only his name to go on.

It took about a half hour to get there. During the trip, I wrote in my notebook as well as I could given the bumpy road. I was trying to come to grips with what we had learned in Loa-Majra. I made a list of things that seemed to confirm Preeti's claims and those that raised questions about it.

The most powerful items on the pro side involved the multiple confirmations of Preeti's identifications. There were also some additional details that could not be explained by nonverbal prompting—like the fact that Preeti noticed the absence of Sheila's married sister and asked about her by name.

On the con side: Though the parents had attempted to make a connection between Sheila's wounds and Preeti's birthmarks, under close questioning it became obvious that their memory was confused. Likewise, the mother's version of the son's dream had Sheila saying, "I'm coming back," while the son's memory of the dream was virtually the opposite: "You won't see my face anymore." Both could indicate a desire on the parents' part to make the case seem better than it was.

Also vaguely troubling was the fact that the father had said that when he arrived at Preeti's home to meet her for the first time, Preeti was already there. Preeti's family had said the father arrived while Preeti was still in school.

Finally, the tantalizing possibility that Preeti's "memory" of having "fallen from above" was related to Sheila being knocked ten to twelve feet into the air by the impact of the car, as the magazine reported, had been contradicted by an eyewitness.

Nevertheless, I reckoned that all of those confusions could be written off. Maybe the mother remembered the son's account of the dream more clearly than the son remembered the dream itself. Maybe the magazine's account of Sheila's accident was closer to the truth than her brother's memory—he was very young at the time, and memories of traumatic events are not always clear. Maybe the parents' contradictions indicate normal imperfections of memory rather than bias—nobody remembers details perfectly; getting a few wrong is normal, no big deal.

Except that memory was what the evidence for this case was built on.

～

We arrived in Kharkhoda and parked on the village's teeming main street. Open, glassless storefronts lined both sides of the dirt street, selling everything from incense to Internet software as fat pigs and pathetic curs competed over the sewage that flowed at their feet. By now, I had come to grips with the sensory bombardment by imagining it to be something out of the Middle Ages, when European cities were beginning to mushroom out of overgrown villages, filthy and out of control but irrepressibly vital—my cultural roots.

Satwant and the driver got out of the car and disappeared down a narrow cobbled lane that stretched between the continuous brick walls of adjoining compounds. Stevenson sat in the back, and I was in front, my window half open in the afternoon heat. A faded blue bus churned up the street, people hanging from every window. Something about one of them, a woman, drew my attention. She was leaning precariously far out of the bus, her face pale and distressed. As the bus came closer, I watched her begin moving rhythmically, her mouth opening and closing as if she were trying to speak. Then a green stream gushed from her throat, pulsing once, twice, three times as the bus passed by. The stream arched in the air and splattered in the street. I felt scattered drops fly through my window just as I comprehended what I was witnessing. Bicyclists barely swayed to avoid tracking in the puddle. An immense pig rooting in garbage on the side of the road looked up, then waddled casually into traffic to begin licking up the mess.

I glanced back at Stevenson. He was deep into his files, apparently oblivious to the digestive pageant ongoing just outside the car. "That's India for you," I muttered under my breath, wiping the side of my head as thoroughly as possible with a used napkin that I found in my pocket. I resolved not to give it another thought.

Satwant had been gone a long time when the driver returned alone. "Follow me," he said. "We have found the man you were looking for."

The lane went back a long way, with even smaller lanes running off it to the right. We passed by four or five before turning right ourselves. Trickles of sewage ran down the street in bricked-in gutters on either side. Not far along this lane, the brick walls gave way to thick masonry. Through an opening in the wall, I could see an elaborate two-story house. Either a stereo system or television blared out music from *Saturday Night Fever* through the open sash windows.

The milkman's house was a half block down, a very humble brick dwelling at the rear of a narrow dirt courtyard, its one touch of relative affluence a phone booth–sized concrete bathhouse at the front of the courtyard beside the water pump. A plastic shower curtain hung across the opening.

The milkman's name was Ranbir Singh. (Singh, I discovered, was a common last name among Hindus and Sikhs—it means "lion," connoting a fierceness of faith—and Ranbir was no relation to Karan Singh.) He confirmed the story that we had heard from both families, but added an essential detail: Preeti's family hadn't just ignored her pleas to be taken to Loa-Majra, they had disciplined her for denying that she was Preeti.

"When I came to milk the buffaloes, I heard them yelling and slapping her. She was crying and she came to me and hugged me and said, 'Please take me to my own village.'"

The milkman, disturbed by the incident, went to the only person he knew from Loa-Majra, the woman who would eventually pass the word of Preeti's claims along to Sheila's family.

The milkman told us that when the woman first went to speak to Preeti, Preeti immediately recognized her and called her by name. He hadn't witnessed this, but that is what the woman told him.

He was present when Karan Singh came to meet Preeti for the first time, and, once again, we were given a slightly different version of what happened. He agreed with Karan Singh that Preeti was present when the men from Loa-Majra arrived. From there, his version differed: Karan Singh had said that Preeti stared at him for a while, then went back to playing until her mother asked her if she could point out her "father." As the milkman recounted it, though, Preeti ran to Karan Singh as soon as she saw him, and hugged him.

Ranbir showed us back to the car. He carried a heavy stick. "The dogs," he said, by way of explanation. We followed him around the back of the house, down a lane that we hadn't seen before. A succession of dogs, barely more than hair, bones, and teeth, snarled at us as we walked around large sinkholes filled with mud. He waved the stick menacingly. The dogs backed off, then circled around and followed us like sinister shadows. When we got to the car, he told Satwant that a woman had been bitten just the day before and that the dog had been rabid—a fact I was happy not to have known until I was stepping into the car.

We had one more stop: the woman who had carried the news of Preeti's claims from the milkman to Karan Singh's family.

It was early evening, and when we arrived at the woman's compound, several families were preparing for dinner, lighting the cooking fires by using a handful of twigs to kindle a large disk of dung, which burned like charcoal when it caught. Babies cried in the background. The woman we had come to interview was only an outline beneath the dark scarf wrapped twice around her face. She repeated much of what we had already heard, but insisted that when Karan Singh came to see Preeti, he first came to this house where we now sat. Preeti was sent for. It was then, not later at Tek Ram's house, that Preeti identified Karan Singh as "her" father.

"That's three versions of the recognition, now, or maybe four, if you count the milkman's contention that Preeti ran to him right away as a separate version," I observed when we were finally on the road back to Delhi. "The only thing everyone seems to agree on is that Preeti recognized him, at some point, in some location."

"I think this woman is just trying to improve her role in this story," Satwant said.

"Yes, you see that sometimes in these small villages," Stevenson agreed. He folded his hands in his lap. We drove on in silence for a minute. Then he said, "Well, I think the skeptics would have a good time tearing that case apart."

Satwant looked at him quizzically.

"What do you mean?" she asked.

I turned to face her. "Allow me," I said. "You have this child who's unhappy with her parents. She's convinced her parents don't love her. And maybe the woman we just interviewed isn't the only one from Loa-Majra who married into the village. Maybe there are three or four other women who know of Karan Singh and his family. And maybe Preeti is in the village one day and she hears a couple of these women reminiscing about the old days, and they mention a teenage girl named Sheila who was killed, and they also mention the father's name and the mother's name and say how much they grieved for the girl. And Preeti thinks, 'Maybe I'm not really from this family that is mean to me.

Maybe those parents who missed their daughter so much are really my parents. And maybe I'm that girl who died.' Because even at a young age she's heard about rebirth. So she starts saying, 'You're not my parents. My father's name is Karan Singh.' The milkman hears that and passes it along. The dead girl's family wants to believe their dead daughter has returned. So they come to see the girl, and there's this big crowd. When they ask Preeti who 'her father' is, she goes to the person everyone is staring at, and Karan Singh takes this as complete confirmation. Similar things happen when he takes her back to his village. Maybe she might even begin to make mistakes at first—she heads toward the wrong person—but she sees people inching away from her or shaking their heads, so she finds the right person. And when she asked where the married sister was? Maybe she had earlier overheard someone say, 'It's a shame that Munni couldn't be here to see this.' And it is no great leap in this culture to assume that the reason a sister would not be at home is because she is at her in-laws."

Satwant watched me with something between hurt and wonder. When I finished she asked, "Is that what you really think?"

I thought about that for a minute.

"No," I said.

13

City of Glass and Glamour

We took the early express train to Agra, home of the Taj Mahal, and watched the sun rise over central India's treeless plain. "These air-conditioned cars are of recent vintage," Stevenson observed dryly. "You aren't really getting the full Indian rail experience."

I got enough of it when we stepped off the train. Porters and beggars swarmed around us and followed us into the parking lot in a clot so dense that we couldn't take a step without bumping into a dozen outstretched arms. Monkeys scampered on the station's tin roof, excitedly hopping off and on from along a rusted drain pipe. As we huddled against the growing mob, a crisp English voice rose above the din.

"Dr. Stevenson!"

"Charlie!" Stevenson exclaimed as a handsome, pale face broke through the crowd toward us. "Charlie is the last of the Anglo-Indians," Stevenson said to me as he approached. "Indian mother, English father. I've known him for years."

As Charlie reached us and took up Satwant's bags, the rival prospects gave way grudgingly.

"Is this your new car?" Stevenson asked as he folded himself through the heavy doors of a polished Ambassador taxi.

"Mine is in the shop, sir," Charlie said. "This is borrowed, so I can only take you to the hotel. I can't go out of town on those dirt roads you like to travel on."

"That's a shame," Stevenson said. "How's your brother, Charlie?"

"Dead, sir. Drank himself to death, I'm afraid."

"I'm sorry to hear that, Charlie."

We passed walled estates, a military installation, and a police station, as well as signs pointing to the Taj and the Agra Fort, a massive ancient battlement that was the city's secondary tourist attraction. Our hotel loomed above a typically squalid crossroads, but inside a gated crescent planted with shrubs and flowers, it maintained the spit and polish necessary to please the mostly European tourists on hand to see the Taj, which, a sign in the lobby announced, was visible from the roof.

We dumped our bags and hired a car—not an Ambassador this time, but a tiny Maruti microbus apparently constructed from the same material that they use to make Pepsi cans. I sat in front, a vertical windshield and nothing else between me and the road, which, given that the road was constantly filled with animals and vehicles of boggling description, made me feel as if I were front-row center in a three-dimensional Imax movie.

Agra appeared older than the parts of Delhi we had seen; it was a conglomeration of ruin and grandeur, mostly ruin, crumbling along a maze of overbuilt streets that led, finally, to a narrow suspension bridge spanning a river trickling anemically through broad mud flats. Black buffalo drank in the brown water, the white onion spires of the Taj Mahal rising majestically in the distance.

Two hours out of Agra, on the outskirts of the industrial city of Firozabad, we turned off on a dirt road into a maze of narrow, close alleys with shop wares spilling from every opening and a mass of humanity defying the restricted space. The front window of the microbus pressed so closely against the back wheels of bikes and hindquarters of oxen as we inched through the mob that I kept pressing against my seat in a futile attempt to gain breathing space. The brick walls closed within inches of the sides of the van; the road ruts carved deeper and deeper into the dirt. Our driver refused to yield to the impossible conditions, revving his engine and spinning his wheels and beeping his horn until we finally found ourselves in the heart of bricked-in hell, wedged into an alley simply too narrow even for the insanely determined to navigate. We squeezed out of the van through the space permitted by the barely open doors, then stepped down to the gouged earth, attempting to avoid the sewage seeping from one rut to the next, trickling weakly in the hot sun.

We set off, Satwant stopping to ask directions every few feet. The environment overwhelmed me, and the dominant impression was: dung. Wherever we turned, dung: stacked and carved into great cones reaching above my head, scattered among shreds of garbage and human waste, floating in a fog of dust rising from the ground. At one point, an exhausted camel blocked our path, laying across the alley in a mucky cess. We picked our way around his matted flanks. Filthy children closed behind us, pursued themselves by flies, both following us over the last hundred yards to our destination. Satwant stepped on a board bridging a sewage trench and ducked into an opening in the brick wall—or, more accurately, a loosely stacked pile of bricks—into a tiny dirt courtyard no more than fifteen feet wide and thirty feet deep. This was the home of a little girl who claimed to remember the life of her cousin who had burned to death in a shack in this same slum.

Satwant discovered the girl through a survey conducted by an assistant. In just six weeks of canvassing the area, the assistant turned up more than 150 potential cases. This one particularly appealed to Satwant because it involved a birthmark possibly related to a previous life. The subject was still very young, four or five years old. From the time she could talk, her parents said, she claimed to have been her cousin, a girl burned to death at the age of fourteen while assembling the thin metal or glass bracelets called bangles that are worn everywhere in India and increasingly in the West. Their manufacture was a cottage industry in the slums of Indian cities; children and women would labor all day, taking unjoined metal rings and fusing them over kerosene-powered candles—literally, a poor man's welding torch. The work was tedious and dangerous. The family said that the fourteen-year-old had been sitting on a woven mat, working, when the lamp fell and set the mat on fire. Nobody was there to help put the fire out, and it quickly overcame her.

As Satwant understood it, the family claimed that the little cousin was born with marks on the backs of her legs that mimicked the pattern of the woven mat, as if it had been burned into her skin.

Stevenson had pursued similar cases for twenty years. All too familiar with the frustrations of verbal testimony like that we had just experienced in Delhi, he saw the mute evidence of birthmarks—corresponding in some cases to medical records of wounds to a previous personality—as a possible antidote.

The tiny courtyard of the compound quickly filled with relations and onlookers. We sat on the wooden benches beneath a thatched overhang projecting from the brick lean-to that was home to the large family. It was in a space just like this, less than a hundred yards distant, that the teenage girl burned and died. The same kind of woven mat that caught fire in the fatal accident lay on the dirt floor of this lean-to.

The children who had been following us crowded into the courtyard. I could sense their ranks swelling behind me, hear them coughing and sniffling and feel their little hands reaching to touch my cotton sweatshirt and nylon backpack with increasing frequency until an adult commanded them to retreat. They briefly obeyed, then moved in again. Sweat trickled down my neck in the stale closeness as every inch of my being rebelled against this circumstance: Could a child really be born to this relentless, miserable existence, then die an agonizing death only to be reborn a few houses away, into another life sentence of welding bangles in the dung?

For the same reason that thought depressed me, it made a powerful argument against those who chalked up these cases to wish fulfillment on the part of individuals and the culture as a whole. If the Hindu belief in reincarnation caused delusions of previous-life memories, why didn't they conform to the basic Hindu belief in karma? In neither this case nor the milkman case was there any hint that the conduct of a previous life had affected the status of the reborn life. Instead, the relation between the two lives seemed random and naturalistic, the way that the location of an oak seedling might relate to the century-old tree from which the acorn fell—governed by proximity, wind currents, and chance, not moral order.

It had been the same in Lebanon. If the innumerable Druse cases were motivated by the desire to reinforce beliefs, why did the average separation between death and rebirth equal eight months when dogma insisted the interval should be nil?

We sat as best we could on the frame of the wooden benches, our knees touching those of the girl's mother, bright-eyed but emaciated, and her father, a graying, careworn man in a soiled white tunic with a maroon-and-white knit scarf around his neck. Satwant said that he manned one of those roadside stalls we had seen on the way in; he was a butcher. A mangy dog tried to insinuate itself under our bench until one of the children thumped it with a stick and sent it shrieking away.

Satwant had a long discussion with the parents without bothering to translate. The mother was particularly animated, and three men standing behind them chimed in from time to time.

The conversation appeared to reach some conclusion, and the woman went into the hut to fetch water in metal cups, then handed them to us one at a time. Satwant turned to me. "The girl's mother was afraid we might take the girl with us," she explained. Stevenson had encountered this reaction before. Once he was trying to interview a child's family when a woman in the inevitable crowd began screaming so loud he could not hear his interpreter's responses. Finally he asked the interpreter what the woman was yelling.

"She's saying, 'Let's kill him before he takes the child away,'" the man reported matter-of-factly. Stevenson eventually managed to extricate himself unharmed. On this occasion, Satwant had preempted the hostility. "I told her that Dr. Stevenson had seen nearly three thousand cases all over the world and that his only interest was to ask a few questions. Then those men behind her started saying to the father, 'What's in it for you?' I told them that he is a scientist and that science discovers things and in the long run everyone benefits. Those men started making fun of it, and they might be a problem later, but we'll see how it goes."

"You think they were expecting you to give them some presents or something?" I asked.

"We used to bring knives, Swiss Army knives, and people weren't happy," Satwant replied. "They thought, 'Here come these big people and they bring something small like that?' That is their perception."

I wondered what they would think had they known that beneath the waist of my faded jeans I was wearing a money belt with a couple of thousand dollars in cash, a credit card with a $15,000 limit, and $1,500 airline tickets—more money than any of these people might see in a lifetime.

And I wondered, too, what it meant that I had so much and they so little.

∽

When the mother returned to the bench, we began the interview. They told us that the girl, not quite five now, began speaking at one year. One of her first complete sentences was, "I was burned." She called her uncle, the dead girl's father, "Daddy," and did not refer to her own father that way until recently. She still sometimes took things from her parents' house and gave them to the other family. One of her first words was the Hindi word for the kerosene-powered candle that caused her cousin's death, and it was always spoken fearfully and accompanied by an acute fear of fire.

As we spoke with the girl's parents, I noticed activity in the shadows beyond the brick hut's open doorway. A young woman was sitting on the straw mat, meticulously polishing her toenails and fingernails. An older woman was seated further back in the dark corner, her hand covering her face.

Satwant must have noticed it as well, because after an extensive discussion she told us, "The PP mother is here, in the house. She is in a bad way because her husband is missing. Her son had gone off to another state and didn't come back for a long time, so her husband went looking for him. The son eventually returned, but he had never met the father. That was eight months ago, and they have never heard from the father again."

Satwant thought that the woman might not be up to speaking with us in front of the entire neighborhood, so asked to speak to her alone in the hut. The woman agreed, and Satwant ducked into the shadowed interior. Stevenson and I smiled and pretended to sip the water that we had been given. We weren't all that interesting to look at, though, and some in the assembled crowd began to drift away.

Satwant emerged ten minutes later and gave us her report: In the months before the little girl's birth, the dead girl's mother had had recurring dreams of seeing her daughter in various places around the quarter. Then, when the subject's mother was in labor, the dead cousin's mother dreamed that her daughter finally spoke to her, saying, "Leave my clothes at my aunt's house." The mother, surprised, asked why, and she said, "Because I'm going to stay there."

These "announcing" dreams were fascinating, but this one didn't do much for the probative value of the case, a typically weak same-family case to begin with. Because of the dream, the girl had been born into the world with a powerful, and possibly self-fulfilling, expectation from her parents that she would remember the life of her cousin.

The only thing to do now was inspect the birthmarks. The mother ducked into the shadows of the lean-to and emerged carrying a crying, greasy-haired little girl, her pretty face marred by an open sore on her upper lip, apparently caused by a chronically runny nose. She picked at it nervously and watched Satwant dig in her bag. She emerged with a plastic-wrapped bolt of blue cloth which she handed to the girl, who stopped crying and turned the gift over and over in her hand.

The father picked his daughter up by the armpits and turned her around so Stevenson could examine the backs of her legs. He leaned close and traced with his fingers the faint, long, thin reddish streaks that ran vertically on the back of both thighs. There was no hint of a woven pattern.

Perhaps sensing our lack of enthusiasm, the parents began telling Satwant that the dead girl had had an enlarged left big toe—the result of an imperfectly healed infection—and that their daughter was born with the same feature. They held out her feet, big toes together. I thought that I could detect some slight difference in size, but wouldn't have bet on it. Satwant took a plastic ruler from her bag and tried wrapping it around each toe. It showed the left to have a slightly larger circumference, but the imperfect flexibility of the plastic allowed plenty of room for error. Also, the chance of documenting the dead girl's toe enlargement through medical records would be nonexistent.

Stevenson wrote down what measurements he could get, then turned the girl's leg to look at the reddish birthmarks once more, tracing them lightly with his forefinger. He sat back, rubbed his chin. "It's all too vague," he said. "Anyone could have these birthmarks. That's why we appreciate the unusual patterns corresponding to something concrete."

Stevenson has had such cases, one of the more dramatic being that of a Turkish man born with a bleeding birthmark on the right underside of his chin. From the time he could speak, the man, Cemil Fahrici, claimed to remember the life of a bandit who had shot himself under the chin after being trapped by police in a burning house. Stevenson didn't invest a lot of hope in trying to verify the man's alleged statements about the previous life. The previous personality had been a distant relative, and there had been some communication between the families involved, but more important, the bandit had been locally famous as a kind of Robin Hood figure, and knowledge about his life was widespread. Finally (as in this case of the "burned" girl), Cemil's father had had a dream the night before Cemil's birth predicting that the bandit would be reborn as his son.

For all those reasons, Stevenson didn't find Cemil's claimed memories to be compelling evidence in favor of reincarnation—except for the birthmark.

By the time Stevenson inspected and photographed the mark, Cemil was in his thirties. It looked like a nickel-sized, half-moon-shaped scar just where the underside of the chin joined the neck.

When Stevenson interviewed the bandit's sister, who had viewed her brother's body up close, and a policeman who had been one of the first to enter the burning house after the suicide, they both agreed that the bullet had entered under the chin and exited the top of the head.

Stevenson had a sudden inspiration. He immediately returned to Cemil and asked if he had any birthmarks on his head. Without hesitation, Cemil reached to the left side of his crown. Stevenson parted the hair and discovered a thin, hairless line just over an inch long. Later, he compared the photo he took of the mark to an autopsy photo of a gunshot exit wound in the same location. It was remarkably similar. Compellingly similar.

Still, it struck me that for as many evidential problems birthmark cases might solve, they carry with them a built-in difficulty: If a child is born with marks reminiscent in some way of a deceased person, that alone might be enough to create a false sense of identification and generate false claims of previous-life memories.

That's not a mere theoretical possibility, either—it happens. In the Turkish bandit case, in fact, another man later came to Stevenson's attention who also claimed to be the same bandit reborn. He had been born with a mark on the top of his head (though no mark under his chin) and claimed to have accurate memories of the bandit's life.

So, barring the possibility of a single soul generating multiple rebirths, that meant that at least one of those previous-life memories was bogus, a lie or a fantasy suggested by the birthmark.

Still, I could imagine a case where birthmarks could provide clinch-

ing evidence of reincarnation: A child would make abundant statements about remembering the life of a person unknown to the child's
family. The child would have birthmarks that did not appear to bear
any relationship to his claimed memories of a previous life. But his
statements would be specific enough to lead an investigator conclu-
sively to someone whose life fit the child's memories exactly.

Only then, in interviewing the family of the previous personality,
would it come out: The deceased person had prominent injuries that related perfectly to the subject's unusual birthmarks.

If Stevenson had never come upon a case quite that perfect, it didn't
mean that one wasn't out there. Of the 150 potential cases in Satwant's
survey, roughly 20 percent involved birthmarks of some kind. Several
of these cases figured prominently on her itinerary for us.

Nevertheless, *this* birthmark told Stevenson little if anything. As we
were about to extricate ourselves from the lingering crowd and this Indian slum, a young girl carrying an eighteen-month-old infant approached Satwant. She was a neighbor, and she had brought her baby
sister for us to look at. The child had only a stump where her left hand
should have been. It quickly became clear that the eighteen-month-old
had not yet said anything that could be related to a previous life, but
something in her mood, according to the girl, had suggested the possibility—though she had no pain from the deformity, she would study
her hand sadly and was sensitive about others looking at it.

"Does she have any phobias?" Stevenson asked.

"She's afraid of cats," said a man who identified himself as the
baby's grandfather.

One of the men in the group beneath the overhang said something
loudly, and the others burst into laughter.

"They're saying, 'Maybe a cat ate her hand in a previous life,' " Satwant reported disapprovingly. "They are being very sarcastic."

Even so, Stevenson methodically took measurements and photographs of the deformed hand, just in case some previous-life claims
surfaced later and came to Satwant's attention. He had a file of such
cases where no specific claims had emerged, including one from Agra
of a boy said to have been born with fifteen small circular marks on
his back and the backs of his arms. The marks were about the size
and shape of wounds from shotgun pellets, and some of them even

had a palpable mass inside that rolled beneath the tip of a finger.

As we left the compound, some of the men who had been having fun at our expense asked to have their photograph taken with me.

The car was not where we had left it. Somehow, the driver had managed to turn it around in the narrows and move it a block and a half farther down the alleyway, pointed toward the main road. As we approached, we saw that the driver's shirt was damp with sweat. It seemed that some of the neighborhood children had flattened the rear tire by slashing it with a nail attached to the end of a stick. He'd already changed the tire—he had had a spare, something that, fortunately for us, Satwant had insisted on checking before we left. Now she was reluctant to drive back to Agra without one.

"If we got stuck on the road out in the countryside here, do you think people would be disposed to help us out?" I asked.

"Not necessarily," she said.

So we found ourselves sitting on the side of the main road opposite a stand made of empty crates that served as the local tire-repair shop. Dealing with the punctured inner tube took a full hour, for reasons not clear to me. The shopkeepers huddled above the tire, rubbing it, pressing it, filling it, letting the air out, and starting all over again. It went on and on, a space of time which allowed me to fully consider a billboard sign a hundred yards up the road.

FIROZABAD, CITY OF GLASS AND GLAMOUR, it boasted.

14

Marked for Life

While we were in Agra, Stevenson wanted to search for medical records relating to a birthmark case in a village three hours to the east. I remembered the long morning spent tracking down the newspaper account of a car accident in Beirut, then multiplied it by the chaos of India, and sat back, resigning myself to an interminable, frustrating day.

The subject of the case was a seventeen-year-old boy. As Satwant briefed me on what she had discovered in interviews with the boy's family, one point immediately intrigued me: For the first time in the cases I had seen, the child's claims concerning a previous life seemed to predate his ability to speak. His parents said that as soon as he learned to walk, every chance he got he would take off toward a neighboring village, which was little more than a mile away. They were constantly running after him, and would have to pick him up and carry him back to their home.

He had been born with two small, circular birthmarks on the right side of his chest; the larger and more distinct one was about an eighth of an inch in diameter. Each was slightly depressed in relation to the surrounding skin, with a thin raised ring around the circumference.

When he could speak, the parents told Satwant, the child pointed to the birthmarks and said, "This is where I was shot."

He also told them his "real name" and gave the names of the men who he said had waylaid him after a night of drinking. The parents knew the names and knew of the murder the boy referred to. It had taken place several years before their son was born, in the neighboring village that so attracted the boy. In addition, the dead man had been a Hindu, and the boy's parents were Moslem. The boy refused to join in the family's prayers, denying that he was Moslem, and insisted that he wanted to return to his Hindu family. That certainly did not please his parents, and seemed to diminish greatly the chance that the child's claims would have been concocted or somehow embellished by them.

Stevenson wanted to find the autopsy report for the murder victim so as to compare the location of the fatal bullet wounds to the subject's circular birthmarks.

Satwant said that the murder took place in 1976. Finding a twenty-year-old autopsy report would be a challenge in Miami. In rural India?

When I told Stevenson of my skepticism, he admitted that it was a long shot. "The odds are one in one hundred, maybe one in fifty if we can get the police to give us a police case number on it," he said. "The thing is, one case with an autopsy report is worth ten without."

We drove out of Agra, passing Firozabad, where we had gotten the flat tire, to the town of Etawah. We found the district police station on the fringe of town, down a dirt driveway, hidden from the main road by an embankment—in the States, I would have probably assumed that the worn concrete structure was an abandoned gas station. The captain, dressed in civilian clothes, sat outside at a wooden table set up in the shade. He asked us to sit while he attended to some other business. There were two plastic chairs beside the table, and another man brought a third from inside the station. The breeze was steady and cool, so I didn't mind sitting there. We waited for about twenty minutes as the captain shuffled through papers, and then he turned his attention to our request. A large cardboard-covered register was retrieved and thumped on the table. The captain opened it to neat, handwritten entries in ink—all of the crimes registered in this district in the mid-seventies. For another half hour he pored over the reports without success. He ran his finger painstakingly across each inked line, and then, when he got to the bottom of the page, he flipped from left to right, working back in time.

When he had exhausted all of the reports for 1976, we were about to thank him and leave. But he flipped back one more page, and sat back in his seat.

"Here it is," he said. The date of the murder was December 1975, a year earlier than Satwant had thought. After three hours of driving and an hour sitting, we had a case number.

"It's still a long shot, but the odds have shifted slightly more in our favor," Stevenson said.

While we were there, a uniformed policeman had walked up behind us and said something to the captain. The captain said something in return, and the man answered shortly and walked away. The captain's face reddened, and he barked ferociously at the retreating policeman, who shrugged his shoulders and kept on walking.

When we left, we discovered what the argument had been about: Immediately outside the entrance, a car, a truck, and a microvan had collided. The driver of the microvan was dead and the body was sitting there. Nobody knew who the dead man was and nobody was willing to take his body away.

The captain had told the cop to at least take the corpse to the town morgue. The cop refused. A half hour later, we saw the crumpled van on the side of the road, the dead man a shadow in the driver's seat. The collision must have happened during the time that we had been sitting in the breeze outside the police station. We hadn't heard a thing.

As we got into the car, I leaned across the backseat and said to Satwant, "Can you ask the driver to try not to get us killed?"

"I already did," she said.

∽

We drove back into town looking for the courthouse, where we hoped to find a case file corresponding to the case number that we had just discovered. The courthouse turned out to be a dingy campus of low-rise, two- and three-story faded-yellow buildings arrayed around a public square. In the center of the square, a well had attracted a line of people waiting their turn at the pump. The whole place was trampled and overrun, the square itself mostly dirt and rotting leaves. In the one patch of what might be called lawn, a few dozen people lay head to foot, sleeping.

We entered the largest building. The entrance hall and all the corridors and stairways leading from it coursed with people moving shoulder to shoulder into the dim interior and echoed with the steady drone of trampling feet and conversation. We followed one stream up the stairs.

As we climbed, I noticed that on the wall opposite the banister, the dirty white paint was marked with reddish-brown streaks the exact color of dried blood. The streaks ascended like a seismograph tracing, following the slope of the stairwell. I couldn't figure out what had caused the strange pattern until I realized that the streaks began, in each instance, at roughly the height of a man's head as he walked up the stairs. I flashed on an image of our driver, pushing open his door at sixty kilometers per hour to spit out a red stream of juice generated by his constant chewing of betel nuts, the local equivalent of a perpetual coffee break. So that was it: decades of expectoration, thousands of people spitting on the wall as they walked up and down the stairs. As we climbed I realized that the red streaks filled every corner of the building, painted the edge of every balcony railing. Wherever you could imagine someone leaning to spit, there it was.

The records room was a large, high-ceilinged affair on the third floor. In the antechamber, six bored clerks sat in wooden chairs watching us skeptically. One of them sprang to our assistance, though, listened carefully to what we were after, and then led us into a larger inner room lined with shelves and nearly filled by an immense wood table. Every surface in the room was littered with heavy ledger books like the one we had seen at the police station. The books were scattered haphazardly, as if they had been dropped from a great height and left wherever they had crashed to earth. The clerk circled the room for a minute, then stood on a chair to pull a volume from the dusty recess of a high shelf. He brought the volume to the table and began to flip through the pages. After a few minutes he closed the book and went back in the front room. We followed.

We found him paging through another ledger at his desk. He looked up when we came in.

"I'm afraid that there was never any suspect accused in that case, and there was never any trial, so we wouldn't have that record," he said. "But perhaps you can get the autopsy report if you go over to the central police station, which is across the street."

"Always ask to talk to the senior man," Stevenson advised as we dodged through traffic—human, animal, and vehicular—to the police headquarters. "If you wind up with an underling, it's completely hopeless."

Satwant did just that, handing over one of Stevenson's business cards. In a few minutes, we were ushered into an immense office that still retained a decayed air of British imperialism about it. A fan spun almost imperceptibly above us as mosquitoes floated in the dim light. The district sub-chief, a man in a yellow short-sleeve shirt with a bottle-brush mustache, sat behind an old desk facing three rows of plastic chairs, writing on a blotter. Standing around him, a handful of other officials talked among themselves. We sat in the front row and waited until the sub-chief stopped writing. Satwant made our request. One of the officials at the sub-chief's side said, yes, that would be no problem, but the others quickly contradicted him.

More officials, both uniformed and in civilian clothes, kept entering the room. Ultimately, ten people collected to argue about whether it was or was not possible to find the record we sought. Thirty minutes later, we received the final verdict: impossible.

Now I was thoroughly convinced we were wasting our time. But Stevenson wanted to check one last possibility—the hospital. It was less then a half mile down the street, another faded concrete low-rise building. Here, at least, we had a contact, a hospital administrator who had actually managed to produce documents in the past. We walked around the side of the main building to a small annex, where the administrator showed us into an empty office with padded chairs lined up against the wall and an air-conditioning unit groaning in the window. In one corner, an ancient blue Frigidaire sat on top of a wooden crate, humming loudly enough to be heard above the AC's condenser. We sat in the room, staring at the walls. After a half hour, Satwant left to check on the progress of the record search. She returned with a bleak report: They could find 1974 and 1976, but not 1975. We sat in the room another forty minutes. I guessed that we had long since been forgotten, so Satwant and I walked into the room where the clerks were sitting around. They weren't happy to see us, but finally agreed to show us where they had been searching. They walked us out into the open-air breezeway to a tall door in the exterior wall: a janitorial closet. At least that's what it looked like—a lightless room lined with ratty shelves on which oversize, yellowing folders stuffed with loose sheets of paper were haphazardly scattered. Many appeared to have tumbled from one shelf to another, or fallen to the floor, shedding papers along the line of descent.

A man stood in the closet, digging through a rotted cardboard box in the corner. I shook my head wearily and started to tell Satwant it was time to pack up and leave. But just then, the man straightened and calmly pulled a legal-size piece of paper from the folder. Our autopsy report.

We went back into the administrator's office and studied the report, an annotated diagram written in English but not always clearly decipherable. The victim had died from a single bullet to the chest, so there was no obvious correspondence for the subject's second, smaller birthmark that was farther down toward the abdomen. Another problem was that the autopsy had the bullet entering at about the level of the right nipple, just to the right of the chest's midline. Our subject's prominent birthmark was both lower and farther to the right than this entry wound. Birthmarks can migrate as a child grows to adulthood, but Stevenson didn't believe that one would move both down and to the right. Moreover, from Satwant's report, it looked as if the birthmark might be too far from the position of the entry wound to reasonably be accounted for by migration since birth.

"Without the birthmarks, this is just another U.P. murder case," Stevenson said as we headed back to Agra. Uttar Pradesh, one of India's poorest and most populous states, was where the majority of his Indian cases originated. Some of those U.P. murder cases presented extremely compelling evidence for rebirth. And, in this case, I still found it provocative that the boy ran toward "his" village even before he could speak and that he had been born Moslem but identified himself as Hindu. But the way Stevenson said "just another U.P. murder" made it clear that he now desperately wanted something beyond provocative; he needed evidence pressed into flesh. It now didn't appear that the case of this seventeen-year-old Moslem boy would provide that.

Even so, Stevenson still wanted to visit the family. He wanted to re-measure the birthmarks and question the mother about their locations at the boy's birth. He also wanted to check on something that he'd seen in the autopsy report: The bullet had entered the chest, traveled diagonally through the torso, and lodged, without exiting, just beneath the skin of the lower back.

"There was almost undoubtedly bruising in that skin tissue before death," Stevenson said. "I want to take a look at that boy's back."

He did just that, spending another entire day in a car slamming his own bruised back on bad dirt roads, only to be disappointed.

"If you wanted to kid yourself," he said after the day-long ordeal, "you could say there's a patch of skin on his back that was slightly different, but I'll have to call that ball out."

Stevenson was making a reference to a conversation we'd had earlier about objectivity and bias in science. He'd said, "Show me a researcher who doesn't care one way or another about the results, and I'll show you bad research," and compared balancing his care with scientific objectivity to making line calls in tennis. As a competitive man, he badly wanted to win. But he wasn't going to cheat by calling a ball that was in out, or vice versa. In fact, it was precisely because he so cared about winning that he paid such close attention to the lines. Someone who didn't care one way or the other was prone to making sloppy calls.

∽

There were other cases we'd seen in India that clearly deserved to be called out, cases that just didn't add up enough to count as valuable evidence one way or the other. But that didn't mean that they weren't fascinating in their own right.

One was a case that had begun right in the Etawah hospital, where we had sat staring at the blue refrigerator while clerks hunted the autopsy report. Years earlier, Satwant and Stevenson were doing research there when they encountered a Dr. Raja Ram. The doctor told them that his son, Kamariliya, had been speaking of a previous life since he was eighteen months old. He used to say, "My car is going to Kanpur," which puzzled his parents because they lived in Agra and had no special connection to Kanpur, a city four hours to the east by train. They had never even recalled mentioning the city in front of the child. As he began to speak more freely, the boy made a series of claims about what they took to be his previous life: He told his parents that he had lived in Kanpur, in a green house he owned near both the train station and the bus station. He said that he had been an engineer who died in a car accident while taking his children home from school. His car, a blue Fiat, had collided head-on with a bus. He had two sons and a daughter—Arun, Manoj, and Sangita, respectively. He said that his wife, whom he loved dearly, was named Alma.

With the father's permission, Dr. L. P. Mehrotra, a psychologist who had assisted in some of Stevenson's earlier Indian research, placed an ad in a Kanpur newspaper in July 1994, asking anyone who found the listed details to closely match the life of a friend or relative to contact him. He got one response—a man named Arun Sahu said that he thought the details matched the life of his father, Drone Sahu, who had died in a traffic accident in 1959, thirteen years before Kamariliya was born.

There were some significant differences between the life of Drone and the child's claimed memories, but Stevenson felt that they were outweighed by the correspondences. Drone did have two sons and a daughter, but the daughter was named Anita, not Sangita, as the boy had said. Close, but no cigar. And not only did the second son have a different name than that given by the boy, he wasn't even born when Drone had died—his wife was pregnant at the time. Kamariliya had spoken of "his" wife with great passion, but the name he called her, Alma, didn't match the name of Drone's wife.

There were two other major discrepancies. First, Drone had not been an engineer. Yet even so, Stevenson had counted that claim as a "questionable" match on the basis of statements made by Drone's family four years earlier that Drone had sometimes referred to himself as an "engineer" because he repaired radios and cars. Second, and most troubling to me, was the fact that Drone had not died in a collision with a bus and not while he was returning his kids home from school. His car tire had blown out as he was driving to a wedding. The car went out of control and slammed into a tree. This seemed all the more significant because Kamariliya had an acute fear of buses that seemed to relate to his memory of dying.

By way of correspondences, Drone had owned both his house and his car, neither of which is common in India now, and would have to have been described as rare in 1959. The house had indeed been green, but had been repainted gray since Drone's death. And it was within walking distance of both the train and the bus station.

Now, Stevenson wanted to go over the various discrepancies with

Drone's family once again. He also wanted to deliver Kamariliya Ram's new address, for the family had moved from Etawah. Despite Arun's belief that Kamariliya had indeed been his father in a previous life, the two had never met.

We took the train to Kanpur and hired a bicycle rickshaw to take us the short distance through the teeming chaos to the Sahu family's address. Stevenson insisted on walking behind us in the rising heat of the busy street because he wanted to measure the distance between the station and the house on his pedometer. Once again, he declined my offer to do the physical labor for him, this time claiming that the instrument had been set to match his stride. Unfortunately, we were on the wrong side of the tracks. It turned out that the alley leading to the house was directly across the street from the train platform, but we had to trek at least a quarter mile out of the way to find a place to cross the tracks, and then walk back up on the other side. From where we turned into the alley, you could see the bus station a few blocks down.

The cobbled, L-shaped alley was lined on either side by deep sewage trenches right at the foot of age-worn, mismatched two-, three-, and four-story buildings. Children and dogs flitted through the street. One little girl squatted over the sewer unselfconsciously. We had to step around a buffalo tethered to a stake, lying indifferently across half the width of stones.

The house where Drone had lived stood at the elbow of the L. The front hallway was so narrow that I nearly had to turn sideways to navigate it. We sat in a tall, narrow living room, the first of three rooms in a shotgun arrangement that stretched to the back of the house. Between the smooth, concrete floor and the ceiling fans, the heat was kept at bay. The walls were painted various tones of purple and featured built-in shelves harboring two televisions, a VCR, and other electronic equipment.

For the occasion, Arun—who had been five when his father died in 1959—had gathered his mother, Drone's wife, and his seventy-six-year-old uncle, Drone's elder brother.

By the standard we had set with other cases, the interview was brief—brief and enlightening. First of all, Stevenson had no mention in his notes of whether the family had said what kind of car Drone had been driving when he had crashed and died three decades ago. Kamariliya had remembered having a blue Fiat.

"I can't remember what he was driving," Drone's brother said. "But in those days, there were only two kinds of cars in India, Austins and Fords."

At some point, Satwant asked Drone's widow if she could ask her a few questions privately. They went in the next room, and we later learned what they discussed. Satwant had wanted to probe the delicate matter of Kamariliya's passionate memories for a woman named Alma, whom he called his wife. Since Alma was not the name of Drone's widow, Stevenson wanted to discover if there was a possibility that the memories of Alma related to a mistress. Satwant approached the subject gingerly, asking the wife an open-ended question about her relationship with Drone. The response was unambiguous: He had adored her, had always been very affectionate, and, in general, they had a great relationship.

So much for the mistress theory, I thought.

Meanwhile, we had moved on to the subject of Drone's occupation. When Stevenson asked about it, the uncle said, "Our family is in the jewelry business. Drone helped out, but he wasn't really interested."

"If people saw him on the street and asked him what he did," Stevenson inquired, "what would he say?"

Again, the uncle answered. "He would say he was a dealer in automobiles and scooters. He would sometimes buy and resell them."

"Well, do you think that because he repaired radios sometimes, he might have thought of himself as an engineer?" Stevenson pressed.

They briefly discussed the question among themselves, then Arun answered: "No."

I was beginning to think that there were two possibilities. Either Kamariliya's "memories" were fantasies, or the life he remembered was not that of Drone Sahu.

In a city the size of Kanpur—about four million in 1959, a multiple of that now—the number of people who might have fit the given details as well as Drone must have numbered in the dozens, at least. Tens of thousands of people must have lived "near" both a train and a bus station. Arun was a common name. There were many green buildings in Kanpur. The requirement of owning both car and house was the most limiting, but it by no means narrowed candidates beyond the possibility of a mistaken match.

It wasn't clear whether Stevenson had misunderstood four years earlier, or if the family had changed its opinion about whether Drone might have considered himself an engineer. When they flatly denied the possibility this time around, in a moment of uncharacteristic frustration, Stevenson said, "Why exactly was it that you responded to the advertisement in the newspaper?"

Arun was unruffled. "There were many things that seemed to match my father," he replied. "And my father died in 1959, but the boy was not born until 1972. That is a long time to remember names. Perhaps when he meets us, he will remember more."

They had already set a date for the trip to Agra for the purpose of meeting Kamariliya.

"Prepare them for disappointment," Stevenson told Satwant, as she rummaged through her notes looking for Kamariliya's new address and phone number.

When Satwant translated the caution, Arun responded, "There's an old Hindi saying: 'There are people who believe in rocks, and if they really believe in them, then they still get something out of it.'

"It's a matter of emotion. When we meet him, maybe we will feel something, and maybe we won't."

&

In the aftermath of our interview, we had several hours to fill before catching an overnight train back to Delhi. We took a cab to a hotel where Stevenson had once been a regular during his earlier trips to India. We found it in shocking decline: A former garden was choked with weeds, the pool was cracked and empty, the lobby deserted, and the top-floor restaurant smelled of urine, had stains and cigarette burns on every tabletop, and offered a menu that was an utter work of fiction. Stevenson and I split a beer, for which they had to send out, and Satwant sipped some tea.

I was tired, and pensive. Did Drone Sahu's case—assuming its flaws to be irredeemable—support the skeptical claim that when families found each other *before* an investigator arrived, they had an opportunity to get their stories straight and smooth over discrepancies?

Of course, Arun's family knew of the discrepancies before our visit, and had every chance to say that, by gosh, Drone *did* think of himself as an engineer, after all. Clearly, however, they felt no need to do so.

Besides, if this were a bogus match, the error may have been created by the investigative process itself: broadcasting details that were not quite specific enough across a city of millions. Who could blame Arun for responding, given the remarkable coincidences that undeniably did exist?

Furthermore, the case of Drone Sahu completely lacked one of the primary features of Stevenson's stronger cases: There had been no meeting of the child and the previous-life family, either before or after the investigator arrived on the scene. It is often the meeting of the families, and the child's recognition of places and people, that provided the strongest evidence of knowledge that could not have been obtained normally. In fact, the families usually relied on these meetings to persuade—or dissuade—themselves that the linkage was genuine.

As it turned out, our all-night train trip would carry us to Delhi for only a brief stay. From there we would catch a plane for a three-hour flight south, as far south as Bombay, to a city called Nagpur. There we would visit with the subject of another "B case"—Stevenson's term for "before" cases, in which a child's claims had been written down *before* any previous personality had been identified.

Unlike Kamariliya's case, in this one, the child had eventually met a family that seemed to fit her claims, and made a substantial number of recognitions that had impressed the investigator.

That original investigator had not been Stevenson or Satwant, however, but an Indian journalist named Padmakar Joshi. Stevenson had not relied on Joshi's account, but on an earlier trip had gone back and interviewed other firsthand witnesses.

We met Joshi for breakfast in a hotel near the Nagpur airport. He was a small, emphatic man who expounded on the Indian political situation with great passion, especially heightened as the country was in the midst of divisive parliamentary elections. His journalistic account of the case had provoked ferocious criticism from Indian skeptics, who claimed that he had manufactured the facts for personal gain. Not surprisingly, he was overjoyed that Stevenson was visiting again. To get as much mileage as he could out of the world-renowned researcher's return, Joshi had arranged for what could only be described as a press conference to follow our interview with the subject, a twenty-four-year-old woman named Sunita Chandak.

According to her parents, Sunita began making statements about a previous life at the age of four. She said that she came from a village named Belgaon and begged her father to take her there.

The intensity of her desire impressed her father, but he was at a loss. He had never heard of a village of that name, but he gleaned some clues as to where it might be; Sunita was very disapproving of the way her mother prepared food, and was always saying things like, "Why don't you serve it this way, like they did in my village?" Her preferences suggested a style of cooking particular to a nearby region. He asked Sunita to say more about the village. She told him that there was a temple, but no school, and that a river ran by the town and hills were nearby.

Sunita's father contacted Joshi and asked for help in locating a town like the one described by his daughter. Joshi discovered that there were twenty-eight villages called Belgaon in the region. Of those, nine seemed to match the child's details.

Over a period of months, Sunita's parents took her to three of the nine Belgaons on Joshi's list. In each case, Sunita said it was not the village she remembered. At this point, Joshi published an account of Sunita's story, along with some other statements that Sunita had made about a previous life, in hopes that it might help pinpoint a past-life family: While she had not mentioned her own name or a family name, she had said that she had a sister named Sumitri and that she had never worn a sari—which Joshi took to mean that she had died as a child, as all adult Indian village women would have worn a sari, but young girls would not.

A reader from one of the six Belgaons remaining on Joshi's list wrote saying that he believed that his might be the village Sunita was talking about: It had all of the geographic features mentioned, and he knew of a family there whose first daughter had died young and whose second daughter was named Sumitra. The dead girl, Shanta Kalmegh, had been born in 1945, and died before the age of six.

In the winter of 1979, when Sunita was five, her family took her to this Belgaon. It was about ninety miles away by road and required multiple bus changes to reach. Upon entering the village, Sunita hesitated briefly, then announced, "This is it." According to people in the village who witnessed the visit, Sunita went on to make a substantial number of identifications.

As usual in these situations, the girl was surrounded by a large crowd from the moment of her arrival. So, because it was impossible to know what kind of prompting the child may have been receiving from the crowd, Stevenson was mostly interested in the recognitions that were spontaneous or contained elaborate information that went beyond what could be suggested by body language or subtle verbal clues.

Sunita was said to have recognized the Kalmegh family's house and to have walked in the house, taken the hand of Shanta's now-aged mother, and said, "This is my mother."

Both of those recognitions were of the sort that might easily have been influenced by the crowd. But others were not so easily explained away.

Sunita noted that "her" house had a raised platform in front when "she" lived there. At the time of her visit, there was no raised platform, but according to Shanta's father and uncle, there had been one when Shanta was alive.

When Sunita was inside the family's house, she said, "This house is completely changed," and indicated a brick wall that she said had not been there. The family confirmed that the wall had been built since Shanta's death. In another place she said, "This is where we used to worship." Again, the family said that this was true—an altar had been moved from the spot after Shanta's death.

During the visit, according to some witnesses, Sunita said that she wanted some milk. Taking a glass from the Kalmeghses' house, she walked to a house not far away. There, she stood by a wall and said, "This is where the window used to be where we bought milk."

The nephew of the person who had sold milk in that house nearly thirty years earlier confirmed that there had been a window at just that spot.

After that, Sunita went to the home of a neighbor and pointed at a spot. To the neighbor she said, "Your father used to write something on a desk here. My father came here and I came with him."

The neighbor said that his father had been a local official and had in fact filled out documents at a desk in that exact spot.

And though Belgaon now had a school, Sunita's statement that her village "had a temple but no school" was true for when Shanta lived there. When Sunita was walking by the school building, she stated, "A grocery store used to be here."

That was correct, according to the village headman, who said that the grocery had been razed fifteen years earlier to build the school.

As evidence, all of these recognitions, however impressive, suffered from their antiquity—Shanta had died around 1950, which meant that all confirmations of Sunita's statements were based on memories almost thirty years old at the time of the girl's visit. But as far as Shanta's family was concerned, Sunita more than proved her claims, and she began a lifelong relationship with them.

She also became a significant personage in Belgaon. On her first visit there, as she was touring the village she pointed to a vacant spot near the school and asked, "Are you going to build a temple here?" There had been no such plans, but the villagers took her question as a sign, and did eventually erect a temple on that spot.

For our visit, Sunita's family had gathered at her husband's family's home, several hours east of Nagpur. It was on a dirt lane among a series of project-like concrete apartment buildings originally constructed alongside train tracks to house railroad workers. Despite its humble appearance, the comfortably furnished one-story concrete house of Sunita's father-in-law, a homeopathic doctor, bespoke relative affluence.

Sunita's parents had come down for the occasion, as had her twin sister, Anita.

Their father, a man with a warm smile and a quick laugh, told us, "I always said to Anita, 'Your sister told me where she lived. Why don't you tell me where you lived?' but she never said anything."

Stevenson was very interested in cases involving twins, for if they were identical twins, it meant that they had come from the same fertilized egg and had exactly the same genes. Thus, the difference in personality between identicals could not owe anything to genetics. The standard explanation was that the differences could be accounted for by environment, beginning with their different positions in the womb and continuing with independent experiences after birth.

Stevenson didn't buy that. Besides, he argued, there were cases of Siamese twins who, though they remained physically joined and literally incapable of experiences independent of the other, had dramatically contrasting personalities. In one famous instance, one of the Siamese twins was a drunk, the other a teetotaler. Stevenson's implication was obvious: Perhaps some of the extreme differences in personality among identical twins could be explained by reincarnation.

Stevenson had compiled a fair number of twin cases, but he faced a purely practical problem, in that distinguishing identical twins from fraternal twins—who were no more alike genetically than normal siblings—was no simple matter. Apparently, "identical" appearance was no guarantee that twins were genetically identical. To be certain, elaborate blood tests had to be done, and not just on the twins, but on the entire family. In India, this would involve not only considerable expense, but persuading everyone involved to travel to a big-city hospital to give blood samples.

Exploring the idea with Sunita's family was one of Stevenson's major objectives for our visit, but he wanted to save that discussion until the end.

The women served fresh fruit, nuts, dates, and raisins and tea on a polished coffee table. Then Sunita's father gave up his armchair to his daughter, a slight, beautiful woman in a white silk sari embroidered with red flowers and green and gold leaves. My guess was that Anita, similarly attired, was a fraternal twin: She was equally attractive, but her face had a slightly different shape. Even so, Stevenson had said that one in twenty sets of identical twins did not look exactly alike.

The first thing I noticed was that Sunita referred to her father as "my Verni Kotha father," identifying him with the town she was born in, as opposed to her "Belgaon father," who was Shanta's father.

"I think she is more attached to her Belgaon family than to us," the father said, laughing.

Sunita quickly denied it. "I still see them on special occasions," she said in a defensive tone. Evidently Sunita's split allegiance was, at least, a somewhat sensitive topic. "But I don't see them any more than my Verni Kotha parents. Maybe when I was living with them they noticed that I missed my Belgaon parents. If you have two children and one of them's in boarding school and the other one's home, you tend to think of the one in boarding school more because you miss him and he's away, but you see the other one all the time. Now that I've moved out and I'm living in my husband's home, I miss both my Verni Kotha and Belgaon parents equally."

We asked her if she still had any visual memories of her previous life.

"Some things I remember," she said. "I remember playing with my younger sister, for instance, but I think much less about it now. It's like when you want to take a test and you study hard, and then go pass the test and forget about it. I wanted to find my village and see my family and when I got most of the things I wanted I didn't think about it so much."

After the plates were cleared, as a phalanx of reporters and photographers waited for the press conference in the front yard, Stevenson decided to pop the question about blood tests. He said that he would finance the trips to Bombay, which was probably the nearest city where sufficiently sophisticated blood tests were available.

A brief discussion with her parents ensued. Turning back to us, Sunita said, "I'm afraid we're not interested. I'm much more interested in finding out about something else. I remember another previous life, but I don't know the names of the village or my family. Perhaps you could help me recall them."

A couple of years after she had returned from Belgaon, when she was seven or eight, she began to be overcome by vivid images of faces looking down on her with great love. She said that she knew them to be her mother and father, but she couldn't come up with any names.

All she knew was that she was an only child, and her parents were very fond of her. Her house was made of cement, and there was a peepal tree in the yard. She could see the railroad tracks from the terrace of the house and she noticed that the local clay was red, in contrast to the yellow clay in this region. Her family had a cloth shop, not in the house, but just down the lane from the house. The only images she had were of being a child.

Satwant said that she planned to return some months hence and asked if Sunita might at that time be willing to undergo hypnotic regression—a technique Stevenson had tried on some other subjects with spontaneous memories, although thus far without much success.

"Yes," Sunita said. "I'm very interested in finding out more."

Sunita's mother groaned and threw up her hands. It was hard to tell if she was feigning exasperation or really felt it. Here was yet *another* set of parents to occupy her daughter's interest and affection. She looked at Sunita and sighed, "I guess our turn always comes last."

15

Sumitra Doesn't Live Here Anymore

Time and space are relative, and, in India, a little bit of space can take an enormous length of time. We set out early one day for a village named Sharifpura, about seventy-five miles northeast of Agra. On an American interstate, it would have been an hour's drive. Given India's ox-ridden roadways, I imagined that the trip would take at least twice that long, and maybe even longer. But I would never have guessed, and barely believed it when it came to pass, that traveling seventy-five miles by car could possibly take six hours.

During that time, I became keenly aware of how precarious was my position in the front of the Maruti. In one instance, as we made our way east on an unmarked strip of pavement wide enough for a single truck, we were confronted by two trucks and a bus, all jockeying for the lead, swinging out onto the dirt shoulder to pass each other as our fragile aluminum vessel hurtled at them. Everybody beeped their horns passionately, but nobody would yield. At the last minute, our driver pulled onto the shoulder, sending the microbus into a spasm of spine-shuddering bounces. The trucks, too, shuddered as they screamed by. This was by no means an isolated occurrence, for us or others: In the first few hours, we saw the remains of three trucks that had shuddered a little too violently and tumbled down the embankment. No way of knowing if they had taken any hired microbuses with them when they went. Meanwhile, pedestrians, buffalo, dogs, children, bicycles, and scooters all wove in and out of the path of approaching disaster.

All of this was of far more than theoretical concern, too, since we had witnessed the aftermath of the fatal accident outside the police station in Etawah, itself a nearly inconsequential addition to the slaughter on India's roads. In the paper we had brought with us from Delhi, there was this story:

Twenty-two people were killed and fifty-two injured in different road accidents in Rajasthan since last evening. Eleven people were crushed to death and seven injured in a collision between a Jeep and a state bus at Jasolpata. Three persons were killed and twenty-eight hurt when a bus from Haryana met with an accident.... Four people traveling in a Jeep were killed and ten others injured when their vehicle rammed a truck.... Three persons were killed and seven injured in a head-on collision in Udaipur....

And on and on. That was in one State, in one day. Stevenson himself told the story of a recent trip to India during which an associate was bounced off the back of a Jeep on a bad road and knocked unconscious. When he came to, he found that he had been robbed.

I tried not to think about any of it, and especially not the quality of emergency treatment we would be likely to find this deep in the Indian outback. As the hours dragged by, I attempted to keep my mind on the published report of the case we were hoping to revisit. Between 1985 and 1987, Satwant, Stevenson, and a University of Virginia associate named Nicholas McClean-Rice had conducted dozens of interviews in and around Sharifpura. The subject of their interest was a young woman named Sumitra. She had been married at thirteen, in an arranged marriage, as was the custom. When she was eighteen, she had a son. A month or two later, she began to experience trancelike seizures that would last anywhere from a few minutes to an entire day. Twice, the trance gave way to an apparent possession in which Sumitra identified herself as another personality—in one case, a woman who had drowned herself in a well, and, in the other, a man from a distant village. These identities, however, were fleeting.

On July 16, 1985, when Sumitra's son was about six months old, she went into yet another trance, this time predicting that she would die in three days. On July 19, Sumitra lost consciousness. Those around her believed that her pulse and breathing had stopped. The blood drained from her face and her friends and family began to grieve.

According to Sumitra's in-laws, she appeared to be dead for about five minutes, then suddenly revived. Upon regaining consciousness, Sumitra professed to not recognize her surroundings. When people called her by name, she responded, "I'm not Sumitra, I'm Shiva." She said that she, Shiva, had been murdered by her in-laws, who bashed her head in with a brick. She was most agitated when she began to ask about the whereabouts and well-being of Shiva's two small children.

Sumitra, now claiming to be Shiva, made many other statements about Shiva's life and death at the hands of homicidal in-laws. She also refused to answer to the name of Sumitra, and she insisted that she did not recognize her son, her husband, her father, or the woman who had raised her as a child (her mother had died when she was very young).

After some weeks, she began to behave again as a mother to her son and a wife to her husband, but continued to insist that she was Shiva, saying she was only caring for the boy because, as she put it, "If I look after this child, God will take care of my [Shiva's] children." She called her husband's previous relationship with her—as Sumitra—"his first marriage."

Shiva/Sumitra now insisted that she was of a higher social caste than the family she found herself living among. She expressed dismay at the idea that she was expected to relieve herself in the fields rather than in a latrine attached to the house. She dressed in a more sophisticated manner and wore sandals instead of going barefoot.

The most arresting difference reported by the family, though, was a marked improvement in her ability to read and write. Sumitra had never attended school and had attained only a rudimentary literacy. As Shiva, she named two colleges that she claimed to have attended, and satisfied her husband and father-in-law that she could read and write with fluency.

∽

A few months later, a man from a town some forty miles distant who believed his twenty-three-year-old daughter Shiva to have been murdered by her in-laws, heard about the case of Sumitra. He traveled the forty miles or so (which I now knew to be about a three-hour trip) to the village Sumitra lived in to see her. When Sumitra was told that "her father" was outside, she ran weeping to see him and called him by the pet name that Shiva had used for him.

The man asked her what nicknames the family had given Shiva, and she mentioned two names, both of which were correct. She went on to make multiple identifications of people in Shiva's life, both from photographs and in person. Shiva's father tried to fool her by saying things like, "Which of the women in that crowd is your mother?" when Shiva's mother was not in the crowd at all, but inside. According to the father, Sumitra passed all his tests.

The circumstances surrounding the real (or, maybe I should say, the original) Shiva's death were mysterious. In May 1985, Shiva's uncle went to call on her at her in-laws' home, where she lived with her husband, according to Indian custom. Shiva, in tears, told her uncle that her mother-in-law and sister-in-law had beaten her. The uncle thought that Shiva was obviously upset, but did not consider her depressed. The next morning, Shiva's in-laws reported to the uncle that the young woman was dead. They told him that she had disappeared from their house that evening, and when they went to look for her, they found her body on the railroad tracks. They concluded that she had committed suicide by throwing herself in front of a train.

The uncle went to see Shiva's body when it was still lying on the train platform, where it had been moved. He noted that the only visible wound was a head injury, and could not believe that a train could have caused no more damage than the head wound. The uncle asked the family to delay the cremation until Shiva's father could arrive in about four hours. They ignored the request and not only began the cremation at 11 A.M. but sped the process by pouring fuel oil on the wood. By the time Shiva's father arrived, his daughter's body had been reduced to ash and bone.

Shiva's father made a complaint to the local police, who eventually arrested Shiva's husband and his father, mother, and sister for murder. Ultimately, however, they were released for lack of evidence.

Sumitra did not "die" and revive as Shiva until two months after Shiva's death. By then, there had been accounts in the local papers about some of the circumstances of Shiva's life and the murder allegations. Nobody in Sumitra's village admitted to seeing the accounts or having any knowledge of Shiva's case, until well after Sumitra made her claims. Even so, Stevenson's case report points out, it would be impossible to rule out the chance that Sumitra or someone who communicated with her had read the newspaper accounts. But still, many of the accurate statements that Sumitra/Shiva had made about Shiva's life—such as the names of the colleges where Shiva had studied—went beyond the information in the newspaper.

As we drove on and on, interminably, through increasingly remote territory with long, straight stretches of pitted roadway traveled by bicyclists and camels and the odd bus, I recalled that when I first heard a quick outline of this case, I thought it might be a powerful argument *against* reincarnation: The subject and the previous personality coexisted—this was clearly not a case of a soul leaving one human body at death then entering a new one at or before birth.

Of course, it was possible (if somewhat creepy) to argue that here was a special case: Perhaps Sumitra did physically die, and Shiva's soul took over the body before physical decay was irreversible.

But what about the earlier trances and the apparent, brief possessions by other personalities? It was even more difficult to explain the earlier possessions in a way that fit any coherent idea of reincarnation. Nobody suggested that Sumitra had physically died before *those* possessions. Where did those personalities come from, and where did they go? Why were they only temporary?

The situation gets even murkier. From the case report:

In the autumn of 1986 [several months after she initially claimed to be Shiva], Sumitra became confused for a few hours and seemed to resume her ordinary personality. Then the Shiva personality resumed control and was still dominant at the time of our last interview in October 1987.

One of the things that had most affected me in visiting these cases was how thoroughly sane everyone had seemed, a gut feeling confirmed by Erlendur Haraldsson's psychological testing that showed no unusual degree of mental pathology among subjects claiming previous-life memories.

But with Sumitra, you had something that looked almost like mul-

tiple-personality disorder. How could "Shiva" have momentarily regained her Sumitra personality if Sumitra had in fact died? The similarity and consistency of the other cases we had studied, and, in a way,
their simplicity, contributed to the feeling that they could be real, part
of the natural order of things—even if, from the Western perspective,
they seemed *super*natural. By contrast, the account of Sumitra's possessions and personality shifts had a disturbing illogic about it, a taint of
body-snatching.

I wanted to know more about Sumitra's momentary resurgence.
The wording in the case report—"seemed to resume her ordinary personality"—was extremely vague for such an important turn of events.

Three hours had come and gone as I studied, and we seemed no
closer to answers. The problem was partly the quality of the roads—
some long stretches were so potholed that our driver had to slow to a
crawl to avoid leaving an axle behind—and partly the unending string
of towns through which we had to pass. As the towns approached, the
road devolved—the pavement turned to brick, then to mud. And in-
variably, the town centers were seized by unholy gridlock, a mad profusion of humanity, traffic, and shacks and dirt and smoke and tires
and shops selling God-knew-what. I had learned to repeat to myself
like a mantra, "This is just the downtown area, a very busy downtown
area," and I tuned out the dystopian aspect—the sewage, the rotting
animal corpses, the unbreathable air—focusing instead on the profusion of life. Wooden carts with big, rough-hewn wooden wheels lum-
bered along behind somnolent oxen. We saw fewer and fewer cars, and
almost no big trucks, the farther behind we left Agra. At one point,
stalled behind the immense rumps of a small buffalo herd, a red hawk
fell from the sky, plunging into the surging crowd to emerge with a rat,
squealing, in its talons.

Every so often, in the relative peacefulness of the countryside, we
asked the driver to pull over to the side of the road so we could get out
and stretch. The backseat, though marginally safer than the front, was
harder and less ergonomically correct. Stevenson was stoically suffering
from back pain at this point, and the periodic breaks were becoming
increasingly necessary. As we walked in circles and touched our toes,
the bicyclists and donkey carts and camel drivers passed by with curious glances.

At one of these stretch stops, I brought up to Stevenson Sumitra's puzzling reemergence and asked why the account of it was so cryptic.

"Our only source for that was the husband," he said, "and he was not the most reliable witness."

I asked if they had pursued the point with others in the village. If they had, Stevenson didn't remember it clearly. It was frustrating, for much about the case was compelling. Even if you believed a barely literate country woman could have gotten hold of a newspaper that circulated primarily in a town hours distant and thoroughly absorbed the details of Shiva's life, what about all the recognitions attributed to her? What about the accurate statements about Shiva's educational résumé, and her knowledge of the pet names for Shiva, her father, and Shiva's two children—none of which had been covered in the newspaper account?

And what of the sudden reading and writing abilities attributed to Sumitra, abilities that would seem to be totally out of reach of someone of her background and situation?

I asked Satwant if she had observed Sumitra read and write. She had: The girl had been shy about demonstrating her proficiency, but ultimately agreed to give Satwant a writing sample.

"I would say that she was writing at a fourth- or fifth-grade level," Satwant said. "Certainly not a college level. But based on everything we learned about Sumitra before the change, I would have expected at *most* a first-grade-level ability."

"It's odd to think that there would be *some* improvement, but not nearly the improvement you would expect to see from someone instantaneously transformed from semiliterate to college educated," I said.

Stevenson, once again folded into the backseat, said, "Well, it's sort of like a master pianist sitting down to play a broken-down piano. It wouldn't sound the same as if he were playing his own highly tuned piano. You have to allow for the new instrument."

By this juncture, there were no longer any "main roads," only paths through the countryside that occasionally diverged. Stevenson had long since lost confidence in the directions that he had jotted down a decade earlier, so at every opportunity, we stopped to ask the way to Sharifpura. Our efforts met with distressingly inconsistent results. Then we came up short at a point where two logs lay across the road, the gap between them blocked with a rubber tractor tire. A man with a long stick stood beside the logjam. When we stopped, he walked to the driver's open window demanding a "road development" toll. "Highway robbery," I thought. The driver consulted with Satwant, then handed the man a bill. The man, in turn, walked into a shack at the side of the road, from which another man sat behind a wooden table watching us unpleasantly. The man with the stick returned and, incredibly, handed the driver a printed receipt. Then he pushed the tire aside with the stick, and we were on our way.

A few minutes later we finally encountered someone who seemed certain of how to get to Sharifpura. We turned off the road, crossed a rotting wooden bridge over an irrigation canal, and found ourselves driving along a deeply eroded dirt path through lush fields sprinkled with yellow mustard flowers. A half mile up the path, the field disappeared into a vast clay pit where people dug ever deeper, using the clay to cast bricks that they dried in the sun then piled in great stacks—hundreds of thousands of bricks stretching into the distance.

Beyond that, the wheat grew higher, the ruts deeper. The car kept bogging down in the muck, but the driver seemed determined to get us all the way to the village. Instead, he got us all the way stuck in the mud.

It was late, almost two, and we decided to walk the rest of the way and leave the driver to figure out how to get the car back on solid ground. As we stepped out, surrounded by the green fields and the blue sky, the sun beginning to dip down to the west, back the way we had come, it hit me for the first time: However long it took to conduct our interviews, we still had a six-hour trip back to Agra. Six hours to the nearest toilet.

We struck off through the fields, and an odd procession we made. Stevenson, with his sport coat and overstuffed briefcase (which he had refused to relinquish), in the lead, followed by Satwant carrying her bag and her camera, then me, with my backpack slung over one shoulder. A few hundred yards beyond the car, we passed two women hoeing weeds in the wheat row. They stopped to watch us pass.

We turned a corner on the path and Sharifpura appeared. It was like no village I'd ever imagined I would see, made entirely of materials that could be collected close at hand and assembled without machinery—roofs of thatched reed and walls made of a mixture of mud, straw, and dung.

The path through the fields became a meandering road through the village that circled the village well and radiated out to each family's compound. The compounds were encircled by smooth, dun-colored walls on an elevated base of the same mud, straw, and dung material. The exterior wall merged seamlessly with the walls of the shelter, more deserving of the term "house" than the brick lean-tos we had visited in other villages. The thatched roofs, supported by columns made of crooked sapling poles set on a pile of bricks, overhung the walls. The snaking branches of tropical hardwoods spread above the brown thatch of the roofs. Children squatted over clay marbles in the dirt. Cattle lapped water from cisterns.

Now we had attracted a crowd. A couple dozen people followed us up the road as we made our way to Sumitra's family's compound. We ducked under the thatched eave surrounding the outer wall and entered the courtyard through double doors of rough wood, followed by half the village.

Sumitra's mother-in-law, a short woman with graying black hair who wore an orange sari and green turquoise bangles on each wrist, took the invasion with aplomb.

"Sumitra lives in Delhi now," she told Satwant shortly. "She hasn't lived here for seven years."

As we stood in the sun, absorbing this news—a twelve-hour trip for nothing—Satwant asked for Sumitra's address in the city.

"I don't have it," the mother said. "I haven't heard from her."

"I don't think she's telling us the truth," Satwant confided. I tried to study the woman without being obvious about it. She frowned and worked a bangle on her left wrist. Meanwhile, onlookers continued to arrive and the large courtyard was filling up. Then, the crowd parted to let in a small boy. People pointed at him, and someone said something to Satwant.

"They're saying that's Sumitra's son," Satwant translated. "And they say that after she became Shiva, she had another child with her husband, a girl, and that she's in the village, too."

This was suspicious, to say the least. Sumitra and her husband had left two children to go to Delhi, and the children had never heard another word from either of them?

"I don't believe this," Satwant said, echoing my thought. "She's not telling us for some reason."

Satwant turned back to the mother-in-law.

"Maybe your husband could tell us," she said.

"My husband wouldn't know anything that I don't know."

I felt the crowd closing in. I scanned the faces, but the mood was hard to read. Fifty, maybe sixty people crowded around us. I thought about the car stuck in the mud. I thought about the pile of bricks stacked just outside the wall.

The mother-in-law said something harshly. Satwant translated: "She says, 'You keep coming back. Why do you keep coming back? We've answered all the questions.'"

Then she pointed at Satwant's camera and continued in the same harsh tone. I thought she might be complaining that they'd promised to send photographs on their last visit and failed to send them, but it turned out they had gotten photographs and now wanted more.

"Should I offer to take a group picture?" I asked.

"I think that might help soften her up a bit," Satwant said.

When the offer was made, the woman's demeanor changed. She said that she wanted to wait until her husband got home, then went into the house to arrange herself. A few minutes later, Sumitra's father-in-law emerged from the crowd by the front door. He was a gray, leathery-skinned man. He and his wife lined up for pictures with Sumitra's son between them.

Afterward, Stevenson decided that we might as well ask some questions, and so did manage to ascertain that Sumitra had maintained her claim to be Shiva, at least until she left the village. Otherwise, however, the effort produced mostly chaos. Everybody responded at once, and then laughed at the responses, then argued about the laughing. One man, sitting up close and shouting the loudest, trying to monopolize the discussion, reeked of liquor.

At one point Satwant said of him, "This man's really scaring me, I think we should leave."

"Is he saying anything threatening?" I asked.

"No, but he's obviously really drunk and he's just scaring me."

We were asking generally if anyone had any clues to Sumitra's whereabouts. One man in the back shouted, "Maybe if you spent three thousand or four thousand rupees you could find her address in Delhi."

"Are you saying that you know her address and you're willing to sell it to us?" Satwant asked.

The man quickly backed down. "Oh, no, no, no. We're not saying that. We're just saying that it costs so much going to Delhi that you'd end up spending three thousand or four thousand rupees."

But I knew that he had meant more than that. Here we came with our cameras and our new clothes and our car and driver, and these villagers had to be thinking, They're spending so much money. Why don't they give a fraction of it to us? That was the reality, and I could feel the tension it created. They were denying that they were asking for money, but there was nevertheless an underlying resentment.

Satwant believed that Sumitra/Shiva was right there, hiding in the hut. To check her theory, she asked the mother-in-law if she could go inside with her and speak to her alone.

"Why?" the woman asked. "What do you want to go in the hut for?"

∽

I began to think it was time to make a graceful exit, but Stevenson kept saying, "Let's ask them one more question."

We were there for an hour.

When we finally left, the entire village followed us into the fields, walking all the way to the car, hemming us in tightly, jostling us as we navigated the treacherous muddy ruts. Stevenson slipped or was bumped and fell into the high wheat. I helped him up, and we limped the rest of the way.

The driver had gotten some men to help him push the car out of the mud, and now it was turned in the right direction and a hundred yards back, on higher ground. We left to waves and shouted good-byes.

When we bumped back onto the paved road, Satwant said, "I have real reservations about that case."

I thought I knew what she meant. The most interesting piece of new information to come out of our interview was the fact that Sumitra and her husband had moved for about a year to Delhi once before, when Sumitra was eighteen, just before her trances began.

It wasn't much, but the timing was suggestive. Maybe Sumitra had liked her life in the city; maybe she had had a chance to improve her reading and writing while she was there. The prospect of returning to her husband's isolated village might have set off acute depression.

When she heard of the murder of an upper-caste girl of about her age in a nearby town, she fastened on it as an alternative personality, a way out of her newly circumscribed life. The trances might have been real—a function of a nervous breakdown.

Shiva's father, motivated by his desire for revenge against the in-laws, might have seized on Sumitra's claims because they supported his belief that the in-laws were guilty of murder. His testimony regarding Sumitra/Shiva's feats of identification could all be tainted by that ulterior motive.

Once again, though, a tidy little argument explaining away the evidence had to get a little untidy at the end. Shiva's father, for instance, was far from the only source confirming Sumitra's numerous recognitions. If this was a conspiracy to make Sumitra look believable, Shiva's entire family—plus several of Shiva's friends and acquaintances—had collaborated in the fabrication.

We took a different route back to Agra, but despite newer roads and fewer towns, it proved no faster. The final hours found us in pitch blackness, the stars dimmed to nothing by the smoke from cooking fires, the world invisible outside the windows save for the headlights of trucks and buses thundering toward us through the haze. I began to feel that we were tempting fate—time after time, we'd go bouncing off the road to avoid a truck only to come up on a nearly invisible cart or scooter, forcing us to swerve violently to avoid a collision. Between the grim focus of our work and the twelve hours of driving, a mood had invaded the car. I missed my family. In India, unlike Lebanon, there had been no ready e-mail access, and aside from a few hurried phone calls in the international phone booths on noisy street corners, I hadn't communicated with them at all. I felt the distance—*half a planet*—keenly and I knew that whatever genuine dangers I faced were amplified by my isolation and the threat it implied. I tried to quiet my thoughts and get a true measure of my feelings: Did the *possibility* of reincarnation give any comfort at all in the face of these morbid thoughts? The answer came to me: I don't want another life, I want *this* one.

Stevenson began to talk about a lecture that he was scheduled to give in Virginia to a convention of scientists interested in subjects on the fringes of mainstream investigation. What are the irreducible elements of science? was the question he planned to explore.

Basically, he said, he wanted to pare away some of the conventional expectations. One thing was repeatability, the idea that you have to have an experiment that can be repeated at will. He felt that he suffered in his peers' opinions because his studies concerned a spontaneous phenomenon that couldn't be re-created in the lab. "You can't re-create a meteor impact or a volcanic explosion," he said. "That doesn't mean you can't do meaningful research on them."

"But there *is* a kind of repeatability in your research," I countered. "Any investigator could go back and interview the same people you interviewed, cross-examine them, recheck the relevant documents. Of course . . . they might want to think twice before going all the way to Sharifpura."

I couldn't see if I raised a smile in the dark. After a minute of silence, he continued.

"Predictability is another one," he said. In traditional science, to be valid, a theory must give rise to predictions that can then be put to an experimental test. Stevenson, for instance, had predicted that the man who claimed to be a Turkish bandit would have a mark on the top of his head to go with the mark under his chin, and he had been correct. But that was the exception. Stevenson couldn't predict the flight pattern of a soul, or which child would begin remembering the life of which dead neighbor. Did that mean that his work was invalid?

Again, I thought that he might be overlooking a point. "But you *can* make predictions, and I think they are pretty powerful ones," I said. "You can predict that a serious survey in any of the places where you now have cases will turn up new ones. You can predict that when investigators interview subjects and witnesses in those cases, they will find evidence that children made correct statements about a person's life that cannot be shown to have been learned in any normal way."

Stevenson ticked through some other points. Falsifiability, for instance—the idea that for a theory to be valid, there must be, at least potentially, some way to prove it is false. Some critics would ask, "How can you prove someone *wasn't* reincarnated?"

But I don't think Stevenson was asking for that. All anyone had to prove in order to get him to pack up and go home was that reincarnation was not the most plausible explanation for what he had observed.

I talked around that for a long time, but when I was finished, he seemed just as gloomy as ever. I was foolish to expect otherwise. He was closing in on 3,000 cases, in which key features asserted themselves over and over again. He had been at this for almost four decades, and, in all that time, he had barely registered on the scale of mainstream science. Now, he knew, his time was about up.

"There's an old aphorism," he said heavily. " 'Science changes one funeral at a time.' There is a powerful conservatism among the scientific establishment. You don't persuade people with your evidence. They have to pretty much die off for new ideas to come to the fore."

I thought about that in silence as a new set of high beams began to wax in the night, taking aim.

Then he asked me straight out: "Why is it people can't accept this evidence?"

People? Why can't *people* accept it? Or me? Was he asking me to declare one way or the other?

I replied cautiously. "Well, it certainly makes reincarnation appear possible, but is it likely? We don't know what a soul is. We don't know by what mechanism a soul could leave one body and enter another. There's so much that just isn't known, and I think that's the problem."

"But what other explanation is there for what we've seen? I've gone through every other possibility, and by elimination reincarnation must be what explains this."

Something in me felt a little desperate. I wanted to stall. "Well," I said, "I think it certainly . . . reincarnation certainly is one reasonable explanation for what we've seen. But I'm not absolutely convinced that there isn't some subtle combination of cultural force and ESP that might create some of these cases, between some kind of extrasensory perception and some cultural cueing and unconscious storytelling. . . . Maybe some basic human need is being expressed by a collective unconscious here, and the force of this collective unconscious is creating these cases somehow. . . ."

But as I listened to myself talk, I thought, God, does that *really* sound likely?

My head ached from thinking about it. I was learning what Stevenson had learned years ago, that the perfect case always seemed to be beckoning from around the corner—but then, when you made the turn, you just ran into more questions. It felt as though some force hovered above us, seeding these cases with just enough compelling evidence to make them impossible to dismiss, but never quite enough for any one of them to be proven beyond doubt.

Still, the logical gymnastics required to explain "normally" any single case were enough to give pause. And going through those same gyrations in case after case after case.... Pretty soon, reincarnation began to seem like a less fantastic alternative. If I accepted even *one* of the cases as genuine, I had to accept many, if not most of them. If reincarnation were possible, even once, then it instantly became a far simpler explanation for Shiva, the milkman, and the others than was the strained chain of conspiracy and coincidence that I had to cook up to explain them all away.

And I asked myself clearly, for the first time: Given all that I'd seen and heard, why couldn't I simply accept reincarnation as real?

There was something stopping me, some factor I could sense but not quite grasp.

Part IV:

The United States
Children Next Door

16

A Land Called Dixie

When I returned to the States and recounted my experiences, I often heard the same refrain: Why aren't there any cases *here?*

But I also found that before long, instead of listening, a surprising number of the people I spoke to were telling me stories about their own children or children they'd heard about that seemed to them suggestive of previous-life memories.

Most of the stories were fragmentary and vague and didn't add up to much more than evidence that children were fascinating creatures. One woman told me her daughter used to say, "I remember when I was in the sky," while another said that when her teenage daughter was not yet two, the little girl stood at the top of the stairs looking down on her reflectively for a few moments, then said, "I'm glad I chose you."

I remembered my own daughter's utter horror of hula hoops, of all things. She'd encounter one in a toy closet and scream bloody murder. Past-life phobia? Or inexplicable quirk of a developing brain?

More to the point, my son used to preface certain observations by saying, "When I was a daddy . . ." A few days after I got home from overseas, I asked him if he remembered saying that.

"I was just little then," he told me. "I didn't know how to say it right. I meant when I *become* a daddy."

I suppose that I could have seen that as an example of how a child becomes conditioned by our society to disregard and censor possible past-life memories. But like most of the things I heard, the original statement was so fragmentary, it didn't bear much examination.

Still, a few stories went further. A neighbor who taught nursery school said that she once had a little girl in her class who was always talking about when she lived in Virginia, going on at great length about it. One day, my neighbor asked the girl's mother how young the child had been when they came to Florida from Virginia. The mom looked puzzled. "We never lived in Virginia," she said.

A woman who once worked as a nanny told me that a child she had cared for had told a long tale that began, "Before I was me I lived in San Francisco and my best friend's name was Bonnie and we drove in a van and got killed."

There was no way to know what I would find if I could track down these children and question their parents. Maybe the child who talked about living in Virginia had enough other memories to pinpoint a time and a place. And the girl who talked about dying in San Francisco in a van with her best friend Bonnie had already come a long way toward permitting the identification of a possible previous personality. If I looked through San Francisco traffic fatalities for five to ten years before the girl was born, I might be able to find a Bonnie who died with at least one other woman in a van accident.

Of course, my friend didn't even remember the girl's name, or if Bonnie was really the name of the friend whom the child claimed to remember dying in a van with.

I was telling these stories to my friend Gene Weingarten, a *Washington Post* writer and editor and one of the most skeptical individuals I have ever known, the kind of guy who would rather feed his hand into a meat grinder than admit to believing in paranormal phenomena. Gene let me finish. Then he said, "You remember that story about Arlene's brother, right?"

Arlene, Gene's wife, had been raised in Connecticut, the daughter of multigenerational Northeasterners. However, as soon as her younger brother, Jim, could speak, he would say, "I was born in Dixie."

No, his parents, would correct him, you were born in Bridgeport, Connecticut. But Jim would insist: "I was born in Dixie."

"It wasn't just that he kept saying it," Arlene told me when I asked her about it. "It was that word—*Dixie*. We didn't know anybody who used that word. Who would use that word in Connecticut in the 1960s?"

I asked her whether she or her parents ever thought that it might have anything to do with a previous-life memory.

"Are you kidding?" she said. "We just figured it was more evidence that he was a weird kid."

Then the family took their first road trip south, to Florida.

Arlene only had a foggy memory of the trip, but thought that her mother would probably remember it clearly. I called her mom, Phyllis Reidy, who now lives just up the Florida coast from Miami.

"I remember we had a real load—my husband, my mother-in-law, the two kids, and myself in our red station wagon," she recalled. "There was no interstate in those days, of course, so we drove all the way down old U.S. 301. Arlene was nine and Jim was six. One of the first things Jim had ever said was, 'I'm from Dixie.' He said it all the time. And he spoke oddly, too. We always said it sounded like he had some kind of accent. We used to ask him if he was from Boston, and he said, 'No, I'm from Dixie.'

"We may have said something like, 'What do you mean you're from Dixie?' But it never really went any further than that. We didn't question kids in those days.

"Then, when we drove into the South, he got all excited, started talking a mile a minute about how his grandmother and grandfather came from Dixie and his mother and father did, too, and I said, '*We're* your mother and father,' and he said, 'No, you're not,' just flatly, like that.

"We were in Georgia, just south of the South Carolina line, and he really started going nuts. 'I'll show you where we used to live,' he said. 'There it is! It's way up there, up that hill and in back of those trees.' "

"Did he describe the house?" I asked.

"It was an 'old house' was all he said."

"Did you pull off the highway to go look?"

"We couldn't be bothered," she said. "After that trip, he never talked about being from Dixie again. The accent lasted about two weeks after we got home, then it disappeared."

"We were just glad he shut up about it," Arlene laughed when I retold her mom's version of the story.

Although Phyllis said that she didn't think Jim would even remember the incident, I got his number and called him. Jim Reidy is now a television engineer living in Massachusetts.

"I don't remember much more than my mother told you," he said at first.

"Do you just remember it as a story your family told about you?" I asked. "Or do you remember having actual memories from before your trip into Georgia?"

"I remember I could describe the house," he said. "I could always picture that house—the porch swing, the weeping willow, the picket fence. I also remember my parents."

"You mean your and Arlene's parents?"

"No, I mean my parents in that house. Their faces are blurry, but I remember they were aristocratic, people of influence. And I was the baby, spoiled rotten. Everyone fussed over me. That's all I remember."

"What did you make of all that?" I asked. "Did you think maybe you had been reincarnated?"

"Not really," he answered. "We were Irish Catholics, and reincarnation didn't really fit into that picture. But it got me to thinking, maybe there were parallel universes, or some such thing."

One thing for sure, I thought: Checking this out any further couldn't have been more difficult even if it had involved another dimension. I suppose that I could drag Jim down old U.S. 301 into Georgia and see if he recognized the house. But in the unlikely event that it had survived, and the even more unlikely event that he pointed it out again, then what? All he remembered was that at some point an aristocratic couple with an only child had lived in a house with a porch swing and a weeping willow. In the pre-1960s South, that was pretty much standard fare.

Practically speaking, the whole thing amounted to little more than an amusing anecdote, but still, I couldn't stop thinking about it. Here was a family who not only didn't believe in reincarnation—they never even considered it. And they certainly had never heard of Stevenson or any of his case studies, which hadn't even been conducted when this took place. Yet, except for the lack of any family interest whatsoever, the case's form was identical to the Lebanese cases. With his first sentences, a child asserts that he is not from "here," but from somewhere else. These aren't his parents, his parents grew up in Dixie, like their parents before them. *I'll show you where we used to live . . .*

It certainly began to answer the question, "Why aren't there any cases here?"

There *are*. If I just came across these by chatting with people I know, what would a systematic search turn up?

Even Stevenson hasn't systematically searched for American past-life cases. But, through referrals, and people calling when they see mention of his work in the media, he has collected more than a hundred nontribal American cases of children making statements about previous lives, and has investigated a number of them in depth.

As a group, the children have fewer specific memories than the children we saw in Lebanon and India. They don't tend to talk about places or personal names as much, or at all, making identification of a specific previous personality unlikely. In fact, the only American cases Stevenson has found in which children have said enough to clearly identify a previous personality and provided verifiable statements about their lives were "same-family cases," as in a little boy claiming to remember the life of his grandfather.

However, regardless of how compelling the facts of such same-family cases might be, they had two built-in weaknesses. One, a clear motivation—grief and the desire for the return of a loved family member—existed for parents to unconsciously manufacture such a case. And, two, obvious normal ways existed for a child to learn enough about a dead family member to fabricate specific "memories" of that person's life.

While we were sitting in the Paris airport waiting for our flight to India, Stevenson had told me about a same-family case that he was investigating in Chicago. The mother, a waitress at Dunkin' Donuts, had a tragic experience with her first child—a boy who died at three of invasive cancer. He had had a tumor in the right side of his head and another in his left eye, and one of his legs was crippled. Before his death, he had learned to walk with the aid of crutches. But he soon relapsed to the point where he had to be hospitalized, then quickly slipped away.

The mother was devastated and continued to mourn even after having two more children. When she gave birth to her fourth child, a boy, she became convinced that he was her first son reborn. The child had birthmarks and defects that matched the dead child's problem areas: a nodule on the head at the tumor site, a left-eye defect where the first boy had had another tumor, a defect in his leg that would make him walk with a limp, and a birthmark on the chest at the location where doctors had inserted a feeding tube into the first son as he was dying. This birthmark had even oozed once.

The problem with the case was that the mother's prolonged and profound grief for her dead child created an overwhelming possibility that the case was more wish-fulfilling fantasy than evidence of reincarnation. Any correspondences between birthmarks or defects and the first son's illness could be a coincidence, a coincidence that triggered her belief that her first son had been reborn. And the brevity of the first child's life, coupled with the mother's passionate desire to believe, would make any later statements by the child about alleged previous-life memories almost totally worthless as evidence.

I knew that even the best conceivable same-family case would still have the built-in weakness of the child being surrounded since birth by potential sources of information about his alleged previous life. Still, I wanted to see one up close. For one thing, this type of case made up a large percentage of Stevenson's American collection.

Stevenson had mentioned that he had just such a case very close to home, in Charlottesville. Soon after returning from India, I flew up to meet him. At my request, he had contacted the family and they had agreed to talk with me.

"I don't mind going back for another visit anyway," Stevenson told me. "I've got a few things I want to double-check."

So, one morning, we drove together into the picturesque rolling hills south of Charlottesville, just east of the Blue Ridge Mountains. The case involved a boy, now nine, whose family believed that he remembered the life of an uncle who had died as a teenager in a tractor accident twenty years before the boy was born.

The family agreed to meet with me on the condition that I not identify them by their full name or precise location. They lived in a tiny trailer-sized home on a small plateau nestled among fabulously beautiful wooded hills.

"Everything you can see is our land," the boy's aunt said as I stood on the front stoop, craning my neck. She was the eldest sister of the dead uncle. A tiny woman, no more than four feet tall, she worked as a guidance counselor in a local school. Her much larger baby sister, Jennifer, was the boy's mother. She greeted us in the dark living room where the boy, Joseph, was flopped in a big armchair. He barely glanced at us as we came in, then quickly returned his attention to Saturday-morning cartoon shows. He was chubby, like his mom, a round-faced kid with bowl-cut sand-colored hair and the vulnerable look of someone other children might pick on. His aunt later remarked that his schoolmates derisively called him "farm boy" for living so far out in the countryside.

"The funny thing is, none of those kids would know a city if one rolled over 'em." She chuckled, shaking her head.

The uncle, a high school dropout named David, had died when a tractor he was driving rolled over, crushing his chest. Joseph had been born with severe asthma, his mother said. It kept him out of school quite a bit.

"My parents were all but destroyed by David's death," the aunt said. "Nobody talked about it. And certainly nobody mentioned him in casual conversation by the time Joseph here was born. So there really wasn't any way he could have heard any of this stuff."

"This stuff" was a series of statements that Joseph had made, which seemed to fit his uncle's life. He had pretty much always called his grandmother "Mom," and mostly referred to his mother by her name, she said, but nobody thought too much of it—after all, she and Jennifer both called Joseph's grandmother "Mom" as well—until Joseph began to say other things.

"One time, he was sitting on the sidewalk at my folks' house just staring up at the roof and we was watching," his mother said. "He called my mom and he said, 'Hey, Mom, do you remember when Papa and I got up there and painted that roof red for you and it got all over my feet and legs? Boy, wasn't you mad!'

"Mom said, 'Joseph?' He didn't answer. She said, 'My God, Jenny, that was David talking to me just now. Because David painted the roof and got into one mess, got more paint on him than on the roof.'

"The thing was, we painted that roof red in 1962, and since then it's been green.

"Then we were going by Route 11 and he said, 'When I was growing up, there was no houses there. There used to be all woods we went hunting in.' And another time we were going by the Farm Bureau and he said, 'I remember that used to be a cornfield. I used to help pick corn with a guy named Garth Clark and Stanley Floyd.'

"I said, 'Oh, really?' and he said, 'Yeah, and we got into an argument over a pair of work boots.'"

We asked if she knew the names, if they had indeed been men David had known.

"I don't know the names," she said. "But there's lots of folks named Clark and Floyd in this county."

Joseph made other similar statements from time to time, his aunt said, but he always spoke of them as if he didn't distinguish those "memories" from his own life. "He said to me, 'When are we going to play with the sheets on the clothesline like we used to?' When we were kids, David and I used to play with the sheets on the clothesline. But we haven't hung any sheets on a clothesline for twelve to thirteen years. We dry sheets in a dryer, like everyone else."

He never told anyone that his name was David, or said anything like "I was your brother and now I'm your son," Jennifer said. Once, though, when she showed him a picture of David in a family album, he said, "That looks just like me."

"David looked absolutely nothing like Joseph," Jennifer said.

As Stevenson went over some questions that he had concerning an earlier interview, I read through that session's transcript. When I got to one particular section, I very nearly said "Uh-oh" aloud—it was about Joseph's "spirit friend" named Michael.

For years, Jennifer said, Joseph had had an imaginary friend named Michael. She could hear her son talking and saying Michael's name when he was alone in his room. He even bought toys for Michael, and when he added to his own collection of hats, he got one for Michael too, "so they wouldn't fight over them."

"I think it's funny if I get in an argument with Michael and I throw my car, it just goes right through him," Joseph once told his mother.

"He thinks I can see him," she said.

Could she?

"Sometimes the hair stands up on your back or something, or a cold wind goes by you. Once he took my little niece Jamie to play with Michael and she came back saying, 'I don't like playing with Michael. They're mean to me.'"

She also said that sometimes the dog growled when Joseph said Michael was around. Michael hadn't been around for a while. "He got mad at me and left," Joseph said.

Joseph had never given Michael a last name or mentioned any connection with his dead uncle. But his mother said that once, when they were driving past a cemetery, Joseph said, "Let's stop and look for Michael's grave. It's somewhere with an American flag on it."

Lots of children had imaginary playmates, and people believe in all sorts of things—just because Joseph was one of those children, and his mother at least entertained the idea that Michael might be something other than a child's imagination, didn't necessarily make their reporting about Joseph's statements concerning his dead uncle's life less reliable.

But as Stevenson had said once before, I sure wouldn't want to take this one to court.

As we were about to leave, we asked if there was anything else they could remember that Joseph had said or done.

"Oh, I'm sure there were lots of things," his aunt said. "But we never wrote them down or anything."

Then, as we were walking out the door, she was saying something about tying Joseph's shoes when Jennifer piped up. "There's something I forgot! When he was little, he used to insist on us buying shoes a ton too big for him. He'd say, 'Mom, I know what size I wear, a size eight.' It was a real pain. He wouldn't drop it. We actually had to buy him a pair and take it home and make him wear it to prove to him it was way too big."

"What was David's shoe size?" I asked.

But I already knew the answer.

17

The Edge of Science

That week in Charlottesville was a busy one for Stevenson, for it coincided with the annual conference of the Society for Scientific Exploration, of which Stevenson was a founding member. Stevenson had spoken of it in Lebanon and again in India; he had great hope that the group might serve to combat the isolation of parapsychological study, and help bring those like himself working on the fringes of accepted science closer to the mainstream.

I didn't think it any coincidence that the meeting was on Stevenson's home turf: He was an eminence in this group, spoken of reverentially by its members. Earlier in the week, he had given the equivalent of the conference's keynote address. He spoke then on a subject that we'd discussed into the night on the way back from our uncomfortable encounter in Sharifpura, arguing that the kind of field research we'd undertaken was valid science, even though it didn't meet all of the standards of the lab.

I did not hear the speech, but read it as it was printed in the conference program, which I found tucked into a manila envelope that was waiting for me at my hotel's reception desk. It was expressed in his usual formal language, but, even so, its conclusion compressed into three sentences forty years of sometimes frustrating experience, as well as his fervent hope for the future. "Difficulties arise when reported observations seem to conflict with 'facts' that the majority of scientists accept as established and immutable," he wrote. "Scientists tend to reject conflicting observations. . . . Nevertheless, the history of science shows that new observations and theories can eventually prevail."

Stevenson was so much in demand that he even called on me to sub for him in his weekly 8 A.M. tennis game at a nearby sports club. (Given Stevenson's astonishing stamina during our travels, I wasn't surprised to discover that his regular partners—who ranged in age from late forties to late seventies, Stevenson being the oldest—played a respectable brand of doubles.)

Him being so busy, I was left with plenty of time to wander the campus—it was just across the street from my hotel—and drop in at some of the conference lectures.

This was my first opportunity to explore one of the most spectacular campuses in the country, and it was a wonderful time to do so, as summer had made a premature late-May arrival. The trees were in full leaf, and the afternoon temperatures pushed into the high eighties. The University of Virginia is a monument to the genius of Thomas Jefferson; an idealized version of an idealized moment in time. The grand domes, lush walled gardens, and tree-shaded lawns that stretched lazily along promenades of red brick and white columns cast a powerful spell. I could feel Jefferson's stalwart optimism, his unlimited confidence in the mind of man. At the dawn of the nineteenth century, when the campus was built, the universe seemed to be rapidly yielding its secrets to science. Soon, it must have seemed, there would be no mysteries left. All of Creation would be as orderly, serene, and well tended as this campus.

It had been more than a year since I had first visited Stevenson here. Since then, I had found myself compulsively reading books on things like quantum theory and research in biochemistry and artificial intelligence. It was the kind of nearly impenetrable stuff that had always stood on the border of my awareness, a marker for the dark and craggy frontier between modern science and my understanding.

What little I knew of that frontier I had gathered obliquely, in the form of a vague sense that the advance of science had been more spectacular than even Jefferson could have dreamed, but ultimately less satisfying. Certainly, I knew, not all the mysteries had been plumbed after all.

I had no better understanding of the specifics than most people did. But now I had a reason to explore that border, a need to understand if there was anything out there that might somehow shed light, however indirect, on what I was seeing.

When I walked out of high school physics, I knew that even electrons and the particles that made up an atom's nucleus weren't the "basic building blocks of matter" that physicists had always been hunting for. And I also had an inkling that once you got into the world of matter at the subatomic level, things got pretty squirrelly. Stuff stopped acting in a way that connected with human experience.

What I didn't fathom was that the whole science of the subatomic world was based on mystery. Physicists trying to observe these particles discovered that they couldn't say where a particle was if they were measuring its momentum, and they couldn't say how fast it was moving if they knew its location. That didn't mean that they weren't skilled or knowledgeable enough to do it—it meant that it was literally impossible. Particles simply didn't occupy space or move through it in a way that was definable in any familiar, quantifiable sense. And while the very essence of these particles was entirely different from anything ever seen before, there was something even stranger going on, too: These particles came in pairs, and if one of a pair was separated from the other, interactions involving one would still have an effect on the other. The question became, How?

Some scientists thought that there had to be some physical cause, some kind of extraordinarily fast message that was delivered from one particle to the other. The problem with that, though, was that the particles were too far apart for any physical phenomenon to cross the space between them quickly enough to deliver the message—the velocity would have had to exceed the speed of light, which is impossible.

That left an inexplicable synchronicity, a phenomenon for which there was no known, definable reason or identifiable mechanism. To this circumstance physicists assigned the perfectly inelegant but perfectly apt term "nonlocal cause."

I also discovered that the tenet that I learned in high school, that "matter can neither be created nor destroyed," had been an early casualty in the campaign to get to the root of all things. It turned out that matter was just another form of energy, and that energy itself was a little difficult to pigeonhole, as it could exist, or at least its potential could exist, in absolute nothingness. Literally, out of nowhere, *something* could pop into existence; energy and matter could be created from the void—and vanish back into it again.

All of the borders of what we thought of as reality were less well defined than we imagined.

Even time itself was far from the unchanging frame that most people counted on. My vague understanding of Albert Einstein's discovery of relativity hadn't prepared me for the degree to which time depended on where, and under what conditions, it was observed. Both gravity and velocity literally changed the shape of time and space.

It was hard to say which seemed stranger—time moving more slowly on the peak of Mount Everest than at its base, or the idea that time was just another coordinate—a fourth dimension—in the overall reality of a universe where past, present, and future are simply different aspects.

In some sense, now, then, and what is to come might exist—to use a word really only appropriate to a three-dimensional world—simultaneously. And that's the problem; our language isn't set up to deal with four-dimensional reality, and neither is our experience, because our experience is absolutely wedded to *sequence,* to the idea that one time—the present—exists and all others are remembered or imagined.

What would it be like to see the world in four dimensions?

It seemed impossible to conceive, but a metaphor occurred to me that helped give me at least a gut sense of it: I imagined that all I could experience was two-dimensional space. In that two-dimensional existence, a dot appears out of nowhere, then spreads outward in a larger and larger circle, until it suddenly vanishes.

In reality, however—that is to say, in three-dimensional space—the phenomenon would not suddenly appear and disappear, or change in any way. It would just be a cone, at rest in a three-dimensional space. But a two-dimensional creature moving through three-dimensional space on a flat plane would have no choice but to see the cone only in terms of two dimensions, and in terms of sequence: a ripple spreading from a single point. I would not be able to imagine what a cone was, much less that it existed *before* I moved through it and remained after I had left it behind.

Maybe all of these strange phenomena that science had uncovered, and some it hadn't yet acknowledged, presented a similar "cone effect." Maybe they all only appeared puzzling to three-dimensional creatures doomed to drift through four-dimensional space seeing only the shadows of things outside of their spheres of awareness.

And who were "we" anyway? Geneticists, biologists, and computer scientists had been beating each other up for decades trying to be the first to create, or, failing that, to duplicate—or, failing either, merely to *define*—consciousness. None of them had even glimpsed a solution.

Which left us . . . where? In a state of paralyzing awe?

That's not a final destination that would have pleased Jefferson. That dissatisfaction, it seemed to me, at least partially explained the gathering at the far end of Jefferson's lovely, lazy lawn. The Society for Scientific Exploration was a very loosely conjoined federation of scientists who saw a gap between what mainstream science had failed to explain and the scientific orthodoxy that tended to brand certain ideas as too radical to discuss.

Not all of the society's members were proposing radically contrary ideas, as Stevenson was. In fact, some were debunkers above anything else. But all were at least interested in trying to apply a scientific approach to subjects sneered at by the mainstream, things like the evidence, or lack of it, for the existence of UFOs, life after death, ESP, psychic healing, or even the mechanism that accounts for the fact that women living together tend to have synchronized menstrual periods.

To say that this produced a mixed bag of speakers and attendees was a desperate understatement. Topics ranged from the sober—"A center to test the efficacy of selected complementary and alternative therapies in reducing pain and distress in selected patient populations"—to the delirious—"The heart is not a pressure pump forcing inanimate blood to flow as water is forced to flow in pipes. Quite the contrary . . . its propulsion system derives from three sources: self-propulsion, momentum . . . and by far the most important, the herein discovered force of cosmic levity . . . obscured for 300 years by the false theorized concept of Borelli and Newton."

The force of cosmic levity?

Some of the attendees weren't scientists at all, but borderline paranoid cases looking to fuel the inner voices that whispered of unspeakable conspiracies afoot to keep them from the truth, whatever that might be. As I entered the auditorium one afternoon, I was cornered by a woman smoldering with barely supressed rage. "You're a journalist," she said. "Tell me why all the newspapers are suppressing the *real* photographs from the Mars expedition."

I knew instantly what was bugging her: The pictures that showed the "face of God" formation on the Martian surface to be nothing more than a pile of rocks.

"Anyone can see that the first photo—the one that clearly shows a face—is much higher resolution than the supposedly superior photos the newspapers ran after the flyby. Somebody got old, bad-quality photos and substituted them for the real ones," she went on, gaining momentum. "Either that, or they were doctored."

"But why would anyone *want* to hide the truth about that?" I asked.

"That's what I'd like to know," she said, glancing to either side as if she feared we were being watched.

The thing was, this woman was rubbing elbows with some unquestioned intellects. One of the lecturers, a demographer from Johns Hopkins University named David Bishai, had come down to deliver a talk on the migration dynamics that would explain why the population explosion did not *automatically* disprove reincarnation. Bishai himself doesn't believe in reincarnation, but he was watching television one night and saw someone on one of those "scientific mystery" shows saying that not enough humans had ever lived to supply a sufficient number of souls for today's population.

"It was just obviously wrong," Bishai said. First of all, he pointed out, the best estimates of the number of humans who have ever died far exceeded the number now living. But even if that were not true, he continued, it wouldn't matter. He drew a diagram on the blackboard in the front of the auditorium, showing a line dividing two hypothetical states, A and B. A was the world we knew, into which people immigrated through birth and out of which they emigrated through death.

"Let's start with the assumption that humans come from we know not where and go to we know not where, a place we'll call State B. I think we can all agree on that."

From the auditorium, a series of ascending semicircular rows of seats, a voice rose up in protest: "But you're assuming they all come from and go to the same place."

Bishai turned from where he was writing on the blackboard and squinted up into the audience.

"Okay," he said. "We *can't* all agree on that. But let's just say that *wherever* they come from or go to, we'll lump it all together and call it State B."

His point: Even assuming that no "new souls" could be created, State B could have possibly begun with an enormous number of souls. As the population of living humans increased in State A, the population decreased in State B, but there could still be a tremendous reserve, which might allow for unlimited population growth here in State A.

He was right. It *was* obvious. I remembered my discussion months earlier with Ricardo, the Christian ecologist, on the terrace overlooking downtown Beirut. He'd thrown up his hands when, at a world-population conference, his Druse colleague refused to acknowledge the population explosion as evidence against reincarnation. I wondered what Ricardo would have thought of David Bishai.

∽

I hadn't come to see Bishai—he just happened to be speaking when I arrived. I wanted to catch Jim Tucker, a thirty-nine-year-old child psychiatrist who had begun working with Stevenson five years earlier. Stevenson spoke highly of Tucker, and though he wouldn't say so, I wondered if, to some degree, he thought of Tucker as a potential successor.

Tucker was to speak about cases he had studied in Southeast Asia, in Burma and Thailand, that involved the custom of marking the body of a dead relative with charcoal or some other substance in the belief that when the deceased's soul was reincarnated, the infant's body would bear a birthmark in the same location.

A thin, dark-haired man with sharp features and a gentle presenting style, Tucker showed some impressive slides comparing charcoal marks on a corpse with a child's birthmarks—they looked almost identical. And he pointed out something of particular interest to me: In "experimental birthmark cases," as he called them, same-family cases could actually be more compelling than cases involving strangers. As he explained, the odds against a family finding a birthmark on a child in the same spot as a mark made on a corpse might not be that great if they could include in their search *any* child known to them—after all, they might then have hundreds of babies to choose among—but the odds against the corresponding birthmark showing up on a child in the immediate family were astronomical.

And yet that was what seemed to have happened in many of the cases that Tucker had investigated.

I noted that Tucker had the same, calm detachment that Stevenson had charmed me with the first time I met him. Tucker, too, spoke in a quiet voice that was nonetheless perfectly audible in the large auditorium.

"There are several possible explanations for this phenomenon," he said. "One is that birthmarks correspond to experimental marks purely by coincidence, or in conjunction with faulty memory by the marker. Another interpretation is the one of maternal impression—that is, that the mother's expectation of having a baby born with a birthmark influences the creation of just such a mark. The third explanation is that some of the cases represent a reincarnation of the previous personality."

After the lecture, I found Tucker in the lobby and introduced myself. I asked him how he had gotten involved in this kind of research.

"Until five years ago, I never gave reincarnation a second thought," he said, but he had run across Stevenson's books and become interested. The coincidence that Stevenson also lived and worked in Charlottesville registered, of course, but Tucker may never have acted on his interest if he hadn't happened to read a report in the local newspaper about a study of near-death experiences in cardiac patients that Stevenson's division was conducting. He called and volunteered to help evaluate medical records that would show whether the patients were or were not near death when they had their experiences. Once he began coming to division research luncheons he became increasingly interested in the research on children who claim to remember previous lives.

Tucker asked me if I had read the skeptical criticisms of Stevenson's research. I told him that I had, and was unimpressed by most of them.

"Of all the arguments," I said, "the one that still seems to me to carry the most weight is the fact that Alzheimer's patients lose every aspect of their personality—their memories, their abilities, their temperaments. And it all disintegrates in direct correspondence to the physical deterioration of their brains. The question is, if partial destruction of the brain destroys all the aspects of a person that might be reincarnated, how can we imagine that anything can survive total destruction of the brain?"

"There's a standard response," Tucker replied. "And I think it's a good one: It's like a radio. If you smash the radio, it's not going to be playing any music. But that doesn't mean the radio waves have disappeared. It just means there's nothing to receive them.

"The skeptics would respond, 'Where does the radio signal come from?' You might as well ask, 'What happens inside a black hole? What came before the Big Bang?'"

I ran into Tucker one other time before I left town. We had another long talk, at the end of which he expressed a frustration that I had long suspected Stevenson felt as well.

"I wish we could move on to attempting to understand the mechanisms behind these cases," he said, "instead of constantly trying to establish this as a legitimate phenomenon."

"The problem is," I said, "if you start talking about how the soul migrates before you know what a soul is and before people accept that that's what your cases prove, you just look silly."

He nodded with a weary look. This was not the first time that that thought had occurred to him.

∾

My turn to participate in the SSE conference came in its closing session: I was one of five panelists in a discussion on how the media covered science. We each had prepared a ten-minute set piece on some related topic, but we soon discovered that the real reason for our being there was to allow conferees to vent an immense bitterness about the way "alternative" scientists were dismissed, or even abused, by journalists. The panel consisted of three reporters—from the local TV and radio stations and the Charlottesville newspaper—and another friend of mine from *The Washington Post,* a writer named Joel Achenbach. I had been invited largely because the man organizing the conference knew that I was writing a book about Stevenson, and I suggested that he invite Joel, who was writing a book, as Joel said, "about aliens."

Joel, one of the smartest people I knew, had worked for me at the *Herald* doing a column called "Why Things Are," which explained science to the masses, with attitude. He told me that his book, among other things, debunked the idea that alien life had ever visited Earth, via UFOs or otherwise. In so doing, though, he was also talking about how science worked, and defending the very conservatism and rigidity that some at the conference decried.

I had thought that this would make him a natural for the SSE panel, and I was right. Joel not only stole the show, but managed to nearly incite a riot by insisting that the scientific mainstream was mainstream for a reason: It made sense, it didn't go off the deep end or jump to conclusions or engage in conspiracies to suppress truth. It simply insisted that things be proven in scientifically rigorous ways that can be repeated and potentially disproven in objective experiments.

For this he was denounced roundly by an orator in the audience, a man who insisted that Joel was deluded to think that mainstream science was anything other than an orthodoxy aimed at the suppression of contrary ideas, and he a tool of that oppression. The man said that he himself had helped to prove the effectiveness of cold fusion—nothing less than a potential source for unlimited, free, clean energy. And yet his advances were being ignored because the mainstream held that cold fusion was impossible and journalists like Joel slavishly believed what the mainstream dictated.

"If he really has discovered how to make cold fusion work," Joel said afterward, "I don't think he'd *need* anyone to believe him. He could just light up Washington with a bottle of water, and call it a day."

It was nearly dusk then, and we were driving into the lush hills outside Charlottesville in my rental car, swooping around luxurious curves cast in green shadow, spiraling through the woods toward Monticello, Jefferson's design showplace of a home. In addition to working together for years, Joel and I had briefly been roommates, when I first came to Miami and Joel was fresh out of Princeton. That was years ago, but something about cruising around aimlessly brought those days back strongly.

"So what's the deal with your guy Stevenson?" Joel asked.

I told him about what I'd seen in Lebanon and India as well as in the last couple of days in Virginia. I told him that after more than a year and traveling nearly around the world, I couldn't dismiss any of it. Yet, for some reason, I couldn't quite say what I actually believed, either.

He said all the things I expected him to say: How could anyone seriously talk about reincarnation when nobody had the slightest idea what a soul might be, or if such a thing existed at all? And, if souls did exist, how did they occupy a body, or move from one to another? All the things the children seemed to know that seemed to defy explanation? Yes, that was fascinating. But it made a good book, he said, not good science. However unlikely the chain of coincidence and conspiracy would have to be in order to account for these cases normally, that chain of normal occurrences had to be the working theory. In the absence of compelling reasons to believe in souls and soul transfers in and of themselves, a rational person had to choose the unlikely over the unexplained.

"Believe me, I've been thinking all those things," I said. "It's just . . ."

The sun had slipped behind the line of hills to the west. A sweet, humid wind moved through the car. And I knew. Finally, I knew what had been haunting the back of my mind ever since India, maybe even before.

"You want to hear a long story?" I asked.

"Sure."

"When I was fresh out of college—this was the Bicentennial, the summer of 1976—a friend and I decided to drive around the country until our money ran out. A typical *On the Road* fantasy. This trip turned into a marathon conversation. We drove, and we played our cassette tapes, and we talked. Being that we were guys in our early twenties, we talked mostly about women. A theme developed for me before we even got off the East Coast. There were a couple of women in my life, and I realized that I was associating each of the women with a different vision of my future. One was safe, expected, almost a retreat. The other was dangerous, risky, a leap of faith. And as the trip progressed, and we played our tapes over and over, each of those women, and each of those attitudes toward life, came to have a theme song in my mind. The safe retreat was Dylan, 'Shelter from the Storm.' The wild, dangerous one was one of those desperate Springsteen songs from *Born to Run*, 'She's the One.'"

"Two great songs," Joel said.

"Damn straight. And they both had a real hold on me. Both the women and both the songs. And my friend and I talked this stuff inside out and upside down. Talked about it the way it can only be talked about when you're twenty-two, unemployed, and driving down an empty highway an hour before dawn toward a place you've never been before.

"Anyway, as you can imagine, this discussion went on ad nauseum as we headed out west and the spaces got wider and emptier. We visited some people we knew in Phoenix, and then we headed toward LA, which had always been our intended destination. On the way, we were going to stop and hike into the Grand Canyon. But it was already afternoon, and we decided to stop instead in a campground an hour to the south, spend the night, then get to the Canyon early the next morning.

"The campground was just a flat plain nestled at the foot of some hills. There were a few trees around, but it was fairly wide open. A dirt path headed in from the road for maybe half a mile, with three loops of primitive campsites coming off it—no water or electricity, just a bare dirt spot for a tent, a picnic table, and a fire ring. There was nobody there. We were completely alone.

"We drove past the first two camping areas and took the furthest spot on the last circle, set up camp, made a fire, and decided to hike up one of the hills. It was late afternoon by this time, and as we climbed higher, it got darker. We started talking about The Dilemma again, and it was really starting to drive me crazy. 'Which woman?' quickly became 'which life?' and the more we talked, the more crucial it seemed to figure out which was the 'right' decision. Everything seemed to reflect the basic choice. Was taking the bold course, doing the unexpected, courageous, or just foolish? Would it lead to glory or doom? Was doing the safe thing solid and reasonable, or cowardly, the first step into a life of tedium and regret?

"And it began to reflect in more immediate decisions. Should we go on to LA as we'd planned? Or turn around and plunge into Mexico, which to us was terra incognita? Should we head back to Florida and look for jobs, as we'd always assumed we would? Or just stay out West, settle down in Phoenix, and start completely fresh—no money, no contacts, nothing but untapped potential?

"You get the idea. This was *it,* the clear turning point. The indecision, the complete inability to see what was the truth and what was the delusion, was agony to me.

"We walked and talked for hours, and by the time we got back to the campsite it was full night. I was exhausted. My brain literally ached. We were standing there, poking the fire with sticks, and my friend said, 'Maybe we should just get back in the car right now and head for Mexico.'

"The idea really appealed to me. It was bold, impulsive, adventurous. But then I started thinking how tired I was, how we'd probably end up pulling off the side of the road in the middle of nowhere and sleeping in the car, feeling stupid that we'd left this nice empty campground and given up seeing the Grand Canyon.

"My head was going to explode. I screamed, 'Wait a minute! That's the same decision as all the rest.' Suddenly I could see how I'd been chasing my tail for hours, if not weeks. 'I'm not doing this anymore,' I said. 'I'm just going to wait for a sign.'

"Instantly, the ache in my head vanished. I felt a bottomless silence wash over me, and we stood there in the dark, listening to the hiss of the fire.

"Absolutely no more than sixty seconds later, we heard the faraway sound of a car engine moving through the night. It faded, then got louder. Then we saw the sweep of headlights through the trees. The headlights would disappear and then appear again as the road rose and dipped. Finally, we could see that it was a van, coming down the dirt path. Remember, the campground was utterly deserted. But the van passed by the first circle, then the second, then it turned in to ours and came around all the way to the end, stopping at the very next site."

Joel jumped in his seat and slapped the dashboard. "Oh, shit," he said. "This better not be the Springsteen song."

"The side door of the van slid open," I went on, "and the sound slapped us, the wailing voice, the grinding guitars, the pounding keyboard. Springsteen. 'She's the One.'"

"Oh, *shit!*" Joel said again.

"It played through the first three-quarters of the song, then it got to the point where he sings, 'And you try just one more time to break on through . . .'—then it just stopped, with that little electronic rip, like someone punched the off button. The lights went out, the door slammed shut, and it was just us again. Perfect silence. We never heard another sound. Not voices. Not rustling. Nothing."

Joel laughed.

"My friend and I just looked at each other. Then I said, 'It's funny—you ask for a sign and you get one. A big, garish, blinking neon sign. And you *still* don't know what it means.'

"My friend said, 'Isn't it obvious?'

"And I knew what he meant. It was *obvious* what he meant: The 'sign' was telling me to take the bold path, go for the dangerous woman, throw caution to the wind. And if someone had just described the scene to me, I would have thought the same thing. But standing there, in the middle of it, I never even considered that. It was instantly clear to me that this inexpressibly absurd coincidence was in no way a practical guide to which set of specific decisions I should make. It was too *weird* for that, at once too immense and too trivial. I had the intense certainty that the universe was laughing at me, at my self-involvement, and the oddest thing happened: The anxiety I felt simply vanished.

"Even though I immediately sensed that the 'sign' wasn't what it seemed, it was years before I came to see it the way I still do. For some reason, I was given this gift, this weird, irrefutable demonstration that there is more to the world than its surface. That whatever we're all about, whatever the universe is, it is far more than just some empty, mechanical, material machine. There is some . . . force out there, something beyond knowing, that we can nonetheless—on some level—feel, and see and interact with. My petty life, and all my personal concerns, in some way connected up with something so big, so far beyond myself, that it could choreograph a little performance like that tailored perfectly to what was going on in the mind of one confused kid.

"I mean, *really*. An empty campground in the middle of nowhere in the middle of the night. And these two kids standing there, discussing everything in terms of two songs over a period of *weeks*, and within sixty seconds of saying, 'I'm going to wait for a sign,' a *van* shows up, plays that one song, nothing more, then shuts up? I would have thought it was some kind of hallucination, except my friend was right there—I have a witness! And the next morning at dawn, we were finally just getting to sleep when we hear the van door open, the tape player crank up, the last bar of the song blare out, then the door slams shut and the van roars down the road."

We had been driving for a long time now. We should have seen Monticello minutes ago. Clearly, I had taken a wrong turn somewhere, zigged where I should have zagged, and we were way out in the Virginia countryside. I did a U-turn in the middle of the road and headed back the way we had come.

"There's no question that's a great story," Joel said. "And I don't personally question that it happened exactly as you remember it. But I don't think that there is some magic cutoff where an unlikely event then translates into 'evidence' of some entirely new phenomenon. What's the phenomenon, exactly? How could your brain or feelings cause the van, and the driver, to pull up? Give me a theory behind the event and then some way to test it.

"What you have is a very unusual event and no theory to explain it other than that there is some kind of larger phenomenon that connects the minds of human beings with physical realities. Implicit is that if other people are trying to decide who to go out with, it might cause you to drive up in a van and play a certain Springsteen song. I don't personally feel that I am under some kind of controlling force emanating from other people's brains. The easiest solution to the situation, if you ask me, is to say that although it was a one-in-a-zillion situation, it did not require any strange phenomena to happen—it only required that someone drive up in a van near where you were sitting, and put on Springsteen. And that's what someone just happened to do, unrelated to your situation. That's my guess.

"The problem with the paranormal is that by definition it tends to be so far outside the norm as to be theoretically unmeasurable. So you can't disprove that it's there—you can't prove or disprove. So I can't rule out the possibility that there was some connection between your thoughts and the van pulling up. I just don't think it's likely."

Now I laughed.

"That's it," I said. "That's the connection between this and those reincarnation cases. I knew there was a connection, and I just couldn't quite make it: *The argument is exactly the same.* I have a set of events that seem impossible to explain in any normal way. I have testimony, and a corroborating witness. You say, 'There's no way to do an experiment to prove or disprove.' I say it would definitely be worth looking for other cases where witnesses allege similar events, and try to establish how likely it is that they can be explained by fraud or delusion. It just so happens that in my own case, I don't have to wonder if the witnesses are reliable, if they're kidding themselves, or flat-out lying. Anyone else might have to wonder about that, but I don't, because I *know* it happened.

"So, then, the question becomes, Okay, it happened, but what does it mean? You say, 'Maybe it's a coincidence.' Fine, but I'm willing to say flat out, *no way*. No way that was completely unconnected to what was happening in my life. Just as now I'm willing to say flat out that there is no way all those kids and all those families and all the other witnesses are simply lying or deluded or wrong. Those kids knew stuff they shouldn't have known. I'm accepting that.

"But in my case, even though I accepted that what happened at the campground wasn't a coincidence, I didn't accept what seemed like the obvious explanation for the sign's meaning. It just felt wrong.

"And I think it's the same thing with saying, 'These kids know what they know because they are reincarnated.' That seems too simplistic to me. Too linear. It's assuming we know things we don't know, like what 'time' is, for instance, or 'personal identity.'

"So I think I'm reaching the same conclusion I reached the first time, that these children are less important for what they say about the specifics of what happens after we die, than for what they say about how the world works—that it's mysterious, that there are larger forces at work, that—in some way—we're all connected by forces beyond our understanding, but definitely not irrelevant to our lives."

Finally, Monticello's iron gate appeared before us. Closed and locked. I looked at my watch. We had time to return, go for a run, and still make the convention's closing banquet. As I headed back toward campus, Joel, as usual, had the last word.

"I'm not arguing with that as a personal insight," he said. "Just don't think it's science."

Only later did I think of a retort: If it's not science, maybe it should be.

18

Chrysalis

"You must be lucky, like me," Stevenson had written just before I flew up to Charlottesville. "I have spoken with the mother in the case I told you about on the phone. She has agreed to talk to you. Unfortunately, because of previous commitments, I will not be able to accompany you."

I did feel lucky. This would be the last family I interviewed, and it filled a gap of sorts. It was an American case in which the life the child remembered was that of a stranger. And not only that, but there also was a chance that it might be the first nonfamily American case where the previous personality could be identified.

In fact, it was eerily similar to the story Arlene Weingarten had told me about her brother Jim, the boy from "Dixie": A young boy in Virginia had been obsessed with cowboy boots and blue jeans from a very early age. He refused to wear anything else, and constantly talked about "his" farm. One day his mother was driving with him out in the country, and he started yelling, "That's my farm."

So far, the parents had made no attempt to verify that statement.

I drove about two hours out of Charlottesville to a new suburban development just off the interstate. It was one of those places where the design of everything from mailboxes to roof shingles was specified by the owners' association, and an overgrown lawn was considered high treason. A construction pit had been landscaped into a "scenic" duck pond; hardwood saplings grew in every yard and were just beginning to cast some shade. Even though the gimmickry was always apparent, the large two-story houses built around winding lanes did manage to lend something of a New England village feel to what had, until very recently, been hardscrabble Southern farm country.

It felt odd pulling the rental Ford into a driveway in the middle of such a familiar 1990s-America setting knowing that in a few minutes I'd be asking the kinds of questions I'd been asking in the stone houses of the Shouf mountains and the mud huts of Uttar Pradesh.

Debbie Lentz was thirty-five, a fresh-faced redhead with the informal, no-BS directness and flat intonation of the California girl that she was. She and her husband owned two health spas in town, a business that Debbie had built through the sheer force of her own will. She had been an aerobics instructor at a spa that went out of business overnight, leaving her out thousands in unpaid salary and commissions, and sticking dozens of her clients with worthless memberships. Her choice was to get locked out of the building, or to persuade her clients to pay again for what had already been stolen from them. She sold $35,000 worth of new memberships in two weeks, and she never looked back. Now she owned that building and another one like it, and had become something of a pillar of the business community. (It was mainly for that reason that she didn't want to go public with her real name, which is not Debbie Lentz.)

"You'd have to know the people I deal with," she told me as we sat at her kitchen table, looking through sliding-glass doors at a garden she had pledged to beautify in the coming year. "They would think all of this was flaky."

Debbie herself had never thought much about reincarnation or other New Age spiritual obsessions. She counted herself among those millions of Americans who moved comfortably in the secular world and didn't give much thought to spiritual matters beyond a general sense that "good things happen to good people."

Still, she'd had a hard road to get to the point where she was comfortable with the idea that she was a good person, and that good things happened to her. Her father, a young writer who had worked with Rod Serling, died of a heart attack when she was three. Her mother remarried a man who turned out to be an abusive drunk who disliked children.

When I asked her whether she ever had an intuitive sense, one way or another, that personality survived death, she said this:

"There were so many times when I lay awake at night in my bed crying out with all my heart for my father. And all I felt was this nauseating emptiness inside, this absolute sense that he was not there."

Then, eleven years ago, after she'd married and moved east, she discovered that she had cancer: two tumors in her right groin.

"The radiation therapy destroyed the ovary on the right side," she said. "The left ovary was saved, but two years later I had a real bad pregnancy and my doctor panicked and took out the left ovary because there was blood everywhere. So when I woke up and he told me that, I knew I could no longer have children, because I knew my right one was not working."

Blood tests confirmed that she was no longer producing estrogen. She was in menopause at twenty-four. The doctors put her on estrogen-replacement therapy.

Debbie had gotten us both tall glasses of ice water. ("You can't drink too much water," she chirped, ever the fitness coach, as she slid the glass toward me.) Robert, her five-year-old, came in from outside.

I had seen him in the side yard as I came in, riding around in circles on a multicolored Hot Wheels trike. I noticed, too, that he was wearing shorts, not blue jeans. But he did wear big, black rubber boots that kept slipping on the trike's pedals. Now he marched up to the kitchen table, a cute blond with blue eyes and a serious expression.

"Mom, I'm bored," he announced.

"I'm having a conversation," she told him. "Go get a game, or watch Nickelodeon. We'll go to the dollar store this afternoon."

"But Mom!" Robert started, then stomped off to do as his mother said.

"This is the first time that we've had him in shorts," Debbie said. "He refused to wear anything but blue jeans. He would only wear cowboy boots from the time he could speak. He told me that's what he wanted, cowboy boots, and that was all there was to it up to about a year ago. He wouldn't be caught in any other shoe. He wore his cowboy boots with his bathing suit to the pool."

"Hey, Robert," I called across the room. "How come you like cowboy boots so much?"

He was lying on his stomach in front of the TV, lazily kicking his leg on the floor. He didn't look up. "I just like 'em," he said.

Debbie sat down opposite me and picked up where she had left off. "I was on estrogen for five, six years, and I just wasn't feeling good,

so I went to my oncologist and he thought I was sick again with another tumor because of my symptoms—really tired, really sluggish, my
hair was falling out, I was hot and cold and real sensitive to the
weather. So he was getting ready to perform a lot of tests and I left the
doctor's office and just out of the blue I thought: I'm pregnant. It was
just the oddest thing. I went and got one of those tests and it was positive. I called the doctor and went back up there and he did a blood test
and he said, 'Debbie, it's the same test that we utilize to find a tumor
and it'll come up positive because there's a tumor. You're not pregnant.'
And I said, 'Yeah, I am.' So I left and went to my obstetrician the next
morning and they did an ultrasound. I was pregnant."

A mixed blessing, her doctor told her. "She said my chances of my
reproductive system coming back and producing a healthy baby after
the menopause and the radiation treatments I'd had were one in a million. Those were literally the numbers.

"But the real fight was my oncologist didn't want me going through
a pregnancy because he thought it might bring to life dormant cancer
cells. It was this real catch-22, and they kind of argued back and forth.
So then they said I needed this test, I needed that test. And they'd keep
calling me with all these new ideas about what deformity the baby
might have. And I just said to my husband, 'You know, there's a greater
plan at work here. There's a reason. It doesn't matter if he doesn't have
legs, if he doesn't have eyes, it doesn't matter to me. So why go through
all these tests?'

"The obstetrician wanted to do a fetal scan at five months, and I
said, well, that'd be fine. So they did the fetal scan and he was perfect.
There was nothing wrong with him. He was sitting there sucking his
thumb and he had all his fingers and toes. You could see everything. So
then they said, 'Well, he'll probably have Down's syndrome.' "

He didn't. In fact, he seemed unusually bright.

"We were at the grocery store one night, and it was really cold in
there, and his dad was holding him and he looked at me and he said,
'Cold.' And I'm: 'Oh my God, that kid is six months old.' "

Robert spoke in complete sentences at twelve months.

"He just always seemed to understand what we said to him," she
said. "Like, we never had to teach him 'around,' 'beside,' 'in front of,'
'behind'—he knew what those meant from the day he was born. A little
crawling baby and you'd say, 'Behind you,' and he'd turn right around."

Now Robert was back with a board game in his hands. "How do you play Chutes and Ladders?" he asked.

"Why don't you take it out and see if you can figure it out," Debbie suggested. Robert flung himself back in front of the TV and began to unfold the game board.

"What was the first time where you thought he might be talking about a previous life?" I asked.

"It began as a joke. My husband and I would be out in public and Robert would always be talking about, 'My farm,' and people would say, 'Oh, you live on a farm,' and we'd say, 'No, that was in his previous life.' So we would joke about it—literally joke about it."

Robert was about two then. The Lentzes lived about a half hour to the north of their present home in an older suburban area. "There were some farms around, but Robert never had a reaction to them. It was always 'at my farm.'

"The older he got, the more his vocabulary improved, the more he'd say. At three, we learned that he smoked at age thirteen in the shed. That came up out of the blue: 'Mama, on my farm, when I was thirteen we were smoking.' But it hit me. Ever since he could walk, he would pick up a stick, he would pick up a pencil, he would pick up anything, and pretend to smoke. Neither my husband nor I smoke. We won't even be around smoke. And at day care he's not around it at all.

"What else would he talk about? He'd talk about tractors, he'd talk about farm things, working on the farm, waking up on the farm, cows . . . There were always cows on his farm. Oh, and he said that a shed had been blown down in a storm.

"Not too long ago, maybe this past winter, he and I were sitting there watching TV and my husband made a fire and it got real quiet and all of a sudden he said, 'My mom used to stand by the fire when she was pregnant.' And he said, 'Mama, let me show you.' And he went over and he stood there and he said, 'She would rub her tummy and it would be real big and she'd stand and warm herself on the fire.' And then we'd ask him, 'How many children did she have?' And he'd say, 'Six.'

"At one point, the lady who takes care of him out of her home said, 'Debbie, what is with this farm?' And I said, 'Has he talked to you about it?' because I'm not gonna tell anybody much about anything because I don't have a clue what's really going on. So we sat down for about an hour and our notes were identical. He had a mother who 'left him' and he had a mean sister, and a green tractor, and a black pickup truck. Everything was identical. And that's what's so interesting. You can talk to kids and the story changes all the time, but when you have one story since birth that never changed, it was almost incredible."

Sometimes, though, when Robert was telling her about his farm, his voice would change. "You could hear it. He'd get like a sing-song voice. And that's when the make-believe would come in. The story would start getting a little crazy, like, 'There was a Ferris wheel at my farm.' You knew when it was over."

We had been talking now for more than an hour. So far, I'd found what she'd been telling me fascinating. But it underscored the power of what Stevenson had shown me overseas: children behaving very much like Robert, but making statements that were far more specific, statements which later proved to be true about a stranger's life. It was that corroboration that changed everything, that made all this odd behavior demand some explanation beyond a dismissive "they're kids."

Before I'd been to Beirut and India, that's how I would have explained what Debbie was telling me: an evocative tale of how mysterious kids could be and how they can't always distinguish between reality and fantasy. And I would also have guessed that Debbie was kidding herself, thinking that she could hear a difference in Robert's tone when he began talking about something ludicrous like a Ferris wheel on his farm. I would have figured it all of a piece, just another bit of evidence that the whole thing had grown out of a lively imagination.

I looked at things differently now, however—I'd seen what I'd seen, and I had no choice but to take all this somewhat more seriously.

There were other things about Robert that seemed highly unusual, Debbie said. For instance, from the time he could talk, he had a precocious interest in motorcycles.

"We'd be driving down the road and hear a motorcycle coming up behind us and he'd say, 'Mom, that's a Harley.' And it would be. That's the amazing thing: He could tell a Harley from a Suzuki. I have no idea how. And he loved the black leather outfits, the long hair, the earrings, the tattoos. Once, we were out someplace, and Robert just couldn't keep his eyes off a man behind me. The man was covered in tattoos, head to toe, and Robert said, 'Oh, Mama, that is great . . . Look at that man!'

"And the man heard him, and I turned around and the man starts laughing and says, 'Oh, man, is that a mother's worst nightmare or what?' "

"Anything else about Robert that seems out of place like that?"

"Well, we don't eat meat, but when he was at his baby-sitter's one night, she barbecued a steak. He was nine, ten months old and he couldn't get enough of it."

"Did you ever ask him what his name was when he lived on the farm?" I asked.

"Yeah, I never got that. He'd say something about the farm, and then it was over with. He wouldn't answer questions about it. He was not interested in discussing it with you. He was *telling* you."

In November 1995, Debbie said, she and her husband bought the house where we now sat. "We lived here for about six months or so, and we would go all the way to 301 every time we had to go to the grocery store. And my husband said, 'You know, there has got to be a quicker way.' So, one day, we decided that we would take a right at this road before you got to the highway and see if that got us there. As soon as we veered to the right, Robert, who was three then, was in the backseat going nuts, screaming and yelling, 'My farm, this is to my farm, Mama, this is it, this is where it's at!' It made your hair stand on end.

"So we drove, and I said, 'Honey, I don't see any farm. There's your elementary school where you're going to go when you go to big school.' And he said, 'No, no, I know it's here, I know it's here, I know it's here.' We had never been down this road, my husband and I, nor him, and we kept past the elementary school and my gosh, in the fork of the road is a farm, and he's just ballistic. 'This is it!' But he'd always talked about a shed on his farm, and I said, 'Well, honey, there's a farm here but there's no shed that you've talked about.' He goes, 'Keep going, Dad! Keep going, on the side . . .' We drove past the house, and looked to the right, and there's this old big shed on the side. And he pointed and said, 'See, I told you. See, Mama?' When we passed the house, a white brick house right in the fork of the road, we saw cows grazing."

A few months later, someone gave Debbie a book by a woman named Carol Bowman who believed that her own children had recalled past lives during hypnotic regression. I'd seen the book early on in my research and found the children's hypnotic recall typical of other hypnosis-inspired past-life "memories" that I'd read about: The children were allegedly recalling lives from several generations in the past, but providing no details that couldn't easily have been gleaned from a romance novel or made-for-TV movie.

Given what she'd been through, though, the book hit a chord with Debbie. She contacted Bowman, who wrote to Stevenson. Stevenson and his young associate, Jim Tucker, interviewed Debbie and began to look into the brick house that had sent Robert into a frenzy.

Stevenson found some interesting material. The house had been owned by the same family since 1962, and the man who had bought the house had died in November 1992, just four months before Robert was born. The obituary in the newspaper said that he had been eighty-two, and described him as a "Realtor and farmer."

Apparently, the surviving family members still lived there.

"Robert doesn't get excited when we go by there anymore. He doesn't say much about it now. And I haven't gone, 'cause—" She stopped abruptly. I had the feeling that she had never really put the reason why she hadn't gone into words, not even to herself. "—'Cause . . . what do you say?"

I asked her what she believed about Robert's memories now.

"I don't really know what to believe," she said, then thought of something else. "There's another story. One of the moms at Robert's day care has a daughter, Ashley, almost two years old. She has a heart murmur and she has a scar over her heart—what looks like a scar. She was born with it. She's never had anything happen to her heart; there's no reason for the scar.

"Ashley does not talk, she's almost twenty-four months and she doesn't talk. But she's afraid of certain men who look alike—dark hair. There's a phobia there."

"Is there anything about Robert that makes you wonder if it's related to a previous life?"

"The thing I talked to Carol Bowman about, the thing that made me want to pursue this, was his tempers. They seemed to not be normal. If something doesn't immediately go his way, he might throw a tantrum, which a lot of kids do, but he would say things like 'I hate my life.' Just things of great magnitude. When he gets on a tirade, you can't reach him. When he was a baby, I remember, I would just hold him and hold him until he couldn't squirm anymore. But I always had this feeling that these tempers were of such a great nature for such a little child. Carol and I thought possibly it might be related to his memories, that his mean sister might have done things to him, that something had happened to him."

Then there were the tattoos and the motorcycles. "Maybe he had hung with the wrong group, whatever. Maybe this man was depressive. Who knows?"

The phone rang: Robert's baby-sitter.

"She's willing to talk to you, if you want," Debbie said.

I got directions. The sitter lived a half hour away on the other side of town. As I gathered my stuff together, I remembered something that I hadn't asked Debbie.

"Does Robert have any birthmarks?"

"You know," Debbie said, "Dr. Stevenson asked me that, and I said no. But I'd forgotten the ones on his head. Robert has one here"—she pointed just above the hairline slightly to the right on top of her head—"and here." She moved her finger back to the crown of her head, just to the left of center.

"I always knew they were there. They were there when he was born. And he was bald for two years. But I just had remembered it when we were at the pool the other day. His hair's still so thin that when it got wet you could see his scalp. And the thought just came over me: I wonder if this old man has old pictures, if he had lost his hair, if he had any marks on his head. And that's far-fetched, I have no clue, but it would be interesting, and I think I need to tell Dr. Stevenson.

"Robert, come here for a second, honey," she called. Robert came and stood by his mother, who parted his hair to reveal a small raised mole near the front of his head, and a larger, darker one on the crown.

"Actually, this one kind of bothers me," she said, gently fingering the large one. "I was going to take him to the doctor. It's too dark. It really gets a lot of sun when he swims and I've been having skin cancer taken off me every three months . . ."

Just before noon, I left to drive across town through heavy traffic to the baby-sitter's house. I'd been at Debbie Lentz's house all morning, but everything felt incomplete. I wasn't accustomed to hearing only one side of a case, being deprived of an interview with the previous personality's family to see how much, or how little, of what a child had said corresponded to an actual life.

While I tried to keep my mind on the complicated set of directions I'd been given, I really only wanted to turn around and say, "Let's go to the house."

But Debbie had been unable to go herself, and I wasn't sure it would be right to push her to do it. With every second, I was moving away at fifty-five miles per hour. I'd talk to the baby-sitter, go back to Charlottesville, and never know what would have happened if we had knocked on that door.

Of course, I missed the exit, and had to circle back. When I arrived at the house, a small, split-level clapboard home in a working-class neighborhood, I knocked on the sliding-glass door on the lower level. Inside, I could see a garage that had been converted into a nursery, and a half dozen small children were running around. The sitter, a blond woman named Donna, came to the door and said, "Tom? Debbie just left a message for you to call her."

There was no answer at her home number. "She must have taken Robert to the store," I surmised.

"I've got her cell-phone number," Donna said.

Debbie picked up on the third ring.

"You left a notebook," she said. "I didn't know how important it was."

"You going to be back in about an hour?" I asked.

"I can be."

"Okay. I'll come pick it up then."

I hesitated.

"Debbie?"

"Yeah?"

"You feel like knocking on the door?"

I think she'd been waiting for me to ask.

"Will you do the talking?"

"Sure, if you want."

"Let's do it, then."

～

The baby-sitter repeated the whole story, of how Robert had kept talking about his farm, how she'd asked Debbie about it, how they'd compared notes and found that he'd told them the same things. I talked to her for a half hour, then headed back across town. I arrived to a problem: Robert was waiting for the older boys who lived across the street to get home from school so he could play with them. He didn't want to go anywhere.

"We're going to go see your farm," Debbie said, coaxing him.

Suddenly, Robert transformed, and it was just as Debbie had described. He started stomping his foot and screaming in an anguished voice, "No! I want to play with the boys! This is so STUPID! I HATE you! Why are we doing this? I hate you! I hate you! This is STUPID! STUPID! STUPID!"

Still, we climbed into Debbie's sports truck and took off, Robert screaming in the back. Debbie just kept talking to him, calmly and firmly. When he quieted for a minute, I used the opening to ask what he had gotten at the dollar store. And he told me, just like nothing had happened—the anger was gone as abruptly as it had come.

The white brick house at the fork in the road was barely a mile away. As we rode past the perimeter, I could see the outbuildings that Debbie had taken to be sheds. I looked over at Robert, who was sitting quietly now. He leaned forward and said, "We had a Ferris wheel here."

I looked at Debbie. She didn't seem to have heard. She gripped the wheel tightly. "I'm real nervous," she said.

We pulled into a tree-shaded drive, stopping in a large open area in front of the house. A little girl who had been swinging on an elaborate play set in the yard ran toward the house. I wondered if the old man's wife had moved, or if this might be a granddaughter.

"Is your mother here?" I asked the girl.

She stopped and turned to face us, confused. "No, no," she said. "I'm here for day care."

A young woman emerged from the house.

"Do you live here?" I asked.

"With my mom and my grandmother," she said. "My mom takes care of these kids. She takes in children for day care."

"Would it be all right if we talked to your mom?"

She walked up the steps and pulled open the screen door. "Mom! Some folks are here to see you."

A sweet-faced woman in her mid-forties, pear-shaped, appeared in the door. "Come on in," she said with an Old South Virginia drawl. "My name is Lynn."

I walked into the foyer, cool and dark after the bright sun outside. Doors on three sides led into the rest of the house. The kitchen was straight ahead; it was large and looked well used. Debbie followed right behind me, and I noticed Robert clinging tightly to her back.

I hadn't given any thought to how I would broach the topic. I could feel Debbie's eyes on me.

"This little boy is absolutely convinced he once lived here," I said.

Lynn looked puzzled. "Oh, honey," she said. "That's impossible. We've lived here for years and years."

"The thing is," Debbie added, "he thinks he had a previous life here."

Lynn's mouth opened slightly, mouthing an "oh!," but I could see her repress her surprise. She looked at Debbie with a combination of skepticism and sympathy.

"Well, sweetheart," she began. "I don't think so. I always listen to what kids have to say, but my daddy had this place for years and years. I think he's had it for thirty-five to forty years."

"The boy keeps talking about the farm he had," I explained. "And he's convinced that this was it."

I could see something like a look of relief in her eyes. "It's never really been a farm since my daddy had it," she said. "He was a Realtor."

"Did your dad have any hobbies, anything he really liked? Robert keeps talking about motorcycles."

"I had a friend who was killed on a motorcycle," she said, shaking her head slowly. "My dad never was fond of 'em." She paused, thinking now.

"He had trucks, though."

"Oh really," I said. "Do you remember any special color?"

"White," she said. "He had white trucks."

I was keeping a mental tally. No farm. No motorcycles. Trucks, but no black truck.

"Was he a smoker?" Debbie asked.

"Oh, yeah. My daddy was a smoker, bless his soul."

"You don't happen to know when he started smoking, do you?"

"Early," she said. "Eighteen? I don't know. In his teens, I reckon."

"Robert mentioned getting in trouble for smoking in the shed when he was thirteen," I said. "You ever hear any story like that?"

She thought for a second. "Well, not about my daddy, but my daddy's brother—he lived in that big house behind us, it was all one property back then—one time when they was teenagers, my daddy and him were walking down to take their clothes to the laundress, this black woman who lived on the property, and he was smoking and he flicked his cigarette and it burnt down the whole laundry, just burnt it down. They got in deep trouble for that, of course."

She thought some more. "We did have some cows. And some pigs. And we grew some soybeans in here, too. He used to load 'em into his truck and take 'em up to the market."

Pigs? Cows? Soybeans? Sounded like a farm to me. And there was the obituary; "Realtor and farmer." And Robert had talked about carrying "grass" from his farm in the back of his truck.

Still, he hadn't given many specifics. He'd said he had six brothers and sisters. Lynn said that there were eight kids in the family, a discrepancy of one. Robert had talked about a shed blowing down in a storm—didn't ring a bell with Lynn. Her dad had never talked about a "mean" sister; he had nothing to do with tattoos. He did wear jeans and cowboy boots, but that wasn't exactly unusual. There was the fact that he'd died just before Robert was born, but so had thousands of other old men on farms, no doubt.

Seems like you have to call this ball out, I was thinking.

And then I remembered something I'd forgotten to ask.

"Did your dad have any marks, any scars on his body?"

"He did have a lot of fibroids that he had to get removed, fibroid tumors. I've been cursed with them, too," Lynn sighed. "I just had to get one removed. We had to get one big one removed from my dad shortly before he died."

She definitely had my attention now.

"Where was it?" I asked.

"Well," she said. She cupped her hand, almost as if she were forming the contours of a growth, then she tilted her head toward us and placed her cupped hand on the crown of her head, slightly to the left of center—exactly where Robert's big mole was.

She looked at me, then at Debbie. She was on the verge of crying.

"My father was a wonderful man," she said, her voice constricted. "He died when he was eighty-seven. Almost six years ago now, and look at me. I still tear up talking about him. He was the sweetest man, just so kind to women. If he ever saw a pregnant woman he was just so kind to her. He'd ask, 'Can I get you anything, darling?'

"When I was pregnant with mine, he was always asking, 'Can I get you a pizza?'"

She laughed, tears starting to run down her cheek. She patted her round belly. "I guess I still have that much of my daddy," she said.

She turned to Debbie.

"If there's any part of my father in your boy, I'd just be so grateful," she said.

From the darkness through the door on the right, a herd of children rumbled toward us, then past, leaving swirling trails of laughter as the screen door hissed closed behind them. Outside, the swings squealed to life amid shouts and murmurs. Lynn bent toward Robert. "You want to go out and play with the other children?" she asked. Robert's face was buried in his mother's back. He was sobbing violently.

Debbie tried to turn to him, but he clung desperately. "What's wrong, Robert?"

Lynn crouched down.

"Now don't cry, sweetheart," she said. "You should never be ashamed of anything you say. You can tell me anything you want. I always want to hear it. I always tell people I'm coming back as a butterfly. I swear I believe it. When I come back, I'll be flapping my beautiful wings."

Back in the car, Robert was quiet again.

"Why did you cry back there?" I asked him.

"I dunno," he said. "I just did."

"Did you think it was interesting, talking to that lady?"

His eyes widened, and he nodded, with big, emphatic nods.

When we arrived back at their home, Debbie asked, "Was that lady familiar to you, honey?"

"Yes," Robert replied. He paused and looked up at her. *"Why is that, Mom?"*

Acknowledgments

I will be forever in awe of Dr. Ian Stevenson's courage in allowing a journalist he hardly knew to accompany him on research trips on three continents, permitting scrutiny of his life's work without limit or complaint. His graciousness was reflected in his associates, Dr. Satwant Pasricha in India, Majd Abu-Izzedin in Lebanon, and Dr. Jim Tucker in the United States, as well as in the office staff at the Division of Personality Studies at the University of Virginia, all of whom went far beyond the call of duty to assist me.

I am indebted as well to a number of people who read the work in progress and offered invaluable advice and encouragement, especially Lisa Shroder, Joel Achenbach, David Fisher, Stephen Benz, Bill Rose, and John Dorschner.

I also want to thank Bob Tischenkel, who brought the work of Brian Weiss to my attention and cowrote with me an article on Weiss that appeared in the *Miami Herald*'s Sunday *Tropic* magazine, a story that I later drew from in composing chapter two of this book.

Writing this book would not have been possible without the support of my agent, Al Hart; the expert guidance of my editor, Fred Hills; and the understanding of Doug Clifton of the *Miami Herald*, who gave me all the time I needed.

Selected Bibliography

Almeder, Robert. "A Critique of the Arguments Against Reincarnation." *Journal of Scientific Exploration* 11, no. 4 (1997): 499–526.

Capra, Fritjof. *The Tao of Physics.* Boston: Shambhala, 1991.

Edwards, Paul. *Reincarnation: A Critical Examination.* Amherst, N.Y.: Prometheus Books, 1996.

Mills, Antonia, et al. "Replication Studies of Cases Suggestive of Reincarnation by Three Independent Investigators." *Journal of the American Society for Psychical Research* 88 (July 1994).

Penrose, Roger. *Shadows of the Mind: A Search for the Missing Science of Consciousness.* New York: Oxford University Press, 1994.

Stemman, Roy. *Reincarnation: True Stories of Past Lives.* London: Judy Piatkus Publishers, 1997.

Stevenson, Ian. *Ten Cases in India.* Charlottesville: University Press of Virginia, 1972.

———. *Twelve Cases in Lebanon and Turkey.* Charlottesville: University Press of Virginia, 1980.

———. *Twenty Cases Suggestive of Reincarnation.* Charlottesville: University Press of Virginia, 1995.

———. *Reincarnation and Biology, Vol. 1: Birthmarks and Vol. 2: Birth Defects and Other Anomalies.* Westport, Conn.: Praeger, 1997.

Weiss, Brian. *Many Lives, Many Masters.* New York: Simon & Schuster, 1988.

About the Author

Tom Shroder has been an award-winning journalist, writer, and editor for more than twenty years. A fourth-generation author (his grandfather was Pulitzer Prize–winning novelist MacKinlay Kantor), Shroder is the Sunday Style section editor of *The Washington Post*. From 1985 to 1998, he was editor of the *Miami Herald*'s *Tropic* magazine, where, among other duties, he edited nationally syndicated humorist Dave Barry. In 1996, he and Barry concocted, and he edited, a serial novel with help from the likes of Elmore Leonard and Carl Hiaasen. The novel became the *New York Times* best-seller *Naked Came the Manatee*.

In 1995, with coauthor John Barry, Shroder published the critically acclaimed *Seeing the Light,* a biography of Everglades naturalist photographer Clyde Butcher written as a nonfiction novel. He lives in northern Virginia with his wife, Lisa, an editor and writer, and his two children, Emily, ten, and Sam, eight. His eldest daughter, Jessica, twenty-one, is a senior at the University of Florida and, with a professionally produced one-act play to her credit, the family's fifth-generation writer.